FOUR KINGS

FOUR KINGS

Leonard, Hagler, Hearns, Duran and
the Last Great Era of Boxing

GEORGE KIMBALL

MAINSTREAM
PUBLISHING

EDINBURGH AND LONDON

First published in Great Britain in 2008 by
MAINSTREAM PUBLISHING COMPANY
(EDINBURGH) LTD
7 Albany Street
Edinburgh EH1 3UG

ISBN 9781845963590

Segments of this work originally appeared in somewhat different form on the boxing
websites TheSweetScience.com and BoxingTalk.com, whose encouragement is gratefully
acknowledged. The arguments comprising the Leonard–Hagler debate between George
Kimball and Hugh McIlvanney quoted in Chapter 11 were originally written for
Boxing Illustrated and *Sports Illustrated*, and are reproduced herein with permission

A catalogue record for this book is available
from the British Library

Typeset in Baskerville and Futura

Printed and bound in the UK by
CPI Mackays, Chatham ME5 8TD

To Marge, Darcy and Teddy, whose love, patience, understanding and encouragement sustained me in difficult times.

CONTENTS

FOREWORD BY PETE HAMILL

THE YOUNG MIGHT NOT believe it now, but there was once a time when men who engaged in the most violent of sports were also artists.

As prizefighters, they had simple, primitive goals: above all, to win, preferably by rendering their opponents unconscious. Their hands were gloved, but they wore no protective helmets, no masks. Boxing was always a tightly focused drama of one man against another man. It was, at its worst, a crude blood sport. But occasionally, a few men would appear who possessed rare skills: power, elegance (in the best sense of that word), intelligence, guile and courage. Above all, courage, which they called 'heart'. The fighters' own definition of 'heart' also included the ability to endure pain while moving through it to victory.

When more than one man emerged with these qualities, fans and writers began to whisper about a Golden Age. If the men who made violence into art were all about the same size and weight, and the outcome of the matches was never certain, they spoke more loudly. This book is about the last Golden Age of boxing. That is, it is about a time when the matches themselves transcended the squalor of the business side of the sport and focused only on the men who fought.

If the young have any doubts about this era of pugilistic marvels, they must read George Kimball. So must people with white in their hair who remember it in their own blurry way. Kimball will tell all of them about the men named Duran and Leonard and Hagler and Hearns. He will evoke the rascals, too, the hustling spear-carriers

9

at the show. He will make the electricity return to packed arenas. But he will speak about heart, too, and fear. They should listen to him carefully because Kimball is a superb witness. He was there. He was there in the training camps. He was there for every minute of every round of every fight. He was there in the dressing-rooms of the losers. Listen to the tale. It's about a Golden Age. Perhaps even the last such age in the poor battered sport that Kimball, and a lot of the rest of us, once cherished more than all others. But it was not a myth. It was as real as a cut over a brow, as real as a hook to the jaw, as real as all great art.

Pete Hamill
New York

PREFACE

BY THE LATE 1970s, boxing had lapsed into a moribund state. Interest in the sport, which traditionally revolved around the heavyweight division, was on the wane. Muhammad Ali, who had beaten Leon Spinks in 1978 to win the heavyweight title for the third time, had announced his retirement and would never again be a champion. In early 1980, the World Boxing Council (WBC) heavyweight title belonged to a former Ali sparring partner, Larry Holmes, the World Boxing Association (WBA) version to the even more obscure John Tate and Mike Weaver.

Beginning in 1980, the sport was resuscitated by a riveting series of bouts involving an improbably dissimilar quartet who would all eventually fight as middleweights. Between them, Sugar Ray Leonard, Marvelous Marvin Hagler, Thomas Hearns and Roberto Duran would fight one another nine times over the decade. Like Ali and Joe Frazier, Jack Dempsey and Gene Tunney, Sugar Ray Robinson and Jake LaMotta, they brought out the best in each other, producing unprecedented multimillion-dollar gates along the way.

Through fortuitous coincidence, Leonard, Hagler, Hearns and Duran matured into greatness in an era in which other sports seemingly conspired to back away and allow boxing to approach the prominence it had enjoyed in the days before baseball and football overtook it in the public consciousness. Major League Baseball experienced debilitating strikes in 1980, 1981 and 1982; the NFL underwent a 57-day strike in 1982 that wiped out much of the regular season, and a lockout in 1987 led to many games being played with scab, or 'replacement' players. Both the 1980 and 1984 Olympic Games were marred by significant boycotts.

Nor did it hurt that the rivalry between the four took place in a domestic climate of relative tranquillity. The last American troops withdrew from Vietnam five years before Leonard fought Duran to inaugurate the series in 1980. The last of the bouts between them, Duran–Leonard III in 1989, occurred 13 months before the first Gulf War commenced.

Each of the nine bouts between the four men was memorable in its own way, and at least two of them – Leonard–Hearns I in 1981 and Hagler–Hearns in 1985 – are commonly included on any list of the greatest fights of all time, while the controversial outcome of another, the 1987 Leonard–Hagler fight, remains the subject of spirited barroom debates to this day.

Between them these fascinating Four Kings of the ring won 16 recognised world titles. In 1989, the date of the last meeting between them (Leonard–Duran III in Las Vegas), the aggregate record of the quartet was 229–15–4. Eight of those losses (and two of the draws) had come in fights against one another.

Put another way, as of 7 December 1989, their records, excluding their fights against each other, were 33–0 (Leonard), 46–1 (Hearns), 60–2–2 (Hagler) and 84–4 (Duran). Each of the four beat at least one of the others, and each of them lost to at least one of the others. Theirs is a shared legacy, and, like John, Paul, George and Ringo, their names are destined to be forever linked.

Leonard, Hagler, Hearns and Duran were fighters. They didn't set out to save boxing from itself in the post-Ali era.

But they did.

And we may never see their like again.

1

IN THE BEGINNING . . .

ON 7 MAY 1973, what may have been the finest collection of American amateur boxers assembled under one roof in a non-Olympic year convened at the Hynes Auditorium in Boston for the National Amateur Athletic Union (AAU) Championships.

Most of the Olympians who had represented the USA at the star-crossed Munich Games a year earlier – including Sugar Ray Seales, the lone American gold medallist – had joined the professional ranks. A new and promising group of boxers (though few could have guessed just *how* promising) had moved up through the ranks to replace them.

The field of 324 included nine future world champions. Four of the boxers who would win a record five gold medals in Montreal three years hence were in attendance, three of them as participants, but just one of them, featherweight Howard Davis Jr, would prevail in Boston. Davis beat LeRoy Veasley, the All-Service champion, in the 125-pound final.

Another Montreal gold medallist-in-waiting, sixteen-year-old Ray Charles Leonard, who had yet to begin calling himself 'Sugar Ray', defeated two of his future professional opponents, Bruce Finch and Pete Ranzany, on his way to the light-welterweight final, where he was outpointed by yet another boxer he would defeat professionally, Randy Shields.

Leon Spinks was knocked out by D.C. Barker in the light-heavyweight final. His younger brother Michael had been eliminated

13

in the regionals of the 165-pound class, but he had accompanied Neon Leon to Boston. Both Spinks brothers would win Olympic gold three years later, and both would eventually become heavyweight champion of the world.

Another future world champion, 18-year-old Aaron Pryor, won the lightweight championship, while Marvin Camel, J.B. Williamson and Arturo Frias, who would all capture world titles at a professional level, were eliminated in earlier rounds in their divisions.

Other participants included Roberto Elizondo, who would twice challenge for the lightweight title, Wayne Hedgepeth, who would later become a world-class referee in New Jersey, and Tommy Brooks, who would train many world champions, including, briefly, both Mike Tyson and Evander Holyfield.

Brooks, the future son-in-law of Hall of Fame trainer Lou Duva, experienced one of the more humiliating moments of the week when his trainer, former light-heavyweight champion Archie Moore, expressed his displeasure over Tommy's performance in his middleweight semi-final against Terry Dobbs by angrily slapping him in full view of the spectators as he sat on the stool between rounds.

The unquestioned star of the week was not one of the future Olympians but a 19-year-old apprentice machinist from nearby Brockton. Marvin Nathaniel Hagler won all four of his bouts, two of them by knockout, and upset Dobbs, the twenty-four-year-old US Marine Corps champion, in the 165-pound final.

Although Hagler was the lone New Englander to win a national title at the Hynes, the Boston newspapers barely acknowledged his presence that week until the night he beat Dobbs and was voted the Outstanding Boxer of the tournament. In one report on a preliminary-round bout, a Boston paper had called him 'Nagler'.

The local press had collectively hitched its star to what appeared to be a better story for the local angle. Robert C. Newton had boxed for the Naval Academy in his college days. Upon graduation from Annapolis, he had been commissioned an officer and had spent the next four years in the service, three of them aboard a destroyer, the USS *Finch*, off the coast of Vietnam. Upon his discharge, he had enrolled as a graduate student at Harvard and resumed his amateur boxing career. Newton was a few weeks away from receiving his Master's degree from the Ivy League school when he defeated future world champion Hilmer Kenty in the first round of the AAU tournament.

Bobby Newton won two more bouts that week, but the bandwagon ground to a halt when he lost to Pryor in the 132-pound final. Boston reporters turned, with seeming reluctance, to Hagler to fill their notebooks.

In provincial New England boxing circles, Hagler was considered an outsider. He had moved to Brockton from New Jersey just three years earlier and had been boxing for only two years. He represented an obscure gym operated by brothers Guarino (Goody) and Pasquale (Pat) Petronelli, who had been in business only since 1969, and when he reported for duty at the Hynes he was sporting a shaved head, a look that had yet to become fashionable.

Throw in the menacing scowl he had already adopted for those occasions when he was focused on the business of fighting, and it helps explain why sportswriters took one look and ran the other way that week – at least until they could no longer ignore him. Even after he won, the account of his triumph in the following morning's *Boston Herald American* described Hagler as 'a Newark-born middleweight'.

In the final round of the championship bout, Hagler knocked Dobbs down twice, and the Marine took another standing eight-count.

'The ref saved Dobbs,' Hagler would recall later.

A few months earlier, Hagler had reached the 156-pound final of the National Golden Gloves tournament in Lowell before losing to Dale Grant of Seattle, Ray Seales's half-brother. The two might have met again in Boston, but fate intervened when Reinaldo Oliveira, who had qualified as the New England representative at 165, declared his intention to turn pro and was thus disqualified from participating. Hagler, who had made the team at 156, was allowed to move up to 165. There was no New England representative in the 156-pound division and Grant, as expected, breezed through the field to win.

'I'd actually thought Marvin was too small for 156, and I couldn't believe it when he entered at 165 and won,' recalled Emanuel Steward. In the 1980s, Steward would win multiple Trainer of the

Year awards, but in 1973 he was still in the early stages of building an amateur powerhouse at an inner-city Detroit gym called the Kronk Recreation Center. 'And Marvin fought a lot of seasoned guys in that tournament.'

'Marvin hurt everybody he fought in this tournament,' Sam Silverman, then the pre-eminent Boston boxing promoter, told reporters. 'He was easily the best puncher in the whole show.'

Hagler was named the tournament's Outstanding Boxer. Having won 42 of his 45 amateur bouts, he might have been considered the brightest prospect of all as a future Olympian, but the night he accepted his trophy from Boston Mayor Kevin White, Hagler announced that it had been his last amateur bout. 'You can't take a trophy and turn it into a bag of groceries,' he said.

'Win or lose, I was turning pro,' Marvin would recall years later.

Six days after the completion of the AAU Championships, he knocked out Terry Ryan in the second round of a fight at Brockton High School for the first of what would ultimately be sixty-two professional wins. Hagler's take-home pay for the Ryan fight was $40.

Four years later, an Olympic medal in hand, Sugar Ray Leonard would earn $40,000 for his professional debut. By then, Hagler had fought 33 pro bouts and might have earned $40,000 all told, but he had done it the hard way.

■ ■ ■

Eleven months earlier, on 26 June 1972, a crowd of 18,821 – more than had watched any lightweight fight in history – had packed Madison Square Garden to see the estimable Scots champion from Edinburgh, Ken Buchanan, defend his World Boxing Association title against a scrappy Panamanian named Roberto Duran.

Duran had turned 21 a week earlier and was but a few years removed from life as a street urchin in his homeland, but he wasn't a complete stranger to New York audiences. When Buchanan had defended his title against Ismael Laguna the previous September, Duran had knocked out Puerto Rican journeyman Benny Huertas in the first round of a supporting bout on the card.

'Duran blazed out of his corner and finished Huertas in about a minute,' Vic Ziegel would recall in *Inside Sports* eight years later. 'He was awesome. But I couldn't help noticing that he neglected to shower after the fight. "Duran hardly worked up a sweat," I wrote, "and a good thing, too, because he didn't bother to shower."' Duran, Ziegel found out years later, hated the line.

The title fight was Duran's first US main event, the first time all eyes would be trained on him, and he left an indelible impression.

The champion, who brought a 43–1 record to the fight, weighed in at 133½, a quarter-pound more than Duran, who was undefeated at 28–0. Duran, comfortably ahead by margins of 9–2–1, 9–3 and 8–3–1 on the scorecards after 12 rounds, was going to win the fight anyway, but the outcome turned on an almost grotesque display of savagery.

Late in the 13th, the two were wrapped up in an exchange so spirited that neither seemed to hear the bell. Referee Johnny LoBianco tried to grab Duran from behind to pull him away, but as he did so, the Panamanian unloaded an uppercut that came up from the floor and caught Buchanan squarely in the groin, beneath his protective cup.

Buchanan writhed in agony on the canvas and eventually staggered back to his stool. There, he was visited by both the ringside physician and LoBianco, who eventually waved his arms, signalling that the fight was over.

Although 18,000 pairs of eyes had seen the low blow, LoBianco apparently had not. Under the rules, Buchanan could have been granted five minutes to recover from a punch below the belt. The referee also had it in his power to penalise Duran for the infraction, or even to award the fight to Buchanan on a foul.

None of those things happened. Roberto Duran was the new lightweight champion of the world, and all people would remember was that a man Budd Schulberg described as 'a Panamanian street dog' had stopped Ken Buchanan with a punch to the family jewels.

While his career didn't end that night, Buchanan was never the same fighter. The critical punch from Duran ruptured his right testicle, and he still experiences discomfort from the injury 35 years later.

'I still get a pain there,' Buchanan told Duran's biographer, Christian

Giudice. 'I'll have it till the day I die. I told Roberto "I'll never forget you. Every time I take a piss I'll think of you."'

■ ■ ■

When Derrik Holmes learned of plans to initiate a boxing programme at the Palmer Park Recreation Center in 1970, he was eager to give it a try but hesitant about showing up alone. He persuaded his best friend to accompany him.

Ray Leonard, then 13 years old, was reluctant. His brother Roger had been boxing for a few years, and on the few occasions Ray had gone to the gym to watch he'd found himself wincing whenever he saw his older sibling get punched in the face. But Holmes was determined, so he agreed to tag along.

Holmes would box professionally, accumulating a 17–3–1 record that included an unsuccessful 1980 challenge for Wilfredo Gomez's World Boxing Council junior featherweight title. It was not immediately apparent that his friend Leonard might be even more gifted.

'Of the four boys in my family,' Leonard would later recall, 'I was probably the *least* likely to become a boxer. My three brothers were good at sports, and from the earliest time I can remember they all played football and basketball and had done well. I wasn't an athlete. I wasn't even athletically inclined. I relied on my mother for everything. Once when I was very small I did go to the gym with Roger, and he talked me into putting on the gloves. I cried when I got punched in the nose. I didn't like it a bit.'

Dave Jacobs and Pepe Correa each claim to have initiated the boxing programme at Palmer Park. Ollie Dunlap, the director of the rec centre, who would become Sugar Ray's closest friend and confidant, recalls that it was initially Roger Leonard's idea, and that while Correa, who had taught boxing in the army, was also involved, 'the paperwork I did for the boxing programme had Dave Jacobs's name on it'.

Jacobs, an AAU featherweight champion in his youth, would later become the salaried head of the boxing programme at Palmer Park, but in 1970 he was an unpaid volunteer and still earned his living driving a delivery truck.

When Jacobs asked Leonard what he knew about boxing, the 13 year old struck a pose reminiscent of John L. Sullivan's fighting stance. It was all Jake could do to keep from laughing out loud.

Those who would later describe Leonard's 'choirboy' looks were actually spot-on in their assessment. Up until the day he put on the gloves at the Rec Center he had been an accomplished member of the choir at St John's Baptist Church in Washington. Once he faced a choice between the two, the choir didn't stand a chance.

'My mother always used to tell me, "You sound like Sam Cooke" or "You sound just like Ray Charles,"' Ray reminisced. 'But I think she was just being kind. My sister Sandy was the real singer in the family.'

Ray Charles Leonard was born in Wilmington, North Carolina, on 17 May 1956. That he grew up in a traditional nuclear family makes him unique among the Four Kings. He was the fifth of seven children born to Cicero and Getha Leonard, and at the age of four he moved with his family to Washington DC.

Cicero, the son of a sharecropper, had boxed in the Navy during the Second World War. He found work at a Washington produce market and in time was promoted to night manager. Getha worked days as a nurse at a convalescent home, which ensured that one parent was always home to attend to their growing brood. By 1966, they were able to purchase a home in Palmer Park, Maryland, a lower-middle-class, predominantly black enclave just across the District of Columbia line.

'Palmer Park wasn't a ghetto, but it wasn't what you envision when you think of suburbia, either,' recalled Ollie Dunlap, who had played on Michigan State's 1966 national co-championship football team. After graduation, he had signed with the Washington Redskins as an undrafted free agent and had a largely unproductive stint on the taxi squad. Although Dunlap later played for the Toronto Argonauts of the Canadian Football League, he continued to make the nation's capital his off-season home, and after leaving football found work as the full-time director at the Palmer Park Rec Center.

'To my way of thinking, it was only a "sport" if its name had the word "ball" in it,' said Dunlap. 'Football, basketball, baseball . . . But when Roger came to me and proposed the boxing programme, I said, "Sure, why not?"'

Correa, in any case, soon departed Palmer Park ('for personal reasons') to begin his own inner-city boxing club in Washington and Jacobs took charge of the Palmer Park boxing programme. He was shortly joined there, at Dunlap's behest, by an insurance broker named Janks Morton.

Morton and Dunlap had been football teammates in Toronto (after being cut by the Browns and Redskins, respectively) and had become friends almost immediately. In addition, Ollie knew that Janks was a former boxer. Jacobs, Morton and Dunlap weren't dreaming about producing an Olympic champion; they were just looking for another way to keep kids off the streets.

The initial outlay for the boxing programme was $45 – the cost of two pairs of gloves. The Palmer Park Rec Center didn't have a proper boxing ring, nor would there be one until 1976, by which time the programme's most illustrious graduate had already won an Olympic gold medal. The young boxers sparred in a makeshift 'ring' marked off with tape on the basketball court, a condition that made the Palmer Park boys acutely aware of the importance of balance. In the absence of a ring mat to cushion one's fall, a misstep or a knockdown could be doubly painful. Initially, boxers had to clear the gym whenever someone wanted to play basketball, but as Jacobs's charges began to assert themselves in matches throughout the area, the rec centre devoted the 1–5 p.m. time slot exclusively to boxing.

Over the next few years Palmer Park accumulated a prodigious collection of trophies, many of them won by Leonard, who, once he learned the basics, proved to be the most naturally gifted boxer Jacobs had ever seen.

In Jacobs's recollection, Leonard had weighed 'a hundred pounds, soaking wet' the day he walked into the rec centre with Derrik Holmes. A year later he had added 25 pounds, virtually all of it muscle, and when in 1971 the 15 year old soundly defeated Bobby McGruder, generally regarded to have been the Washington area's best amateur featherweight, Jacobs realised that he might have something truly special on his hands.

'Up until then I'd boxed in the Novice class,' recalled Leonard. 'McGruder's opponent that night fell out and somebody said, "Well, we've got this kid . . ."'

'I said, "Sure, I'll fight him," and I not only beat him, I beat the *hell* out of him,' said Leonard. 'That was the end of Novice fights for me. I'd only been boxing competitively for a year, but I fought in the Open class after that.'

In less than two years, Leonard had come to dominate in metropolitan Washington boxing. By 1972, it was time for him to move on to the national stage. That spring he won the Golden Gloves national lightweight title, a prodigious leap that allowed him to entertain hopes of making that year's Olympic team.

'The first time I saw him was in 1972 at the Eastern Olympic Trials in Cincinnati,' recalled Emanuel Steward. 'He was just a baby-faced little kid and he fought a much older guy, Greg Whaley, in the semi-final. Whaley was a real strong fighter who was favoured to win the trials and go on to Munich – and he was *from* Cincinnati, fighting on his own home turf. Ray put on such a show that everyone was saying, "Where did this little kid *come* from?" They gave the decision to the other guy, but Ray had beat him up so bad that Whaley couldn't fight the next night.'

Greg Whaley didn't go to the Olympics either.

In fact, he never boxed again.

'It turned out Ray had lied about his age, and even if he *had* won they couldn't have let him go,' said Steward. 'He was barely 16 years old.'

Boxers were required to be seventeen to box in *all* international senior competitions, not just the Olympics, but this didn't stop Leonard from representing his country in two pre-Olympic meets against a team from the USSR in Las Vegas that summer.

When Rolly Schwartz asked Leonard how old he was, the boy smiled sweetly and said 'Seventeen, sir.' Schwartz, the chairman of AAU Boxing, only had to take one look at Ray to know he wasn't, but he allowed him to fight anyway.

'Rolly Schwartz knew I was underage, but he also knew I could hold my own with pretty much anyone,' said Leonard.

'The truth of the matter,' said Schwartz, 'is that he was already the best amateur lightweight in the United States.'

At the first meet, Leonard knocked out his Soviet opponent with the first punch he threw, a left hook to the face. In the next, against Valery Lov, he was knocked down in the first when the Russian caught him with his guard down.

From the canvas, Leonard looked up and saw Joe Louis and Redd Foxx, seated together, laughing at him. Furious and embarrassed, he climbed to his feet and stopped Lov in the third round.

The following year, both major boxing championships took place in Massachusetts – the Golden Gloves at the Lowell Auditorium in March and the AAUs in Boston two months later.

'I'd become very involved with amateur boxing by '73 and, in fact, my heavyweight Johnny Hudson won the Gloves championship in Lowell,' said Steward. 'I'd seen Leonard box the previous year, but Lowell was the first time I actually met him. Dave Jacobs came to me and asked for some help. He was afraid Ray was going to be overweight for his final match.'

Nearly 17, Leonard was still growing and was struggling to make weight for what would be his last bout at 132 pounds. Steward and Jacobs used tape to seal the bathroom door in the motel and, turning the hot water on full blast, converted it into a makeshift steam room. That and half an hour's worth of exercise helped Leonard shed the requisite two pounds with minutes to spare, but, recalled Leonard, 'It felt like it took forever.'

Ironically, he was matched in the final against Hilmer Kenty, a boy from Columbus, Ohio, who would later move to Detroit and become Steward's first professional world champion.

'Ray won a close decision over Kenty, and Hagler lost to Dale Grant in the middleweight final,' said Steward, whose brightest prospect, 14-year-old Thomas Hearns, was still back home in Detroit. 'I developed a relationship with those guys, and even though Marvin and Ray later fought Tommy, I've always had a close relationship with them. It was like we all kind of grew up together.'

None of Steward's boxers qualified for the AAU Championships two months later, but he attended as a spectator. Leonard had moved up to light-welterweight, where he was outpointed by Randy Shields in the championship match, while Hagler won at 165.

After the disappointment of the 1972 Olympics, when Seales was the only US fighter to return home with a gold medal, Rolly Schwartz had been given a brief to revamp amateur boxing in the hope of restoring American dominance in the sport. Schwartz arranged a heavy schedule of international competitions over the two years leading up to the 1976 Olympics – but took care never to show the rest of the world a full-strength American squad.

Leonard won both the Gloves and the AAU titles in 1974 and was on the US team that boxed in Eastern Europe that summer. On that trip, Leonard incurred what would go into the books as the final two losses of his 150-bout amateur career.

In Moscow, he dominated Anatoli Kamnev, only to have the judges award the verdict to the Russian champion. When the decision was announced, the pre-glasnost crowd erupted in a chorus of whistles and jeers. Kamnev appeared to share their sentiment. He walked across the ring and presented Ray with the trophy he had just won.

In Warsaw a few days later, Leonard floored Kazimier Szczerba three times in the final round, the last for good, but after Szczerba had been counted out, the Polish referee ruled that the knockout punch had been delivered after the bell had sounded and disqualified the American. Szczerba had to be propped up in the ring to receive his medal.

'Ray Leonard was fantastic,' said Emanuel Steward. 'He was more exciting than anyone I'd ever seen. Early in 1976, he came to Detroit and trained at the Kronk Gym for several days. The kids called him "Superbad" and pretty much adopted him. During the Olympics, the Kronk looked like a Ray Leonard shrine. There were pictures of Ray all over our gym.'

Leonard repeated as AAU champion in '75 and then went to Mexico City, where he won the light-welterweight gold medal at the Pan-American Games. By then, the secret was out. Asked by ABC boss Roone Arledge which American athletes bore watching at the upcoming Montreal Games, Howard Cosell predicted that 'Sugar Ray Leonard will be the Olga Korbut of the 1976 Olympics'. (The 'Munich

Munchkin', Korbut was a tiny gymnast from the Soviet Union who had captured the hearts of television viewers all over the world with her performance at the 1972 Games.)

He was an enormously talented boxer, but Leonard's other attributes made him even more appealing to the network. He was telegenic and articulate, with a ready smile that exuded charisma.

'All the attention was new to me, but I honestly didn't mind it,' said Leonard. 'When I was 16, someone interviewing me had asked, "What do you want to be when you grow up?" I think he expected me to say "a champion", or something like that, but I said, "I want to be *special*." And in Montreal that's exactly how I felt – special.'

ABC televised all six of Leonard's Olympic matches, in which he defeated a Swede (Ulf Carlsson), a Russian (Valery Limasov), a Briton (Clinton McKenzie), an East German (Ulrich Beyer) and a Pole (his old friend Kazimier Szczerba) on his way to the final, where he would face the formidable Cuban Andrés Aldama.

ABC's showcasing of Leonard added to the pressure. Sports editors watching on TV back home were on the horn to their Olympic correspondents demanding that they join the Leonard bandwagon. As the week wore on, each time he ventured out of the Olympic Village Leonard was trailed by an ever-growing pack of reporters, each searching for some titbit of information television viewers didn't already know. By the time he squared off with Aldama, most of America was aware that Leonard would be boxing with a photo of his high-school sweetheart Juanita Wilkinson tucked into his boot for inspiration.

'People seem to think that was about image, but it wasn't,' said Leonard. 'It was just about scoring brownie points with my girlfriend. I did it for Juanita, that's all.'

If anyone had bothered to ask, Leonard might also have revealed that Juanita was the mother of 'Little Ray', his two-year-old son.

US boxing coach Pat Nappi told Baltimore columnist Bob Maisel that 'Sugar Ray Leonard is the best amateur I've ever seen – and that includes Muhammad Ali'. Aldama had stopped all four of his preliminary opponents leading up to the final, but Leonard handed him a pair of standing eight-counts in the last round, handily winning the fight (5–0 on points) and the gold medal. All of his wins had come via decision.

He was joined on the victory stand by four other Americans – flyweight Leo Randolph, lightweight Howard Davis and brothers Michael (middleweight) and Leon (light-heavyweight) Spinks. It is generally acknowledged to have been the greatest team triumph in Olympic boxing history. (The Americans won nine golds in Los Angeles eight years later, but the Soviet and Cuban boxers boycotted those Games, considerably diminishing the accomplishment.)

Although Leonard had surely been the face of the 1976 Olympics and had captured the hearts of his countrymen, the panel of boxing officials who selected the Outstanding Boxer of the Games hadn't been watching ABC. Howard Davis won that trophy.

In an interview with Cosell immediately after the gold medal match, Leonard said that the Aldama fight had been his last. 'I'm finished,' he insisted. 'I've fought my last fight. My journey has ended. My dream is fulfilled.'

The kid with the captivating smile and the all-American looks hoped to capitalise on his Olympic triumph with promised commercial endorsements. Leonard, who had already accepted a Congressional Scholarship, said he would hang up his gloves and enrol as a full-time student at the University of Maryland, where he planned to major in communications. After that, he hoped to go to law school, perhaps at Harvard. The next time Americans saw his face it would presumably be staring at them from a Wheaties box.

He rode back to Maryland with his family, the gold medal hanging from the rear-view mirror of the crowded van Cicero Leonard and Dave Jacobs had driven to Montreal. On the Beltway, they were intercepted and then accompanied by a police cruiser, sirens blaring.

Joined by local politicians and dignitaries for an impromptu motorcade, the Leonards were whisked away to a civic reception in downtown Washington, where, before a crowd of well-wishers, Sugar Ray repeated his intention to retire.

'This medal is all I ever wanted,' he said. 'I will never be a professional fighter, I promise you that. It's time I started a new life.'

Two days later, the *Washington Star*, in a front-page story, broke the news that Juanita Wilkinson had filed an application to receive $156 a month in welfare payments and that Prince George's County had in turn filed a lawsuit on her behalf against the Olympic hero.

The paternity suit came without warning. Leonard had never denied paternity of his son. Somewhat embarrassed officials explained that they had merely been following a pro forma procedure mandated by a recently enacted law intended to winnow out welfare cheats, but the damage to his public image was both immediate and devastating.

'Several companies who had expressed interest in me backed away,' said Leonard. 'When the news broke about the paternity suit, all hell broke loose, and it killed a lot of deals. Juanita started getting threats. My family blamed her for the suit and jumped on her.'

As the promised endorsements evaporated before his eyes, Leonard realised that the carefree life of a college student was no longer an option. If he was going to capitalise on his Olympic triumph, he was going to have to go to work, and the obvious choice of occupation would be the one he knew best.

'It was the only career where I wouldn't have to start out at the bottom,' said Leonard. 'I already had a pretty good résumé.'

■ ■ ■

Unlike the bureaucrats of Prince George's County, the denizens of El Chorrillo, the desperately poor slum area into which Roberto Duran was born in 1951, did not place a high premium on formalities such as matrimony. His mother, Clara Samaniego, would eventually give birth to nine children by four different men. His father, Margarito Sanchez Duran, had also fathered another of Clara's sons, but the boy, Alcibiades, died of heart disease as a toddler and was buried in a municipal graveyard in Panama City.

Roberto's father was a US soldier of Mexican descent, and once his tour of duty in the Canal Zone was up, he disappeared. He was subsequently stationed in California and in Germany, and upon leaving the service he married and settled in Arizona. He might never have been heard from again had it not been for his son's successes. Duran was a grown man, a world champion and purportedly wealthy, by the time his father deemed it propitious to make contact.

Margarito Duran had been a street fighter of some repute and when he abandoned Roberto, it was later noted, 'the only thing he left his son was his punch'.

With jet-black hair and the dark, piercing eyes that Joe Frazier would later liken to Charles Manson's, Duran was nicknamed 'Cholo', the Panamanian designation for one of mixed white and Indian blood. Although Clara did her best to raise her disparate flock of children, Roberto was often left to fend for himself on the streets. From nearly the time he could walk, he hustled for change, shining shoes and selling newspapers. The latter occupation often required that he defend himself against older newsboys who tried to steal his allotment of papers. Fistfights for street-corner turf were not uncommon, and young Cholo more than held his own.

Food was scarce; unable to care for him, his mother literally gave the boy away on several occasions. When he wasn't eating as a guest of the families of his friends, Duran lived by his wits, often foraging like some feral animal among the garbage cans of Chorillo.

His formal education ended in the fourth grade. Duran's older brother, Toti Samaniego, told Christian Giudice that Roberto had 'tried to hit a male teacher and then tried to kiss his female replacement'. Duran's own version (in a *Sports Illustrated* profile) held that 'in school one day a kid came over to hit me, and I moved. We exchanged positions, so his back was toward the steps. I hit him and he fell over backwards and down the steps. And they threw me out.'

He followed Toti to a boxing gym at the age of eight and had his first amateur bout a year later. He knocked down his opponent three times, but – possibly because the other boy was the referee's son – he lost the decision.

Boxing out of the Cincuentenario Club in Panama City, the young Duran attracted the attention of an established local trainer, Nestor (Plomo) Quinones. Although he weighed less than 100 pounds, he enjoyed prodigious success, much of it against opponents who were both older and larger – and many of his best fights took place *outside* the ring.

Duran was 15 and walking his girlfriend home from a dance when they encountered half a dozen rowdy drunks who attempted to accost the young lady. In a few frenzied moments, Roberto knocked out five of the assailants. The sixth knifed him with a grazing blow to the back just before the police arrived.

Duran, the girl and his five victims all spent the night in jail together; the sixth guy got away. Only later did Duran learn that the man who had tried to stab him was the husband of one of his aunts.

The oft-repeated tale of Duran vs the Horse has so many versions that it is difficult to separate fact from legend. In some accounts he was 15, others 16. Ray Arcel would later claim to have witnessed the incident and Arcel, who became his trainer, didn't meet Duran until he was 20. Duran's manager, Carlos Eleta, later told the *New York Times*'s Michael Katz that the incident had taken place in the Panamanian jungle, winning Duran a bet with some workers. What everyone seems to agree on is that Duran scored his one-punch equine knockout years before Alex Karras, as Mongo, performed a similar feat in Mel Brooks's *Blazing Saddles*. In some versions it was a body shot. In others, Duran dropped the beast with a punch behind the ear.

He was indisputably 16 years old when he knocked out the favoured Buenventura Riosco to win the national light-flyweight title, and with it an expected berth in the Pan-American Games in Canada. Duran's record at that point was 29–3. He had beaten virtually every worthwhile amateur in Panama, but once again boxing politics intervened. A soldier from the Panamanian National Guard was picked to go to Winnipeg.

Shortly thereafter he was approached by Quinones, who found him working at one of his odd jobs.

'I was painting houses for $1.50 a day,' Duran recalled to Giudice. 'Plomo comes in and says, "Duran, you want to make $25 to fight – win, lose or draw?"'

Quinones didn't have to ask twice.

'Who do I have to kill?' asked Roberto Duran.

On 23 February 1968, Duran made his professional debut in Colon, in a four-round bout against a countryman named Carlos Mendoza.

He won every round and captured a unanimous decision. Afterwards he was approached by Carlos Eleta, the millionaire Panamanian sportsman.

Eleta and Duran had actually met five years earlier. Eleta had looked out his window and spied a boy poaching coconuts from a tree on his property. This was not an unusual activity for the young Duran, who often swam across a canal and returned with sacks full of fruit to feed his family. Once, Pat Putnam related in a *Sports Illustrated* profile, the weight of the stolen fruit weighed him down so much that on the return journey he began to sink and he had to be rescued by his accomplices.

Even having caught him red-handed, Eleta admired the youngster's audacity and invited him into his house and fed him lunch that day. The two hadn't laid eyes on one another again until the night Duran knocked out Buenventura Riosco. Eleta, it turned out, had planned to manage Riosco.

Now he had a different plan. He wanted to manage Duran.

Educated in Europe and the United States, Carlos Eleta Almaran owned a newspaper, radio and television stations, and an airline. He was the Panamanian representative for several US corporations and was well connected to the rich and powerful of many nations. (The ailing Shah of Iran recuperated as his guest on an island owned by Eleta.) He operated the most successful racing stable in Panama. And he managed boxers.

Duran was nominally managed by a Panamanian jockey named Alfredo Vasquez. Instead of bankrolling Duran's career, Vasquez had tried to hit *him* up for money. When Eleta offered the jockey $300 for Cholo's contract, Alfredo jumped at it.

For Duran, it was a propitious career move.

Over the next ten months the teenaged Duran had eight more fights. He knocked out seven of his opponents in the first round, the other in the second.

For the first two years of his pro career, Duran campaigned as a featherweight. In his last bout at that weight, in 1970, he stopped future world champion Ernesto Marcel in ten at the Gimnasio Nuevo Panama in Panama City.

Though Duran feared no boxer, he idolised at least one: born in

1943, Ismael Laguna had been fighting professionally for eight years by the time Duran won his first pro fight, and in March 1970 Laguna regained his status as a Panamanian national hero when he scored a tenth-round TKO of Mando Ramos in Los Angeles to reclaim the world lightweight title, five years after he had lost it.

'Someday,' Duran had told Laguna, 'I will be as good as you – or better.'

Laguna's second reign as champion proved to be short-lived. In his second defence, he lost his title on a split decision to Ken Buchanan in Puerto Rico. Looking to climb back into the rankings, in his next outing Laguna fought a rematch with Lloyd Marshall, a useful New Jersey lightweight who hadn't lost in eight years before Laguna beat him at Madison Square Garden back in 1968. In March 1971, Laguna won a ten-round decision over Marshall at the Gimnasio Nuevo Panama.

Two months later Duran was matched against Marshall in the same venue and stopped him in four. Afterwards, Duran presented the gloves he had worn to a visiting American youngster. Ten-year-old John F. Kennedy Jr had been seated at ringside as a guest of his host, Carlos Eleta.

Laguna's reward for beating Lloyd Marshall was a return bout against Buchanan. Duran's was his first fight in the United States.

On 13 September 1971, Laguna lost a unanimous decision in his title rematch with Buchanan at Madison Square Garden. On the undercard, 20-year-old Roberto Duran knocked out Benny Huertas at 1:06 of the first for his 25th win in as many pro fights.

■ ■ ■

Born in West Virginia, Emanuel Steward moved to Detroit at the age of 12 and boxed out of the Brewster Recreation Center, where the young Joe Louis had honed his craft. Winning the bantamweight title at the 1963 Golden Gloves was the pinnacle of his amateur career. Married at an early age, he never seriously entertained the notion of turning pro and became a licensed electrician for Detroit Edison.

When his younger brother, James, expressed an interest in following in his older sibling's footsteps, Emanuel took him to an inner-city gym called the Kronk Recreation Center. He shortly found himself giving pointers to other boys in the gym and signed on as a part-time boxing coach there.

Even in its early days, the Kronk embodied Steward's team concept. Boxers were thrown together, irrespective of weight class, for hellish sparring sessions in the dank, steamy gym, but once they stepped out of the ring they were members of a fraternity, blood brothers forged in the cauldron of a shared experience only they could understand.

Initially, the Kronk colours were blue and red, but when a Kronk alumnus returned on leave from the service, he brought along his red-and-gold Marine Corps boxing robe, which he donated to the gym. Gold was added to the colour scheme.

Kronk boxers wore matching gold-and-red trunks, and the more accomplished members were awarded handsome letter jackets, which they proudly wore, both on the streets of Detroit and to the national competitions to which they soon began to travel.

'Boxing in Detroit was dead, period, until I came along and started my group,' recalled Steward. 'But within a few years we started winning things and people started to pay attention to the Kronk boxing team.'

■ ■ ■

Thomas Hearns was born in Memphis, but like Steward he had moved to Detroit at an early age and was raised on Detroit's east side. Although he had the quintessential pug's nose, it didn't come from boxing. Hearns had broken his nose in a bicycle accident when he was nine, before he'd ever laced on a pair of gloves. As a result of that injury, he experienced nasal problems throughout his career, and years later would undergo surgery for a deviated septum.

'Tommy must have been ten, and didn't weigh more than eighty pounds when he first walked into the gym,' said Steward. 'He was always a skinny little kid, all through his amateur career. Even though he wasn't one of the top fighters in our gym right away, he was always special. He always gave it his best effort and he always worked hard.

'Back then we were the only gym that travelled. At other gyms, a kid might get two or three fights when the city recreation tournament came around, and outside of that they might have got two or three other fights at most. But from 1969 on I took our kids on little out-of-town trips,' recalled Steward. 'I'd load 'em all into my car and we'd drive off to Columbus or Chicago for the weekend, and of course they loved it. When a kid came from a house with no father and a lot of poverty, that meant a lot.

'At first, out of maybe ten kids Tommy might have been the sixth-most talented,' added Steward. 'Sometimes he'd lose three in a row, but he was always gracious and grateful. Whenever we got back he'd make it a point to say, "Thank you, Mr Steward, for taking me on that trip."'

Two years younger than Leonard and four years Hagler's junior, Hearns was a few steps behind his future rivals in his progression through the amateur ranks. Only 14 at the time, he didn't accompany Steward to the 1973 Gloves and AAU tournaments, but by 1975 he had earned his first berth in the National Golden Gloves.

'He weighed about 110 pounds, but he surprised me,' said Steward. 'He lost to Mike Ayala, who went on to win the bantamweight championship that year. Ayala had had 238 amateur fights. I don't think Tommy had even had 20.'

Hearns, recalled Steward, 'was real quiet, but he always tried hard, even when he lost. And even though he was always so thin, he only lost to the top fighters. He lost to Ayala, who won everything, in 1975. Then in the AAU that year I let him go up to 126, and he lost a decision to Ronnie Shields, who also won everything at that weight. The next year he lost in the Gloves 132-pound final to Aaron Pryor, and in the AAU final he lost to Howard Davis.'

Just a few months later Davis would be named the Outstanding Boxer of the 1976 Olympics.

'Tommy didn't go to the Olympic trials,' said Steward. 'He was still a year or two behind those guys, but he *did* have Howard Davis hurt in the second round of their fight.'

Like Marvin Hagler, Hearns also had to overcome the fact that he had come from virtual obscurity.

'Nobody ever outboxed Tommy, even then,' insists Steward. 'He was a master boxer. But you've got to remember the politics of this era in amateur boxing. Rolly Schwartz, who headed up the amateur programme, was from Cincinnati, and of course the metropolitan New York organisation was also very strong. It seemed like one or two of Rolly's fighters got through to the final every year, no matter what.'

'Guys like Pryor [from Cincinnati] and Davis [New York] would throw these little flurries to make it look good, and of course the judges all knew these guys. They were politically well connected, but *nobody* knew Tommy. He was just a skinny little guy from a Detroit club and nobody knew who he was. This was all a new experience for me, too, and nobody from Michigan had any clout whatsoever,' said Steward. 'A couple of Tommy's fights against Pryor, for instance, were very close, but you always knew the Cincinnati guy was going to get it.'

Hearns had made enough of an impression that he was picked to box on a team of American amateurs sent to Europe after the '76 Olympics. It was his first taste of international competition and he won all of his matches.

'Then something happened between 1976 and 1977,' said Steward. 'Tommy just blossomed. Up until then, like a lot of tall kids, he'd move up a weight division each year but he'd have grown another two inches in height, so he was getting bigger but he wasn't getting any stronger. But beginning at the end of 1976, he went up to 139, but he didn't grow taller in height. For the first time, you could actually see muscles develop. He was physically much stronger than he'd ever been.'

By early 1977, Leonard had turned pro. Dave Jacobs phoned to ask Steward if Hearns could come down to Maryland to spar with the Olympic champion.

'Tommy stayed at Jacobs's house for several days,' said Steward. 'Dave called me up and told me Tommy and Ray had boxed at Palmer Park. He said the whole place was packed, and what was amazing is that Tommy had outboxed Ray. It was a good workout and nobody got hit clean, but Ray had problems with Tommy.'

'The thing is, Tommy was an amateur, I was a professional, and he was younger than I was,' recalled Leonard of the episode. 'I never even dreamed that just a few years down the road Tommy would wind up being one of my biggest rivals and foremost adversaries. I still thought of him as a young kid.'

Young Hearns's progress became even more evident when the national tournaments rolled around that spring. In the semi-final of the 1977 National Golden Gloves, Hearns faced Ronnie Shields, who had beaten him the year before. He knocked Shields out on his way to winning the Gloves championship, and then added the AAU title by outpointing Bobby Joe Young. (A decade later, Bobby Joe Young would administer the first and only defeat of Aaron Pryor's professional career.)

Emanuel Steward had been grooming his stable of amateurs for nearly seven years. Now it was time for the next step.

'I always knew they would turn pro eventually, and when they did, I would too,' said Steward. 'That was the plan all along.'

On 25 November 1977, a month after his 19th birthday, Thomas Hearns was one of four Kronk boxers to make their professional debuts on a card at the Olympia in downtown Detroit. In the main event, Mickey Goodwin knocked out Willie Williams in the first round. Hearns stopped Jerome Hill in the second round of their prelim. It was his first professional win and before he was done there would be 60 more of them.

■ ■ ■

Unless you spent a lot of time around the New England club fight scene 30 years ago, or worked as a Massachusetts prison guard, chances are you've never heard of Dornell Wigfall, but if there hadn't been a Dornell Wigfall, there might never have been a Marvelous Marvin Hagler.

By the time I met Wigfall, he was in his second go-round as a pro. He'd gone 17–3 as a middleweight before he went to prison for over five years, and he went 3–3 as a light-heavyweight after he got out. By then, he had developed one of those spectacular jailhouse physiques, honed by hours of lifting in prison weight-rooms, but he had no chin at all. He had become a professional Opponent, and in his last two fights he got knocked out in Atlantic City. The last I heard of him he was back in the joint, doing time again, at the state prison in Walpole.

34

Two of Wigfall's early losses were to Hagler, but the first time they met, in an unsanctioned street fight in Brockton, Wigfall was the clear-cut winner. A notorious street tough, Wigfall had accosted the 16-year-old Hagler at a party, taken him outside and in Hagler's recollection, 'kicked my ass', embarrassing him in front of his friends and compounding the humiliation by stealing the jacket off Marvin's back.

The day after this encounter Hagler showed up at a Brockton gym operated by Vinnie Vecchione. (More than two decades later Vecchione would have his moment of nationwide fame when he rescued his heavyweight, Peter McNeeley, from Mike Tyson in Tyson's get-out-of-jail fight.) Hagler sat down and quietly watched the boxers go through their paces. He came back for several evenings in a row and never said a word to anyone. Nobody said a word to him, either.

'The funny thing was, Wigfall was a fighter in that gym,' said Angie Carlino, who would later become Marvelous Marvin's personal photographer and confidant. 'Marvin didn't even know that at the time. He sat there and watched for a week, and I guess he didn't like the way Vinnie operated. You've got to remember, Marvin was a very shy kid.'

The next day he walked across a parking lot and climbed the stairs to the Petronelli Brothers' Gym.

Though born and raised in the shoe-factory town Rocky Marciano called home, Goody Petronelli had departed Brockton at an early age and served 20 years in the United States Navy, where he compiled a 23–2–1 record as an amateur welterweight and later coached the boxing team at the Great Lakes Naval Air Station. By the time he was discharged in 1969, he had risen to the rank of Chief Petty Officer in the navy's Medical Corps, a background that he would utilise in establishing himself as a cut man par excellence.

'I've got stuff in this bag,' he once told me, 'that'll stop a bullet hole.'

Lifelong friends of Marciano, Goody and his brother Pat had arranged to go into partnership with the retired heavyweight champion in a Brockton boxing gym. On 31 August 1969, Goody had driven halfway across the country, discharge papers in hand, when he heard on the car radio that Rocky had been killed in a plane crash.

Pooling their resources and underwriting the enterprise with a construction company they operated by day, the Petronellis opened the doors to the planned gym anyway.

When the new arrival shuffled into the gym and looked around for a place to sit, there was no indication that the fortunes of three men were about to be changed.

On his first night, Hagler once again watched in silence. On the second, Goody walked over and asked with a smile, 'Hey, kid, do you want to learn how to fight?'

'That's what I'm here for,' said Marvin. Goody told him to come back the next night and bring along his gear.

Gear? All he had was a pair of cut-off jeans and some tennis shoes.

'When a new kid comes to the gym, I sit him down and give him a list of the pros and cons,' said Goody. 'I explain that if he does well, it will teach him self-respect and make him a better person, but I warn him that there's nothing easy about it. He'll have to work hard and get up in the morning to do roadwork. It will cut down on his social life. And no matter how good he might be, he's going to get hit, and he's not going to like it.

'When I asked him if he still wanted to do it, he said, "Yeah. And one day I'm going to be the champion of the world."'

Goody thought the kid didn't know what he was talking about. He laughed and put his arm around Hagler.

'That's great, son,' he said. 'When you're the champion, I'll be your trainer.'

Somewhat to his surprise, the new boy came back the next night, and the night after that. 'Most of them don't,' said the trainer.

'It didn't take long to realise that he was progressing faster than most of the other kids,' said Goody. 'I asked him why and he told me he'd been practising. "Practising? How?" I asked him. He told me when he went home at night he practised throwing the combinations he'd learned in front of a mirror.'

'I met Marvin a couple of months after he started going to the gym,' recalled Carlino. 'I was down at the Fargo Building in Brockton, where they used to do amateur fights, and Pat Petronelli says, "Hey, Angie, you want to take a picture of this kid?"

'"Who is he?" I asked, and Pat said, "He's Short Stuff Hagler."

'I took a few pictures, but I had to show him how to hold his hands to pose,' said Carlino. 'He had on a pair of grey gym shorts and he was still wearing sneakers. He was completely green.'

■ ■ ■

On 12 July 1967, Newark had erupted in a riot that gripped the city for the better part of a week. Thirteen-year-old Marvin Hagler had initially watched with fascination as looters scurried about on the street below, but after a bullet crashed through the window, his mother, Ida Mae Lang, ordered her six children to crawl on the floor when they had to go from room to room lest they expose themselves to the gunfire. For days the family were prisoners in their tenement flat.

Anna Jones, the social worker attending the public housing project where Hagler's family lived, was the mother of the poet and playwright Amiri Baraka. Then known as LeRoi Jones, Baraka was himself arrested (though acquitted two years later) on gun charges during the 1967 episode he prefers to describe as 'the Rebellion'. In Baraka's recollection, it took over a year before his mother was able to help Mae Lang relocate her family to Brockton, where she had relatives.

'They finally tore those projects down a couple of years ago,' said Baraka. 'Until they did, you could still see the bullet holes in the walls of the buildings.'

Brockton itself was a city in some decline, but people weren't shooting each other on the streets – at least not on a regular basis.

Back in the Newark projects, Hagler's contact with members of the Caucasian race had been limited almost exclusively to policemen. He had by his own acknowledgement been a loner in Newark, and now in Brockton, where he knew no one, he felt even more alone.

'It took a long time before he could relax in the presence of white people,' said Goody Petronelli. 'I wouldn't call him suspicious, but Marvin was always wary. He is to this day, as a matter of fact. He really has to know someone to trust them, but eventually he came to trust me and Pat. We all grew in that relationship together.'

In two and a half years, Hagler would come to dominate New England amateur middleweights, but Petronelli wasn't sure what he had until 1973, when Hagler followed his near-miss against Grant in the Golden Gloves final with a clean sweep in the National AAU Championships.

Although 'Stuff' (abbreviated from the original 'Short Stuff') would remain his gym name, somewhere along the line a scribe described him as 'Marvelous' Marvin. Hagler liked the sound of that and adopted it as his *nom de ring*, although both television announcers and newspapermen seemed reluctant to use it. ('The *New York Times* was willing to call Leonard "Sugar Ray", but they wouldn't let me put the "Marvelous" in front of "Marvin",' recalled Michael Katz.) It would be some years later that he went to court and had his name legally changed from Marvin Nathaniel to Marvelous Marvin Hagler.

By '73, Hagler had fathered a young son and entered into what would be a short-lived marriage; both factors contributed to his decision to jump straight to the pro ranks.

Naturally right-handed, Hagler had favoured a southpaw stance. Because Hagler seemed more comfortable that way, Goody had left him alone, but eventually he began working him as a right-hander in the gym. Hagler boxed as a southpaw in winning the AAUs, but he turned around and fought from an orthodox stance when he knocked out Terry Ryan a week later.

Goody Petronelli and Hagler's first promoter, Sam Silverman, had initially reasoned that since many managers were reluctant to pit their fighters against southpaws, it might be easier to book fights for a right-handed Hagler, but after just three outings Silverman advised Petronelli to 'turn him back to southpaw'. 'He's more devastating that way,' he said.

Although he would be listed as a southpaw for the rest of his career, Hagler had become virtually ambidextrous. He could, and often did, befuddle opponents by switching from one to the other in the middle of a round.

In his fourth pro outing, Hagler got the fight for which he had originally gone to the gym. Dornell Wigfall was 8–0 when the two met in Brockton in October 1973. Although he was rocked by at least one punch from his former tormentor, Hagler exacted revenge by winning a solid decision that toppled his old nemesis from the ranks of the unbeaten. (When they met in a rematch two years later, Hagler would knock Wigfall out in six.)

Hagler began to shave his head while he was still an amateur. The orginal notion was strictly utilitarian – it had occurred to him that it might cause a foe's gloves to slide off his head – but the combination of the shiny head and goatee also provided a vaguely Mephistophelian cast and the suspicion is that Marvin rather liked the reaction this produced when an opponent sized him up for the first time.

The look, though it would later become popular among athletes of all stripe, was still somewhat novel in the mid-1970s. As he was making his way towards the ring for one of those early fights, Hagler overheard a couple of punters making a friendly wager on the outcome. 'OK,' one of them told his seatmate, 'I'll take the black Kojak.'

Although he was dominating local opposition, Hagler might as well have been fighting in a vacuum for all the attention he was getting.

'Never mind what happened in the amateurs, they had trouble getting his name in the papers until he became world champion,' recalled Angie Carlino.

'The Petronellis were greenhorns when it came to publicity, but Sam [Silverman] had his own guy, Bill Ebel. The papers never sent photographers to the fights, so I'd take the pictures, take them home and develop them, then deliver one to the *Herald*, one to the *Globe* and leave the rest with Ebel at Sam's office on Canal Street. He'd put captions on them and send them out to the suburban papers,' said Carlino. 'If we were lucky and it was a slow news day, they might use one.'

'And in those days, Brockton was even worse,' added the photographer. 'The Petronellis' gym was right next to the Brockton *Enterprise*, and when he ran shows down there Sam would hold a press conference at the Genova Café, which was literally across the street from the paper. The *Enterprise* wouldn't send anybody across the fucking *street* to cover it. The *Enterprise* still didn't consider Marvin a Brocktonian. To them, he was still a kid from Newark.'

During those early years Hagler was sometimes overshadowed by a fighter from his own gym. Pat Petronelli's son Tony was initially considered the more promising of the two, and at one point he owned the United States Boxing Association (USBA) light-welterweight title. Tony's career took a wrong turn in 1976, when he was so soundly whipped in a world title fight against Wilfredo Benitez that he flunked a brain scan before his next outing. Although he passed a subsequent EEG and was cleared to fight again, he never regained his earlier form. Tony boxed sporadically over the next few years before retiring with a 41–4–1 record.

In August 1974, Hagler met Sugar Ray Seales in what was billed as a marquee match-up of what had been the country's top amateur middleweights of the two preceding years. The 1972 Olympic champion was by then 21–0 as a pro. Hagler was 14–0, but had yet to fight outside New England. Not only was the bout televised, it took place at a television station, in a ring erected in a studio at Boston's WNAC-TV.

Before an audience of invited guests, Hagler prevailed by decision to hand Seales his first loss. A rematch was arranged for November, this time in Seales's home town, at the Seattle Coliseum. One judge, Clay Nixon, scored the fight 98–96 for Hagler, 4–2–4 in rounds, but was overruled by two compatriots, Frank Pignataro and William Kidd, who returned identical 99–99 scorecards. That a professional boxing judge would score eight out of ten rounds even was improbable enough, but that two of them would do it in the same fight was absolutely flabbergasting.

The draw represented the first semblance of a blemish on Hagler's record, but it didn't make the big fights any easier to come by. In 1975, Silverman matched him against another unbeaten middleweight, 29–0 Johnny (Mad Dog) Baldwin, secretly half-hoping that a loss might make it easier to move Hagler. Once again, Hagler won by decision.

As 1976 dawned, Hagler had been fighting as a pro for nearly three years. His record was 25–0–1, but no one outside the boxing game knew his name. Those inside it, on the other hand, were inclined to give him a wide berth.

As Roberto Duran's trainer Ray Arcel was fond of saying, 'Tough times make monkeys eat red peppers.'

■ ■ ■

Still in his 20s, J. Russell Peltz was the director of boxing at the Spectrum in Philadelphia, a venue that would shortly become familiar to American moviegoers as the scene of Rocky Balboa's battle with Apollo Creed. With former champ Joe Frazier on the downside of his career, Philadelphia didn't harbour any real-life heavyweight Rockys, but the misnamed City of Brotherly Love was a hotbed of middleweight contenders. Bennie Briscoe, Willie (The Worm) Monroe, Bobby (Boogaloo) Watts and Eugene (Cyclone) Hart, any one of whom might have won a title two decades later, performed regularly on the enormously successful shows Peltz was running at the Spectrum.

'We had all these middleweights and we needed guys for them to fight,' said Peltz. 'My recollection is that Sam Silverman approached me, because I wouldn't have gone looking for a left-hander.'

'We knew if we were going anywhere we had to fight "the iron",' said Goody Petronelli, 'so we went to Philadelphia.'

For a purse of $2,000, Hagler was matched against Watts on 13 January that year. He arrived in Philly early and trained at Joe Frazier's gym. The former heavyweight champion was impressed by what he saw but warned Hagler, 'You've got three things going against you. You're black. You're left-handed. And you're good.'

At a pre-fight press conference, Hagler, undoubtedly at Silverman's urging, uncharacteristically attempted to beat his own drum by reciting a poem describing what he would do with Watts.

Although Hagler appeared to dominate the fight, referee Hank Cisco called it even and, worse, both judges scored it for Watts. It was a home-town decision so egregious that Peltz was embarrassed. On his way to the dressing-room to console Hagler, he ran into Silverman sitting forlornly outside.

'Sam, I'm sorry,' Peltz told the old promoter.

'Ah, I been around forever,' Silverman replied with a dismissive wave of his hand. 'I'm used to it.'

'Later that night, Allen Flexer, the president of the Spectrum, came to my office,' recalled Peltz. 'He asked me "How can they *do* this?"'

'Welcome to Philadelphia, Marvin Hagler!' read the headline in the next morning's Philadelphia *Inquirer*. In the *Daily News*, columnist Stan

Hochman spoofed Hagler's pre-fight verse with his own poetic view of the verdict:

> *Marvelous Marvin, a fighter from Brockton*
> *Came to the Spectrum and barely got socked on*
> *Boogaloo Watts up he did carve*
> *But guess what happened to Marvelous Marv?*

'It might not have been the worst decision of all time,' said Peltz of Hagler's first career loss, 'but it was a pretty bad one.'

Two months later Hagler returned to the Spectrum, this time to fight Willie (The Worm) Monroe. Monroe was 32–3–1. Sixteen months earlier he had lost a decision to Watts.

'Monroe was originally supposed to have fought another Massachusetts middleweight, Vinnie Curto, that night,' said Peltz. 'Even then Curto was notoriously unreliable, and we had a feeling he might not show up, so I'd been in contact with the Petronellis.'

Somebody had to take a fall for the Watts debacle and it had been Sam Silverman. Hagler's promoter had been thrown overboard, and Pat Petronelli was now doing the negotiating. Two weeks before the 9 March date he sent Peltz a telegram agreeing to a $2,000 guarantee against a percentage of the gate to fight Monroe.

'I still have the telegram, because Pat and Goody later claimed they'd taken the fight on a few days' notice and Hagler wasn't ready,' said Peltz. 'That just wasn't true.

'Monroe didn't mind fighting Hagler, because against Boogaloo he hadn't been exactly devastating,' added Peltz. 'Marvin had just plugged away and outworked Watts.'

A blizzard enveloped Philadelphia that night, effectively killing the gate. The diehard, mostly black fans from North Philly still came down on the subway, but the suburban crowd that regularly patronised the Spectrum shows couldn't reach the venue. The announced attendance was 3,200. Hagler received his guarantee, but that was all.

'In my mind, that remains the only fight Marvin Hagler ever lost,' said Peltz. 'Monroe had the best fight of his career. Willie just had one of those nights every fighter dreams about.'

Although it would be reported in Boston as another home-town larceny, most agreed that Monroe did enough to win. Even Hagler seemed unsure.

'How did Watts ever beat Monroe?' he wondered in the dressing-room.

'I have a few things to learn,' added Marvin. 'But I have a feeling Willie already knows them.'

Before the Petronellis returned to Brockton they met with Peltz. Having jettisoned Silverman, they needed someone to help them move Hagler. Peltz was young, energetic and knew his way around the boxing netherworld. If he would throw in with them, Pat and Goody offered to cut him in on a piece of the action.

Peltz declined. Thirty years later, he still slaps himself in the head when he remembers his next sentence: 'If you can't beat guys from Philly, what am *I* going to do with you?'

Hagler's next trip to Philadelphia has been described as the crossroads fight in his career. It was. He had lost to Watts and he had lost to Monroe, and if he'd lost to Cyclone Hart as well Marvin Hagler might have been reduced to an Opponent.

'If he couldn't beat Gene Hart, he *would* have been an Opponent,' said Peltz. 'If he'd lost to Hart, we couldn't have used him again.'

Hart's record was a modest 30–6–1, but a year earlier he had outpointed Ray Seales on what would be the last card staged by the legendary Philadelphia promoter Herman Taylor, and in his next outing had battled Briscoe to a draw.

But on that night in September of '76, Hagler walked right through him. From the middle rounds on, Hart's corner was in chaos.

'They were arguing through the whole fight,' recalled Peltz. 'At one point I heard Hart tell his trainer, Sam Soloman, "Aw, the hell with it. Why don't you just throw in the towel?"'

After eight rounds, Soloman did.

The win over Hart earned Hagler a rematch with Monroe. His confidence bolstered by the earlier win, The Worm agreed to travel to Boston to meet Hagler on his own turf.

This time Hagler didn't leave it to the judges. In the final round of a 12-round fight, Hagler caught Monroe with a right uppercut followed by a straight left and knocked him out cold. Goody Petronelli would forevermore describe the combination as 'the Willie Monroe punch'.

Eddie Futch and George Benton worked Monroe's corner that night. After the fight, Futch came to Hagler's dressing-room to offer his congratulations.

'It seemed like every time we had Willie do something, Marvin did something else,' he told Goody Petronelli.

▪ ▪ ▪

Don King had spent several months negotiating with ABC in developing the United States Boxing Championships, a year-long tournament that would take place over 1977. The field, King had promised the network, would be 'comprised of the best fighters in the USA'. Howard Cosell enthusiastically embraced his role as host and commentator.

ABC agreed to underwrite the enterprise, paying King $2 million and handing over another $200,000 in matchmaking fees to the promoter's henchmen Al Braverman and Paddy Flood.

The Ring magazine, the self-described 'Bible of Boxing', agreed to verify records and rankings, but as matchmaker Teddy Brenner pointed out, 'If *The Ring* is the Bible, then maybe boxing needs a New Testament.'

Although many other top boxers were also ignored in the selection process, the exclusion of Marvin Hagler was the most egregious. It subsequently came to light that virtually half the boxers in the tournament had ties to King, Braverman, Flood, *Ring* editor Johnny Ort or Chris Cline, another King-controlled manager.

While Hagler was ignored, the middleweight field included Johnny (Mad Dog) Baldwin, who had not had a single fight since Hagler defeated him a year earlier. Another competitor was Ike Fluellen, a Bellaire, Texas, policeman who had also been inactive for a year. Fluellen subsequently confirmed that he had been assured a spot in the tournament if he signed with Chris Cline. Shortly thereafter two fictitious bouts, both against non-existent Mexican opponents, mysteriously appeared on his record and – *voilà!* – Fluellen abruptly found himself the tenth-ranked middleweight in the world.

'If I'd stayed retired,' Fluellen would later say, 'maybe I could have become champion.'

Although his exclusion would ultimately become Exhibit A for the prosecution, Hagler and the Petronellis initially coveted a place in the United States Boxing Championships. Goody even fired off letters of protest to both *The Ring* and ABC.

'King and his people wanted to take over Marvin's career,' Goody later explained to journalist Jack Newfield. 'They insisted me and my brother surrender all our rights to Marvin, if they let him into the tournament. King would have become his new manager if he won. We don't do business that way.'

Petronelli revealed that even after being rebuffed, King attempted a back-door manoeuvre and approached Hagler's mother about gaining a spot in the tournament in exchange for dumping the Petronellis.

'Marvin wouldn't do that,' said Goody. 'He told King "We're all in this together."'

Alex Wallau, a 27-year-old ABC researcher and associate producer with an abiding interest in boxing, attempted to alert his bosses to the fact that something was amiss. With the assistance of Malcolm 'Flash' Gordon, a counter-cultural iconoclast who hawked a mimeographed sheet called 'Tonight's Boxing Program' for 35 cents a copy outside Madison Square Garden, Wallau prepared an extensively documented memo detailing the odoriferous proceedings afoot.

Braverman attempted to discredit both. In a mimeographed imitation of Flash's publication he called 'Boxing Beat', Braverman labelled Gordon 'a beatnik pothead with body odour' and a 'faggot . . . who hates girls'.

And in a threat overheard by several ABC colleagues, Braverman shook a finger in Wallau's face and told him, 'In the old days we knew how to take care of enemies like you. Bums like you used to be found laying in the gutter.'

While his superiors at ABC were still mulling over Wallau's memo, *Sports Illustrated* hit the stands with a laudatory blow-job praising the US Boxing Championships. The magazine's usually respected boxing writer Mark Kram unabashedly defended both King and the tournament, and even quoted Johnny Ort as saying, 'It's going to bring fresh air to the game.'

ABC, at Cosell's urging, removed Wallau from its boxing broadcasts.

The crooked 'tournament' had kicked off amid a display of patriotism with a card telecast from the decks of the carrier USS *Lexington*, and the second series of bouts took place at the US Naval Academy at Annapolis. The third took place at King's alma mater, Marion Correctional Institution in Ohio. (There to cover the proceedings, Associated Press scribe Ed Schuyler said to King that Marion 'looked like an easy place to escape from'. 'It wasn't,' replied the promoter.)

In the aftermath of a ludicrous decision that had gone against him in Annapolis, heavyweight Scott LeDoux interrupted Cosell's post-fight interview with winner Johnny Boudreaux by aiming a karate kick at Boudreaux. (He missed and instead kicked Cosell's toupee off. Howard tried to quickly replace it and conducted the subsequent interview with his hairpiece on backwards.)

LeDoux, with the ABC cameras rolling, unleashed a barrage of accusations of fixed fights and rigged ratings. The loss remained on LeDoux's record, but the outburst did result in the convocation of a grand jury in Maryland, and the FBI was shortly looking into the proceedings.

ABC didn't cancel the tournament until 16 April. By then, federal investigators had determined that King had made cash payments to, among others, Johnny Ort, and that Ort and fellow *Ring* editor Nat Loubet had obligingly falsified the records of numerous participants.

King, predictably, claimed that he had been 'betrayed'. He labelled Ort 'a Judas' and made a public spectacle of firing Braverman and Flood. (Not long afterwards, with less fanfare, King determined that they 'should be considered innocent until proven guilty' and reinstated both men.)

The Ring's reputation was so devastated by the disgrace that it took decades to recover. Several journalists were also tainted by the scandal, among them Mark Kram, who was quietly dismissed by *Sports Illustrated*.

Howard Cosell somehow emerged from the tawdry episode unscathed. Much to Howard's chagrin, so did Wallau. Reinstated to his position at the network, Wallau was given a $4,000 raise and a $10,000 bonus. Thirty years later, Wallau is the president of ABC.

Another whistle-blower, Scott LeDoux, became a boxing commissioner in his native Minnesota.

Flash Gordon, alas, seemed to drop off the face of the earth and hasn't been seen around the boxing world for years.

In retrospect, Braverman and Flood probably did Hagler a favour by keeping him out of the scandal-plagued ABC tournament, but neither he nor the Petronellis viewed it that way at the time.

It seemed, in fact, to be only further evidence that the boxing world was conspiring against him.

■ ■ ■

In the summer of 1977, Hagler found himself relegated to a spot on the undercard of Sugar Ray Leonard's fight against Vinnie DeBarros at the Hartford Civic Center. Leonard's bout, televised by ABC, earned him $50,000. Hagler got $1,500 for fighting Roy Jones Sr, the father of the future light-heavyweight champion. Both Hagler and Leonard scored third-round TKOs.

'Then in August we made the rubber match with Monroe for the Spectrum,' said Russell Peltz. 'Michael Spinks, who'd won an Olympic gold medal the year before, was also on the card, and we drew about 8,000.'

Beforehand, Goody warned Hagler, 'This time don't wait 12 rounds.' Marvin apparently listened.

In the second, Hagler nailed Monroe with a right hook followed by a left hand that caught him flush on the chin. Monroe crashed back into the turnbuckle, and when he attempted to regain his feet he was reeling around the ring. The referee stopped it at 1:45 of the round.

Hagler grabbed the ring announcer's microphone and called out Bennie Briscoe.

Although he was an African-American who shaved his head like Hagler's, Briscoe had a certain cross-over ethnic appeal as well, since he had converted to Judaism and wore a Star of David on his trunks. In the 1970s, he had inherited Ruben Carter's designation as 'the best middleweight never to win the title', having come up short in three challenges for the championship. He lost a decision to Carlos Monzon in 1972 and then, in 1974 in Monte Carlo, was KO'd by Rodrigo Valdez in a fight for the vacant WBC title. It was late in 1977 that he got his last shot at the championship. By then, he was 34 years old. Following the retirement of Monzon, Briscoe once again fought Valdez for the vacant championship in Italy but was outpointed on all three cards. Then, in February 1978, he lost another decision, this time to future champion Vito Antuofermo at Madison Square Garden.

By the time his fight against Briscoe could be made, Hagler had disposed of previously unbeaten Mike Colbert and twice stopped British Commonwealth champion Kevin Finnegan on cuts. The two Finnegan fights were sandwiched around an eighth-round TKO of Doug Demmings in a nationally televised bout for the United States middleweight title in Los Angeles.

Hagler–Briscoe, on 24 August 1978, brought them flocking to the Spectrum.

'It was the largest indoor crowd for a non-world championship fight in Pennsylvania history: 14,950 people,' said Peltz.

Given its build-up, it was a disappointing fight. Hagler was cut badly in the first round.

'It was a bad one,' recalled Goody. 'It might have been the worst cut I'd ever had to work on. Bennie Briscoe used that big, bald head of his and split Marvin right open.

'Before the round was even over, I told Pat to keep the referee and doctor away from the corner, because I was afraid they'd stop the fight. The cut was right above the eyebrow, and at the end of the round I was up there in the corner even before Marvin got back. I slapped compression right on it and loaded it up with, uh, medication, and held it there. By the time the doctor got up there and made me pull the compress away, the blood had stopped. They let the fight continue, but I told Marvin to just stay outside and box.'

Once Petronelli staunched the flow of blood, Hagler was careful to keep out of harm's way for the rest of the night, dancing in circles and outboxing his older foe.

Hagler easily took the decision. Briscoe won just one round on one judge's card, three on the other's, and two on referee Tommy Reid's. Incensed by Hagler's refusal to engage him, Briscoe refused to shake hands afterwards.

Whether Hagler's seemingly timid performance was due to the cut, or whether he showed Briscoe too much respect remains a subject of debate.

'I think it was a bit of both,' said Peltz. 'But you've got to remember, Bennie was 35 years old, and in those days that was *really* old. Briscoe had no legs left, so his only chance would have been if Marvin had stood right in front of him and tried to go toe-to-toe. Hagler would have been foolish to fight him any way other than the way he did.'

Hagler, in any case, emerged from the Briscoe fight with Bennie's 'title'. For the next two years, people would be calling *him* 'the uncrowned champion'.

■ ■ ■

While Hagler had trouble interesting big-time promoters, Ray Leonard found himself fighting them off.

Once it became clear that Sugar Ray was going to turn pro, he surrounded himself with a trusted cadre from his amateur gym. Dave Jacobs and Janks Morton had been the volunteer boxing coaches at the Palmer Park Recreation Center and would remain in Leonard's corner together for the boxer's first 28 pro fights. Ollie Dunlap, the former Michigan State running back who directed the rec centre, became Team Leonard's 'chief of staff'.

Michael G. Trainer, a successful Bethesda attorney, was initially brought aboard to handle the legal and financial aspects of Leonard's career. Although Trainer had no experience in boxing, Morton, who played on the Wildwood Manor Exxon softball team for which the lawyer pitched (and later managed), vouched for his honesty and intelligence.

When Morton initially broached the idea of representing Leonard, Trainer admitted, he had no inkling of what the boxer's services might be worth.

'Do you think he can make $20,000 a year?' wondered the lawyer.

'More like $100,000,' Morton told him. Morton's estimate would also prove to be a lowball figure.

Few, particularly Mike Trainer himself, could have guessed that for the next decade he would be one of the most influential figures in the sport.

The final piece to the puzzle, Angelo Dundee, was initially approached by Washington publicist Charlie Brotman and retained – for a 15 per cent cut of Leonard's purses – with the title of 'manager'. Although Dundee, who had risen to fame as Muhammad Ali's trainer, would be the chief second in the corner and would 'polish off' his training in the weeks before a fight, Leonard felt it important for symbolic reasons that Jacobs, who had laced on the first pair of gloves he had worn back in Maryland, retain the title of 'trainer'.

Sugar Ray Leonard, Inc. was following the lead of the original management group overseeing the career of the young Cassius Clay when it aligned itself with Dundee. When Angelo accepted the role, it was on the condition that he would have complete approval over the young fighter's opponents.

■ ■ ■

Born in Philadelphia to immigrant Italian parents, Angelo Mirena was one of three brothers who would change their name to Dundee. Joe, the eldest, had adopted it as his *nom de guerre* when he became a professional boxer, and Chris, who would become a manager and promoter, also took the name. When Angelo Mirena was discharged from the army after the Second World War and hooked up with Chris in New York's busy fight scene, it seemed only natural that he would call himself Dundee as well.

By the 1950s, having served his cornerman's apprenticeship under Lou Stillman, Dundee was rising to prominence as a trainer, with Carmen Basilio and Willie Pastrano among his pupils. Following Chris's lead, he relocated to Miami Beach, where, operating out of the famed Fifth Street Gym, he would guide the fortunes of a trio of great Cuban boxers (José Nápoles, Sugar Ramos and Luis Rodriguez), teaching himself Spanish along the way.

After the audacious Cassius Clay won the Olympic light-heavyweight gold medal in Rome in 1960, he turned professional under the guidance of the so-called Louisville Group, a consortium of businessmen from his Kentucky home town. They, in turn, enlisted Dundee as Clay's trainer, a position he would retain throughout the career of the man who would become Muhammad Ali.

Dundee was not only an insightful strategist and master of the psychological game; he knew the tricks of the trade as well. In the fourth round of a 1963 fight in London, Henry Cooper floored Clay with a left hook that left him dazed and woozy. Concerned that his man might not fully recover between rounds, Dundee noticed a small tear in one of his gloves and, with his finger, surreptitiously exacerbated the damage. The ruse bought valuable time, allowing Clay to regain his senses while a new pair was brought from the dressing-room. He stopped Cooper on cuts a round later.

In Clay's epochal 1964 challenge for Sonny Liston's heavyweight title (a bout promoted by Chris Dundee), Angelo once again saved the day. Blinded in the fifth round by a foreign substance that may or may not have come from Liston's gloves, Clay wanted to quit and ordered Dundee to cut his gloves off. Instead Dundee sponged out the eyes as best he could and literally threw the challenger back into the ring with orders to run. Clay survived the round and took the title when Liston quit on his stool, failing to answer the bell for the seventh round. (Within days Clay announced that he had joined the Black Muslims and would henceforth be known as 'Cassius X'. A few weeks later he was given the name Muhammad Ali by Elijah Muhammad.)

By the time he signed on with Sugar Ray Leonard, Inc., Dundee had already trained a dozen world champions. Leonard would be his 13th.

Dundee had not been the only candidate for the job, but two other future Hall of Famers had essentially taken themselves out of the running: Eddie Futch, by insisting that Leonard would have to move to Philadelphia, where he then trained his boxers, and Gil Clancy, by demanding the titles of both manager and trainer.

While the titles assigned to the members of Team Leonard tended to blur traditional roles, the division of responsibility was clear. Dundee would approve the opponents and prepare Leonard for fights, while Jacobs and Morton would share the day-to-day training work. Charlie Brotman would be in charge of public relations and

Dunlap would arrange scheduling and logistics. Trainer would handle contractual matters.

■ ■ ■

Don King had weighed in with what was on paper by far the largest offer, a guaranteed $200,000, to promote Leonard's career, but after reading the fine print Trainer realised that its terms would virtually turn Leonard into an indentured servant, and rejected it.

Trainer, by his own estimate, knew next to nothing about boxing when he agreed to oversee Leonard's affairs, but he undertook a diligent study of the business side of the sport and came away convinced that there had to be a better way to do it.

'Why should what the fighter earns be dependent on what the promoter will pay him?' asked Trainer. 'Why don't we just put on the fights ourselves and *hire* a promoter?'

Following another lead from Ali's early career, Trainer initially rounded up 21 Maryland businessmen, most of them members of the softball team for which he and Morton played. The investors put up $1,000 apiece on the understanding that their investment in Sugar Ray Leonard, Inc. would pay an annual return of 8 per cent. As it turned out, the seed money was hardly needed – it was repaid in full from what CBS paid to televise Leonard's pro debut a few months later.

'The difference between our arrangement and Ali's was that Ray still owned 100 per cent of himself,' said Trainer. 'From a business standpoint, it wasn't the shrewdest investment these guys ever made, but they were mainly in it for the fun – it was kind of like having your own team to root for in the NCAA tournament. By the time we bought them out, each of them made $80 for their $1,000 stakes. Fortunately, none of them was really doing it for the money. They just wanted to help Ray get started.'

Instead of going the traditional route, Team Leonard hired Daniel E. Doyle Jr to be its promoter of record. A successful college basketball coach (at Trinity) who had dabbled in many aspects of the sporting world, Doyle took out a promoter's licence in several states. Trainer – or more accurately, Sugar Ray Leonard, Inc. – paid him a flat fee.

On 5 February 1977, when Leonard took on Luis Vega at the Baltimore Civic Center, CBS paid him $40,000 for his maiden voyage. Vega was a journeyman from Allentown, Pennsylvania, who had begun his career in convincing fashion, with seven wins and two draws in his first nine fights, but he would lose twenty-seven of his last twenty-nine, and there wasn't much tread on the tyre by the time he met Leonard. Leonard won all six rounds on all three cards for a unanimous decision.

In May he faced 10–1 Willie (Fireball) Rodriguez, and once again pitched a shutout, winning all six rounds on the judges' cards. Although there were no knockdowns, Rodriguez received a standing eight-count from referee Terry Moore in the third.

In his third pro outing, with Hagler performing on the undercard, Leonard stopped Vinnie DeBarros in Hartford, Connecticut. The bout represented the first instalment on a $350,000, six-fight contract Trainer had negotiated with ABC.

By his fifth fight, Leonard was playing Las Vegas, though not as the headliner. His opponent at Caesars Palace was an undistinguished Mexican welterweight named Augustin Estrada, and Leonard knocked him out in five. In the main event, Ken Norton outpointed Jimmy Young in what was billed as a World Boxing Council heavyweight eliminator. (When, a few weeks later, Leonard's Montreal teammate Leon Spinks – who had upset Muhammad Ali to win the heavyweight championship in his eighth pro fight – signed for a return bout with Ali, in contravention of WBC rules, the organisation stripped Spinks and declared Norton its champion. Norton thus became the only heavyweight champion in history to lose all three title fights in which he participated.)

The road map Dundee had plotted out for Leonard was far from random. As A.J. Liebling eloquently noted in *The Sweet Science*:

> In any art the prodigy presents a problem. Given too easy
> a problem, he gets slack, but asked too hard a question
> early, he becomes discouraged. Finding a middle course is
> particularly difficult in the prize ring . . . The fighter must
> be confirmed in the belief that he can lick anybody in the

world and at the same time be restrained from testing this belief on a subject too advanced for his attainments.

'Sometimes Angelo Dundee doesn't get the credit he deserves for what he did with Ray,' said Emanuel Steward. 'I've heard guys in our business say, "Shit, *anybody* could have trained Muhammad Ali and Ray Leonard," and in a sense they're right. It's sort of like coaching a Michael Jordan. He's bound to make you look good, no matter who you are.'

Or, as the legendary George Gainsford once put it, 'I'm the greatest trainer who ever lived. I trained Sugar Ray Robinson.'

'Ali and Leonard were truly gifted boxers who were going to be great fighters no matter who trained them, but, to me, the finest work Angelo did was in the managerial role,' said Steward. 'Angelo picked the right opponents that allowed Ray to develop into a complete fighter. He put him in with tall guys, short guys, old guys, young guys, left-handed guys and right-handed guys, guys who could punch and guys who could box. They gave him free rein to do it, and there was a reason for each and every one of them. He made the right matches, just as he'd done with Ali early in his career.'

From the outset Leonard's career trajectory differed from the norm for nascent pros. Boxers usually began with four-rounders, eventually graduating to six- and eight-round fights, but Leonard started with six-rounders and was scheduled for eight by his fourth pro fight.

And while promising young boxers traditionally got their feet wet in the pro game by taking on unskilled novices and used-up bums, Leonard, in his entire career, faced only two opponents with losing records – Vega, his first victim, and Estrada, who played the foil in his Las Vegas debut.

ABC was so pleased with the ratings of Leonard's fights that it had upped the ante. Under the terms of a new deal with the network, he would be guaranteed a million dollars a year for five weekend-afternoon bouts. By July 1978, he was 12–0 when he was matched against Dickie Ecklund at Boston's Hynes Auditorium. Ecklund was 11–3 at the time, and his career would shortly go off the deep end as he succumbed to the temptations of drugs. (Years later he would make a successful return to boxing as the trainer of his younger brother, junior welterweight Micky Ward.)

A 1974 federal court edict ordering the desegregation of the public school system had produced what Bostonians referred to as 'the busing crisis'. Four years later the racial tension was still very much in evidence.

'That fight was the first time I'd been exposed to racial taunts,' said Leonard. 'Not from Ecklund or any of his fans, but there was a concentrated element there, and I could hear them shouting nigger this and nigger that.'

The Ecklund fight was also noteworthy because it featured the first recorded knockdown of Sugar Ray's career.

As knockdowns go, it wasn't much. Most agree that Ecklund stepped on Leonard's foot as he delivered what didn't appear to be a particularly lethal punch, but referee Tommy Rawson gave him a count and it went into the books as an official trip to the canvas. It would be six more years, in another fight in Massachusetts, before Leonard would go down again.

'I'll tell you one thing, though,' said Leonard. 'Dickie Ecklund was tough. Just think what he might have done if he'd been sober.'

Dundee had invoked an old trick of the trade to cure another long-standing Leonard malady. As an amateur, Ray's hands had painfully swollen after nearly every fight. Both for sparring and in actual fights, Dundee addressed this by placing a Kotex pad beneath the tape when he wrapped Leonard's hands, and the homespun remedy produced immediate improvement.

In his next outing after the Ecklund fight, Leonard almost fought Tommy Hearns.

Since it didn't happen, we can only ponder what might have been had Leonard and Hearns met not in their primes and not amid the glitter of Las Vegas but three years earlier, in a grimy New England mob town.

In August 1978, Dundee was out of the country, on a cruise with his wife, Helen, and unreachable by telephone, when ABC called to offer Leonard a televised fight against Hearns.

The bout would take place at the Providence Civic Center in September. The $100,000 purse, which would come from the $1 million extension Leonard had signed with the network, sounded right, and Leonard's people provisionally accepted the offer. The contract would be formally signed at a press conference in Providence the following week.

By then, Hearns had been fighting professionally for just ten months. His record was 11–0, but he had fought just once outside Michigan and never on national television, while Leonard had improved by leaps and bounds since that sparring session a year earlier. Trainer, Doyle and ABC could be forgiven if they were unimpressed with Hearns's credentials, but Dundee knew better.

At 11.30 the night before the scheduled press conference, Doyle was at the summer basketball camp he ran at the Westminster School in Connecticut when he got an urgent call from Dundee, who had just returned from the cruise and received the message.

Angelo's first words were, 'Are you nuts?'

'We can't take this fight,' ordered Dundee. 'We're not fighting Hearns.'

'Why?' asked Doyle.

'Ray isn't *ready* for Hearns,' Dundee told him. 'Not now, but in a year or two he will be. And by the time he is, this fight is going to be worth much, much more than we're talking about now.'

'Based on the terms of his managerial contract with Ray, Angelo had the right to veto the opponent,' recalled Doyle, now the executive director of the Institute for International Sport in Kingston, Rhode Island. 'At first, some others in the Leonard camp weren't happy about the decision.'

Instead of Hearns, Leonard fought Floyd Mayweather on the Providence show. Like Dickie Ecklund's, Mayweather's career would shortly be derailed by drugs. Like Ecklund, he would also go off to prison, only to emerge as a top-notch trainer of, among others, his enormously talented son, Floyd Jr, and Oscar De La Hoya.

Mayweather was the first Top Ten contender Leonard faced. Ray knocked him down twice in the eighth round before the fight was stopped in the tenth.

When the bout against Leonard evaporated, Hearns took a fight with *his* first ranked opponent and on 7 September, two nights before Leonard fought Mayweather, the Hit Man knocked out Bruce Finch in three rounds in Detroit.

'Then in October of that year a group of us went to see Hearns fight Pedro Rojas in Detroit,' recalled Doyle. 'Those of us who had been opposed to Angelo's position realised that we'd been wrong. A Leonard–Hearns fight, when it happened, was going to be worth a *lot* of money.'

Leonard would have been paid $100,000 for fighting Hearns in 1978, exactly what he received for beating Floyd Mayweather. Hearns's end would have come to $12,500.

■ ■ ■

In 163 amateur bouts, Thomas Hearns had knocked out only eight of his opponents. As a professional, he dispatched the first 17 men he fought.

At six-foot-one he was improbably tall for a welterweight, but by now he was built like a linebacker from the waist up. Ron Moore, a Detroit auto-parts manufacturer who served as the promoter for many of those early cards involving the Kronk boxing team, likened him to another Detroit creation.

'You could take the best designers at Fisher Body and they couldn't build a better body for a boxer than Tommy Hearns's,' said Moore.

'Forget "Sugar Ray" Leonard,' matchmaker-turned-promoter Teddy Brenner told Michael Katz at the time, 'the young boxer who most resembles the original Sugar Ray [Robinson] is this young kid Hearns – he's tall and slender with knockout power in either hand.'

With Hearns knocking out opponents left and right, Steward bestowed upon him the nickname that would become his *nom de guerre*.

'Tommy's like a Hit Man,' the manager observed. 'He does his business and then gets out of town.'

Steward knew Hearns was good but was still not quite sure *how* good. 'You've got to remember, this was a whole new ball game for me, too,' he recalled. 'A bunch of my kids had turned pro together, but it was a new experience for me.'

The epiphany came in January 1979, when Hearns, in his 15th

pro bout, was matched against Canadian veteran Clyde Gray in Detroit.

'Gray was ranked No. 2 in the world and everybody said he was too much for Tommy at this stage of his career,' recalled Steward. 'They were probably right. He was a very seasoned fighter. Tommy had all knockouts up until then, and that night was the first time he didn't knock his opponent out right away. From the fifth round on he was running out of gas.'

It was, in fact, the first time Hearns had ever *fought* a fifth round. All of his amateur bouts had been scheduled for three rounds and only one of his professional fights had lasted into the fourth.

'By the ninth round, Gray was really coming on, and Tommy was looking tired. Before the tenth, I told him to just go out there and try to box, hoping we could win the decision. He just looked at me, and then he went out there and knocked Clyde Gray out in the tenth,' said Steward. 'To me, that was star quality. That night is when I knew I might have something sensational on my hands.'

Like Robinson against Gene Fullmer, Hearns had knocked Gray out while moving *backwards*.

Up until now Hearns had been considered a local phenomenon, little known outside Michigan. It was time to start trying to get him noticed around the rest of the country.

Alfonso Hayman, Hearns's 18th foe, became the first to go the distance when they met at the Spectrum in Philadelphia that April. (Hearns emerged from the bout with two sore hands. Steward blamed the 'cheap gloves' provided by Russell Peltz and vowed never to fight for him again.)

In May, Hearns topped a card at the Dunes in Las Vegas, where he stopped another respected veteran, Harold Weston. At one point, Weston appeared to have Hearns in trouble, but an accidental thumb produced a detached retina that ended Weston's career.

In June, Hearns returned to Detroit to fight Bruce Curry in a main event at the Olympia. Curry was 20–4. Two of the losses had been in Madison Square Garden fights against Wilfredo Benitez, who had gone on to win the WBC welterweight title. In one of those, Curry had knocked Benitez down three times but lost a split decision.

'Tommy got a bad cut early, and I was afraid they were going to stop it,' said Steward. 'But he went to war. It was like Ray Robinson against Randy Turpin. Tommy was unbelievable. He knocked Curry out in the third.'

■ ■ ■

Born in Indiana in 1899, Ray Arcel had been raised in Spanish Harlem and educated at Stillman's Gym. During the Roaring Twenties he enjoyed a highly successful partnership with Whitey Bimstein, and over the course of the Great Depression he tutored the likes of Barney Ross, Jack (Kid) Berg and Sixto Escobar, and handled the great Benny Leonard, who had been forced to make a comeback after losing much of his money in the stock market crash.

Arcel had worked the corner of James J. Braddock on the night the Cinderella Man turned back into a pumpkin against Joe Louis, and of Ezzard Charles when he lost to Rocky Marciano. In between he had handled so many members of Louis's infamous Bum of the Month Club that Jimmy Cannon dubbed him 'The Undertaker'.

The iconoclastic Arcel often found himself in conflict with the powers-that-be. In the early 1950s, he went into partnership with Sam Silverman, the Boston promoter who two decades later would launch Marvin Hagler's career, packaging a 'Saturday Night Fights' series for ABC.

The enterprise put him at odds with not only the mobbed-up International Boxing Club but also the so-called Managers' Guild, a New York-based organisation which also operated at the behest of boxing godfather James A. Norris. In 1953, Arcel was standing outside the Hotel Madison, adjacent to the old Boston Garden, in conversation with fellow manager Willie Ketchum when a man sneaked up behind him, pulled a lead pipe out of a paper bag and smacked him on the head.

Arcel spent 19 days in the hospital, much of it in a coma. When he revived, he decided to get out of boxing for good.

For many years thereafter, Sam Silverman never left his office without first slipping a flunky a few bucks to go out and start his car.

It has been said that it took Roberto Duran to bring Arcel back to boxing after an 18-year hiatus, but that isn't entirely accurate.

Twenty years earlier, Arcel had handled a Panamanian pug named Federico Plummer for Carlos Eleta. In 1971, Eleta was grooming Alfonso (Peppermint) Frazer for a title fight against junior welterweight champion Nicolino Locche of Argentina and pleaded with Arcel to come to Panama to train his prospect. Arcel, who brought along his trusted assistant Freddie Brown, agreed to put the finishing touches on Frazer. Eleta had also suggested that Arcel might be interested in working with his other youngster, Duran, but Arcel demurred, preferring to concentrate on Frazer.

But Arcel and Brown were seated at ringside the night Duran destroyed Benny Huertas in his American debut, and they liked what they saw. A month later they were in Panama, with Frazer, when Duran fought the Japanese veteran Hiroshi Kobayashi. Although Duran would recall his opponent only as 'some Chinese guy', Kobayashi had in fact held the World Boxing Association junior lightweight title from 1968 until 1971, and had been dethroned by Alfredo Marcano less than three months before he fought Duran.

When Duran knocked him out in seven, Arcel became a believer.

Once Arcel and Brown assumed control of Duran's training, there were the expected moments of friction with Plomo Quinones, who felt his authority was being usurped, but for the most part the three appear to have coexisted without major incident. Brown handled the day-to-day conditioning, but at Arcel's insistence did not attempt to tinker with Duran's style.

'Don't change a thing,' Arcel had ordered his deputy.

Duran had two more fights – a decision over the wily Cuban veteran Angel Robinson Garcia and a first-round stoppage of Francisco Munoz – before he fought Buchanan for his title at the Garden.

After winning the lightweight championship, Duran interrupted his celebrations just long enough to score two first-round knockouts in Panama before returning to New York for a non-title fight against Esteban DeJesus, a 32–1 Puerto Rican trained by Gregorio Benitez, Wilfredo's father, at the Garden.

By all accounts, he was undertrained and unprepared, and incurred what would be the only loss of his first 72 fights. Duran went down from a left hook in the first round, but that was merely a harbinger of things to come that night. DeJesus won on all three scorecards: judges Bill Recht and Harold Lederman had it 6–2–2 and 6–3–1 respectively, while Arthur Mercante, the referee, scored it 5–4–1 for DeJesus.

Duran would later blame the lingering effects of a car crash in which he had been involved a few weeks before the fight, but his handlers knew better. When he, Eleta and Arcel repaired to a Manhattan restaurant later that evening, a disconsolate Duran was in tears.

'You didn't lose that fight in the ring, you lost it in training,' Eleta admonished him.

Duran would meet DeJesus in a rematch two years later. Once again Cholo went down in the first, but this time he got up and knocked DeJesus out with a right to the head in the 11th.

Duran would rule the lightweight division for the next half-dozen years. Apart from the first DeJesus fight, he won 33 times, 25 of them by knockout, and made a dozen defences of his championship – and on several occasions embellished the reputation for savagery he had established in the Buchanan fight.

In his first title defence, Duran hit Jimmy Robertson with a right hand in the first round that knocked three of the American's teeth out. Then he knocked Robertson out for good in the fifth.

Hector Thompson was an Australian Aborigine who had killed a man in the ring. Unimpressed, Duran knocked him out in eight.

In a 1975 defence at the Gimnasio Nuevo Panama, Duran put Ray Lampkin down with a left hook that left the American in convulsions, twitching on the canvas. Although Lampkin was rushed to the hospital, Duran insisted that he hadn't even landed his best shot.

'If I had,' he told reporters, 'he wouldn't be in the hospital. He'd be in the morgue.'

Six months later, Duran fought a fellow named Pedro (El Toro) Mendoza in a non-title bout in Nicaragua. Mendoza was a local favourite, held in such esteem by Nicaraguans that the country's dictator, General Anastasio Somoza, had personally asked Duran to carry El Toro long enough to avoid embarrassing him, but Cholo couldn't help himself and knocked him out in the first round. Bobby Goodman, then a Don King publicist, was in Managua for a WBA convention and had gone to watch Duran, along with another of

King's fighters, Wilfredo Gomez, perform that night, and recalled a wild melee in the ring afterwards.

'Some woman, I think it was Mendoza's wife, jumped in the ring and made a beeline for Duran,' Goodman recounted to Al Goldstein in *A Fistful of Sugar*. 'He just whirled around and flattened the broad with a right hand, better than the one he starched Mendoza with.'

'The thing about it was, there was nothing contrived about any of it,' Goodman recalled to me more than three decades later. 'Some guys try to create an image by acting like some kind of animal, but not Duran. He actually *was* a fucking beast.'

In his 12th title defence, Duran met his old foe DeJesus, who had by then acquired the WBC version of the lightweight title. The rubber match took place at Caesars Palace, in January 1978, and Duran reunified his championship with a 12th-round TKO.

Although he would not formally relinquish the belts for another year, the third DeJesus fight would be Duran's last as a lightweight. To this day, his name would be included on any list of the two or three greatest lightweights of all time, but by 1978 he had been struggling for years to make the 135-pound limit, and he could do it no longer.

Duran had already won five fights as a welterweight by June 1979 when he was matched against the estimable Carlos Palomino, who had held the 147-pound title for three years before losing it to Wilfredo Benitez earlier that year. Duran firmly established his welterweight credentials, winning nine of ten rounds on all three cards at Madison Square Garden, and might have qualified for a title challenge there and then.

Benitez had other ideas. Duran could wait. Benitez's handlers had an offer on the table that would pay him more than a million dollars for what looked to be an easier fight. Against Sugar Ray Leonard.

■ ■ ■

Leonard's march towards a title challenge had reached a furious pace by 1979. In the first nine months of that year, he fought eight times, all of them against respected opponents.

In January he took on Johnny Gant, a veteran of fifty-eight pro fights, and stopped him in eight at the Capitol Center in Landover,

Maryland. In February he travelled to Miami Beach, where he flattened the Canadian junior middleweight champion, Fernand Marcotte, in eight. It was Marcotte's 60th pro fight, Leonard's 19th.

In March he went to Tucson to face Daniel Gonzalez, who was 52–2–4 going into the fight, and knocked him out in two minutes.

In April and May he won decisions over, respectively, Adolfo Viruet at the Dunes in Las Vegas and Marcos Geraldo in Baton Rouge, though the latter was hardly perfunctory. Geraldo, a rugged Mexican middleweight, was, at 160 pounds, by far the biggest opponent Leonard had ever faced, and early in the fight he hit Leonard so hard that a dazed Sugar Ray complained to Dundee that he was literally seeing three Geraldos in the ring.

(Dundee summoned the time-honoured cornerman's advice in these confounding situations: 'Aim for the one in the middle.')

Leonard recovered to post a comfortable decision, but it would be eight years before he would face another full-blown middleweight.

In June of '79 Leonard met Tony Chiaverini, a tough former college football player with a 30–3–1 record. Chiaverini quit on his stool after four rounds.

In August he faced yet another contender, Pete Ranzany, whom he had beaten as an amateur in Boston six years earlier, when Ray was a sixteen-year-old prodigy and Ranzany a US Army Sergeant. This time Leonard stopped him in four.

In September he was matched against Andy Price at Caesars Palace in a bout for the North American welterweight title. It was Leonard's first scheduled 12-rounder.

Virtually every one of Leonard's 1979 fights had been shown on network television, as the Price fight would be. Americans were by now more familiar with Leonard's face than they were with that of the heavyweight champion, which was the reason Leonard–Price (along with another bout, pitting Duran against Zeferino Gonzalez) had been added to the bill, the ostensible main event of which was Larry Holmes's title defence against Earnie Shavers, the hard-punching Cleveland heavyweight Ali had nicknamed 'The Acorn'.

Price was a 25-year-old Californian with a 27–5–3 record, but he was known as a spoiler in the welterweight division, having rung up wins over both Carlos Palomino and Pipino Cuevas in non-title fights. Earlier in his career he had been managed by the actor Burt Reynolds, but by the time he met Leonard, the singer Marvin Gaye had his contract.

During the week of the fight, Leonard was the centre of attention. Duran also seemed to attract more interest than Holmes. When 'Manos de Piedra' worked out at the Sports Pavilion, Leonard was among the curious onlookers.

Holmes went down from a thunderous right in the seventh round, but rose to stop The Acorn in the 11th. Duran seemed at times to struggle against the aptly named Speedy Gonzalez but posted a comfortable win by decision.

Leonard–Price lasted less than three minutes. In the first round, Leonard landed a solid left hook-overhand right combination that knocked Price into the ropes, and jumped straight on him, turning his foe into a speed bag. There were at least a dozen rapid-fire, unanswered punches, the last of them a big right hand that put Price down. He tried to rise, teetered for a moment and collapsed in a heap, where he lay for a full minute before he was carried back to his stool.

The quick knockout did not entirely please Dundee. Because of their stylistic similarities he had hoped to use the Price fight as a tune-up for Benitez, but the brevity of the bout had obviated its value as a learning experience. On the other hand, it had once again been an awesome display of another side of Sugar Ray Leonard, one that seemed to impress even Duran's handlers.

'In another year,' said Freddie Brown, with a shrug to Hugh McIlvanney, 'he could even be ready to try Duran.'

■ ■ ■

Marvin Hagler had also been active during this period, though not all of his campaigns were in the ring. Already angered by Hagler's exclusion from King's US Boxing Championships, a pair of powerful Massachusetts politicians had been enlisted in his cause, demanding that he be allowed to fight for the middleweight championship.

After the Briscoe fight, Hagler fought a Texas veteran named Willie Warren at the Boston Garden and stopped him in seven. On the undercard, an up-and-coming Italian-born New York middleweight named Vito Antuofermo had fought Kansan Mike Hallacy in a bout memorable largely because Hallacy appeared to accomplish the unthinkable and out-bled Antuofermo, prompting Don Dunphy's immortal ringside call: 'That's Antuofermo with the white trunks and the red blood and Hallacy with the green trunks and the red blood.'

Since the beginning of 1979, Hagler had scored a first-round knockout of Ray Seales in their third meeting and knocked out Bob Patterson and Jamie Thomas in a pair of New England fights, but he seemed no closer to the brass ring than ever.

Hagler had by now aligned himself with Sam Silverman's one-time associate, Anthony (Rip) Valenti. Prior to Silverman's 1977 death, the grandfatherly Valenti had primarily focused on amateur boxing – he had been the promoter of record for the 1973 AAU tournament where Marvin had made his first big splash – and his sphere of influence was limited to New England. Hagler had come as far as he had while keeping himself clear of entangling alliances, but now it was time to strike a deal. Even Rip agreed that what Marvin needed now was a promoter with some juice.

The United States might have been the epicentre of boxing, but not of the middleweight division. The great Argentinian champion Carlos Monzon had ruled the 160-pounders for most of the decade, and the middleweight title was securely controlled by Top Rank's Bob Arum and Arum's Italian partner, Rodolfo Sabbatini.

Between 1970 and 1979, there had been 25 middleweight title fights. Seventeen of them had taken place in Europe, seven in South America. During that span, only two American-born fighters had challenged for the championship, and the only middleweight title fight to take place in the US had been Monzon's defence against Tony Licata at the Garden in 1975.

The *New York Times*'s Michael Katz, who had become the fourth estate's most prominent booster of Hagler's cause, had suggested to the Petronellis that their surest route to a title fight would be to align themselves with Arum, but, recalled the Wolf Man, 'They were rightly paranoid about promoters, following Hagler's absence from the Don King tourney.

'I had received letters from Ted Kennedy and from Tip O'Neill, threatening that they would hold congressional hearings if I didn't get Marvin a title shot,' recalled Arum. 'Most of my middleweight fights had been in Europe, so I didn't know much about Hagler, other than that he was a terrific fighter and that King had fucked him over by keeping him out of that tournament. But I knew I didn't want Congress on my back.'

Arum did not realise that the sabre-rattling on the part of the politicians had been the result of some prodding by former Brockton mayor George Wainwright, whose eccentric lawyer son Steve now represented Hagler and the Petronellis.

'But it wasn't like I went out and *recruited* Hagler. I knew Rip Valenti because we'd done closed-circuit business with him in the past. He brought the Petronellis down to my office in New York,' continued Arum. 'Rip assured me Hagler was the real deal and that the Petronellis were good people. It turned out to be a fortuitous thing for all of us.'

The long-term contract arranged that day called for Hagler to fight an Argentine middleweight named Norberto Cabrera, who owned an earlier win over champion Hugo Corro, on the undercard of Antuofermo's challenge to Corro in Monaco that summer, with the understanding that if he performed up to expectations his next fight would be against the winner.

The Hagler party was headquartered in San Remo, on the Italian Riviera, providing Hagler his first glimpse of the country in which he would later box and, eventually, live. (Antuofermo trained in the south of Italy, near his old home in Bari.)

The pre-fight press conference also took place in San Remo and was conducted in French, Italian and Spanish. Periodically Hagler heard his name mentioned, but had no idea what the speaker was saying. He turned to Michael Katz and said, 'I feel like a piece of meat.'

'The Petronellis didn't bring any sparring partners,' recalled Katz, 'because Arum had assured them that there were plenty in Europe and that it would be cheaper. That was "yesterday". When "today" dawned, Marvin's only sparring was against Goody, holding the mitts, so for the first few rounds against Cabrera, Marvin was effectively getting in the sparring he'd missed.

'The French crowd, which adores middleweights, was going "*Ooh-la-la!*" at Marvin's brilliance,' remembers Katz, 'and by the time the referee, Stanley Christodoulou, stopped it, I swear the only thing holding Cabrera up was Hagler's uppercuts.'

On 30 June 1979, Marvin Hagler stopped Cabrera at the Chapiteau de Fontvielle in Monte Carlo. In the main event that night, Antuofermo won a split decision to take the middleweight championship from Corro.

Hagler–Cabrera had been taped by ABC, to use on the telecast in case the title fight ended prematurely. After Hagler's bout but before Antuofermo's, Howard Cosell approached Katz at his ringside position and said, 'You call that a great fighter? I was just on the phone to New York and told them not to put that piece of shit on the air!'

'You must have a piece of that guy,' Cosell muttered to Katz as he walked away. The Wolf Man and a colleague from *Sports Illustrated* seated next to him were left staring with mouths agape.

Only later did the reason for Cosell's outburst – and for his reluctance to allow his call of the Hagler–Cabrera bout to see the light of day – become clear.

The network had done a 'live-for-tape' call, which could not be re-dubbed. Cosell, who had berated Hagler's performance (a virtuosic one, in the eyes of most other observers), had, at the fight's denouement, turned his scorn upon the referee for stopping the bout.

'Cosell was pissing all over Christodoulou, saying he was in bed with Arum, he should never work another fight, he should be run out of town,' revealed Katz. 'Someone in the ABC truck interrupted to tell him through his earpiece, "Howard, he stopped the fight because Cabrera's corner threw in the towel."'

Arum was true to his word. On 30 November 1979, Hagler, in his 50th pro fight, would meet Antuofermo for the middleweight championship of the world at Caesars Palace, but much to his chagrin he would once again be playing second fiddle to Leonard. Antuofermo–Hagler was relegated to the undercard of Leonard's coming-out party – his challenge to Benitez for the WBC welterweight championship.

'I had promoted the Benitez–Palomino fight, so I still had options on Benitez,' said Arum. 'Even though Trainer had already made his deal with Benitez, he still had to go through me. I think that may have been my first dealing with Mike Trainer.'

Trainer had already negotiated the terms with Benitez's manager, Jimmy Jacobs. He had also sidestepped the fight's eventual promoter in arranging the site before he came to Arum with the arrangement.

Caesars Palace was anxious to host Leonard's first title fight. Bob Halloran, a former Miami sportscaster who was by then the president of Caesars Sports, had telephoned Angelo Dundee to ask about Trainer, whom he had never met.

'He's a small lawyer with one secretary,' Dundee told Halloran. 'And when he's not in the office he's usually on the golf course.'

Halloran was a former scratch golfer who often played with the casino's high-rolling customers. He phoned Trainer and in the course of the conversation baited the hook by saying, 'I hear you play a bit of golf. Are you any good?'

'How many shots do you want?' asked Trainer.

'Say no more,' Halloran told him.

A few days later, said Halloran, 'I flew into National, rented a car and drove to Bethesda. When I pulled up in front of Mike's house, he was out on the lawn, wearing a pair of shorts and swinging a golf club.

'By the time we got to the tenth hole that day, we had a deal,' said Halloran.

Caesars agreed to post a site fee of half a million dollars to host the Benitez–Leonard fight.

The agreement Trainer brought to Arum promised the challenger an unheard-of $1 million purse, the champion $1.2 million. Hagler's purse, by contrast, was just $40,000. Although it was a career-high payday, it was precisely what Leonard had made for his maiden voyage, and what Andy Price had been paid for serving as Sugar Ray's foil two months earlier.

Arum covered his investment by peddling, for $1.9 million, a package of three world championship fights to ABC for a night-long boxing marathon that would fill the network's entire Friday night prime-time slot. Antuofermo–Hagler was the second of the title bouts. The other would be Marvin Johnson's challenge to WBA light-heavyweight champion Víctor Galíndez of Argentina.

'I'd already sold the telecast to ABC, but at that time the sanctioning organisations were flexing their muscles, and [WBC president] José Sulaimán, in his infinite wisdom, decreed that we couldn't even have a championship fight from the other organisation on the same card as a WBC fight,' recalled Arum. 'Sig Rogich was the head of the Nevada commission, and he went along with Sulaimán.

'We had no alternative but to move the Galíndez–Johnson fight to New Orleans and use a split feed for the telecast,' Arum said. 'So then to help the live gate at the Superdome, we put on a co-feature using another up-and-coming young welterweight, Tommy Hearns.'

Although Hearns's decision over Mike Colbert wasn't part of the ABC bill, clips of it were shown on that evening's telecast after Johnson stopped Galíndez in the 11th. For many television viewers, that night provided their first exposure to both Hagler and Hearns.

Dismissive of Antuofermo's punching power, Hagler referred to the champion as 'Vito the Mosquito' and handed out souvenir fly-swatters at the pre-fight press conference.

Antuofermo, who realised he could not hope to match Hagler's quickness or boxing ability, tried to force the fight to the inside, but Hagler could brawl as well as box, and by the middle rounds of their 15-round bout, the champion's face looked like somebody had used a fungo bat on an overripe tomato.

'Marvin was at his best over the first half of that fight,' recalled Katz. 'He was landing combinations, hitting Antuofermo with everything he threw. Only Vito's chin kept him in that fight.'

After 12 rounds, Hagler appeared to have built up such a commanding lead that he could not possibly lose. Warned by the Petronellis to stay out of the corners and away from the ropes, he boxed conservatively down the stretch.

'I think it was more than protecting a lead,' opined Katz. 'Remember, at this point Hagler had never gone 15 rounds, and he'd only gone

12 once. He seemed to be trying to husband his energy to conserve himself for the later rounds, and the more cautious he became, the more Antuofermo came on.'

By the 14th, Vito could sense his title slipping away and charged headlong at Hagler, resulting in a spirited exchange from which Antuofermo emerged having sprung a few new leaks. And in the 15th, although Antuofermo fought furiously, Hagler caught him with at least one uppercut that nearly lifted him off the floor.

As the combatants and their handlers milled about in the ring after the final bell, referee Mills Lane asked Pat and Goody Petronelli to move to one side. 'I want to be facing the camera when I raise Marvin's hand,' explained Lane.

Then came the announcement of the judges' cards. Duane Ford had it 145–141 in Hagler's favour, reflecting the opinion of most ringside observers, but his scorecard was offset by that of Dalby Shirley, who had scored the fight 144–142 for Antuofermo. The third judge, Hal Miller, had it even at 143–143, thus rendering the verdict a draw that allowed the Mosquito to retain the title.

'I promoted both Antuofermo and Hagler, but I thought Marvin won at least eight rounds and Vito no more than four,' said Arum.

There were howls of protest from the crowd and most sportswriters excoriated the decision. The long-suffering Hagler, whose paranoia didn't need much prodding, was convinced that he had been victimised by 'Vegas judges' in a betting coup.

'It was a terrible decision,' said Katz. 'If they'd had punchstats back then, they probably would have had Hagler outlanding Antuofermo 3 to 1 – and remember, Vito couldn't punch.'

It was unquestionably a bad decision, but, on the other hand, neither did the 15 rounds of the Antuofermo fight, taken in sum, represent Hagler's finest hour as a boxer.

As he walked towards his dressing-room at Caesars that night, Hagler was intercepted by Joe Louis.

'You *won* that fight,' the Brown Bomber told him. 'Don't give up.'

Through gritted teeth Hagler replied, 'I'll be back in the gym tomorrow.'

Bob Halloran was himself a Massachusetts native. Later that night he ran into the Speaker of the House of Representatives. Tip O'Neill was no more pleased by the decision than Hagler was.

'You can tell the promoters,' O'Neill warned Halloran, 'that if Marvin doesn't get another title shot, there *will* be an investigation.'

Divorced, Hagler had recently taken up with Bertha Walker, a single mother of two from Brockton. He had promised that the two would wed once he won the title and she had flown to Las Vegas in anticipation of that outcome.

'Late that night, I was at a post-fight party at Caesars when I stepped out into the corridor and ran into Marvin and Bertha,' remembered Michael Katz. 'They were walking hand-in-hand down the hall.'

'We're getting married anyway,' Hagler told the Wolf Man. 'No matter what the judges said, as far as I'm concerned I *am* the middleweight champion. I *know* I won that fight tonight.'

Hagler's indignation would be exacerbated when Leonard dispatched the previously unbeaten Benitez in a performance so convincing that by midnight any residual outrage over the Antuofermo verdict had been relegated to a footnote.

■ ■ ■

Born in the Bronx but raised in Puerto Rico, Wilfredo Benitez had been a boxing prodigy. He had turned pro two months after his 15th birthday and was only 16 when he topped a bill at Madison Square Garden's Felt Forum in New York. Benitez became the youngest world champion in boxing history when, at 17, he outpointed Colombian Antonio Cervantes to win the WBA light-welterweight title, and three years later he won the WBC welterweight crown when he dethroned the legendary Carlos Palomino at Hiram Bithorn Stadium in San Juan.

Benitez had fast hands and (as Hagler stablemate Tony Petronelli had learned back in 1976) sneaky knockout power, but his real forte lay in the fact that he might have been the slickest defensive fighter ever to lace on a pair of gloves. Possessed of an otherworldly combination of split-second reflexes and an uncanny sense of anticipation, he seemed to avoid punches before the opponent even decided to throw them, a gift which had earned him the sobriquet 'El Radar'.

'To me, Benitez's greatest attribute was his agility,' recalled Katz. 'I never saw a guy better at bending backwards from his waist to avoid punches.'

Wilfredo had been schooled by his father, the noted Puerto Rican trainer Gregorio Benitez. Before the Palomino bout, Gregorio had sold his son's contract to Jacobs, the erudite New York fight-film collector – reportedly for $150,000 in cash, 10 per cent of Wilfredo's future earnings and a pair of tickets to each of his fights. Teddy Brenner, then the president of Madison Square Garden Boxing, had been the go-between in brokering the arrangement, and when his involvement came to light Garden owner Sonny Werblin was not pleased. It cost Brenner his job.

Although Benitez was undefeated in 39 pro fights, the oddsmakers had installed Leonard as a 4–1 favourite and in the run-up to their anticipated encounter *The Ring* magazine featured a story headlined 'Why Benitez Will Lose His Title'. Its purported author was Gregorio Benitez.

Gregorio would explain that he was trying to motivate his son, whose distaste for training was nearly as legendary as his defensive skills.

■ ■ ■

Watch highlights of Leonard–Benitez nearly three decades later and you might think it was a one-sided fight. You'll see Benitez going down twice, Benitez bloodied from the middle rounds on, and Benitez being rescued, apparently from a terrible beating, in the 15th round.

In fact, for much of the evening it was Sugar Ray's most difficult fight to date. As advertised, El Radar often seemed to make himself invisible, causing Leonard's punches to whistle harmlessly past his head. Although Leonard seemed to dominate the early going, the usual flash-and-dash the public had come to expect was curiously absent. Leonard would later reveal that the night before he had received a telephone call from Muhammad Ali, who, after wishing him luck, had cautioned against showboating in the title fight on the grounds that it might alienate the judges.

'Benitez gave me my introduction to psychological warfare,' said Leonard. 'Watch a tape sometime of the stare-down before that fight. I'm literally chomping at the bit, about to bite clean through my mouthpiece, and he's just standing there, calmly staring at me. I learned from Benitez, and later from Duran, the importance of being relaxed at the start of a fight.'

In the third, Leonard embarrassed Benitez when he knocked him down with a jab.

'When I knock most guys down, it's pretty much over,' said Leonard. 'I tried to knock him out, but I couldn't. I don't know how many punches I missed. Benitez was the most elusive and talented boxer I'd ever faced.'

Shortly thereafter Benitez adapted his tactics and began to emulate the challenger, counterpunching so adroitly that Leonard would later say, 'It was like fighting myself in the mirror.'

Not everyone at ringside was impressed. Said veteran boxing writer Barney Nagler in the *Daily Racing Form*, 'Leonard took Sugar Ray Robinson's nickname. Maybe he ought to give it back.'

From the corner, Dundee urged Leonard, 'Go to the body.'

The sixth round produced a collision of heads. Benitez got the worst of it, coming away with a gash high on his forehead that bled for much of the night.

In the seventh, Benitez incurred a stinger to his wrist while landing a jab and fought the rest of the round with his benumbed left arm seeming to dangle from its socket. But when he came out for the eighth, he flashed a smile at Leonard and stuck his tongue out before going on the attack.

Benitez appeared to be battling his way back into the fight, but in the 11th Leonard drove Benitez into the ropes and unleashed a left hook that sent his gumshield flying. Although it might have impressed the judges, the resultant respite was probably more beneficial to Benitez than to Leonard. Referee Carlos Padilla called time before sending Wilfredo back to the corner to have the mouthpiece rinsed, allowing Benitez to catch a breather by the time hostilities resumed.

If nothing else, the Antuofermo–Hagler fight an hour earlier had provided a cautionary tale for the challenger, and Leonard fought the 15th like a man determined to erase any doubt in the minds of the judges.

'I've always believed in closing the show,' said Leonard, 'but I think somewhere in the back of my mind was what had happened in Hagler's fight, too. I'd been watching that one on TV in my dressing-room and when they announced the decision I was thinking, "Damn. No *way* Marvin didn't win that fight."'

Leonard hurt Benitez with a straight right in that final round, and then moved in to land a spectacular flurry of punches topped off by three successive hooks that buckled the champion's knees.

Benitez instinctively lowered his head and groped his way towards Leonard, hoping to tie him up, but as he did he walked right into a punch Leonard hadn't thrown all night – a left uppercut, which sent him sprawling to the deck.

Only seconds remained in the fight. Benitez managed to get to his feet, and backed unsteadily towards the ropes as Leonard closed in. Sugar Ray landed two or three more punches before Padilla abruptly raced in between the boxers and signalled that the fight was over.

Leonard raced across the ring, vaulted himself into position atop the second strand of ring ropes and thrust his gloved fists into the air.

Many among the crowd of 4,500 at the Caesars Sports Pavilion howled in protest over the referee's seemingly precipitate intercession. The 1–4 odds on Leonard had been prohibitive enough that there wasn't a great deal of action either way on the outcome, but there had been heavier betting on the 'go/no go' proposition. The sports books had offered 6–5 odds on whether the fight would last the full 15 rounds, and at least one prominent Las Vegas gambler, Billy Baxter, had wagered $50,000 that Benitez–Leonard would not go the distance.

There were only six seconds left in the fight when Padilla intervened. Not only does the timekeeper pound the canvas to signal the referee when ten seconds are left in a round, but in Nevada the corner-posts are also equipped with red lights that are illuminated at the ten-second mark. It seemed inconceivable that Padilla didn't know that the fight was virtually over and that another punch could not have been thrown before time expired had he merely stepped in and broken the fighters.

The question on a lot of people's minds was then, and remains to this day: was Carlos Padilla rescuing Benitez, or was he rescuing Billy Baxter?

'According to a possibly apocryphal story I've often heard,' said Katz, 'Padilla was chased out into the desert that night by distraught gamblers. I saw Padilla stop a similar fight where the only action was go/no go, with seconds remaining and the fighters far apart.'

'I didn't know anything about any betting line,' said Leonard with a chuckle, 'but I was certainly glad when he stopped it. I was exhausted. I'm not sure I could have lasted another six seconds.'

The outcome, it turns out, was not in dispute either way. After 14 rounds – *before* the final knockdown – Leonard had led by margins of 137–130, 137–133 and 136–134 on the judges' cards. Less than three years removed from his Olympic triumph, and after just his 26th professional fight, Sugar Ray Leonard could call himself the welterweight champion of the world.

2

LA FACE-À-FACE HISTORIQUE

Duran–Leonard I
Stade Olympique, Montreal, 20 June 1980

AFTER SUGAR RAY LEONARD won his first world title by stopping Wilfredo Benitez for the WBC welterweight in November of 1979, there loomed an obvious candidate for a big-money fight, and his name was not Roberto Duran.

In early 1980, the Mexican welterweight José Isidro (Pipino) Cuevas was boxing's longest-reigning world champion, having won the WBA title in 1976 and defended it on ten occasions.

A showdown between the two 147-pound claimants seemed not only natural but inevitable, and the groundwork for the fight was laid after Leonard's first WBC title defence, a fourth-round, one-punch knockout of England's Davey (Boy) Green in March 1980.

A deal for a Leonard–Cuevas fight to unify the welterweight title had actually been reached, with the approval of both sanctioning bodies, but the proposed match-up rapidly began to unravel amid charges of backroom politicking involving some unlikely bedfellows.

Although Leonard was the standard-bearer of the World Boxing Council, the organisation was headquartered in Mexico, and WBC president José Sulaimán implored his countryman Cuevas to step aside and pave the way for a Duran challenge to Leonard. (A cynic might have noted Sulaimán's cosy relationship with Don King at work in these machinations: Leonard–Cuevas would have been a big fight on which King would not have made a single peso.)

The World Boxing Association, whose title Cuevas held, was based in Duran's home country, and the military government there turned the thumbscrews on a pair of Panamanian nationals, WBA president Rodrigo Sánchez and Elías Córdova, the chairman of the organisation's championship committee.

Colonel Rubén Paredes, who headed up the National Guard of Panamanian dictator General Omar Torrijos, paid a visit to the WBA offices and strongly intimated that it would be in Sánchez's best interests to pull the plug on Leonard–Cuevas. Paredes represented the muscle for Torrijos, whom he would later, albeit briefly, succeed. Torrijos's principal *padrone* was Carlos Eleta, Duran's influential backer, but the Duran camp denied having exerted undue influence.

'We never pressured anyone,' insisted Luis Enriquez, a Duran adviser who served as Panama's honorary consul in New York. On behalf of his people's government, said Enriquez, 'We merely asked the WBA to do what was right for the sport of boxing and the people of Panama.'

To which the curmudgeonly New York scribe Dick Young replied, 'On behalf of the New York *Daily News*, I would like to say one word: *Bullshit!*'

Leonard's attorney, Mike Trainer, recalled that 'some very influential people' wanted to see a Leonard–Duran fight come off before Cuevas got his crack at unifying the title, but for public consumption it was announced that Cuevas was withdrawing from the proposed Leonard fight due to an injury incurred in his April bout against Harold Volbrecht.

Even with the WBC now endorsing a Leonard–Duran match, there remained several obstacles to be overcome, among them that there was no contract, no site, no purse structure and no promoter.

Both Leonard and Duran were technically promotional free agents, but Bob Arum, as the promoter of the aborted Leonard–Cuevas fight, could claim some currency with Leonard. King had Eleta's ear and tried to negotiate on Duran's behalf, leaving Trainer convinced that the flamboyant promoter was more concerned about Don King's interests than about Roberto Duran's. Trainer and Arum then decided to try an end-run around the self-described World's Greatest Promoter, flying to Panama to take their case directly to Carlos Eleta.

But they had underestimated King's intelligence network. (Very little happened in the world of boxing that King didn't know about; he had better spies than the CIA.) As they waited to board their flight in the first-class lounge at Kennedy Airport, King, who just 'happened' to be stopping by, joined them.

A bizarre conversation ensued, in which the rival promoters refused even to acknowledge the other's presence, conducting their discourse through Trainer, who was seated uncomfortably between them. At last, the lawyer had had enough.

'Look, this is ridiculous,' he told them. 'There's plenty enough in this for everybody. Either you two guys work this out or I'm going to Panama by myself.'

■ ■ ■

Then as now the sport's pre-eminent promoters, Arum and King, could not have come from more diverse backgrounds.

A native New Yorker, Arum was in his youth a Talmudic scholar who had been educated at NYU and at Harvard Law School. In 1961, on the recommendation of his Harvard classmate Richard Goodwin, a top adviser in the Kennedy administration, he became an assistant US Attorney under Robert F. Kennedy.

King had grown up a street tough in Cleveland and, about the time Arum was prosecuting federal tax cheats, had risen to become the overlord of the Cleveland numbers racket.

The position sometimes required that he act as his own enforcer. In the 1950s, he had shot and killed a man in what was ruled a justifiable homicide. In 1967, while attempting to collect a delinquent account from a gambling associate named Sam Garrett, King so savagely stomped Garrett in a street confrontation that, as he later described it, 'much to my regret, the gentleman subsequently expired'.

Convicted of manslaughter, King used his three-year, eleven-month stretch at the Marion Correctional Institution to educate himself, devouring the works of Shakespeare, Aquinas, Voltaire and, apparently, P.T. Barnum. King also emerged having mastered a new language of his own creation, a dazzling locution that combined Ebonics with polysyllabic malapropisms.

Both men had risen to prominence in the sport on the coat-tails of Muhammad Ali. In 1962, Arum had been dispatched to investigate suspected tax fraud in connection with that year's Sonny Liston–Floyd Patterson rematch, whose ancillary rights were controlled by the notorious conservative lawyer (and Bobby Kennedy arch-enemy) Roy Cohn. On the night of the bout, Arum had agents waiting to pounce on the box-office receipts at every closed-circuit venue in the country.

It was a major coup for the young lawyer, who was nonetheless astonished to realise just how much money could be made in boxing. A few years later, after John F. Kennedy's assassination had rendered his future in the Justice Department unpromising, he approached former NFL star and Ali confidant Jim Brown with a suggestion:

'Why can't we do what Roy Cohn did, only better?'

Brown brokered an introduction to Ali, and Arum wound up the titular promoter for the heavyweight champion's 1966 defence against George Chuvalo in Toronto. The first fight Arum promoted would also be the first one he had actually seen.

'When it came to boxing, I was a complete neophyte,' recalled Arum. 'A few days before the fight I was in the hotel coffee shop when Chuvalo's managers, Irving and Abe Ungerman, sat down and joined me. One of them asked if I thought there was any way their guy could win the fight.

'I didn't want to let on that I knew nothing about boxing, so I said, "The only way Chuvalo can beat Ali is to hit him in the balls, and to keep hitting him in the balls."

'Well, the night of the fight Chuvalo must have hit Ali low a dozen times. Ali won, but afterwards in the dressing-room at Maple Leaf Gardens he was in absolute agony. I was afraid to confess my part in it, but as I was in there commiserating with him this balding guy with a microphone shoved his way into the dressing-room. I turned around and pointed at him and said, "You! Get the fuck out of here!"

'That,' said Arum, 'was how I met Howard Cosell.'

Arum's nascent promotional firm, Top Rank, would go on to stage most, though not all, of Ali's fights in the 1970s. During Ali's post-exile comeback, Arum also served as his personal attorney, even for fights he did not promote.

That he had assimilated the necessary nuances of the sport became evident when *Newsday*'s Bob Waters caught Arum red-handed in what might charitably be described as a misstatement. When it was pointed out that he had said precisely the opposite just 24 hours earlier, Arum responded with what should have become his personal entry in *Bartlett's*: 'Yes, but yesterday I was lying. Today I'm telling the truth!'

King, after his release from prison in September 1971, had an even faster track to the top. In 1972, he promoted an Ali exhibition staged for the benefit of a Cleveland hospital (the show might well have benefited the hospital, but it benefited King considerably more) and in early 1974 he separately approached both Ali and heavyweight champion George Foreman with promises of then unheard-of $5 million purses.

King came away with contracts bearing the signatures of both boxers. What he did not have, of course, was $10 million, but that oversight was shortly corrected via a mechanism that would become a hallmark of Don King promotions: OPM – Other People's Money.

King's sometime partner Hank Schwartz prevailed upon British millionaire investor John Daly to provide some of the cash, and, hoping to boost tourism in his emerging nation, President Mobutu Sese Seko of Zaire dipped into the national treasury for the rest. Thus was born the Rumble in the Jungle, and while his role had been more that of matchmaker than promoter, King would claim much of the credit. He emerged from Zaire as the veritable face of that epic fight.

When 1980 dawned, Ali had retired for the third time, having regained the heavyweight title from Leon Spinks a year earlier, and the championship had two claimants. King promoted Larry Holmes, the WBC champion; Arum, John Tate, who owned the WBA belt. Both promoters had been cagily attempting to lure Ali out of retirement, each hoping that The Greatest would confer legitimacy on his half of the championship by challenging his man, but that March Arum's quest had been dealt a severe blow when Tate was knocked out, in the 15th round, by the even more obscure Mike Weaver. This calamity occurred on the same night – 31 March – and on the same televised card that Leonard KO'd Davey (Boy) Green.

Although they had joined forces in an earlier marriage of convenience to promote the 1975 Ali–Frazier III Thrilla in Manila, Arum and King roundly despised each other. In recent months, Arum had likened King to Idi Amin, and King had described Arum as 'a snake' and 'a Jewish Hitler'.

'Think,' said Dr Ferdie Pacheco (Ali's personal physician and later an NBC broadcaster) 'of King as a sledgehammer and Arum as a stiletto.'

They would make strange bedfellows indeed, but the result of their meeting at Kennedy Airport was the establishment of a new promotional super-firm called BADK, Inc. BADK would promote exactly one card – Duran–Leonard I – before dissolving in acrimony shortly after the gate receipts were tallied.

Trainer would later explain that he had wanted both promoters involved all along – Arum for his unchallenged expertise in the vagaries of closed-circuit television, and King because he would almost certainly have devoted his energies to undermining the promotion had he been excluded. (As the Scottish scribe Hugh McIlvanney once noted, expecting King to play by the rules is 'like asking a wolverine to use a napkin'.)

Once it became clear that Duran was seeking a $1.5 million guarantee, negotiations became frighteningly easy.

'We can do that,' said Trainer, who tried not to betray his surprise. After joining forces with Arum, King failed to improve Duran's guarantee at all, but did double the promoters' share he would split with his new partner, from $1 million to $2 million.

'It was almost embarrassing,' Trainer recalled the final tally, in which Duran collected a career-high purse of $1.65 million. Leonard, who in lieu of a purse had taken the site fee and an 80 per cent upside of both the closed-circuit and foreign-rights television sales, wound up with nearly $10 million – by far the most any boxer at any weight had ever earned for a single fight. (The previous record had been the $6.5 million Ali got for his third fight against Ken Norton.)

The Quebec Olympic Installation Board, still smarting from the cost overruns of the Olympics four years earlier, ponied up a $3.5 million guarantee (all of which went to Leonard) against the live gate, banking on the allure of the biggest fight of the year and Leonard's residual popularity from the 1976 Games.

The intriguing match-up between the stylistic boxing virtuoso and a man widely regarded as a barely domesticated animal was scheduled for the night of 20 June. Leonard was 24 years old, Duran 29, and their combined records were 98–1.

For a fight that would be billed as *La Face-à-Face Historique*, the 78,000-seat Stade Olympique was scaled from $500 for ringside seats to $20 tickets in the upper-deck nosebleed sections. Tickets in those denominations moved briskly from the outset, but, in the run-up to the fight, sales for the mid-range tickets, priced from $75 to $300, were disappointing.

The bout was formally announced in April at a press conference at New York's Waldorf-Astoria. Leonard wore a business suit, while Duran was resplendent in jewels.

'Leonard was sitting on one side of the dais, Duran the other,' recalled King's matchmaker Bobby Goodman of the Waldorf gathering. 'I watched Leonard stare at Roberto as he ate. There was fruit on the table, and Duran just picked up the grapefruit with his hand and pushed it into his mouth, gnawing his way toward the centre. Leonard seemed very taken aback.

'Then came the steak. As Ray was politely cutting his steak, Duran jammed a fork into his, picked up the entire steak and started tearing at it with his teeth like a hungry lion. Leonard blinked a couple of times and looked away. He must have been thinking, "This guy is a friggin' *animal*!" I'm sure it was the precise mindset Duran was seeking.'

When it came his time to speak, Leonard, presumably to show he was *not* going to be intimidated, promised, 'I'm not just going to beat Roberto Duran, I'm going to *kill* him.'

It was an unfortunate choice of words.

'I don't know why I said that, or where it came from,' reflected Leonard. 'It was uncharacteristic of me. Duran had been pushing all the buttons. Whenever he got close, he'd curse or shove me or act like he was going to hit me, just a total lack of respect, and I let myself get angry.'

'When Leonard told him in New York, "I'm going to kill you," he made a grave mistake,' Duran's octogenarian trainer, Ray Arcel, told Baltimore sportswriter Alan Goldstein. 'If he had said that to Roberto on the street, Mr Leonard would still be stretched out in an alley.'

Duran remained in New York for the initial phase of his training, sparring at Gleason's Gym with Teddy White and with a young New York pro named Kevin Rooney, who would later distinguish himself as Mike Tyson's trainer. The Duran camp then relocated to Grossinger's Resort in the Catskills.

'Grossinger's was still in its heyday, and it was a tremendous place to train,' recalled Goodman. 'The food was fabulous, and Duran was an instant hit with the guests and the visiting media. The ski lodge at Grossinger's was closed for the spring, so that became his private training quarters.

'Duran was focused and serious, so much so that it became difficult getting sparring partners to stay in there with him. He was getting that sharp,' said Goodman. 'Ray Arcel would come up weekly to check on his progress, but Freddie Brown was in charge of the camp.'

Brown, who had been in the fight game since the Depression years, was an old-school trainer. He is generally acknowledged to have been the inspiration for Burgess Meredith's razor blade-wielding 'Mickey Goldmill' character in Sylvester Stallone's *Rocky* films.

About once a week, Goodman would look out his window and see Brown, his bag packed, trudging off towards the reception area.

'This would happen whenever Duran wouldn't get out of bed to run,' Goodman recalled. 'Freddie would go to his room and pack his bag. Invariably, you'd then see Duran chasing him across the lawn in his underwear, shouting, "Freddie, don't leave! I run!"

'After several weeks, the instances of Freddie walking out grew less frequent. Duran was getting into tremendous condition. I don't think he'd ever trained this hard for a fight – before or since.'

Once he hit peak condition, said Goodman, 'he almost toyed with his sparring partners. Cus D'Amato sent Kevin Rooney up to Grossinger's, but Duran just played with the willing Rooney, who would keep coming but could hardly lay a glove on Duran, who could be a defensive magician when he wanted to. He would just put his gloves on his waist, plant himself right in front of a guy and they would *still* have trouble landing anything clean.'

Rubén Blades, the Harvard-educated salsa singer and bandleader, often came up to Grossinger's to hang out with Duran. Lou Goldstein, the resort's long-time director of activities, who years earlier had invented a game called 'Simon Says' for the amusement of the guests, would sometimes be joined by Duran for his after-dinner programme at the resort.

Leonard had opted to remain nearer to home. He based his training camp at a Sheraton in New Carrollton, Maryland, just off the Capital Beltway, and did his morning roadwork at nearby Greenbelt Park. He didn't exactly splurge on sparring partners, using Don Morgan, a journeyman welterweight who had made a career of losing to bigger-name opponents, and a local amateur named Mike James. Roger Leonard, the champion's somewhat less talented older brother, and 'Odell Leonard', who identified himself as Ray's 'cousin', also shared time in the New Carrollton ring.

'Odell wasn't my cousin,' recalled Ray. 'His name was Odell Davis, and he'd showed up at the gym in Palmer Park one day with a Mohawk haircut, saying, "Where's Sugar Ray Leonard? I'm gonna kill him!" He started hanging around the gym and became sort of a fixture there. One day he asked about the people my family had known in North Carolina and then he said, "We must be some kind of cousins." I said, "Whatever," but, next thing you know, he's getting fights by calling himself "Odell Leonard".'

At the champion's request, the sparring partners all wore T-shirts with 'DURAN' stencilled across the front.

'I have a tendency to ease up when I spar,' Leonard explained to Philadelphia *Bulletin* scribe Ray Didinger. 'But I see that name and I want to tear the other guy's head off.'

A few weeks before the fight, publicist Charlie Brotman arranged an open workout at the Sheraton. Sportswriters from up and down the East Coast were invited to come in, watch Leonard spar and engage in a Q-and-A session afterwards.

It was there that Didinger asked Leonard if he'd ever reflected on how things might have gone had he been able to stick to his original plan after the Olympics and never turned pro.

'I'd still be under pressure, but a different kind,' he told Didinger. 'I'd be a senior at the University of Maryland, getting ready to take my final exams and wondering what I was going to do after graduation. I'd be plain old Ray Leonard again, and I wouldn't have to worry about looking at Roberto Duran's ugly face next week.'

'And,' he added, 'I'd be a whole lot poorer.'

Apparently unpersuaded that Duran's knockout prowess had travelled with him to the 147-pound division, the oddsmakers posted Leonard as a 9–5 favourite. A preponderance of boxing experts shared that view.

In a June issue that featured the two boxers on its cover, *Inside Sports* polled a select panel of insiders. Muhammad Ali, Gil Clancy, Sugar Ray Robinson, Jimmy Jacobs, Red Smith, Bert Sugar and Edwin Viruet (who had gone the distance with both Leonard and Duran) all picked Sugar Ray to win.

Harold Lederman liked Duran, albeit for the wrong reasons ('He'll get Leonard late'), while Cus D'Amato was, it would turn out, pretty much right on the money: 'If Duran has the will to apply his skills with determination and courage, he will neutralise Leonard's ability.'

The final tally favoured Leonard by a 7–2 margin, with one abstention. The tenth member of the *Inside Sports* panel, Arthur Mercante, still hoping that he might be named the referee, declined to pick a winner.

'The casting is perfect,' said Angelo Dundee. 'You have Sugar Ray, the kid next door, the guy in the white hat, against Duran, the killer, the guy with the gunfighter's eyes. It's the kind of fight where you *can't* be neutral!'

While the fighters were still in training camp, King dispatched Bobby Goodman to Montreal for a site survey. In the customs line at the airport, he was surprised to run into Arum.

'When are Teddy and I going to get together on the matches?' asked Goodman. The Leonard–Duran fight was an Arum–King co-promotion and he had expected his matchmaking counterpart, Top Rank's Teddy Brenner, to share the duty of putting together the undercard.

'The card's already been made,' Arum replied.

Goodman was somewhat taken aback, and when he voiced his objection, Arum replied, 'That's too bad. If Don has a problem, we'll go to arbitration – and the guy handling that is Mike Trainer.'

Goodman interpreted Arum's undercard coup as a declaration of war. Brenner, hoping for a win that would put John Tate back in line for another world title shot, had matched the former WBA champion against the Canadian heavyweight champion, Trevor Berbick.

'So we reached out for Berbick, set him up in camp and got him some great sparring to get him ready for an upset over Arum's contender,' recalled Goodman.

A month before the fight, Duran began experiencing severe back spasms and a specialist was summoned to Grossinger's. Members of the camp were sworn to secrecy, but the condition was bad enough that Luis Enriquez seriously contemplated asking for a postponement.

■ ■ ■

Though the eyes of the boxing world were fixated on Leonard and Duran, both Hagler and Hearns were closing in on title shots of their own.

In February 1980, three months after the draw with Vito Antuofermo, Hagler was matched with middleweight contender Loucif Hamani at the Cumberland County Civic Center in Portland, Maine. Hamani was a Paris-based Algerian with a 20–1 record, but he had never fought in the United States, nor had he ever faced an opponent of Hagler's calibre. Hagler knocked him out in two.

Hagler got the opportunity to avenge his first career defeat when he fought Boogaloo Watts two months later. Once again the bout took place in Portland, and once again it didn't get out of the second round.

In May, he fought Marcos Geraldo in Las Vegas. The Mexican had given Leonard a world of trouble when they fought in Baton Rouge a year earlier, and Hagler had his problems as well, but he did enough to win seven of ten rounds on the scorecards of all three judges.

Hearns had also kept himself busy. In February, he travelled to Las Vegas, where he knocked out 'Fighting Jim' Richards on the Larry

Holmes–Lorenzo Zanon undercard. A month later he was back in Detroit to fight Angel Espada, a former WBA welterweight champion, in the main event of a card at Joe Louis Arena. Hearns stopped Espada in four. In that evening's co-feature, Hilmer Kenty stopped WBA lightweight champion Ernesto España in nine to become Emanuel Steward's first world champion.

On 31 March – the same night Leonard knocked out Dave (Boy) Green at the Cap Center – Hearns KO'd Santiago Valdez at Caesars Palace. Employing a split feed from three separate venues, ABC had shown title bouts originating in Landover, Knoxville and Las Vegas. Hearns–Santiago had been part of the Larry Holmes–Leroy Jones card at the latter venue but was not included on the telecast.

In May, the Hit Man returned to Detroit to fight veteran Eddie Gazo at Cobo Hall. Gazo, a Nicaraguan, had just a few years earlier held the WBA junior middleweight championship. ('At the time, he might have been the worst champion in history,' claimed Katz.) Hearns knocked him out in the first round.

The Hit Man's record was now 28–0. His next fight, scheduled for later that summer, would be against Pipino Cuevas for the WBA welterweight title.

■ ■ ■

Duran arrived in Montreal a few days before Leonard and polished off his sparring at the Complex des Jardins. The assumption had been that Leonard would have retained his popularity among the locals who remembered him from the 1976 Games, but Duran, who wore a T-shirt saying *'Bonjour, Montreal'* at his workouts, quickly captured the hearts of the Québécois.

The boxers worked out in the same ring at des Jardins. The gym had been converted from an old ice hockey rink. The novelist Leonard Gardner (*Fat City*), in Montreal to cover the fight for *Inside Sports*, watched both boxers prepare; one afternoon he saw Leonard knock Mike James down with a right hand.

Gardner was not the first to notice that Duran had never quite mastered another time-honoured practice of boxers-in-training. The Panamanian, observed the novelist, skipped rope 'like a drunk'. In a Cleveland gym, I once saw a similar display of ineptitude; Duran kept getting himself tangled up in the jump-rope. Since skipping rope is universally one of the very first exercises a nascent boxer learns, this also struck me as a pretty startling revelation. It was sort of like encountering a football player who couldn't do jumping-jacks.

Michael Katz insisted that Gardner and I were both fooled, and that Duran, when he set his mind to it, could be a dazzling, rope-skipping virtuoso: 'If he skipped rope "like a drunk", he must have been imitating a drunk,' said the Wolf Man.

Duran's work in the gym nonetheless made an indelible impression on Gardner.

'I saw him land a right hand that left me spellbound,' Gardner recalled 27 years later. 'It reminded me of some of the great fighters I'd watched on television as a kid – just a picture-perfect punch. But what impressed me even more was his exuberance. He was so full of energy and seemed to really enjoy what he was doing. I was at the gym one day and when he finished he was ready to leap right out of the ring. The ring was a good four or five feet off the floor, so this absolutely terrified Ray Arcel and Freddie Brown, who seemed to be watching over him every second. Arcel was old, but he could move pretty fast. He raced over and helped Duran down from the ring to make sure he didn't jump and turn an ankle or something.'

'Later that night when I got back to my hotel, I phoned a friend in California,' said Gardner. 'I advised him to bet on Duran.'

Dundee, who would turn 60 a year after the Montreal fight, was regarded as a venerable figure ('He's been around the fight game longer than the Marquis of Queensberry,' wrote Didinger), but he was a spring chicken compared to Arcel and Brown.

'Those two guys are older than water,' said Dundee of Arcel, who was 82, and Brown, 73. As a young cornerman in New York in the late 1940s, in fact, Dundee had learned many tricks of the trade from the courtly Arcel, whose experience went back to the days of *Benny* Leonard.

Freddie Brown could also claim a lengthy boxing pedigree. In Marciano's corner a generation earlier, wrote Gardner, Brown had acquired 'a degree of immortality as the cut man who closed the rip on Rocky's nose in his second bout with Ezzard Charles'.

'Arcel, when he's not screaming, sounds like the chairman of a college English department,' noted Vic Ziegel in describing the venerable duo. 'Brown is a white-haired man with a nose that resembles a low flush in clubs. His sentence structure is equally dazzling.'

Duran and his boisterous travelling party were booked into the staid Hotel Bonaventure. Leonard and his crew, once they arrived in Montreal, took up residence nearby at the more modern Le Regence Hyatt.

Their sumptuous digs were a far cry from the Leonard family accommodations in Montreal four years earlier. During the 1976 Games, of course, Ray had stayed in the Olympic Village, but his parents Cicero and Getha, wife-to-be Juanita, Dave Jacobs and several Leonard brothers and sisters had driven to Canada together in a beat-up Volkswagen van they nicknamed 'the Sardine'.

The ladies had shared a single room in a budget motel, sleeping on beds, chairs and the floor. Jacobs, Cicero, Roger and Kenny slept in the Sardine, which was parked on the street nearby, and made occasional forays to the motel room to sneak in a shower.

Now, in 1980, Duran's and Leonard's respective headquarters were only a few blocks apart and it was inevitable that there would be chance encounters in the days leading up to the fight. Roberto Duran might not have spoken much English back then, but that didn't mean he couldn't give Leonard the finger whenever he saw him.

One morning Leonard's sister Sharon was walking down the street when she looked up and saw Duran leering at her from a passing car, 'flashing a message', wrote Chicago *Sun-Times* scribe John Schulian, 'that did not require an interpreter'.

'Once his *wife* even gave my wife the finger,' said Leonard. 'Duran was just weird.'

The macho gamesmanship took its toll on Sugar Ray. Dundee would later admit to the *New York Times*'s Dave Anderson that Leonard 'got out-psyched. Duran abused Ray, and Ray couldn't handle it. Duran would see Ray walking with his wife in the streets in Montreal and he'd yell, "*I keel your husband. I keel your husband!*" The night of the fight, Ray wanted to *keel* him. Ray wanted to *fight* the guy, not box him.'

Twenty-seven years later, Leonard conceded that Duran did a

masterful job of winding him up. 'I don't think it was *calculated*,' said Leonard. 'It was more a case of Duran being Duran. He had that bully's mentality, and he *always* tried to intimidate opponents. But he *did* challenge my manhood, and I wasn't mature enough to know how to respond. All I could think about was retaliating.'

The hirsute Katz, in Montreal to cover the fight for the *New York Times*, dropped by Duran's hotel one morning to find the lobby filled with Panamanian militiamen, zealously guarding Duran and swatting away any hotel guest who might venture too near. Duran spotted Katz across the room and, shooing away his protectors, walked over and hugged him. The two chatted for a moment and, as they parted company, Duran winked at Katz and told him, 'I hope you bet *beeg* on me.'

'So I did,' said the Wolf Man.

The boxers reported to the Quebec commission offices on Monday for their pre-fight physicals. Shortly thereafter Arcel got a phone call in his hotel room, informing him that Duran's ECG had revealed an irregularity – an unexplained arrhythmia – and that the fight might be in jeopardy.

'How can he have a heart condition?' asked Arcel. 'Duran doesn't even *have* a heart.'

Arcel informed Eleta, who phoned Torrijos, and by nightfall the foremost cardiac specialist in Panama was en route to Montreal on a private jet.

The next morning Duran underwent a four-hour battery of tests at the Montreal Institute of Cardiology and was cleared to fight. The cause of the irregularity on the initial ECG was never confirmed, but it was widely speculated that it could have been precipitated by diet pills Duran had consumed in a frenetic attempt to shed extra poundage in the days before the fight.

If that was the case, the diet apparently succeeded. At the weigh-in, both made the welterweight limit with ease. Leonard weighed 145, and Duran was just half a pound heavier.

In retrospect, believes Leonard, 'I probably came in too light for that fight.'

José Sulaimán, the WBC president Arum once described as 'a fat Mexican dictator', had elected to stay at the same hotel as Leonard.

Sulaimán had further enraged the Duran camp when he appointed Carlos Padilla as the referee.

It had been Padilla, remember, who the previous November had intervened to stop Leonard's fight against Benitez with six seconds left in the final round, and more recently had appeared somewhat squeamish in working the first Alan Minter–Vito Antuofermo fight. In the opinion of Brown, who had been in Antuofermo's corner, the referee's disinclination to let Antuofermo work inside had cost his man the title.

Brown complained that whenever Antuofermo worked his way inside under Minter's jab, the Englishman would grab him, and when Vito continued to punch with his free hand, the referee would break the fighters.

'I want a referee that'll let my fighter fight,' moaned Arcel.

At the weigh-in, Arcel made it a point to lecture the Filipino referee. Arcel plainly hoped to gain an advantage for Duran when he reminded Padilla that the customers had paid to see the two boxers, not him.

'Give us a great fight,' he told the referee. 'The whole world is going to be watching. Let them fight.'

'The night before the fight, several of us were having a drink at the bar atop the Hyatt when José Sulaimán sat down and joined us,' recalled Katz. 'He told us that night that he had instructed Padilla to let the fighters fight. I think this had a lot more to do with the conduct of the fight than anything Ray Arcel might have said to the referee.'

With the advance sale less than half the house, the local promoters had been relying on a big walk-up crowd the night of the fight, but it began to rain early that afternoon and a steady drizzle continued to fall as the preliminary bouts got under way.

In its original concept, Stade Olympique was to have a retractable domed roof, which would be opened and closed by cables suspended from a 500-plus-foot tower. On the drawing board, the roof resembled the lid of a giant teapot. Inhospitable weather, a protracted labour dispute and engineering foul-ups had delayed its completion, and the 1976 Olympics had taken place in the open air.

The tower remained, but four years later the 60,000-square-foot roof was still in Paris. The roof wouldn't be installed until 1986, and in 1991 it collapsed, raining 55 tons of concrete into the fortunately unoccupied interior. The cost of the stadium had initially been estimated at $120 million, but by the time the Expos fled to Washington in 2006 the figure topped a billion dollars, and 8 per cent of the price of each pack of cigarettes purchased in Quebec was going to defray the debt service from an Olympiad held three decades earlier.

That the roof was still not in place for the Duran–Leonard fight proved a boon for those who had purchased tickets in the cheap seats, most of which were protected from the elements, but the ring had been set up in the baseball infield, between the pitcher's mound and second base, meaning that the prime ringside seats were at field level and fully exposed.

Ushers in the $500 sections walked about dispensing ponchos. When they ran out of those, they distributed plastic rubbish bags for the high-rollers to wear over their clothes.

Paid attendance would eventually reach 46,195. Had the Expos been able to draw such numbers, they would still be in Montreal today, but on this evening it translated into nearly 32,000 empty seats. Far from recouping its investment, the Quebec Olympic Installation Board would be driven even further into the hole.

The ringside press seats were also exposed to the elements, and many of us watched the undercard from beneath the roof, in the stands above the first-base line. Others watched from the comfort of the Expos' press room.

Tragedy would visit the proceedings in the second bout of the evening, a rubber match between lightweights Cleveland Denny and Gaetan Hart, who had split two earlier meetings. In the final minute of their ten-round bout, Hart rained a succession of unanswered blows to the head of Denny.

Far too late, the Canadian referee, Rosario Ballairgeon, tried to stop the fight, but even in his belated intervention he was hopelessly out of position. Ballairgeon stood behind Hart, frantically waving his arms, while Hart, unable to see the referee, kept pounding away at Denny.

Once Hart was pulled away, Denny keeled over, his head thumping off the canvas. For several minutes he lay there as chaos reigned in the ring. The moment remains etched in Leonard Gardner's mind:

'I'd never seen anyone die in the ring before, though I've seen it since,' said Gardner. 'It seemed apparent that that had happened, even at the time. Denny seemed to change colour before my eyes. He looked like he was turning grey. It was a weird thing to see, or to *think* you've seen.'

Eventually a stretcher was summoned. Denny, still convulsing, was strapped to it and wheeled from the ring. By then, Michael Katz and I had made our way back down to ringside, and as we looked at him on the gurney, Denny's eyes had rolled back into his head, evincing only white, and his gumshield was still clenched between his teeth.

'I think we both knew right then he wasn't going to make it,' Katz recalled a quarter-century later.

'You've got to get that mouthpiece out!' I told one of the paramedics.

A familiar face emerged from the mob surrounding Denny.

'I've been *trying* for the last ten minutes,' a weary Ferdie Pacheco told me.

The Fight Doctor, scheduled to work as part of the broadcast team, had followed his instincts and his Hippocratic Oath, abandoning his TV position to assist the stricken boxer.

My *Boston Herald American* colleague, Tim Horgan, had been assigned to write the Duran–Leonard lead that night. Now what appeared to have been a preventable tragedy might also be an important story. After quickly conferring with Horgan, I jumped into a cab and followed the ambulance bearing Cleveland Denny to Maisonneuve-Rosemont Hospital.

Denny was scheduled for immediate surgery to relieve a subdural haematoma, but no other information seemed to be forthcoming. Denny's wife, Clarine, had accompanied him in the ambulance, but less than an hour later, on the advice of the hospital staff, she summoned another cab and returned to the stadium.

'Well, if *she's* going back to the fight, *I'm* going back to the fight,' I reasoned.

Denny would linger for nearly two weeks. His brain stem had probably herniated when he hit the floor. He was pronounced clinically dead on 2 July, but his wife elected not to remove him from life-support systems, opting to rely on prayer. He lasted five more days before he died on 7 July.

In my absence, a pair of Canadian middleweights, Eddie Melo and Fernand Marcotte, had battled to a ten-round draw, but I got back in time to see the conclusion of the semi-final, which on another night might have provided comic relief.

In what was supposed to be the first step in the rehabilitation of John Tate, Arum had matched him against the Canadian heavyweight champion, Trevor Berbick. Fighting in the same city where he had been ingloriously knocked out by Teofilo Stevenson in their Olympic semi-final four years earlier, Tate had more than held his own for eight rounds, but in the ninth Berbick caught him with a big right hand, and Tate responded by turning his back and literally running away.

As Tate fled across the ring, Berbick chased him, still throwing punches, the last of which caught the American on the back of his head and knocked him headfirst through the ropes. Landing with a belly-flop on the canvas, Tate came to rest with his head dangling over the edge of the apron, a position he retained as he was counted out. The only perceptible movement from Tate came in the involuntary twitching of his legs, and in that instant it crossed more than one person's mind that we might have been looking at two ring fatalities in one night.

'Tate landed almost directly in front of Bob Arum,' remembered Michael Katz. 'Arum had a look of shock on his face, and even as the referee was counting I could hear the unmistakable – *Heh! Heh! Heh!* – of King cackling from across the ring.

'I looked over at him and said, "Don't tell me you've got Berbick, too!"'

King enthusiastically nodded his head. Yes, he did.

Duran, the first of the main event competitors to make an appearance, seemed so eager to fight that he almost raced from the dugout to the ring, accompanied by the beat of drums. When Leonard approached centre stage, his wife and sister climbed atop their chairs, dancing as they sang, '*Hey, Sugar Ray!*'

I also seem to recall that once they reached the ring, the principals were forced to stand through three different national anthems, and that, as usually happened in Montreal, the rendition of 'O, Canada!' turned into a contest between the French- and English-speaking segments of the crowd, each trying to drown out the other by singing in its preferred tongue.

As the boxers were introduced, another division of loyalties became evident. Despite his history in the venue, Leonard was far from an overwhelming crowd favourite. The cheers for Duran were even more pronounced, and boos and whistles could be heard amid the applause that greeted Leonard's name.

Leonard, for possibly the first time in his career, was even outswaggered. Duran exuded confidence. Leonard, despite a nervous smile, looked like a man about to face a firing squad.

'This was a big fight, bigger than anything I'd ever experienced before,' said Leonard. 'I can remember looking around at all those people in the stadium, looking at myself on the big TV screen, and thinking "Wow. This is *huge*." I was in awe from the sheer magnitude of it.'

Whether Leonard's hand speed and ring quickness would offset Duran's street-fighting tactics would quickly became a moot point. For much of the night, Leonard tried to beat Duran at his own game.

The tone for the evening was set at the opening bell, when Duran charged straight out of his corner and tried to hit Leonard in the balls with the first punch he threw.

Duran spent most of the opening three minutes trying to bull his way around the ring, and Leonard spent most of it trying to shake his way clear. Duran landed the best punch of the round when he speared Leonard with a right-hand lead, and Ray responded by shaking his head to indicate that he hadn't been hurt.

When a boxer does that, it is usually a safe bet that he has been.

In the second, Duran caught Leonard high on the head with a left uppercut that knocked him backwards into the ropes. Stunned, Ray tried to clinch, but even as he grappled and looked to the referee for help, Duran kept pounding away.

'Starting out, I'd given him some head movement and a few little feints, but then Duran caught me with an uppercut and just knocked the shit out of me,' said Leonard.

Katz recalled the same punch as a right-hand lead. 'The shock to me was that Duran had hands as quick as Leonard's,' said the Wolf Man. 'Ray was hurt by that punch and he didn't recover for *rounds*.'

Before the fight, Dundee had predicted that 'the key will be Ray's left hand', but Leonard hadn't shown that weapon. On the other hand, he *had* answered another question that hadn't been asked in his 27 previous fights.

'I showed I could take a punch,' he said.

Duran continued to punish the champion over the next two rounds, pounding Leonard with solid right hands, and while Leonard sometimes landed spectacular flurries of punches, he spent much of the evening allowing himself to be pushed around the ring. Although he had been expected to set the tone with his jab, Leonard failed to establish a rhythm that would allow him to use it, and when he tried to go on the attack, Duran was able to rely on his superior counterpunching.

The Leonard camp would later complain that Padilla (with, perhaps, Sulaimán's pre-fight admonition ringing in his ear) had abetted Duran's rough-housing by allowing him to escape unpunished when he held and hit, or used his elbows and forearms to manoeuvre Leonard around the ring. From the corner, Dundee pleaded for the referee to be more assertive in breaking up the frequent clinches.

As he recalled these early stanzas two decades later, Manos de Piedra told his biographer, Christian Giudice, that Leonard (or, perhaps, Dundee) had committed a tactical blunder by smearing his body with Vaseline. The theory had been that the ample coating of grease would cause Duran's punches to slide off, but by the fourth round the substance had been transmitted to Duran's gloves. When Leonard tried to tie him up, which was often, Duran was able to yank his hands free and resume his attack.

Although he was ostensibly the quicker man, Leonard already had rope burns on his back from the numerous occasions Duran had driven him to the edge of the ring. Ray was no longer even trying to dance. In her ringside seat, Juanita Leonard had begun to sob.

Leonard finally sprang into action in the fifth, unleashing dazzling combinations of punches that impressed the judges, if not his opponent. 'I couldn't tell you why,' Leonard said of the abrupt change in approach beginning with the fifth. 'I think my fighting instincts just took over.'

Duran disdainfully sneered in response, but when it was over it was clear that Sugar Ray had claimed his first round.

The sixth saw Leonard once again become the aggressor, using his jab to set up combinations. Now Ray was forcing Duran to tie *him* up.

'By then, I felt I was in control of the fight,' Leonard recalled to his Boswell, Al Goldstein, 'but the one thing that concerned me was Duran's head. He was using it as a weapon. Every time I moved inside, he tried to butt me.'

By the seventh, the fight had turned into an all-out street war, and by the time it ended both men looked so tired that it was hard to imagine this fight lasting eight more. I thought Duran had probably won the round, but all three judges scored it even.

As the two engaged in a toe-to-toe brawl in the eighth, stadium ushers rushed to Juanita's ringside seat. Overcome by the intensity of what she was watching, Ray's wife had fainted.

Dave Jacobs, working the champion's corner with Dundee and Janks Morton, looked as if he was about to pass out himself.

'*Box!*' he kept pleading.

'Be the boss!' Arcel ordered Duran.

The ninth round produced another vintage Duran move. He charged into Leonard, butted him squarely in the forehead and then, as Ray clinched, raked his head across his eyes. Leonard, once he extricated himself, wiped himself with his glove to check for blood.

Once again, all three judges scored an even round.

'Leonard showed tremendous courage,' an admiring Arcel would say later. 'Duran landed some body shots that would have shook Hitler's army, but Leonard kept fighting back.'

The tenth was on the way to being another close round until Leonard clocked Duran with his best punch of the night, an overhand right that came out of nowhere and rocked the Panamanian in his tracks.

The 11th was another non-stop, three-minute brawl. Leonard, who opened with a right-hand lead followed by a staccato flurry to the body, probably did enough to win it, but Duran fired back in kind and was battling at its end, setting the stage for the 12th, in which Duran would win his last round of the night.

The 13th proved to be Leonard's most dominant stanza of the evening as he dug into Duran with a left to the body followed by two rights to the head. Later in the round, the second half of a left-right combination snapped Duran's head backwards.

Leonard continued to jar Duran with combinations in the penultimate round, but the challenger countered by putting his head down and charging forwards to tackle Ray in an effort to smother the onslaught.

From the corner, Dundee shouted, '*Why don't you break 'em, Padilla?*'

Leonard closed the show with a dazzling final round that impressed all save Duran, who, playing to the crowd, mocked his opponent. Apparently confident of victory, Duran did a little Leonardesque dance and pointed to his chin, daring Leonard to hit him one more time.

When the final bell sounded, Leonard reached out and tried to tap Duran with his glove, but Cholo appeared to ignore the gesture. Both boxers were quickly engulfed in a mass of humanity as cornermen, posses and officials poured into the ring.

When Duran reached his corner, I saw him suddenly wheel and, pointing to his own genitals, unleash an incomprehensible torrent in Spanish.

'*What did Roberto say?*' I asked my pal Jose Torres, the former light-heavyweight champion.

'He called him, you know, a pussy,' said Torres. 'A cunt.'

Leonard Gardner seemed to think that Duran was addressing his remarks to Wilfredo Benitez, while my own impression was that he had been looking right at Sugar Ray when he did it. As it turned out, we were both wrong. Cholo's invective was directed toward *Roger* Leonard.

'Right after the bell rang, Roger came charging out of the corner, running straight at Duran,' said Ray. Duran responded pretty much the way he had to Pedro Mendoza's wife and dropped Roger in his tracks with a single punch.

'Duran just *nailed* him,' said Ray. 'There was so much confusion in the ring that not a lot of people even saw it happen.'

Benitez was, however, a conspicuous presence at ringside. He had been invited by Howard Cosell to sit in on the telecast, but, said Leonard Gardner, 'had abandoned his post to yell insults at Duran'.

'A security guard picked him up and was about to throw him over the ropes into the press section when I convinced him that Wilfredo was a valuable commodity,' wrote Gardner in recapturing the moment.

An eerie silence pervaded the stadium while the verdict was awaited. Sugar Ray Leonard had closed the show, but now the unthinkable had begun to cross his mind – the possibility that he might have lost.

'They'd both been blocking and slipping and rolling and countering,' Gardner remembered thinking. 'To me, it had seemed quite an even fight.'

In the initial reading of the scorecards the French judge, Raymond Baldeyrou, had it 146–144 for Duran. The Italian judge, Angelo Poletti, scored the fight even at 147–147.

For a brief instant it appeared that a fight this close might come down to a split draw, but then came the British judge's card: Harry Gibbs scored it 145 Duran, 144 Leonard, rendering it a majority decision.

Though clearly disappointed, Sugar Ray didn't quibble about the verdict. In his dressing-room, he conceded that Duran had won most of the early rounds in what he termed 'the hardest fight of my career' but pointed out that once he did get untracked, 'I stood my ground.'

'You never fight to a guy's strength, you try to offset it,' sighed Dundee, as he attempted to explain to *Sports Illustrated*'s Bill Nack how the best-laid plan had gone awry. 'It was strictly Duran stuff – elbows, knees, head-to-the-face. The guy who had more practice at that won the fight.'

An hour later Bob Lee, then a WBC supervisor, entered the press room to sheepishly announce that there had been a mistake in the tabulation of the scorecards and that Poletti had actually scored it 148–147 for Duran.

While it made the decision unanimous, the one-point correction didn't alter the outcome, but it made it all the more outrageous in that it confirmed that Poletti, who had flown from Italy to Canada on the promoters' dime because of his alleged boxing expertise, had scored ten rounds of a fifteen-round fight even. It was a cop-out so infuriating that even his fellow judges condemned him.

'Calling ten rounds of a fight even is a diabolical disgrace,' said Gibbs, although in truth none of the judges that night was particularly decisive. Between them they scored 18 of a possible 45 rounds even.

'It was a great fight, and it was a shame that either fighter had to lose that night,' Bobby Goodman recalled 27 years later. 'The way Red Smith put it was very fitting: "Tonight, the man became a legend, and the boy became a man."'

But in the end, Leonard had lost for essentially the same reason Marvin Hagler would lose to him seven years later. Sugar Ray had allowed his adversary to dictate the terms under which the battle was waged. He had fought Duran's fight.

Why had Leonard allowed himself to be drawn into a battle for which he was ill-suited?

'It's hard to think when you're getting your brains knocked out,' supposed Freddie Brown. 'This ain't football, you know. And Duran is like Marciano. He never gives you the ball.'

Like Hagler (who described his alter ego as 'the monster') and Hearns (the 'Hit Man'), Leonard nurtured a disembodied boxing self he referred to in the third person: the street fighter.

'The street fighter was always lurking there somewhere inside me. I knew I could hang with anyone, any size, when it came down to inside fighting,' reflected Leonard. 'Normally the street fighter doesn't come out, because he's controlled, but in this fight I just lost it and he took over.'

■ ■ ■

Having repaired to his dressing quarters, Duran brandished his gaudy new WBC championship belt. Then he looked across the room to Brown and said, tears glistening in his eyes, 'Freddie, you deserve this,' and handed it to the gnarled old trainer.

When the first wave of press arrived, the new champion was asked what had made the difference in the fight. Duran responded by pounding on the left side of his chest to indicate *corazon*.

Was he suggesting that Leonard had *lacked* heart?

'No,' Duran replied through an interpreter. 'If Leonard did not have a heart, he would not be alive tonight.'

'To my mind,' said Michael Katz, 'what happened in Montreal that night was one of the greatest displays of athletic heroism I've ever witnessed. Roberto Duran beat a man who was bigger, stronger, younger, faster – and just plain better – with will power. It was an incredible performance.'

After the fight, Leonard said he was contemplating retirement. 'I was serious, or serious about considering it anyway,' he confirmed many years later. 'It had nothing to do with the decision. I didn't like the fact that I'd lost, but I wasn't demoralised, the way the rest of the guys were. Janks, Dave, even Angelo were devastated. Mike [Trainer] was so crushed that I don't think he even came into the dressing-room.'

Elsewhere in the stadium, Trainer told Bill Nack, 'As far as I'm concerned, [Ray] can pack it in.'

By winning a world title, Leonard had 'accomplished what he set out to do', said Trainer. 'I don't enjoy this. I don't enjoy seeing him get hit.'

'I *was* mentally and physically exhausted,' Sugar Ray recalled. 'I'd never taken such a physical beating. The doctor had to come up to my hotel room later that night and drain blood from my ears.

'It was one of the most physically demanding challenges of my life, but the thing people had always wondered about was whether I could take a shot. I'd never had to before.'

Although he went 1–1 for the evening, Roger was the only Leonard to win a fight that night. Before getting KO'd by Duran, he had outpointed Clyde Gray, the thirty-three-year-old former Canadian welterweight champion who had in the space of eight months the previous year been knocked out by Tommy Hearns, Pete Ranzany and Chris Clarke.

Despite having been embarrassed in the post-fight skirmish with Duran, Roger excitedly proclaimed that he would avenge the family honour.

'I want Duran next,' he told anyone who would listen.

'Roger,' Dave Jacobs said wearily, 'shut up.'

3

STONE vs SUGAR

Leonard–Duran II
Louisiana Superdome, 25 November 1980

In almost any field of endeavour a sequel can either reaffirm or refute its predecessor. Duran's legion of supporters expected him to repeat his virtuosic Montreal performance in the rematch, while Leonard's hoped he would demonstrate that his own had been an aberration. It's safe to say that no one could have anticipated what actually did unfold when the two met again five months later. If Duran had prevailed by indomitable force of will in his first fight with Leonard, his will was utterly broken in the return bout, and while the second Leonard–Duran fight, unlike several of those between the Four Kings, would stake no claim to a position among the great fights of all time, in its own way it became the most celebrated of them all. What took place that night in New Orleans transcended boxing and indeed, the world of sport. Even people who had never watched a fight and didn't speak a word of Spanish now knew at least two of them, and exactly what they meant. The words were 'No mas.'

■ ■ ■

AMID THE POST-MORTEMS FOLLOWING the fight in Montreal, Don King conceded that Leonard's representatives had done a superior job of negotiating. Now, King reminded the press the following morning (neither boxer was present), Duran was in a position to dictate the terms of a rematch.

'We assume they're going to be fair,' said King, who held the promotional rights to Duran–Leonard II. 'It's like a mirror. Mr Trainer was quite adamant in his negotiations for the first fight and did a splendid job for Sugar Ray Leonard. I'm sure that Mr Eleta and I can do the same for Roberto Duran.'

Initially, it was by no means clear that there would *be* a rematch. As Duran embarked on a profligate celebratory tour that would take him and his partying posse from Montreal to Panama and then back to New York, a disappointed and confused Leonard headed off to Hawaii to ponder his own future.

There were days of solitary walks on the beach, evenings in which he seemed to stare for hours at the ocean. But all the while his mind was churning, as he replayed the events of Montreal in his mind.

'I ran on the beach every day, and every day I'd run into people who'd say, "You know what? If you'd fought *your* fight, you'd have won,"' said Leonard. 'The more I thought about it, the more I realised they were right.'

Even though he had willingly walked into Duran's trap, he began to realise, it had *still* been a very close fight. If he could come that close to beating Manos de Piedra fighting Duran's fight, what would happen if he fought his *own*?

Juanita Leonard told Duran's biographer Giudice: 'For a week, Ray never said anything. Then one day he said, "I've got something to tell you, sweetheart. I can't quit fighting." I just looked at him and said, "It took you a while, didn't it?" He was 25 years old. There's no *way* he was going to quit.'

'That conversation is accurate,' said Leonard, 'but by the time I told Juanita I'd already phoned Mike Trainer and told him I wanted the rematch. I didn't need to clear it with my wife first.'

When Leonard told Trainer he wanted to fight Duran again, he also told him to try to make the fight right away.

'That was calculated on my part,' admitted Leonard. 'I knew Duran was overweight and partying big time. I've done some partying myself, but I know when to cut it out. I said to Mike, "Let's do it now, as soon as possible." In retrospect, it was pretty clever of me.'

▪ ▪ ▪

Four days after defeating Leonard, Duran was greeted by 700,000 of his countrymen at a rally in Panama. He wore about his waist the green WBC belt he had 'given' to Freddie Brown a few nights earlier.

On several occasions Duran pointed down to the belt as he spoke, reminding the throng, '*This does not really belong to me, it belongs to you, my people,*' and, more colloquially, '*This thing is hanging there for you guys.*'

Only later, Duran related to Giudice, did he realise that a sizable portion of his audience assumed from the animated gestures that he was referring not to the championship belt but to his '*verga*' – his prick.

From Panama, Duran returned to New York, where he and his friends continued a celebration that lasted the entire summer. By September, the welterweight champion weighed nearly 200 pounds.

In the meantime, King and Eleta had managed to strike a bargain with Trainer that was favourable to their client in every respect save one. Duran would indeed earn the champion's share, an $8 million guarantee that exceeded his wildest expectations. The catch was that the rematch would take place in November.

Eleta was subsequently criticised for taking the autumn date, even though he knew how badly out of shape Duran was. The manager later explained that he agreed to the timetable not because Leonard had demanded it but because if he hadn't, he feared, Duran might *never* stop partying.

'In our country, Duran is like a god,' Eleta later explained to Dave Anderson. 'Everybody is after him to do this or do that, and he is very difficult to control. After he won the title from Leonard in Montreal and returned home to Panama, everyone invited him to parties and his home was turned into a hotel. Training in Panama became impossible. He was 183 pounds before we got him out of the country.'

Duran–Leonard II was once again officially announced at a press conference at the Waldorf-Astoria. At its conclusion, Katz approached Duran and thanked him for the score he'd made in Montreal.

'*Thees time, bet dobble,*' a smiling Duran replied, in English.

'I did,' said the Wolf Man.

At that same press conference, Duran foreshadowed the events of what would prove the critical moment of his life, providing a glimpse into his psyche as he voiced his disdain for Leonard.

'I don't like to see clowns in the ring,' said Duran. 'I like to see boxers. To fight and beat me, you have to come into the ring and fight me. He goes into the ring and tries to imitate Ali, but an imitator is a loser.'

■ ■ ■

'It was a little tougher getting Duran into camp,' recalled Bobby Goodman. 'He had celebrated his win over Leonard with, shall we say, gusto and enthusiasm.

'You've got to remember that now Duran was even bigger in the boxing world than he'd been before. He had now reached a legendary status that transcended the Latino community, and even the sport itself. It made no difference that he didn't speak English. He was *Roberto Duran*.

'Once we got him up to Grossinger's, he went to work – though it was evident it wasn't as hard as he had worked for the first fight. It was fall and the mornings were getting colder. Sometimes Freddie had a hard time getting him out of bed.'

This time Don Morgan served as Duran's principal sparring partner. Goodman also recalls that Kevin Rooney journeyed over from Catskill on several occasions as well.

'[Duran] did the things he'd done that spring – interacting with the hotel guests, meeting with the media – but there seemed to be even more family and friends around,' continued Goodman. 'He went through the motions and got himself into decent shape, but it seemed he didn't spar quite as hard or exercise with the same abandon. He was so sure he could handle Leonard again that this time there was no sense of urgency to his preparations.'

When it came time to break camp and move on to New Orleans, no one was happier than Duran. Not necessarily because he was anxious to fight, but rather because it was getting cold up in the Catskills, and he was eager to get back to a more hospitable climate.

If Freddie Brown, who had done the hands-on training at Grossinger's, was concerned, he apparently didn't tell Ray Arcel. When the older man was asked about the possibility of an upset, he replied, 'If Duran lost to Leonard, he'd be ready to commit suicide.'

■ ■ ■

Leonard had taken much of the summer off, dabbling in television work for both HBO and CBS, in addition to a part-time gig as a sports reporter for a Washington station. He'd done a couple of commercials as well, including a celebrated one in which he and Duran were jointly featured. Their two young sons accompanied the boxers to the photo shoot.

'7-Up approached us with the idea of me and Duran doing the commercials with our kids,' said Leonard. 'I told Mike to let Duran know, "This was found money, easy money, but if he acts the fool in front of Little Ray, it's fucking *over!*" I didn't want him making obscene gestures or threats or the stuff he used to do around my kid.'

'As it turned out, it went fine,' said Leonard. 'While we were shooting it, Duran was a perfect gentleman.'

Leonard once again trained in New Carrollton, but this time his preparations were Duran-specific. One of his sparring partners, Dale Staley, described himself as 'the American Assassin'.

In a bout against Leo Thomas at Washington's Starplex the previous February, the American Assassin had been disqualified for taking a bite out of his opponent. It cost him the fight, but it won him a job in the Leonard camp, where he was encouraged to use his ample arsenal of dirty tricks to emulate Duran.

'Staley was a nasty fighter, and his idol was Duran,' said Leonard. 'I told him, "You can do anything you want, except bite me." The first week or so he was rough, but then I learned to compensate.'

In camp, Staley was free to employ his elbows, arms and head. John Schulian described one sparring session in which Staley grabbed the ropes for leverage and then butted Leonard squarely in the head. Leonard responded in kind, grasping the ropes with one hand and smacking the Assassin in the face with the other.

After Leonard's loss to Duran in Montreal, Dave Jacobs had so strongly opposed the idea of an immediate rematch that he had threatened to quit, and did, when Trainer and Dundee signed to go back up against Duran without a tune-up fight.

'Some people wanted him to fight again before the rematch with Duran, but that would have been useless,' Dundee explained. 'You don't gain anything by fighting less than the best. We know what we have to do to beat Duran.'

The disagreement over the wisdom of the rematch was the stated reason, at least for public consumption, for Jacobs's departure, but there was obviously more to it than that. Jacobs had been Leonard's first boxing coach and his father-confessor at every step of the way, but he had increasingly chafed as he saw his influence waning. Trainer was making the management decisions, Dundee the boxing decisions, and Morton seemed to increasingly have Ray's ear as well. Jacobs still had the position of trainer but lacked the authority implicit in that title. Nor was he being paid what he thought a man in his position ought to be.

Jacobs's departure was a disappointment 'because at one time he and Ray had been very close,' said Mike Trainer, 'but the important thing to remember is that Ray didn't fire him. Ray fired a lot of people over the years, but Dave Jacobs quit.'

Since Dundee wouldn't arrive in Washington until early November, this left Janks Morton in charge of the early preparations. Leonard, who had often sparred as many as fifteen rounds a day before the first fight, never worked more than nine for this one.

In contrast to the corpulent state in which Duran opened camp, Leonard was a model of fitness. He weighed 173 pounds the day he commenced his workouts in earnest and was already down to 160 by the time Dundee arrived, three weeks ahead of the fight.

Angelo, plainly pleased by what he saw, warned that the first time around Duran had mistaken decency for weakness.

'No more Mister Nice Guy,' said Dundee.

'I know what I have to do to beat him this time,' said Leonard. 'It will be completely different.'

Besides, he wondered, 'If he's so tough, how come he didn't knock me out in the first fight, even when I was fighting his style of fight?'

■ ■ ■

In 1923, seeking the largest possible purse for what was by any standard an ordinary defence by his heavyweight champion, Jack Dempsey's legendary manager, Jack (Doc) Kearns, had found willing accomplices among the citizenry of Shelby, Montana.

Appealing to the spirit of boosterism among the frontiersmen,

Kearns persuaded several of the Montana town's leading lights to put up what eventually turned out to be $300,000, in addition to erecting from virgin local timber a temporary stadium that would accommodate what was hoped would be a crowd of 40,000 to watch Dempsey defend his title on the 4th of July against a challenger named Tom Gibbons.

Although the Shelby civic leaders, hoping to put their town on the map, had initiated the entreaty, they were clearly overmatched. As John Lardner described it, 'These men marvelled at Kearns's almost religious attachment to the principle of collecting all the cash in Montana that was not nailed down.'

No one had held a gun to the heads of the citizenry of Shelby, but they shortly found themselves throwing good money after bad, having been persuaded that 'the honour of all Montana' was at stake. After Dempsey decisioned Gibbons over fifteen lacklustre rounds, he and Kearns (who was somewhat weighted down with two large bagfuls of silver) slipped out of town on separate trains and reconvened in Salt Lake City a few days later. By then, the first of what would be four Shelby banks to fail as a direct result of the Dempsey–Gibbons fight had already shuttered its doors.

The town fathers who had hoped to render the town's name a household word had inadvertently done so. Forevermore, 'Shelby', both as a noun and as a verb, would be ingrained in the lexicon of boxing.

And nobody could Shelby the way Don King could Shelby.

Whether King had Kearns's example or his own experience with the Republic of Zaire in mind when he set out to Shelby New Orleans is unclear, but early on in the proceedings it became clear to the World's Greatest Promoter that in spite of the intense interest in the Duran–Leonard rematch, he had a box-office dog on his hands.

As the half of BADK left standing after Duran's victory in Montreal, King had the promotional rights to the return bout. Duran, as the winner of that fight, was seeking a purse comparable to what Leonard had commanded when he was the champion. And Leonard, though willing to take a cosmetic pay cut as the challenger, had already set a high bar for himself with his unprecedented purse in June.

By the time he had both men's signatures on contracts, King was on the hook for an $8 million guarantee to Duran and another $6 million to Leonard. Now all he had to do was find $14 million.

In Montana back in 1923, Kearns had driven up the price of poker with fictitious reports of a half-million-dollar offer from Madison Square Garden to stage the Dempsey–Gibbons fight. In 1980, King fuelled a similar bidding war by obtaining a modest site-fee offer from Caesars Palace and then using it to play the Astrodome in Houston and the Louisiana Superdome off against each other.

The latter 'won' by agreeing to take 90 per cent of the promotion off King's hands for a mere $17.5 million. This obligation was directly assumed by the Hyatt Corporation, whose hotel abutted the Superdome.

Having absolved himself of the attendant financial obligations, King remained the hands-on promoter and retained for himself foreign-rights television sales, which he shared with Neil Gunn, the Superdome official who had been the point man in putting together the financing of the New Orleans enterprise.

In addition to making its pitch for New Orleans civic pride and the anticipated boost the event would provide to local tourism, the Hyatt people were relying on the gate receipts at the 79,000-seat Superdome, where a capacity or even near-capacity crowd would have covered their financial stake. That their projections were wildly off the mark did not become apparent until the week of the fight.

Duran wouldn't be the only one to say 'No mas' in connection with this fight. The Hyatt Corporation never promoted another boxing event.

'Neil Gunn was an awfully nice fellow and we did our best to help him out, but they had vastly overpaid for that fight,' said Trainer. 'They took a beating.'

■ ■ ■

Both men talked a good fight that week.

'I will beat him worse than the first time,' vowed Duran, who undoubtedly meant it. 'This time I'm going to shut his mouth with my gloves.'

Leonard, noting that he had accumulated 'five years' worth of experience in one night' in Montreal, lapsed into the third person when he said, 'I knew that if Sugar Ray fights his fight, he wins. But in that first fight he got into my head, took me out of my game plan.'

Howard Cosell was performing double-duty in New Orleans that week. The night before the fight, the Saints hosted the Rams in a nationally televised Monday Night Football game. The Superdome press box was filled to capacity with boxing writers. After the game we ended up, en masse, at the Old Absinthe House on Bourbon Street.

King had provided complimentary tickets for Larry Holmes, Ken Norton, Michael Spinks and Saoul Mamby, and made sure that the boxers were prominently seated together at ringside. Hearns and Emanuel Steward had also travelled to New Orleans. When word reached King that Thomas Hearns was in town, King had a message for the WBA welterweight champion.

'If Hearns wants a ticket,' said the World's Greatest Promoter, 'let him buy one.'

'We were just there to create some attention,' said Steward. 'It was clear to me by then that Tommy and Ray were going to fight eventually and I truly expected Ray to win the rematch.'

■ ■ ■

Over breakfast at his London hotel in September 1980, Marvin Hagler held up his two fists and declared: 'This time I'm bringing my own two judges with me.'

Ten months had passed since the draw with Antuofermo, and now Hagler was in England, once again poised to fight for the middleweight championship of the world, but this time there would be a different dance partner. The 160-pound championship now belonged to a Briton named Alan Minter.

That Leonard–Benitez/Antuofermo–Hagler joint bill in Vegas the previous November had provided most American scribes' first introduction to Minter. Then the World Boxing Council's top-ranked contender, the Englishman presumably loomed as the next challenger for the winner. Accompanied to Vegas by his father-in-law and trainer, Doug Bidwell, Minter was a ubiquitous presence at Caesars Palace that week, and at one point the late Hunter S. Thompson convinced himself that Minter was stalking *him*.

Thompson began to see Minter in his sleep. Once he peeked around from behind the faux Michelangelo's 'David' statue planted in the corridor to see if 'that damned Minter' might be lurking in the hallway, and on another occasion when he spotted Minter strolling through the lobby, he ducked under a cocktail table at the Galleria Bar to hide from the Englishman.

In Las Vegas, Minter and Bidwell seemed to be inseparable. One night the English boxer and his father-in-law brazenly strolled through Caesars with matching hookers on their arms.

Under normal circumstances, the controversial nature of the Antuofermo draw might have put Hagler in line for an immediate rematch, but since the Mosquito held both the WBC and WBA titles – the only ones extant a quarter-century ago – he was first obliged to defend against Minter. That fight, in March 1980, produced one of the more bizarre scoring discrepancies in the annals of the sport.

Two judges, including one who scored the fight 7–5–3 (in rounds) for Antuofermo, had it reasonably close. The third, Roland Dakin, scored the fight 149–137, or 13–1–1 for Minter. That one-sided scorecard, coupled with allegations of misconduct on Dakin's part, rendered Antuofermo's rematch position even more compelling than Hagler's.

'When Antuofermo fought Minter, Minter won the fight, but the English judge kept signalling to the British television people after each round,' said Arum. 'When the television tapes confirmed that, the WBC ordered an immediate rematch.' (José Sulaimán also announced that Dakin would never judge another WBC title fight, but it didn't take him long to relent: barely a year later, Dakin was back in a judge's seat when light-heavyweight champion Matthew Saad Muhammad stopped the Zambian Lottie Mwale.)

'The English were delighted, of course, because Minter got another payday, but it turned out to be a year after the first Antuofermo fight that Marvin got his shot, and it had to be in England,' added Arum. 'Basically, it had to be in England because of [British promoter] Jarvis Astaire fucking around with the WBC.'

Marvin had bided his time, keeping busy with a pair of fights in Maine, neither of which got out of the second round. (In one of them, he avenged the old Philadelphia robbery by stopping Boogaloo Watts, who would later become one of his most reliable sparring partners. In the other, he solidified his position in the pecking order by knocking out Hamani, the French contender.)

Then, late that spring, Hagler had returned to Vegas, where he outpointed Marcos Geraldo in an ABC fight. Although he won comfortably, Marvin's performance was less than dominating, and when Minter busted Antuofermo up and stopped him on cuts in the eighth round of their rematch at the Wembley Pool in June, the comparative performances combined to produce a growing confidence among British boxing fans that Minter represented the real goods among middleweights – and that Hagler, by implication, did not.

By the time he got to England, Hagler's complement of sparring partners had been reduced to two: journeyman Danny Snyder and Marvin's younger brother, Robbie Sims, who had made his pro debut earlier that year. Snyder, like Minter, was a southpaw, while Robbie, in emulation of his older brother, was essentially ambidextrous and could produce a fair approximation of the Englishman's style.

Snyder had been in England once before. When Mike Baker challenged another left-hander, Maurice Hope, for the WBC junior middleweight title a year earlier, Danny had been the American's principal sparring partner. In a session at the Elephant & Castle a few days before the Hope fight, Snyder accidentally knocked Baker cold. It hadn't been a public rehearsal, but several eyewitnesses from the seemingly omnipresent London fight mob remembered him and at Hagler's first workout at Freddie Hill's Gym, on the second floor of a Battersea pub, the Fleet Street crowd spent as much time interviewing 'the bloke who knocked out Baker in the gym' as they did the American challenger.

Arum had offered Sims a spot on the undercard, but Goody and Pat Petronelli rejected the idea on the grounds that concern about his younger brother could prove a distraction to Marvin. Instead, Robbie's next fight took place five nights later back in the States, where he knocked out Danny Heath in the first round on Rip Valenti's live card at the Boston Garden, staged to accompany the Holmes–Ali closed-circuit telecast at the old Causeway Street edifice.

Another key member of the entourage – and the third man in the corner during the fight – was Hagler's attorney, Steve Wainwright. The scion of one of Brockton's oldest and most prominent families (his father was a former mayor), Steve was a partner in the firm of Wainwright, Wainwright, Wainwright, Wainwright, & Wainwright. Despite his lofty pedigree, on fight nights Steve was now manning the spit bucket, conspicuous in a satin cornerman's jacket with 'BARRISTER' stitched across the back.

Wainwright was partial to tequila, which someone had warned him might be difficult to procure in London. As it turned out, it was readily available in most of the better pubs, but, as a safeguard against a possible drought, he'd brought along a case of the stuff.

Like much of London, Bailey's Hotel had recently been purchased by oil-rich Arabs. It didn't take Wainwright long to make their acquaintance, and within a day or two he'd conducted a crash-course in the ritualistic art of tequila consumption. In what became a nightly routine, around closing time at the hotel bar Wainwright would be joined by a table full of sheikhs in flowing white robes, who would gleefully lick salt from their fists, toss down tequila shooters, suck on limes and break into high-pitched giggles.

During one such bash, Wainwright promised that if Hagler won the world title on Saturday night he would shave his head just like Marvin's.

As a psychological ploy, or so Bob Arum claims to this day, the British promoters had initially assigned Hagler and his party to another hotel, but between the traffic and the all-night noise Marvin couldn't sleep. Bailey's was no doubt considered a demotion, but a blue-collar boxer from Brockton wouldn't have known the difference. Hagler was every bit as comfortable there as he might have been at the more elegant Dorchester just up the street.

Bailey's was located in Kensington, near the Gloucester Road Underground stop. Each morning before breakfast Marvin, along with Goody and the sparring partners, did his roadwork in Hyde Park.

Convinced that he'd been the victim of at least a larcenous decision, and possibly a betting coup, Marvin blamed the outcome of the Antuofermo fight on 'Vegas judges' and vowed never again to leave the outcome to the capricious whims of mere mortals, particularly in a town where hundreds of thousands of dollars might be riding on the outcome at the sports book windows.

Nevada might have been the only place in America where one could legally bet on a fight in 1980, but it wasn't the only one in the world. One afternoon in London I went out and surveyed several bookie shops, where I was surprised to discover that Minter was holding firm as an 11–10 favourite. At that attractive price, I placed a bet on Hagler.

When I got back to Bailey's that day, Marvin was sitting with Pat and Goody in the coffee shop. When I started to reveal the results of my reconnaissance mission, Marvin abruptly shouted, 'I don't want to hear it!' and stormed out of the room. Convinced that the only way he might lose this fight would be at the behest of gambling interests, Hagler was just superstitious enough to believe that advance knowledge of the odds might somehow open the door for hanky-panky.

Although Hagler was an American challenging for an undisputed world championship, Ali was fighting Holmes at Caesars for the heavyweight title a few nights later, so the stateside press contingent was relatively small. Besides myself, Leigh Montville was in London covering the fight for the *Boston Globe*, as was Frank Stoddard for Hagler's home-town Brockton *Enterprise*. (*Sports Illustrated* saved expenses by assigning the fight to its resident Brit, Clive Gammon.) ABC would televise the bout back to the US, but I don't recall seeing Al Michaels or Howard Cosell until the night of the fight.

Antuofermo was there, having wangled a gig as a commentator for Italian television, and most evenings Vito would join Montville, Stoddard, Angie Carlino, Jimmy Quirk and me, along with Bernie LaFratta, who had helped Arum package the European rights, and whatever Fleet Street scribes happened to be around, at our adopted headquarters – the Stanhope Arms across the street, where the publican was an affable Irishman named Peter Flood, thus ensuring that the establishment offered yet another London rarity: a decent pint of Guinness.

The five-hour time difference in our favour, along with the British licensing laws then in effect, sometimes made for an odd drinking schedule.

'The beauty of that trip, if I remember right, is that it was the one time in my life I could get drunk twice a day,' Montville would recall years later. 'We would pound a bunch of beers before the two o'clock closing in the middle of the afternoon, then be back in the bar after watching sparring and writing our stories at night.'

Since both Minter's and Hagler's sparring sessions were conducted in gyms located above pubs (Minter made the Thomas à Becket, in South London, his training headquarters), we often got a head start on the evening session, but somehow the stories got filed.

Another presence who arrived a few days before the fight was Fulgencio Obelmejias, a tall Venezuelan middleweight who had advanced to No. 1 in the WBA rankings and thus loomed the mandatory challenger to the Minter–Hagler winner.

The middleweight championship might have been what had by 1980 already become a boxing rarity – a unified, undisputed title – but the promotional rights were so thoroughly splintered that at least seven men had a piece of the action. Minter's interests were represented by a four-man consortium headed up by Astaire, the Wembley impresario, along with Mickey Duff, Terry Lawless and Mike Barrett. Arum was Hagler's promoter-of-record, but Rip Valenti, the legendary Boston octogenarian who, as Sam Silverman's partner and, later, successor, staged most of Marvin's early fights, also had a piece of the American challenger, as did Rodolfo Sabbatini, a courtly Italian godfather whose mysteriously inherited interest in the 160-pound title dated back to the days of Nino Benvenuti.

'There was a tremendous ongoing dispute, me and Sabbatini on one side and Duff and Astaire on the other,' revealed Arum. 'They were supposed to have a piece of the options on Hagler and I had a piece of the options on Minter. We resolved it by agreeing that whoever's guy won, the others would drop out.'

'Obviously,' added Arum, 'Jarvis and Mickey didn't think Minter was going to lose.'

Mickey Duff had provided the Hagler party with a van and driver to get them around London. The driver was a lovely kid named John who'd been in enough London club fights that his brains were scrambled by the time he turned 21. John was great behind the wheel;

he just couldn't remember directions, so Duff had assigned a co-pilot, an old Welsh pug who couldn't drive but knew London like the back of his hand.

It didn't take Goody and Pat long to notice that the Welshman spent a lot of time on the phone. The assumption, undoubtedly correct, was that he was reporting everything he saw back to Duff and Minter, but since everyone assumed he was a spy for the opposition, Goody made sure he didn't see much.

At his secluded Provincetown training camp, Hagler was famous for putting himself 'in jail', spending most of his waking hours brooding in his room as he mentally psyched himself up for the task at hand. Except for roadwork, sparring and the odd meal in the coffee shop, he followed the same routine in London. It was somewhat surprising then, when a couple of days before the fight he appeared downstairs and asked Steve Wainwright and me if we felt like going for a walk.

We spent a couple of hours strolling the streets of the British capital. Even though shaven-headed American tourists were a rarity in London back then, Marvin for the most part went unrecognised. At a tourist shop, he playfully tried on a London constable's helmet. I still have the photograph of him and Wainwright posing on the pavement, the bobby's hat perched on Marvin's head.

At one point we came upon a building site, which gave Marvin pause to reflect on his previous occupation. For most of his boxing career, Hagler had supplemented his income working as a labourer for the Petronellis' construction firm, as had Tony Petronelli. As Hagler watched the labourers scurry about the London building site he revealed, more with amusement than rancour, that Tony had been given a job as a bricklayer, while he was assigned to be a hod-carrier. For years, Marvin had reckoned that he had the better job of the two – until he discovered the disparity in their hourly wages.

Now that he appeared to be on the verge of supporting his family through his boxing career, Hagler confessed an ambition. He and his wife had talked it over and decided that once they had enough money they ought to open a laundrette. The notion of owning a business appealed to him. People who couldn't afford washing machines still had to wash their clothes, he reckoned, and all he and Bertha would have to do would be sit back and watch them plop quarters into his machines.

In keeping with another long-standing practice, two days in advance of the fight, Goody ordered up the van and had John drive him and Marvin over to Wembley to inspect the venue.

'It's partly to make sure everything's all right from my standpoint, but mostly to familiarise the fighter,' Petronelli explained. 'We talk about how everything is going to go on the night of the fight – which entrance we're coming in, where our dressing-room is, which route we'll take to walk to the ring.'

'I want him to be as comfortable as possible and to know what to expect so there won't be any surprises,' continued the trainer. 'As we stood there looking up at the empty seats, I reminded him that they'd all be full on Saturday night – almost all of them with hostile British fans cheering for Minter.'

Goody could scarcely have imagined how much he had understated the case.

Possibly because they have been disappointed so often for so long, British boxing fans don't need much of an excuse to become overenthusiastic, and Minter himself abetted the jingoistic frenzy in the run-up to the fight when he promised that 'no black man is going to take my title'. By injecting a whiff of racism into the issue, the champion ensured that Hagler's reception at the arena would be nasty.

There was a substantial presence of the anti-immigrant National Front at Wembley that evening and the prevalent mood was further exacerbated by the outcome of the co-feature, which saw a young British middleweight named Tony Sibson knock out the previously unbeaten American Bob Coolidge. Around the arena the bloodthirsty mob engaged in football chants. Many of the spectators had arrived bearing Union Jacks, which they brandished like battleaxes. There were even guys dressed in beefeater costumes.

It didn't help, either, that the concessionaires at Wembley were selling beer by the case. Not even a hard-guzzling Londoner can drink twenty-four beers in less than three rounds, meaning that by the time the fight reached its premature conclusion, many of the spectators had an abundance of ammunition at hand.

'I remember standing there in the lobby of the arena watching all these skinheads buying cases of beer, hoisting them onto their shoulders and trudging up the stairs to the balconies,' recalled Montville. 'I couldn't have anticipated what was going to happen, but I remember thinking that no good was going to come of this.'

'I never saw anything like it,' said Arum. 'It was like a huge, drunken orgy.'

In contrast to the fever pitch of the crowd, the fight itself was almost perfunctory. Less than 30 seconds had elapsed when a Hagler right jab ripped open a gash below Minter's left eye, and Marvin went to work on the cut, using his fists like the hands of a skilled surgeon.

With the crowd chanting, 'Minter! Minter!', the champion fought back, and even nailed Hagler with a good left just before the bell ended the first.

Minter fought bravely in the second, but he was engaged in an uphill battle. Although Marvin was plainly concentrating on the cut, each time he missed the spot he seemed to open up a new one – first above the left eye, then alongside the right one – on Minter's face.

It might have been close on the scorecards – after two rounds, two judges had Hagler up by a point, while one had Minter by the same score – but by the third the ring looked like an abattoir, as Hagler pressed the attack, repeatedly rocking Minter with right uppercuts punctuated by the occasional straight left.

'I always thought in most of his fights Marvin showed too much respect to his opponents,' said Montville. 'He was cautious in the first Antuofermo fight, and he was the same way against Duran and Leonard. But in this one he fought with an absolute fury. Once he had Minter cut – and that was almost right away – it was as if all the frustrations of his career were being unleashed.'

Many of the hooligans were either so drunk or seated so far from the ring they couldn't accurately gauge the extent of the damage to Minter's face, and they erupted angrily when the referee, Carlos Berrocal, stopped the fight midway through the third and led the Englishman to his corner to have the wound examined.

When the blood was wiped away, Bidwell surveyed the damage and nodded to the referee to stop the fight. Berrocal officially terminated the action at 1:45 of the third.

'Marvin beat the shit out of him, and when they finally stopped the fight because of the cuts, they went crazy and started throwing bottles,' remembered Arum. 'In the midst of what should have been a great celebration, everybody was ducking under the ring.'

Initially, there was an angry roar, and then a second or two later the first bottle sailed into the ring, bursting and sending up a spray of beer that flashed under the ring lights. It didn't take long for the rest of the crowd to get the same idea.

As the bottles showered down from the rafters and exploded on the canvas, Pat and Goody Petronelli, Robbie Sims and Danny Snyder all raced into the ring to shield Marvin from the grenade assault.

Harry Carpenter, the English broadcaster calling the fight for the BBC, described the scene as 'a shame and disgrace to British boxing'.

A wayward beer can from the cheap seats aimed at Hagler, in fact, struck Carpenter on the head. The commentator didn't miss a beat as he continued to describe the riot.

'I remember poor Rip Valenti,' said Arum. 'Here Marvin has won the title after all these years, and I had to hold his hand and lead him out of the building. He was trembling.'

Protected by the phalanx of bodies, Hagler was hustled from the ring towards the safety of his dressing-room, which was well attended by London bobbies. Antuofermo grabbed me by the arm and pulled me and Montville in the same direction.

As we tried to make our way to safety, a skinhead made the mistake of whacking Vito over the back of the head with a beer bottle. The Mosquito didn't even blink. He wheeled around and laid the guy out with a picture-perfect right cross.

It may have been the best punch Antuofermo ever threw.

'I always wondered if the guy even knew what had hit him,' Montville reflected. 'When he came to, did he know he'd been knocked out by the former middleweight champion of the world?'

We managed to get through the swarm and into the dressing-room of the new champion. A shaken Cosell eventually crawled from his hiding place beneath the ring to interview Hagler.

Marvin never did get his belts that night. When he departed the arena an hour or two later, remnants of the rioting crowd still lingered outside. One of them heaved a brick and smashed the windshield of the car carrying the new middleweight champion.

By the time we got back to Bailey's, the celebration was under way. A contingent of Hagler's Brockton friends had materialised in the bar, as had his mother, Mae Lang, and Marvin's stepfather, Wilbur. Wainwright broke out the last of his tequila and, as the giggling sheikhs looked on, made good on his wager, allowing Marvin's wife Bertha to shave his head right there in the bar. He retains the Hagler look to this day.

Marvin was indulging himself with a pint of ale. Arum was already contemplating his first defence, against Obelmejias. Pat and Goody were reflecting on the comportment of the English crowd.

'We're never coming back to this place as long as we live,' vowed Pat.

By dispensation of the sheikhs, the hotel bar remained open all night. The morning light was peeking through the windows of the boozy, smoke-filled room when Danny Snyder and Robbie Sims descended the staircase, carrying an American flag they had somehow appropriated. Arum and I decided to reprise a scene from *The Deer Hunter* and broke into a heartfelt if somewhat drunken a capella rendition of 'God Bless America'. The entire room, Marvin included, joined in.

We didn't realise it at the time, but we were inaugurating a tradition. With Hagler facing just one American-born opponent in a seven-bout stretch that began with Minter, the scene would be repeated in venues around the world, as 'God Bless America' became Marvin Hagler's post-fight celebratory anthem.

■ ■ ■

By the time he met the twenty-one-year-old Tommy Hearns in August 1980, Pipino Cuevas had defended the WBA title eleven times and only one of his opponents, Randy Shields, had survived to hear the final bell.

The Mexican champion had been lured to Cobo Hall by the promise of a career-high purse. The card on which Hearns would win his first world title was promoted not by Don King or Bob Arum, but by the new kid on the promotional block, a fast-talking, free-spending huckster who called himself Harold Smith. Smith's promotional firm was called Muhammad Ali Professional Sports, or MAPS. Ali had nothing to do with the operation but had merely leased his name.

The card in Detroit included two other WBA title bouts – Hearns's stablemate Hilmer Kenty's first lightweight defence against Young Ho Oh, and a junior lightweight bout between Yasutsune Uehara and Sammy Serrano. Smith had overpaid for all of them.

'He was regularly paying guys purses that were at least three times too big,' recalled Bob Arum. 'The boxers loved it, of course, but nobody could figure out how he was doing it. He *had* to be losing money every time he ran a show.'

The following year all became clear when it was revealed that Smith's name was actually Ross Fields and that the entire MAPS operation had been a ruse, a money-laundering scheme financed by a computerised theft of $21.3 million from Wells Fargo.

Hearns had a tougher battle with the scale than he did with Cuevas. Although he had been right on target to make the 147-pound limit, the day of the weigh-in Hearns's Detroit pal Quenton (QB) Hines told Michael Katz, 'I gave Tommy some fruit to eat – plums – and they made him overweight.'

According to Hines, Hearns had to be spirited off to a massage parlour – the Oriental Health Spa & Massage Parlor in downtown Detroit – where he was broiled in a sauna to shed the excess weight.

Emanuel Steward, on the other hand, denies the tale to this day.

'Tommy wasn't that kind of kid,' said Steward. 'He never went to no massage parlour. He was about 150 the day before the fight, but we just put him in a rubber suit and let him shadow-box, and he took it off with no problem.'

Hearns, in any case, made the limit with a pound to spare. Cuevas weighed 146½.

The Hit Man's unusual dimensions figured to make him a tough opponent for Cuevas in any case, and the champion appeared to have approached the bout without a firm battle plan. He tried to box in the first round but got caught with a right that nearly put him down.

In the second Cuevas tried to move inside and force Hearns to brawl, with disastrous consequences. Hearns wobbled him with one right, and not much later cold-cocked him with another. Cuevas ploughed face-first into the canvas, where he was counted out by referee Stanley Christodoulou.

All of Detroit celebrated, but no one more happily than Hines, who'd provided Hearns with his pre-fight plums.

'If Tommy hadn't knocked him out quick, he would have had no strength to go on,' sighed QB. 'And it would have been all my fault.'

In a year in which Leonard and Duran met twice and Marvin Hagler won the middleweight title for the first time, Thomas Hearns would be selected as 1980's Fighter of the Year by the Boxing Writers Association. And, making it a clean sweep for the Kronk, Emanuel Steward would win the Al Buck Award as Manager of the Year.

■ ■ ■

On the morning of the Duran–Leonard rematch, rumours abounded that both contestants were having trouble making weight. That morning Leonard was spotted jogging through the French Quarter in what many assumed to be a last-minute effort to shed excess poundage. Duran, who had trained in a rubber corset until a few days before the fight, was reported to be dehydrated and under a physician's care.

Duran was accompanied to the weigh-in by an army of sycophants whose size, noted Bill Nack, 'would have befitted Montezuma'. The oversized posse wove its way in a procession to a ballroom on the ground floor of the Hyatt. Only two uniformed security guards had been assigned to the ritual, and they were quickly overpowered by the Panamanian's entourage.

The result was that the weigh-in, I noted in my dispatch to the *Boston Herald American*, 'was witnessed by more pickpockets than reporters'.

Leonard weighed in without incident, at 146.

Duran peeled off his black motorcycle jacket, T-shirt and Levi's, and also made the welterweight limit with a pound to spare. He then immediately drained the contents of a Thermos of beef broth provided by a waiting attendant and attacked two large oranges before heading back to the Hyatt to eat some more.

'He's dehydrated,' whispered Angelo Dundee.

Janks Morton had been assigned as the representative of Leonard's team to monitor the enemy's trip to the scale. On his way out of the room, Duran glared menacingly at Morton, slammed his fist into his palm and gave him the finger.

By the time we got back up the escalator to the atrium, Duran was making a spectacle of himself in the coffee shop with his customary display of table manners. Having made weight just a few minutes earlier, he was already seated at a table, and, having speared a thick sirloin steak with a fork, he held the slab of meat suspended before him as he leaned forward to rip off huge chunks, which he devoured like a ravenous animal.

At the afternoon rules meeting, Dundee protested Duran's chin-whiskers and asked that he be ordered to shave.

'That beard nauseates me,' said Dundee. 'It isn't good for the clean image of boxing. Besides, beards are unsanitary.'

The common assumption was that Dundee had raised the issue as a psychological ploy, hoping to get under Duran's skin. José Sulaimán cited the WBC rule on the subject, which specified that 'a beard on a fighter will only be accepted if its thickness is not considered a cushion, or that it could cause a cut or a hurt over a cut over [sic] his rival'.

Sulaimán explained that Duran's beard would be OK'd provided it were 'reasonably trimmed'.

What was 'reasonable', we asked.

'Oh, a half-inch, maybe, as long as it's not a cushion.'

With that he reached out and tugged on my beard.

'Yours, for example, would probably be all right.'

'Watch out,' I told him, jumping back. 'Beards are unsanitary, remember?'

At the rules meeting, Carlos Eleta asked, 'Is it a foul if you hold the other guy behind the neck and pull him towards you while you hit him?'

The question was greeted with some amusement, since the tactic was one not unfamiliar to Duran.

Octavio Meyran of Mexico was named the referee, Mike Jacobs,

James Brimmel and Jean Deswerts the ringside judges. Neither side voiced any objection to the officials.

Before the parties were dismissed, the WBC reaffirmed its policy prohibiting 'profane or abusive language', although, we noted at the time, they didn't specify in *which* language.

Afterwards, reporters flocked around the chief seconds.

'Duran is a real cutie, but he has his own rhythm he likes to fight to,' said Dundee, who predicted the Leonard we would see the next night would be a dramatic departure from the one who had fought Duran in Montreal. 'If you want to beat Roberto Duran, he's the type of guy who will get frustrated if he can't do what he wants to do.'

'It's been six months and only one thing has changed,' said Arcel. 'Now Leonard will walk into the ring knowing he can't win.'

Only one of them would be right.

The Superdome had been scaled from $20 to $1,000, and with the prime seats spread across what would normally be the football field, the organisers had developed a unique configuration to improve the sight lines. The ring had been raised, with a second set of ring-posts piggybacked atop one another and securely bolted together.

The rows of the media section surrounding the ring were stepped down, and the ringside photographers were assigned to shoot from a 'well' beneath the ring, thus ensuring the best possible view for the patrons with floor-level tickets.

'It seemed like a great idea at the time,' recalled Bobby Goodman.

Goodman had arranged to beef up the Superdome security force by contacting the athletic departments at several local universities and hiring a number of students from Tulane and Loyola, who were given a crash course in pickpocket-spotting and issued matching T-shirts. The college boys were happy enough with the chance to earn a small pay cheque and watch the fight for free.

Roger Leonard once again fought on the undercard, as did the brother of another world champion, Larry Holmes. Roger outpointed Melvin Dennis over ten rounds, while Mark Holmes knocked out a local middleweight, Bruce Calloway, in five. Two New Orleans boxers who would later challenge for world titles also boxed in that night's prelims: Jerry Celestine dispatched Pablo Ramos in the ninth round of their light-heavyweight fight, and lightweight Melvin Paul knocked out Chubby Johnson in four.

In the co-feature, Marvin Camel, an Eddie Futch-trained Native American from Montana, became the first man in boxing history to lose a cruiserweight title. Camel, who earlier in the year had won the newly minted championship on his second try (his first bout, against Mate Parlov, in Yugoslavia, had ended in a draw), lost a majority decision to Carlos De Leon.

The crowd eventually reached 20,000, a figure that might have been impressive in another venue. The NBA Jazz had routinely drawn larger audiences to the Superdome during the Pete Maravich era, but had nonetheless been forced to move out of town because they were losing money. When Hyatt executives stood on the floor and looked around the stadium, they saw 60,000 empty seats.

A buzz filled the stadium as the combatants made their entrances. In Montreal, both Leonard and Duran had worn white trunks. This time Leonard came out in what Ed Schuyler's AP dispatch described as 'villain black' – black trunks and a tattered pair of black low-cuts, whose gold laces matched the stripes on his trunks.

Duran and his substantial entourage were decked out in matching white tracksuits, and as the procession made its way to the ring they looked like they were on their way to a Moonie wedding. An alarming number of them made it into the ring with the champion and they gleefully waved Panamanian flags as that nation's anthem was played.

Nobody thought of it at the time, but all that excess weight in the ring undoubtedly put an extra strain on the jury-rigged ring supports and probably contributed to the engineering disaster that nearly brought the fight to a halt a few minutes later.

Duran and King might have dictated most of the terms of the rematch, but Leonard retained one psychological ploy. In lieu of the US anthem, the bout was preceded by Ray Charles, the man after whom Leonard had been named, singing 'America the Beautiful'. It was a moving rendition, and an approving Ray Charles Leonard, a confident smile on his face, danced an accompanying shuffle in the corner.

Although Bobby Goodman's loyalties were with Duran, he recalled, 'We got goose bumps' at that moment.

'You could hear a pin drop in the 'Dome,' said Goodman. 'All you could hear was Ray and the music. I'd never put it together that Ray Leonard was named Ray Charles Leonard, but it was like he was singing the song *just* for Leonard, and it must have added a lot of inspiration.'

It did, said Leonard.

'This was *Ray Charles*, my hero, my namesake,' recalled Leonard. 'When he walked towards me he said, "I love you, brother." And then when he *sang*? Forget about it! While Ray was singing, I looked over at Duran and it was like he was thinking, "What the fuck is this?"'

Leonard was determined to correct his strategic failings in Montreal and did so in spectacular fashion. Refusing to be drawn into another street battle, he used his speed and superior boxing gifts to frustrate Duran.

'You could see it right from the opening bell,' recalled Bobby Goodman. 'Duran came out in aggressive mode, but Leonard was dancing, flicking with his jab, moving around in circles as he changed direction. Duran had expected to be meeting the Leonard he faced in Montreal, but it was as if he'd been replaced by a different boxer. You could almost watch the frustration spread across Roberto's face.'

Midway through the opening stanza, Duran lowered his head and bull-rushed Leonard into the ropes. It was a move reminiscent of their first fight, but this time Ray spun around in a graceful pirouette and landed a right hand as he danced away. Near the end of the round Leonard stopped circling long enough to land a solid left-right combination.

At one point in the second round Leonard dazzled Duran with three straight rights, one of which snapped the Panamanian's head back. When Duran charged, Leonard quickly tied him up and, as if to remove all doubt from the judges' minds, finished up by landing two stiff jabs at the end of the round.

Midway through the second round, the middle of the ring abruptly collapsed as if it had developed a sinkhole. The spectators were oblivious to this development, and few of us in the press row noticed it right away.

Bobby Goodman raced from his seat and crawled under the ring. The bolts holding the centre support of the jury-rigged structure had snapped under the tension. The ring was sagging in the middle.

'I've often thought later that this could have given Duran an out,' said Goodman. 'He could have avoided the embarrassing outcome if he'd said he'd twisted his ankle when the ring dropped – or he could have said it was too dangerous and refused to continue. But Duran was too much of a macho guy for that. He just wanted Leonard to be a man and fight.'

Between rounds, Goodman hastily summoned a platoon of the football players he had recruited as security guards. The college boys managed to reposition the centre column and then were ordered to remain there, with the weight of the promotion literally on their shoulders, for the remainder of the fight.

'There must have been ten or twelve of them standing underneath the ring, holding it up,' recalled Goodman. 'They did a great job.'

Duran was still trying to play the bully in the third round and did a better job of it, winning the round on all three scorecards. He pushed Leonard around a bit, landed a few blows to the body and at one point swatted Leonard with a punch to the face. Ray responded by sticking out his tongue.

Manos de Piedra continued his body attack in the fourth. As he pushed Leonard into the ropes, Duran fell down.

A round later, it was Leonard's turn to hit the deck, falling as he backed into a corner trying to fend off Duran's body attack. Both trips to the canvas were ruled slips by Meyran, and when Leonard got up from his pratfall he tagged Duran with a left-right combination. Duran landed two glancing body shots and a right to the head just before the bell to solidify his claim on the round, which he won on two scorecards.

In their first fight Duran had mocked Leonard. Now it was Sugar Ray's turn.

'Round after round you could see the frustration building in Duran,' said Goodman. 'This was a fight that neither he nor his brain trust had ever imagined. Leonard's strategy was brilliant, but it was like he was making fun of Duran. Duran felt disrespected by his tactics.'

In the seventh round Leonard dropped his hands and pointed at his chin. A seething Duran fired with his right, but Leonard pulled his head back and allowed the punch to sail harmlessly past.

Then he stopped in mid-ring and wound up his right arm in windmill fashion, as if he were going to deliver a bolo punch. Instead he punched his seemingly mesmerised opponent in the snout with a jab stiff enough to make Duran's eyes water.

The late Pete Axthelm, covering the fight for *Newsweek*, was seated next to me. We turned to one another, shaking our heads over the act of provocation.

'He might as well have pulled the tail of Duran's lion,' I said, and Axthelm smiled in agreement.

'Doesn't he know,' he said, 'that this is *Roberto Duran?*'

Our thinking was that taunting Duran seemed particularly unwise, because if you *really* pissed him off, he just might kill you.

In retrospect, though, 'it may have been the most painful blow of Duran's life', wrote *Sports Illustrated*'s Bill Nack. 'It drew hooting laughter from the crowd and made Duran a public spectacle – a laughingstock.'

'Leonard could not have shamed Duran more thoroughly if he had reached over and pulled down his trunks,' wrote Ray Didinger.

Calling the fight from his ringside position, Howard Cosell exclaimed, '*Duran is completely bewildered!*'

Leonard kept mugging at Duran, skipping his feet as he went into an Ali shuffle, as he shouted at his foe. Duran was seething as he returned to his corner.

Leonard was clearly winning the psychological battle, but on the official scorecards it was still a fairly close fight after seven rounds. Brimmel had Leonard ahead by a single point, Jacobs and Deswarts by two.

The judges' opinions would become moot a few moments later.

The start of the eighth was momentarily delayed when Meyran sent Duran back to his corner and ordered Brown to remove what the referee had deemed an excessive coat of Vaseline from his face, but when action resumed, the fight had taken yet another turn: in the seventh Leonard had taunted and teased Duran, but in the eighth he was inflicting actual damage as well.

As Ray danced from side to side, keeping his opponent at bay with a graceful jab, an enraged Duran lowered his head and charged the matador. Leonard stepped back and countered with a hard right to the face.

A chastened Duran withdrew to ponder his fate, once again allowing Leonard to keep him at the end of his jab. As Leonard pressed forward, Duran backed towards the ropes, where he absorbed a three-punch combination delivered with lightning speed.

Late in the round, as Leonard once again herded him towards the ropes, Duran abruptly threw up his arms, muttered something to the referee and began to walk away.

From our ringside positions, it was impossible to hear what he had said. It would be left to Meyran to explain to the press that Duran had told him, '*No mas. No mas box!*'

Even though the statement had been uttered in his own language, the Mexican referee did not immediately comprehend that Duran was trying to quit and tried to wave him back into action. Leonard did not seem to grasp it either. He chased Duran across the ring and landed two punches to the midsection. There was no response from Duran, other than to wave dismissively as if to say, 'I'm not going to do this any more.'

'*He quit! He quit! He quit!*' Leonard heard his brother shout from the corner.

It took even longer for the crowd and ringside reporters to figure out the perplexing turn of events, but when Leonard went cartwheeling across the ring and began to climb the ring ropes in celebration it was clear that the fight was over.

'But if you look at the tape, as Duran was walking away toward his corner he turned and suddenly put his fists up again,' said Leonard.

No, Duran hadn't reconsidered his retirement from the fight.

'Roger had come running out of the corner, and after what happened in Montreal, Duran thought he was coming after *him*.'

■ ■ ■

'There was a look of disgust and frustration on Duran's face when he said, "No mas",' recalled Bobby Goodman. 'Everyone was stunned, including me. The great Duran, quitting in the middle of a world title defence? No way, I thought, but it was true.'

Two of the most prominent British boxing scribes were seated side-by-side in the Superdome that night. Hugh McIlvanney, then writing for *The Observer*, had been confident of a Leonard victory, while *The Independent*'s Jim Lawton had penned an advance that was a paean to Duran's 'implacable will'.

'Based on what I'd seen in the last two rounds in Montreal, I didn't think Duran had a prayer,' recalled McIlvanney. 'I'd bet about $300, which was a lot for me, on Leonard. When people asked why, I said, "[Duran] doesn't even want to train, because he knows in his heart he can't win."

'When Duran quit, it took a moment for it to sink in, but then I couldn't resist,' continued McIlvanney. 'I turned to Lawton and said, "Well, James, it looks like the bottom's dropped out of the fucking implacability market."'

■ ■ ■

Duran disappeared in the pandemonium. The press was left to besiege Arcel and Brown for explanations, but in the immediate aftermath the Panamanian's elderly cornermen appeared to be as befuddled as the rest of us.

'The guy's supposed to be an animal, and he quit,' said Freddie Brown moments afterwards. 'You'd think that an animal would fight right up to the end.'

In the long history of boxing, there had been few precedents. In his 1949 fight against Jake LaMotta, the French middleweight champion Marcel Cerdan had torn the supraspinatus muscle in his right shoulder. Though in agony, Cerdan had continued to fight, using only his left, until his corner prevailed upon him to retire. And, of course, Sonny Liston had quit on his stool in his first fight against Ali, failing to answer the bell for the seventh after incurring a shoulder injury. But Duran hadn't looked – or fought – like an injured man.

'Something happened in the ring and I don't know what it was,' Arcel shook his head. 'I thought he'd broke his arm or something. I've never seen anything like it. After the sixth, he said something about his arms feeling stiff, but he's never done anything like this, ever.'

Perhaps, it was suggested, Leonard's making a monkey out of him might have had something to do with it.

'I don't rule it out,' conceded Arcel. 'Leonard controlled the fight and it frustrated him. He just quit.'

Half an hour later, an alternative theory, blaming a 'stomach-ache' resulting from Duran's post-weigh-in gluttony, quickly spread around the press room. Duran was reported to have blamed 'cramps in my stomach and in my right arm'.

'I got so weak I couldn't go on,' Duran was said to have explained. 'Leonard was weak, but I didn't have the strength to pressure him.'

WBC president José Sulaimán told Red Smith that Duran had told him that 'when he threw a right hand in [the eighth] round, something happened to his shoulder'.

Duran never met with the press that night to offer his own explanation. Purported quotes, often contradictory, were supplied by his team.

Although the post-fight press conference took place in Duran's absence, the 'other' welterweight champion made himself available. Tommy Hearns, correctly anticipating a Leonard victory, had brought along a rubber chicken, which he flung at Leonard by way of challenge.

Had Leonard's triumph been accomplished by more traditional means, this might have proved an inspired tactic, but in the midst of the confusion that reigned in New Orleans that night it was a meaningless ploy, and few reporters even took note of it, and, apart from a look of mild annoyance, Leonard appeared to ignore it.

'I didn't feel disrespected,' recalled Leonard. 'I knew it was a spoof. I knew they were just trying to get some attention, so it didn't bother me, but frankly Tommy Hearns and Aaron Pryor were the last things on my mind that night.'

'But just by being there we created more attention than if we *hadn't* been there,' said Steward.

In his moment of triumph, Leonard refused to gloat. The memory of his own feelings in Montreal five months earlier still resonated and when someone suggested that Duran's actions had been those of a coward, Leonard sternly warned, 'Don't put words into my mouth.'

And, oh yes, there was a concomitant communiqué from Duran that night:

'*I will never fight again. I am retiring from boxing now.*'

That night over a hundred sportswriters found themselves faced with the prospect of explaining to their readers something they could barely comprehend themselves.

'*It was as if John Wayne, faced by the guy in the black hat, got a case of shaky knees,*' I began to type.

Once I had finished and filed my story, I turned to the scribe next to me.

'Look at the bright side of it,' I sighed. 'It'll be a long time before we have to sit through the Panamanian national anthem again.'

■ ■ ■

Why Roberto Duran turned tail in New Orleans remains a subject of debate to this day.

'He quit out of humiliation and frustration,' said Leonard. 'It's one of those things that happens to bullies. It's like a guy who jumps off a bridge and halfway down he says, "Damn! I could have gone into therapy!" Duran threw his hands up without realising the repercussions it would have on his legacy.'

My view was that Duran at the time actually believed himself to be committing the ultimate macho act. Emanuel Steward concurs.

'Duran was completely frustrated,' said Steward. 'It was like he was saying, "If you don't want to fight, then *fuck* you. I'm not going to stand here jumping all around after you." In Duran's mind, I think he expected that the crowd would condemn Leonard for having made a mockery of the fight, rather than him for quitting.'

'I think Duran was just saying, "I came to fight and you didn't,"' opined Jim Watt, the Scotsman who had succeeded Duran as the WBC lightweight champion. 'It was as if he was saying, "Look, I'm going home. Here's my phone number. If you decide you'd like to fight, give me a ring. And here's my wife's phone number, too. If it's dancing you want to do, call *her*."'

'The "stomach-ache" explanation was a load of bollocks and nobody believed it for a second,' said Watt in recalling No Mas a quarter-century later. 'There's no doubt in my mind that he quit out of frustration because Leonard was making a mockery of it by dancing around out there, but that's still totally unacceptable. Otherwise everybody who fights Floyd Mayweather Jr would be entitled to quit.'

■ ■ ■

Later, word came that Emile Bruneau, the chairman of the Louisiana Boxing Commission, wanted an immediate meeting with Duran and his handlers.

Bobby Goodman hastily conferred with King, Duran, Arcel and Eleta, essentially to make sure everyone would have his story straight. The 'cramps' excuse concocted by Freddie Brown sounded as good as anything else, and would be difficult to disprove.

Arcel walked back to the meeting, accompanied by an old friend, Newark *Star-Ledger* columnist Jerry Izenberg.

In an anteroom in the bowels of the Superdome, Bruneau had set up a table and chairs, conference-style.

'As soon as I walked in, Bruneau told me they were going to have to hold the purse, pending an investigation,' recalled Goodman. 'I explained that they *couldn't* hold Duran's purse. It had already been paid by a letter of credit lodged with a bank in Panama. All that was required to release it was a newspaper article confirming that Duran had showed up and that the fight had taken place, and it *had* taken place.'

'Well, we're going to have to determine just what we can do to penalise this boxer. We have a responsibility to the fans,' argued Bruneau.

Arcel reminded the chairman that if Duran had indeed become ill it would be just as if he had been injured during the fight, and cited the example of Liston in the first Ali fight.

'I don't know what happened, and if *I* don't, *you* don't,' Arcel told Bruneau. 'I'm not even sure Roberto does. But do not rush to judgement of this man, whose hand you couldn't shake fast enough each time he filled an arena for you.'

'Duran is a gallant warrior,' pleaded Eleta. 'He would *never* quit.'

Bruneau informed the assembled parties that there would be an official meeting of the commission at ten o'clock the next morning. He then dismissed the group, asking Goodman and Duke Durden to remain behind.

A former minor-league ballplayer who had reached the Triple A level in the Dodgers' organisation, Durden was in 1980 the chairman of the Nevada State Athletic Commission, in which role he had often seemed unconscionably close to King. He would later make that relationship official by resigning his position at the NSAC to become a vice-president of Don King Productions. Since he lacked any jurisdiction at what would become known as the No Mas fight, we must assume that he was asked to participate in an *ex officio* capacity.

And, given subsequent developments, it is also reasonable to assume that whatever advice he offered was likely to benefit King.

Conceding that he wouldn't be able to impede the letter of credit in Panama, Bruneau determined that he would impose the maximum fine allowed under Louisiana law, which at the time was $7,500.

After the meeting with Goodman and Durden, Bruneau met with the press, where he exclaimed, 'I've never seen anything like this in all my days around boxing, and we owe it to the people of Louisiana who paid to see this fight to investigate the whole matter.'

While the meeting was taking place beneath the Superdome, Duran had returned to his suite at the Hyatt. Ray Arcel's wife, Stevie, went to visit him there, expecting to offer her commiseration and check on his condition. To her surprise, she found a lively party under way. Surrounded by an entourage that included several National Guard colonels, Duran and his wife were singing and dancing. From all appearances, you'd have thought he'd won the fight.

Before he left his dressing-room, Duran had been examined by his personal physician, Dr Orlando Nuñez, who had, the press had been told, diagnosed Duran's malady as 'acute abdominal cramps'.

Many of us remained sceptical.

'Millions of American women take Midol every day for this complaint,' I noted at the time.

Thom Greer was moved to recall an occasion several years earlier when he'd been covering a women's fight at the D.C. Arena and Jackie Tonawanda's opponent had to quit because of menstrual cramps.

Another scribe, recalled Al Goldstein, said, 'If Duran had stomach cramps, it must have been his guts shrinking.'

After he was dismissed from the meeting, leaving Goodman and Durden to sort things out with Emile Bruneau, Carlos Eleta returned to the hotel, where, like Stevie Arcel, he was shocked to find Duran in the midst of what had all the trappings of a wild celebration.

Eleta angrily drove the money-changers from the temple and then ordered Duran to change clothes. At 2.30 a.m., Manos de Piedra accompanied his manager to Southern Baptist Hospital, where he was examined for the next several hours.

That the tests Duran underwent at the hospital during those early morning hours were unable to exclude the 'cramps' diagnosis confirmed Freddie Brown's quick thinking in concocting an excuse that could not be medically disproved.

Brown later confirmed to Michael Katz that the 'cramps' story had been his own invention. 'If they knew he'd quit back in Panama, they'd have *moidered* him,' said Brown.

A variant explanation promulgated in the hours immediately after the fight held that Duran had become 'nauseous' from something in his diet.

If so, I pointed out, that would make him the first visitor since Andrew Jackson expelled the British in 1815 to leave New Orleans complaining about the food.

Duran's first stop after leaving the hospital was the Hyatt coffee shop, where he polished off yet another plate of steak and eggs. When he appeared before the Commission a few hours later, Duran apologised and insisted that he had withdrawn because he had become ill with cramps.

Bruneau then announced that he was fining Duran $7,500 as the result of his 'unsatisfactory performance'. Bobby Goodman reached into his pocket and produced a cheque for that precise amount. It was made out to the Louisiana Boxing Commission and the funds were drawn on the account of Don King Productions.

Although Duran was sticking to his story, the elder half of his brain trust viewed it with some cynicism.

'*Doctor?*' exclaimed Arcel. 'This guy needs a psychiatrist more than anything else. If anyone had ever come to Freddie and me and said, "This guy will quit on you," I'd have spit in his eye. Duran? Quit? *Never!*'

Three years later, Duran would recall to *Sports Illustrated*'s Bill Nack:

'Leonard knew I had nothing. He was running and clowning because he knew I couldn't do anything. I wasn't going to let myself get knocked out and look ridiculous in the ring.'

'What he did was so much worse,' added Carlos Eleta. 'But he didn't think about *that*.'

'I think something really *was* wrong with him,' Don King told the assembled press the next morning. 'People talk about all the money he made and say he wasn't hungry enough this time. Money comes and goes, but words will follow you forever – especially in Latin America.'

'Yeah, they're checking Duran's birth certificate back in Panama,' cracked Fast Eddie Schuyler. 'They think now he may be a Guatemalan.'

'You guys will write about all this now and cut him up a little bit for a week or two, and then everybody will forget about it,' predicted King. 'But in Panama, they'll *never* forget it.'

A few nights later, Johnny Carson told his *Tonight Show* audience that he had considered inviting Duran to appear on his programme to sing 'The Twelve Days of Christmas'. 'But I'm afraid he'll quit by the eighth day,' quipped Carson.

Duran's surrender was so stunning that it all but overshadowed the brilliance of Leonard's performance, but, Ray pointed out, 'I *made* him quit – and making Roberto Duran quit was even *better* than knocking him out. The fact that he quit and the way he did it doesn't take anything away from my victory. I'm the champion because he couldn't change and I could.'

Interestingly, the term 'No Mas' did not immediately enter the lexicon. Although the Spanish phrase would become synonymous with the New Orleans rematch and Duran's fall from grace, the words 'No mas' were nowhere to be found in Ed Schuyler's AP story read by millions of Americans the next morning, nor did they appear in mine.

Since the fight had occurred on a Tuesday night, the issue of *Sports Illustrated* with Bill Nack's account didn't appear until eight days later, and then it was under a headline – 'The Big Belly-Ache' – that still appeared to buy the 'cramps' story.

The morning after the No Mas fight, General Omar Torrijos

angrily ordered Duran and his entire 36-member travelling party to return to Panama immediately, but the boxer ignored his country's ruler and went to Miami instead. It was weeks later that he went back to Panama, only to discover that in his absence his mother's home had been vandalised, his own house stoned. Newspapers questioned not only his courage but also his masculinity. A makeshift billboard reading 'Duran is a Traitor' was painted on the seawall alongside La Avenue Balboa in Panama City. He heard himself described, variously, as *un cobarde* (a coward), *una gallina* (a chicken) and, simply, *maricón*, or homosexual.

And, in perhaps the unkindest cut of all, the Panamanian government had repealed the special tax exemption it had granted Duran as a 'national hero'. When he came home and tried to cash his $8 million letter of credit, the government grabbed the first $2 million off the top.

Whatever might actually have been going on in Roberto Duran's mind when he said 'No mas', he could hardly have anticipated the consequences. He became the butt of jokes, and even his most ardent admirers deserted him in droves.

'His image had been destroyed in a single moment,' said Bobby Goodman. 'When he got back to Panama, he didn't even dare show his face. He lived like a prisoner in his own home.'

Goodman had been with Duran every day for months on end at his training camps for the two Leonard fights, and knew him as well as anyone.

'Duran had great pride, and the heart and soul of a warrior,' said Goodman over a quarter-century later. 'He was the ultimate warrior who had come ready to do battle, but his opponent changed the rules and he wouldn't submit to being humiliated like that.'

It was, in any case, a moment that would haunt Duran for the rest of his life. Worse still, he had turned his despised adversary into a boxing hero.

Sugar Ray Leonard would no longer be regarded as boxing's pretty boy. He had added a new scalp to his collection. He was now the man who had made Roberto Duran quit.

4

THE SHOWDOWN

Leonard–Hearns I
Caesars Palace, 16 September 1981

AS THE ENTOURAGES OF victor and vanquished spilled into the ring and 23,618 high-rollers, celebrities and boxing aficionados began to file out of the stadium in the direction of the casino's gaming tables, the sky lit up with a gaudy and expensive fireworks display Caesars Palace had commissioned for the occasion.

It was 16 September 1981, and the fight advertised as 'The Showdown' had more than lived up to its billing. For almost 14 rounds of non-stop action, Sugar Ray Leonard and Thomas Hearns had gone back and forth, each getting a nose in front only to be overtaken by the other. It had been a thrilling war of give-and-take, ebb-and-flow, and when it was over only one man was left standing.

But, the beaten Hearns would say, accurately, once it was over: 'We put on a great show for them. If you never see another fight, but you saw this one, that would be enough.'

More than twenty-six years later it remains high on anyone's list of the great boxing match-ups of all time.

Had the two fought, as they almost did, in Providence back in 1978, remember, Leonard would have made $100,000, Hearns $12,500. Three years later, their respective guarantees were $8 million and $5.1 million, and each would earn millions more against what turned out to be a $36 million gross.

Although his introduction to the professional game had been less auspicious than Leonard's, by 1980 Hearns had attracted the attention of boxing insiders, if not the public at large.

After the Cuevas fight, Hearns – posing as the Hit Man, wearing a gangsterish zoot suit with (of course) a tommy gun tucked under his arm – had been featured on the cover of *The Ring* magazine. And it had been the still-undefeated Hearns and not Leonard (2–1 in 1980) who was the reigning Fighter of the Year.

'When we finally made our deal with the Hearns camp, we did things the way I'd always felt a big fight should be done,' recalled Mike Trainer. 'We did all our negotiating with Hearns's representatives and with Caesars Palace first. *Then* we went out and hired somebody to act as the promoter.'

Officially, the promotion was staged by a four-way consortium of Dan Doyle and Shelly Finkel, along with the husband-and-wife team of Dan and Kathy Duva, who headed up Main Events. Their prior experience had for the most part come in the promotion of small club-fight shows in New Jersey.

'Shelly had kind of been the intermediary,' said Trainer. 'He helped work things out with Hearns's people, and he was close to the Duvas. We basically hired them to put on the promotion, and it pretty much put Main Events on the map.'

Doyle, as a reward for his loyalty and past services, was listed as a co-promoter, but, said the erstwhile basketball coach, 'My real job was to raise the capital for the fight and handle the New England pay-per-view sale. Dan, Kathy and Shelly handled a variety of tasks, and they did a terrific job. Bob Arum was later brought on board to help with the overseas markets and to coordinate the pay-per-view distribution.'

Once the match was made, Caesars knew that Leonard–Hearns would be the biggest boxing event it had ever hosted. Although both participants had fought at the casino before, it had been within the cosy confines of the tin-walled Sports Pavilion. For this fight, the hotel constructed a temporary stadium that rose up from what was normally a parking lot. Immediately after the fight it would be dismantled to make way for the Caesars Grand Prix, but, for this one-time use, capacity would be nearly 24,000. The top ticket price was set at $500.

With hotel rooms at the host casino jammed with high-rolling customers, most of the press contingent was relegated to the Marina, a fly-by-night motel up the Strip that would eventually be bulldozed to make room for the present-day MGM Grand.

'How bad is the Marina?' a scribe grumbled. 'When I checked in, the bellhop asked me if I knew where *he* could find any girls.'

Although few realised it at the time, the Showdown was briefly imperilled three weeks before the fight. At Leonard's training camp in Phoenix, one of his sparring partners, a then-unbeaten young California middleweight named Odell Hadley, caught Sugar Ray with an errant elbow beneath the left eye. Although he wasn't cut, the shiner was bad enough that it was initially feared that a postponement might be necessary. After a few days, the swelling subsided. Members of the training camp were sworn to secrecy, and Leonard resumed his preparations.

An even more serious training injury occurred in the other camp, but it wasn't to Hearns. In a sparring session less than ten days before the fight, the Hit Man served notice that he was getting his game face on when he broke Marlon Starling's jaw.

Starling, who would later become a two-time welterweight champion, was to have headlined the live card accompanying the closed-circuit telecast at the Hartford Civic Center. Instead of replacing his bout, local promoters advertised that they would show video clips of the sparring session in which Hearns injured Starling.

Each competitor, in fact, prepped for the Showdown against a sparring partner named Odell. Hearns was also sparring with Odell Leonard, who promoters around the country had been pitching as a 'cousin' of the Olympic champion. That Odell, who would fight Marvin Hagler's brother Robbie Sims on the Boston Garden live show on 16 September, made no attempt to correct the alleged family ties, but once he went over the hill and joined the enemy, the Leonard camp quickly outed him.

'His name is Odell Davis and he's from North Carolina,' said Janks Morton. 'He changed his name after the 1976 Olympics.'

'He's not my cousin,' said Roger Leonard. 'If he was my cousin, do you think he'd be helping the guy who's going to fight my brother?'

■ ■ ■

In the first six months of 1981, Marvin Hagler had made the first two defences of his middleweight title on his home turf, facing Fulgencio Obelmejias in January before meeting Vito Antuofermo in a June rematch.

Obelmejias was 30–0 and rated the No. 1 challenger by the WBA. His first twenty-seven fights had for the most part taken place in his homeland and Mexico, while his last three, all against nondescript opposition, had taken place in Italy.

That Hagler would approach his championship reign with the same dedication he had in the years when he was a hungry outsider was evident the first time we visited him in Provincetown before the Obelmejias fight. All but shuttered for the season, the sprawling Provincetown Inn was a ghostly mansion in January. Hagler rose each morning to run across the secluded dunes at the tip of Cape Cod, emerged from his room once a day for sparring, and spent the rest of his time in seclusion, staring out at the bleak winter landscape.

As a boy in Newark Hagler had kept pigeons in a rooftop coop. In Provincetown he had developed an affinity for the ubiquitous seagulls, some of whom he had even given names. In training, Hagler wore shirts and caps emblazoned with an ominous-sounding, if bizarrely ungrammatical, slogan: *Destruction and Destroy*.

Sometimes Goody and Pat would drop by for a chat, and he would occasionally roust one of his sparring partners for a walk on the dunes, but it isn't a stretch to say that Hagler spent 20 hours of each day alone, much of that thinking about his next opponent – in this case, Obelmejias.

Considering his dearth of high-level experience, Obelmejias performed creditably enough. He didn't win a single round, and was down twice before Octavio Meyran stopped it 20 seconds into the eighth.

Obelmejias had been a mandatory challenger. In his next defence, Hagler was determined to erase what he considered the lone remaining blight on his record.

He had avenged the Philadelphia decisions with Watts and Monroe by knocking out both men. He had removed any lingering doubt over the Seales draw with a first-round knockout in their third meeting.

Now it was time to prove to the world that the Antuofermo draw had been a miscarriage of justice.

Antuofermo's proclivity for being cut was legendary. He had recently undergone a new form of surgery that promised to alleviate the condition. Doctors had gone beneath the tender skin above his eyebrows to shave down the bone, a procedure it was believed would better allow him to withstand punches without bursting open.

'I guess,' a cornerman would say later, 'the operation didn't take.'

Vito didn't have a chance in this one. Hagler was all over him from the opening bell onwards, and Antuofermo's face began to sprout leaks in the first round. A deep cut above his left eye had turned his face into a mask of gore, but Vito the Mosquito pressed bravely onwards. Hagler dropped him in the third, and when Vito emerged from his stool to answer the bell for the fifth, he was followed into the ring by a towel from his corner.

Marvelous Marvin's reign as middleweight champion was off to a flying start, but he would never play the old Causeway Street arena again. The second Antuofermo fight turned out to be Hagler's last in the Boston Garden.

■ ■ ■

The Showdown with Hearns would confirm what those closest to him already knew about Ray Charles Leonard: that beneath the million-dollar smile and the pretty-boy veneer lurked a boxer with the heart of a serial killer.

'People who think he's a nice guy don't know *how* nice he is,' said Dundee. 'And people who think he's a tough fighter don't know *how* tough a fighter he is. He's a nicer guy and a tougher fighter than people realise.'

Emanuel Steward enthusiastically concurred with that assessment.

'One of Ray's greatest attributes was that he was such a strong finisher. He could always close the show,' said Steward. 'Even in the first Duran fight he was the guy coming on over the last few rounds. When people looked at that baby face and small-boned structure, they didn't realise how strong and physical he was, but Sugar Ray Leonard could be a total *animal* in the ring.'

Beyond his respect for Leonard's abilities, Steward had another concern in the days leading up to the Showdown.

'I was afraid Tommy was overtraining,' recalled Emanuel. 'I tried to rein him in, but for the first time since he was ten years old he wasn't listening to me.

'He had this crowd of people around him, and they were telling him, "Ray and Ollie run their camp. Angelo just comes in at the end, and they tell *him* what to do." So he was running in the morning, running again at night. When I told him I thought he was doing too much, he said, "I'm the one doing the fighting."

'A few days before the fight there was a big crowd at Tommy's workout. We were supposed to be through sparring, but Shelly Saltman, who was doing PR for us for that fight, grabbed the microphone and announced that Tommy was going to box.

'I said, "*What?*" I thought I hadn't heard right, but Tommy had told Shelly to announce it. "Yes, I'm going to box," he told me. He went seven rounds with Cave Man Lee and Dujuan Johnson [two future Kronk title challengers] that day.'

Another potential distraction occurred a few days before the fight. At daybreak one morning a tangential Hearns hanger-on who described himself as a 'bodyguard' was cleaning a pistol near the outdoor swimming pool when the weapon accidentally discharged. Although no one was injured, Caesars security officials quietly moved to disarm the Hearns posse, at least until the fight was over.

■ ■ ■

The Showdown would affirm boxing's first undisputed welterweight champion since José Nápoles, but although Leonard held the WBC title and Hearns the WBA belt, neither championship was even mentioned in the contract. Both organisations belatedly agreed to sanction the bout, but when their representatives arrived in Vegas, instead of getting the red-carpet treatment, the tinpot boxing dictators from Mexico and Venezuela discovered that they were expected to stand in the same credential line as everybody else.

When they complained about waiting to have their photos taken, it was presumably to say, '*We don't need no stinkin' badges!*'

'Why do they bother taking these guys' pictures?' wondered Bert Sugar. 'They could get them right off the post office wall.'

In September 1981 Leonard actually owned two world titles. The previous June he and Hearns had laid the groundwork for the Showdown by sharing a bill at the Astrodome in Houston, where Hearns defended his WBA welterweight championship, stopping Pablo Baez in four, while Leonard TKO'd Ayub Kalule in nine to win the WBA junior middleweight title.

The rationale for this joint appearance had been simple. Although the clamour for a Leonard–Hearns bout had commenced shortly after Duran said 'No mas' in New Orleans, Trainer said at the time that while 'boxing people know all about him, the American public doesn't even know who Thomas Hearns *is*'.

It was hoped that sharing the limelight with Sugar Ray at the Astrodome would help correct that deficiency.

The most memorable pre-fight moment in Houston came after Arum's publicist Irving Rudd trotted out what was supposed to be an authentic African witch doctor, ostensibly to boost the chances of the Ugandan-born Kalule by casting a spell on Leonard.

It was a cheap publicity stunt that appealed to the basest stereotypes, and at least one African-American on hand was prepared to denounce it as such. Outside the hotel, Rock Newman – later the manager and promoter of Riddick Bowe, but then a Washington-area sports radio personality – staged an impromptu press conference to decry the 'witch doctor' gimmick and all that it implied.

Newman was wearing white trousers and a white dashiki, and as he stood there berating the 'witch doctor' and railing against the racial overtones implicit in the gag, he was suddenly set upon by a flock of angry crows, who without warning swooped in from the sky and attacked Rock with such ferocity that he was forced to flee in terror.

Score one for the witch doctor.

(Native Texans later explained that everyone in Houston knew better than to wear white in the summer, because the colour was known to antagonise the local crows.)

Leonard, in any case, was allowed to hang on to both belts through the summer. Granted dispensation by the sanctioning bodies, he had until ten days after the Hearns fight to decide which one he would keep.

Sharing the spotlight with Hearns in Houston had brought about Leonard's first day-to-day interaction with the Hit Man. Leonard's impression?

'They ought to lobotomize Hearns, just to see if there's a brain in there,' he said, unkindly.

The remark was widely circulated and would be frequently revived in the run-up to the September fight. Like Muhammad Ali's equally mean-spirited description of Joe Frazier as 'ignorant' and 'a gorilla' ten years earlier, it would serve as bulletin-board material for the opposing camp.

Although the outcome of the No Mas fight seemed to have proved Dundee and Trainer right and Jacobs wrong, the breach was now irreparable. Having completely severed his ties with the Leonard camp, Jake volunteered his services to the enemy. In 1981, Ray's old amateur coach materialised in Las Vegas as a member of Hearns's entourage.

Although Steward welcomed his input, it is questionable how much advance intelligence Jacobs actually contributed. He walked around Caesars in a Kronk Boxing Team jacket and held court for the press, but on fight night Jacobs was not in Hearns's corner.

'I'd known Dave Jacobs for several years,' said Steward. 'We'd been friends since the '73 Gloves. He was part of our camp for the Leonard fight, but he didn't ever give us advice about how Tommy should fight Leonard.

'He didn't have to. I knew Ray Leonard as well as anyone,' said Steward. 'I'd seen him most of his amateur career, I'd coached him on several international amateur teams and he'd come to the Kronk to prepare for the 1976 Eastern Regionals before the Olympics. There wasn't anything [Jacobs] could have told me about Ray that I didn't already know.'

Even though he was technically a member of the Hearns entourage in Vegas, Leonard's old mentor clearly had mixed feelings. Two days before the Showdown, he told the Chicago *Sun-Times*'s John Schulian, 'If they called this fight off, I'd be the happiest man in the world.'

The Nevada State Athletic Commission had assigned the triumvirate of Duane Ford, Chuck Minker and Lou Tabat to be the judges. Sixty-three-year-old Davey Pearl, a fund-raiser for University of Nevada at Las Vegas (UNLV), was named the referee.

At the pre-fight rules meeting, Dundee asked Pearl to be vigilant in monitoring certain Hearns tactics he'd picked up watching films of the Hit Man's earlier fights.

'Watch how many punches Hearns misses and then hits the guy with his backhand,' said Leonard's trainer. 'Or how many times he'll miss with a jab, then hold the guy with his left hand behind the head and throw a right. I warned the commission about these things at the rules meeting.'

'They'll be watching for it,' said Dundee, 'but so will my guy. When Hearns does that, he's off balance, and Ray will catch him with left hands.'

The Showdown loomed a classic boxer–puncher match-up, then, and both participants appeared to subscribe to that view.

'My right hand could make this the easiest fight I've ever had,' said Hearns. 'It's very possible this fight can end very, very quickly. No more than three rounds.'

'Hearns makes mistakes,' countered Leonard. 'He tries to knock out everybody with one punch. I use my mind. Maybe Tommy would too – if he had one.'

'Emanuel Steward is no dummy,' said another interested observer, Marvelous Marvin Hagler. 'I expect Hearns will try to take Leonard out early, and I'm sure he'll be the aggressor. Of course, when that bell rings you never know what might happen. Hearns might not fight the way he's supposed to. But I think he will.'

Hagler would not be an eyewitness to the Showdown. The middleweight champion was again sequestered at his training camp in Provincetown, preparing to make his third title defence, against Mustafa Hamsho in the Chicago suburb of Rosemont, a few weeks later.

Neither Leonard nor Hearns had ever fought as a 160-pounder, but even in 1981 it was apparent that both loomed as potential Hagler opponents.

Marvelous Marvin was doing double-duty the week of the Leonard–Hearns showdown, 'covering' the fight as a guest columnist for the *Boston Herald American*. Before leaving for Vegas, I'd sat down with Marvin in Provincetown for his analysis, and in the days leading up to the bout we spoke each day by telephone.

'The first Duran fight was his toughest test so far, but his fight against Hearns will be even tougher,' Hagler had predicted. 'To neutralise Hearns's reach advantage, Leonard is going to have to stay either inside him or outside him. My guess is that he'll stay outside and box and make Tommy come to him. Leonard is a very good counterpuncher.

'The way Hearns carries his left hand so low looks dangerous, but it really isn't,' added Marvelous Marvin. 'Not if he keeps the proper distance. There's a safe distance and an unsafe distance, and Hearns is awfully quick. If Leonard tries to come inside that left, well, there's a saying in boxing that if he's close enough to hit *you*, he's close enough for you to hit *him*. That's especially true with those long arms Tommy has.'

It had not gone unnoticed that Hearns had a proclivity for running out of gas in longer fights. In addition to the issue of Hearns's punching power versus Leonard's boxing abilities, the matter of the Hit Man's stamina was also called into question.

'Only two of Hearns's fights have ever gone the distance, and his longest fight ever was when he went twelve rounds in beating Randy Shields,' noted Hagler. 'But Randy Shields is the sort of fighter who could make a firing squad look bad.'

But when Hearns was asked about the possibility of the fight lasting into the later rounds, he seemed confident.

'I might be tired, but Ray better not underestimate me,' he warned. 'Tired, I'm still able to break ribs and break jaws.'

At a breakfast with the press a few days before the fight, Hearns was asked about the mind games Leonard seemed to be playing.

'If he's trying to psyche me out,' said Hearns, 'he's not doing a very good job of it.'

The widespread assumption was that the judges would bend over backwards for Leonard and that Hearns almost *had* to score a knockout to win. One of the wire services, in fact, polled out-of-town boxing writers on the matter, and, of seventy prognosticators queried, only one picked Hearns by decision.

Even Emanuel Steward seemed to share the view that the judges would be disposed towards Leonard. 'If the fight goes 15 rounds and it goes to a decision, it will be, uh, *interesting*,' said Hearns's manager/trainer.

The bettors apparently subscribed to the opinion: wagering that the fight would end by knockout was an odds-on, 2–5 proposition.

Leonard had been posted as a narrow favourite when the fight first went up on the board, and remained so until two nights before the fight, when so much Motown money came rolling in that Hearns became a 7–5 favourite.

Having made their cases for the conventional wisdom, Hagler and both trainers allowed themselves some wiggle room by conceding that the fight just might not unfold the way everyone expected.

'Leonard knows he can't run all night,' said Hagler. 'He'll have to give them a show, but I figure he'll try not to mix it up early, hoping that Hearns will get tired and sloppy in the later going.'

'But you never know,' mused Marvin. 'Leonard *might* try to punch with Hearns. He's showed a tendency to do that in some of his more recent fights, especially the last one, against Kalule. If he does that, I think it will be a mistake.'

'People forget that Tommy wasn't always a puncher,' Steward said. 'In his whole amateur career he hardly ever knocked anybody out. He was a boxer then, and he's a boxer now.'

'My guy is gonna back him up,' vowed Dundee, although few expected that to happen.

'One of them will be a loser and the other one is doomed,' said Hagler, 'because the winner gets *me*.'

Steward, Walter Smith and Prentiss Byrd comprised the brain trust in the Hearns camp. Byrd, Steward's aide-de-camp, was a former minor leaguer in the Chicago White Sox system, Smith a retired automotive worker. The colourful fourth figure in the Kronk corner was Don Thibodeaux, a Detroit artist and sculptor with long red hair and an even longer beard, which reached nearly to his navel.

Thibodeaux was successful in his day job – he had once sold a piece (a bust of Muhammad Ali) for $40,000 – but found himself inexorably drawn to the Sweet Science and Steward's steamy, inner-city gym.

Mickey Goodwin, the Kronk middleweight who had been the main event performer on the early Detroit cards on which Hearns boxed, recalled a night when Thibodeaux was working his corner. At the '*Seconds Out!*' command, Thibodeaux had bent over and shoved Goodwin's gumshield back in – and a large mouthful of beard along with it.

'You ever try to get hair out of your mouth with boxing gloves on?' asked Goodwin.

As 16 September dawned, Hagler said, 'I'm sure both of them woke up this morning just wishing this fight was over.'

'The day before the fight I wanted to check Tommy's weight, but he just shooed me away and said, "I'm fine,"' recalled Steward. 'Then when we got to the scales the next day, Tommy was 145. I thought I could see Ray Leonard's jaw drop. Everybody seemed shocked.'

'I was worried right then and there – and with good reason, it turned out,' said Steward. 'Half a tank of gas might get you where you're going, but I don't care what kind of car you've got, if you don't have enough in the tank for a long trip, you're not going to go all the way.'

A lengthy undercard that began under the hot afternoon sun played out as darkness fell across the desert: Tony Ayala Jr, a young junior middleweight prospect promoted by the Duvas, went to 10–0 with a first-round knockout of Jose Rendiz. Heavyweight Tony Tucker, then trained by Steward, stopped Harvey Steichen in three, and Marvis Frazier scored a fourth-round TKO over Guy Casale. In the co-feature, another future world champion, lightweight Edwin Rosario, outpointed James Martinez.

The early prelims had been fought before a smattering of witnesses, but as twilight turned to evening an audience that would eventually reach 23,306 began to file into the makeshift stadium – Kareem Abdul-Jabbar and George Carlin, Bill Cosby and Jack Nicholson, Cher Bono and the Rev. Jesse Jackson, Karl Malden, Bo Derek and John McEnroe among them.

Fans gawked as present and former champions from Larry Holmes to Joe Frazier to Jake LaMotta took their places in the stands. The biggest ovation was reserved for a late arrival, Muhammad Ali, who just a few months later would engage in his final bout, in the Bahamas. The great man whose *nom de guerre* Leonard had appropriated, Sugar Ray Robinson, was also ushered to a ringside seat.

By nightfall the temperature, which had reached a high of 96 degrees that autumn afternoon, had subsided, but under the glare of the lights from the canopy above it was still almost 100 in the ring.

Both participants entered the ring in shimmering white satin robes. Leonard had won a coin-toss to determine the order of procession, so Hearns was the first to arrive. The words 'WINNER TAKES ALL' were emblazoned across the back of his robe. Leonard's said, simply, 'DELIVERANCE'.

'Before the fight started, Tony Ayala, who had won on the undercard, was running up to the ring and calling out Leonard,' recalled Michael Katz. 'It occurred to me then that you never heard anyone calling out *Hearns*. *Nobody* wanted to fight a six foot, one inch welterweight with the power to destroy Pipino Cuevas [and, later, Roberto Duran] inside two rounds.'

When Leonard was introduced, Hearns banged his gloves together in mock applause and then, a menacing scowl on his face, followed Ray across the ring to his corner. This bit of gamesmanship was countered by Dundee, who complained to Pearl about what he considered an excessive amount of Vaseline smeared across the Hit Man's face.

'Just before the start, I was standing up in my seat and I turned to Joe Flaherty and said, "*Let's have a fight!*"' remembered Katz. 'I had no idea who was going to win.'

Dundee and Morton worked Leonard's corner, where they were augmented by Ollie Dunlap and, at least initially, Ray's brother Roger.

Moments after the opening bell, Bob Arum materialised beside the ring apron, shouting, '*Stop the fight!*'

Arum wasn't even the promoter of the Showdown, but he *had* arranged the pay-per-view distribution. He had just been informed that due to a glitch in the cable system, thousands of homes in California were receiving the signal for free. He somehow had it in his mind that Pearl should stop Leonard and Hearns from boxing until the technical difficulties could be overcome, but the referee ignored him.

What unfolded that night turned out to be a symphony in five distinct movements.

The first, comprising the opening five rounds, was a protracted overture in which both combatants performed brilliantly, but pretty much as advertised. While Leonard dazzled with his speed, he seemed wary enough of Hearns's punching power that he wasn't about to mix it up, and Tommy, for his part, used his reach advantage to poke away at Leonard with jabs when he came near enough.

As the first round drew to a close, Roger Leonard excitedly shouted something to his brother. Distracted, Ray looked away as Hearns punched him just after the bell. Pearl jumped between the fighters, but as Leonard stumbled back to his corner Janks Morton shouted down from the ring: '*Kenny, get Roger out of the corner!*'

Kenny Leonard, already wearing a white satin cornerman's jacket, was thus handed a battlefield promotion, and replaced his brother in the corner for the balance of the fight.

Leonard's corner had told him to keep Hearns moving anticlockwise. Most of Hearns's victims, fearing his long reach and superior jab, had allowed him to box in his comfort zone, which was going to his left, and in denying Hearns the jab had exposed themselves to an even more fearsome weapon, his right hand.

Leonard spent much of the early going darting around the ring as if he had an invisible jet-pack mounted on his back. Backwards, forwards, sideways, he flitted from corner to corner, rope to rope, presenting a tantalising target, only to whoosh out of range as Hearns closed. When Tommy landed, it was usually with a glancing blow, and when Leonard scored, he escaped before the Hit Man could exact retribution.

Leonard bent forward from the waist, presenting an even smaller target, but if Hearns was frustrated by the awkward angles at which he was forced to attack he didn't let on. Behind his jab, he continued to walk Leonard down, and the expression on his face was that of a man who knew that sooner or later he was going to catch up with his quarry. Periodically he seemed to smile disdainfully, the ring lights exaggerating the expression by illuminating the flash of his gumshield.

In the third round, the two stopped and briefly went toe-to-toe. Neither man emerged with a clear advantage from this spirited exchange, and after it Leonard seemed to remember where he was and whom he was fighting and got back on his bicycle again. By the end of the round, a telltale welt had begun to form under his left eye.

Whether it was the exacerbated residue of Odell Hadley's elbow three weeks earlier, the result of a Hearns punch or (more likely) some combination of the two remains the subject of some debate a quarter-century later.

Dunlap and Julius (Juice) Gatling, Leonard's equipment man, maintain that it was the former, but Emanuel Steward remains convinced that the puffy eye was the result of Hearns's attack.

'Sometimes a fighter will get cut in training and it will open up during the fight, but I never saw any evidence of swelling on Ray's face beforehand,' said Steward.

Throughout the night, Dundee applied his secret weapon, an Endswell, to Leonard's swollen eye. Although it is now standard equipment in most trainers' bags, in 1981 the contraption seemed a space-age invention. Essentially a miniature flatiron ('Like something you might find in a dollhouse,' noted Pat Putnam), the device was stored in an ice bucket, whence it was retrieved between rounds and pressed against the boxer's face to reduce swelling.

On several occasions Pearl had to move in and separate the fighters after the bell, and at one point Leonard, reprising a playground gesture from the second Duran fight, wound up his right as if to throw a bolo punch and instead threw a left. Hearns responded by sticking out his gumshield in derision.

It wasn't surprising that Hearns was ahead with the fight already one-third over. What was surprising was that he had gained that advantage by outboxing Leonard.

Their mutual respect was such that neither man was willing to go on the attack, and the result was that in this early going Hearns maintained control with his jab and superior wingspan. From a technical standpoint, it was enthralling to watch it unfold, but some of the spectators grew restive.

'There were pockets of booing during the opening five rounds,' said Katz. 'Few boxing fans would cheer the Fischer–Spassky chess matches.'

'For the first five rounds the six-foot-one Hearns was in command, stinging Leonard with his jab and keeping his shorter opponent at bay with his vaunted seventy-eight-inch reach,' Schulian described this initial interlude. 'Unable to get inside where he wanted to operate, Leonard had to fight outside, and he paid in pain.'

The momentum abruptly shifted in the sixth, when Leonard spotted a moment of complacency and seized the advantage: Hearns dropped his right for a split second, and Leonard pounced on the opening to land a vicious left hook to the body that drove Tommy back into the ropes. Steward would later describe it to Putnam as the punch from which Hearns never recovered.

His killer instinct ignited, Leonard treated Hearns's midsection like a speed bag, tattooing him with a barrage of punches to an unprotected body. When Hearns dropped his elbows to protect his ribcage, Leonard merely readjusted his sights and shifted the attack to the head.

Despite the terrible pummelling, Hearns somehow stayed on his feet, and when the bell rang to end the round Leonard seemed to smirk and asked him, 'You all right?'

The seventh was once again all Leonard, and Hearns absorbed such a beating that Steward considered rescuing his man by throwing in the towel. Hearns fought the entire round going backwards, but survived it. Leonard, as a coda to the round, finished it by landing three successive left hooks.

Although Hearns didn't go down, he was legless and all but out on his feet for much of the sixth and seventh. All three judges scored the rounds for Leonard, but not one of them scored either a 10–8 round, as did many scribes at ringside.

'I was ready to stop the fight,' said Steward, 'and if Ray had landed one more solid punch I would have, but Tommy was avoiding them – barely. Then, much to my surprise, Tommy went back to boxing and eventually took control again.'

By the eighth, the roles had reversed: Leonard had become the stalker, trying to walk Hearns down for the big punch that would end it all, and the Hit Man had mounted the bicycle, still dancing away but now firing jabs to cover his retreat.

It seemed as good a time as any for an intermission and, as if by mutual consent, both fighters took the ninth off.

Downshifting, said Dundee, 'was my idea. I was afraid Ray was going to pop a cork in there.'

Hearns needed no encouragement to take a breather but was so wary from the battering he had taken in the middle rounds that it was midway through the tenth – when he was alerted by the restive booing and whistling of the crowd – that he began to assimilate the fact that he was no longer under attack.

Leonard had been presenting awkward angles all night, but now there was a new twist to his posture. His head tilted at an odd angle, swivelled around to compensate for a rapidly decreasing field of vision. If he faced Hearns head-on, he couldn't see the right coming.

But even as he reasserted himself over the 11th and 12th rounds, Hearns withheld the weapon that was supposed to be the ultimate deterrent. Although he was dominating Leonard once again, conventional wisdom had it that this fight would turn on Leonard's ability to absorb Hearns's big right hand. But Tommy never threw the haymaker.

'He kept moving off to the side, so I couldn't hit him with the full force of the punch,' Hearns would later explain. 'I *still* haven't hit him with my best shot. Why didn't I try to land more right hands? Basically, because I don't throw a punch if I know it's not going to land.'

As the 12th ended Hearns seemed firmly in control, and had won over much of the crowd. They were chanting, 'Tommy! Tommy!', and Hearns acknowledged their new-found allegiance by waving his arms like a cheerleader as he returned to his corner.

Across the ring, Dundee towelled off Leonard's face and attempted to communicate the urgency of the situation.

'You're blowing it, son,' he shouted at Leonard. 'You're blowing it!'

Dundee couldn't have known it, but his opposite number was even more worried. Steward's fighter had assumed control of the fight, but he had paid a price.

'At the end of the 12th Tommy came back waving to the crowd, but I was still worried,' Steward said. 'I knew Ray always, always, *always* finished up strong. Even in the first fight with Duran he'd come on those last three rounds and beat the hell out of Duran. He was always physically strong.

'I was talking to Tommy and all of a sudden his head slumped down. He was out of gas. I knew right then it was over.'

Moreover, Hearns was now in uncharted waters. He had never before fought a 13th round.

By now, Leonard's left eye had ballooned so grotesquely that you half expected Dundee to produce a razor, à la Burgess Meredith in *Rocky*, and provide relief by slicing open the haematoma.

'At that point the eye was so badly swollen that somewhere between half and three-quarters of my vision was impaired,' Leonard would recall. 'He was starting to get through with some jabs and some rights because I couldn't see. That's why I wanted to end it quickly. I just pulled it up from my guts.'

Early in the 13th, Hearns stumbled as Leonard shoved him, and then unaccountably dropped his hands again. Spotting the opening, Leonard fired a hard right-hand lead to the head, followed by a left hook that wobbled Hearns in his tracks.

Leonard, smelling blood in the water, abandoned all pretence of elegance. He landed an uppercut and then unleashed an uninterrupted fusillade of at least two dozen rapid-fire punches that drove Hearns across the ring, through the ropes and onto the apron.

Pearl did not rule it a knockdown, and, as Hearns teetered precariously on the apron, one of the judges reached up and steadied his back to keep him from falling over the edge.

'Pearl said he had been pushed,' wrote the Boxing Bard of Scotland, Hugh McIlvanney. 'All of us had better hope we never encounter such pushing in a bus queue.'

'*Get up!*' the referee inexplicably ordered Hearns. (Pearl would later explain that he had meant to say, '*Can* you get up?')

Hearns was helped to his feet, but appeared lost. If ever a situation demanded that a boxer in trouble tie up his opponent, this was it, but at that moment Hearns looked as if he'd never *heard* the word 'clinch'.

He probably hadn't. Prior to the Leonard fight, Steward had boasted that 'you never see a clinch in the Kronk Gym', as if it had been a point of honour. The events of that evening resulted in a revision of that philosophy.

'In his whole career Tommy had never had to clinch,' said Steward. 'Later on, once he learned *how* to do it, he became an *expert* at it – think about the fights with [James] Kinchen and [Juan] Roldán. But in the Leonard fight he never even thought about it, because he didn't know how.'

Left to his own devices, Leonard resumed right where he had left off, battering Hearns with a series of punches that once again knocked him through the ropes. Looking dazed and cross-eyed, Hearns was left draped, half-sitting, across the bottom strand.

'Off the rope!' ordered Pearl.

'*Mmm,*' Hearns groaned, woozily shaking his head.

Pearl, belatedly, began to count. Hearns extracted himself by the time he reached four, but he barely survived the round.

As the fighters returned to their corners, Dundee was on his feet, shouting at Pearl, 'It should have been *two* knockdowns!'

In the corner, Dundee warned Leonard that he still might be behind on points.

'I really didn't think he was, but I figured it wouldn't hurt to give him a little needle,' the trainer said later. But as it turned out, his worst-case assessment was right on the mark.

Hearns might have led on the scorecards, but he was utterly spent. Leonard came charging out of the corner like a sprinter from his blocks to greet him with a left hook.

In the first minute of the round, he sent Hearns reeling with a savage right to the head and followed up with four or five more punches that knocked Hearns all the way across the ring.

Leonard chased Hearns down in a neutral corner and then trapped him there, landing three rapid-fire hooks to the head of an utterly defenceless Hearns. Pearl stopped the fight at 1:45 of the round, and Ray Charles Leonard was the undisputed welterweight champion of the world.

Hearns briefly, though unconvincingly, protested the stoppage before stumbling into the arms of his cornermen. Smiling through his gumshield, Leonard raised both gloves in the air as the crowd roared its approval of what had been a thrilling performance by both men.

'I knew where I was at all times,' Hearns would later recall the final four and a half minutes of fighting. 'I wasn't dizzy or nothing. It just seemed like every time he hit me with a combination I hadn't got myself back together yet before he hit me again.

'It was in my mind to try to hang on and last the fight, even after I was hurt,' admitted Hearns. 'I thought I was in control of myself, but the referee didn't. There's nothing I can do about it.'

All three ringside judges had Hearns in front at the time of the stoppage – Minker by four at 125–121, Tabat by three (125–122) and Ford by two (124–122).

The judges were roundly excoriated by, among others, Hughie McIlvanney, who cited 'a lack of perception and common sense afflicting the three'. (McIlvanney reserved a particular place of dishonour for the late Chuck Minker, whom he described as 'good old Chuck, who should not be allowed out without a guide dog'.)

'I'm not saying Ray should be treated like Muhammad Ali. I'm not saying he should get everything that's close,' moaned an astonished Mike Trainer when the scoring was revealed. 'But, Jesus, give him a fair shake. If you look at those scorecards, it'll turn your stomach!'

The judges' scorecards were indeed a surprise to most ringsiders ('As far as I was concerned,' wrote British scribe Frank Keating, 'each of them was as daffy as Don King's barber'), but Hearns claimed afterwards, 'I thought I was ahead.'

My own scorecard had the fight dead level going into the 14th, meaning that I'd have had Leonard ahead by at least two points with a round to go if Pearl hadn't stopped the fight.

Even Pearl, who didn't have a vote, seemed appalled when he viewed the scorecards.

'I figured Hearns was winning all those light-hitting rounds,' the referee told Pat Putnam. 'But Leonard was doing all the heavy damage. I thought it was close. Jeez, what if I had let the fight go on and Ray just barely won the last round and they gave Hearns the decision? Caesars wouldn't have had to tear the stadium down for the Grand Prix. The people would have done it for them.'

Years later, having viewed the videotape of the Leonard–Hearns fight on numerous occasions, Duane Ford would admit, 'I was off in that fight – but Chuck was *way* off!'

'But that fight actually changed the scoring system in Nevada,' said Ford, who would later become the chairman of the NSAC. 'We'd just gone from the five-point system to the ten-point must system, and the way the rules read in 1981 we weren't *allowed* to score a 10–8 round with no knockdown.'

In an early edition story written before the fight, Katz had noted that Mike Trainer had expressed concern that the judges might be predisposed against Leonard. His theory was that there might be some residual resentment over the way he and Leonard had altered the dynamics of big fights by letting the boxers, and not the promoters, call the shots.

'[Trainer] was very correct,' recalled Katz. 'Chuck Minker was later rewarded by being made the executive director of the Nevada commission.'

■ ■ ■

'I have no qualms about the referee's decision,' recalled Emanuel Steward. 'Some people said because Tommy was ahead on the scorecards he should have been given a chance to finish the fight, but the truth is, if he'd made it out of that round he couldn't even have made it back to the corner, much less lasted another one. His legs was gone. He was cooked.'

'I saw Thomas Hearns hurt, and I never saw that before,' added Steward, apparently as mesmerised by what had taken place as the rest of us. 'I saw Ray Leonard outboxed, and I never saw *that* before, either.'

'When I returned home, a friend thanked me for touting Leonard in my *New York Times* articles,' recalled Katz in a remembrance for TheSweetScience.com a quarter-century later. 'In those enlightened days, *Times* reporters were not allowed to make predictions, and, frankly, I didn't have a clue. What I *did* write, though, was that the fight might resemble a mirage in the desert – that Thomas Hearns would be the boxer and Ray Leonard the slugger.

'I got that part right, and my friend took it to mean that Leonard would win and was able to cash in. But having forecast the role reversals didn't mean I thought the slugger would win – and there was ample evidence that wonderful night that Hearns indeed could have outboxed Leonard to win a decision.'

When they appeared together at a post-fight news conference that night, Leonard and Hearns sounded downright affectionate. Ray even apologised 'for some of the things I said about Tommy – like that he didn't have any brains'.

'There was room for only one of us,' said Leonard. 'We both stood our ground. In my book, we both are still champions. He's a superior athlete.'

Added Hearns: 'I gave my best. I just made a couple of mistakes, and you can't afford to make mistakes against a fighter of Ray's calibre.'

When Leonard ruefully noted that Hearns had landed 'some really solid shots', somebody asked him if he'd ever been in trouble.

'I knew I was in trouble,' replied Leonard, 'the moment I signed the contract for this fight.'

Leonard didn't look much like a man who'd just won a fight. His face was a mess. Later that night, Putnam was with Leonard in his suite when the boxer's seven-year-old son entered the room and got his first look at his battered father.

'Little Ray bit his lower lip, blinking away the tears in his bright eyes,' wrote Putnam.

'Daddy, why do you keep on fighting? Why don't you take up another sport?'

'Like what?'

'Like basketball.'

■ ■ ■

The all-night gamblers were still out in force the next morning when Hearns and Leonard made their separate ways through the casino to meet with the press. Hearns wore a gold Kronk warm-up suit, while Leonard was dressed in white trousers and shirt, a white yachting cap perched atop his head. Both wore sunglasses to mask the evidence of the carnage of the previous evening.

As the two sat side by side, one scribe was moved to note that the pair of them looked like the aftermath of 'a bad night on *Gilligan's Island*'.

'My face,' Leonard recalled later, 'looked like the Hunchback of Notre Dame's.'

There was little discussion of a rematch. Leonard, noting that he had the option of defending either the undisputed welterweight title or his WBA 154-pound championship, seemed disposed to the former, and pointedly invited junior welter champion Aaron Pryor, whom he accused of talking too much, to move up and challenge him.

'Aaron Pryor says he wants to get into the ring with me,' said Leonard. 'He wants to be able to retire – and he *will*, for health reasons.'

Although an obvious big fight loomed against Hagler, Leonard didn't sound eager to have it happen any time soon.

'I think I'll be a middleweight in a year or two,' said Leonard. 'I figure the longer I wait, the older Hagler will get.'

What about Hearns and Hagler, then?

Leonard didn't even wait for Hearns to answer.

'Tommy can have him,' he smiled.

When Angelo Dundee was congratulated for his inspirational work in the corner that night, he shrugged and said, 'Thanks, but Ray did the fighting.'

■ ■ ■

Both Leonard and Hearns would go on to win bigger battles and earn even more money than they did that night in 1981; years later they would even fight one another again. Yet that magical evening in the desert remains, in the estimation of most boxing historians, the greatest welterweight fight of all time. I've covered nearly 400 world title bouts since, but with all its fascinating nuances, Leonard–Hearns I remains the best fight I was ever privileged to watch.

5

TOUGHING IT OUT

Hagler–Duran
Caesars Palace, 11 November 1983

BY LATE 1982, DURAN'S stock had tumbled even further than after the No Mas fight. He had lost a decision in a challenge for the WBC junior middleweight title to Wilfred Benitez (who had by then anglicised his given name by dropping the 'o') and then been solidly outpointed by Jamaican-born journeyman Kirkland Laing.

After the Laing fight in Detroit, Don King had stormed into the loser's dressing-room to unleash an obscenity-laced ten-minute tirade, at the conclusion of which he angrily told Duran he would never promote him again.

At 31, Manos de Piedra hadn't even been placed on waivers. He had been handed boxing's equivalent of his outright release.

Just as his entourage of once-faithful 'friends' had all but abandoned him, virtually every associate who had shared his journey to the top had deserted. Freddie Brown had quit in a dispute over money after the No Mas fight. After washing his hands of Duran in New Orleans, Ray Arcel had relented and returned to work Cholo's corner against Benitez but had been so disappointed in the result that he subsequently sent Duran a heartfelt letter recommending that they *both* retire.

Carlos Eleta no longer even phoned, and appeared to have lost all interest. Only Plomo – Nestor Quinones, Duran's boyhood trainer – remained from the old days.

Luis Spada was a courtly Argentine who had for many years done business as a matchmaker in Panama. Years before, he had told Duran that if he ever needed an extra spit-bucket carrier, he would be his man.

As he contemplated his future, Duran telephoned Spada.

'I don't want you to carry the bucket,' he told him. 'I want you to be my manager.'

Spada contacted Eleta, who confirmed that he was through with Duran and wished him luck.

In the autumn of 1982, Duran presented himself at the offices of Top Rank.

'He was worthless, not worth a plugged quarter,' said Bob Arum, who was disinclined to take on the reclamation project but did so at the urging of Teddy Brenner. The deposed president of Madison Square Garden Boxing had, after an unsuccessful fling at promoting, resurfaced as Arum's matchmaker.

During Brenner's Garden tenure he had staged many of the Panamanian's early fights. He argued that, at 30, Duran hadn't absorbed a lot of physical punishment in the ring, and that if he could only rekindle the fire that had once made him the most feared man in boxing, he might prove a profitable acquisition for Top Rank.

(It was a transaction that would have ramifications for years to come. Prior to signing Duran, Arum had underestimated the Hispanic boxing market, but his experience with Duran's resurgence led to subsequent alliances with Julio César Chávez and Oscar De La Hoya, and ultimately, to the contemporary crop of Top Rank boxers – a roster that includes the likes of Miguel Cotto, Erik Morales, José Luis Castillo, Humberto Soto, Jorge Arce, Antonio Margarito and Julio César Chávez Jr, along with the Spanish-speaking Filipino Manny Pacquiao. Top Rank regularly markets fights to Telefutura, and Arum employs a full-time Spanish-language *publicista*, Ricardo Jimenez, to work alongside press agent Lee Samuels.)

Duran's first fight under the Top Rank banner, a lacklustre decision over Briton Jimmy Batten on the Aaron Pryor–Alexis Arguello card in Miami that November, didn't do much to enhance his image, but there were few witnesses. The main event had ended chaotically, and the Batten fight was the walkout bout of the evening. By the time it started I was filing my story from the football press box high above the Orange Bowl, so far from the ring that it was difficult to see what was taking place, but the boos and catcalls from what remained of the crowd spoke volumes.

In January 1983, on the eve of Super Bowl XXVII in Los Angeles, Duran scored a stunning knockout of Pipino Cuevas at the LA Sports Arena, dropping the former welterweight champion twice before stopping him for good in the fourth. The Cuevas fight represented a giant leap forward in Duran's comeback plans, but it nearly sparked a riot at the venue. The boozy, mostly Mexican-American fans had been solidly pro-Cuevas, and they were outraged over what they considered a poor effort. Eddie (The Animal) López, a Chicano heavyweight from East Los Angeles, stood on the apron of the ring cursing at Cuevas.

As the fighters and their entourages milled about in the ring, a network cameraman on hand to capture Duran's post-fight interview was struck squarely in the back by an object heaved from the stands and immediately felt warm moisture spreading across his back. He feared at first that it might be his own blood, but when he looked down to the canvas, he realised he had been hit by an East LA hand grenade – a makeshift water balloon consisting of a condom filled with freshly produced urine. It had presumably been intended for Pipino.

Arum had told Duran that if he could beat Cuevas he would arrange a shot at WBA junior middleweight champion Davey Moore. The promoter was able to make good on his promise sooner than expected. Tony Ayala, the unbeaten young Texas junior middleweight in line for a mandatory challenge to Moore, was arrested on rape charges (he ultimately spent nearly 17 years in prison), clearing the way for Duran.

The fight against Moore was initially scheduled to take place at the Sun City Casino in the South African 'homeland' of Bophuthatswana, in combination with a Ray Mancini–Kenny Bogner lightweight title match. Both bouts would be prelims to the *pièce de résistance* of the evening, a concert by Frank Sinatra.

'Sinatra had agreed to perform because he was a big fan of Boom-

Boom Mancini,' recalled Arum. 'Then, a couple of weeks before we were to fly to South Africa, Mancini broke his collarbone. When that fight was cancelled, Sinatra cancelled too.

'We had to find a new site for the Moore–Duran fight, and New York seemed a natural. Moore was a native New Yorker who'd won multiple Golden Gloves titles at the Garden. Duran always had a big following among the Hispanics of New York, so we rented Madison Square Garden and put the fight there.

'In retrospect,' added Arum, 'it may have been the best thing that ever happened to Duran. If he fights Moore in South Africa, I'm not even sure he wins.'

(Michael Katz disputed Arum's contention on this point: 'That's bullshit,' said the Wolf Man. 'He thumbs Moore in the eye no matter where they are.')

While Duran was preparing for the 16 June Moore fight, Hagler was training in Provincetown, getting ready for a 27 May title defence against Wilford Scypion at the Providence Civic Center.

Under normal circumstances, once Hagler put himself 'in jail' you couldn't have dislodged him with a bomb, but he had agreed to break camp for a day a week before the fight to participate in a boxing skit with Sugar Ray Leonard as part of Bob Hope's televised 80th Birthday Special at the Kennedy Center in Washington.

The appearance was meaningful to Hagler for a couple of reasons. Not only did the celebrity role with Hope represent the sort of recognition he felt was long overdue, but for one night, at least, it would put him on equal footing with Leonard, whom he continued to regard as his nemesis.

■ ■ ■

After defeating Hearns, Leonard made just one defence of the undisputed welterweight title, a third-round TKO of Bruce Finch in Reno in February 1982. He was to have met Roger Stafford in Buffalo that May, but a routine pre-fight physical revealed a detached retina in his left eye. The Stafford fight was cancelled, and Leonard returned to Maryland, where he underwent surgery at the Johns Hopkins Hospital in Baltimore.

A quarter-century ago, a detached retina was usually considered to be a career-ending injury, but laser techniques were just becoming available, and this was Sugar Ray Leonard.

Leonard booked the Baltimore Civic Center for 9 November, a week after his return from Italy, where he had gone as part of the HBO broadcast team for Hagler's 30 October rematch against Obelmejias. (Obelmejias II had initially been scheduled for 15 July but had been postponed after Hagler incurred a rib injury while sparring in Provincetown.)

Ray had chosen the site of his pro debut for what he promised would be an 'historic announcement'. Over 10,000 tickets had been sold to the public (the proceeds would be donated to the Boys Clubs of Baltimore) and another 2,000 'special guests' had received invitations. Among those on the guest list were Guarino and Pasquale Petronelli and Marvelous Marvin Hagler.

When they met in their rematch in San Remo, Hagler finished Obelmejias off in five, belting him with a right hand that left the Venezuelan sprawled on the deck. Obelmejias was still struggling to regain his footing when referee Ernesto Magana counted him out.

'As soon as I hit him,' Hagler recalled afterwards, 'I *knew* he wouldn't get up. Well, he'd have been a fool if he'd tried to.'

Among the first in the ring to congratulate Hagler was Leonard, who interviewed him for HBO. Once they had disposed of their recap of the fight itself, Marvin turned to Ray with a grin and teased him:

'Let's go for the big one,' Hagler told him. 'The people want to see you, Lenny. They don't want you to retire.'

'I'll think about it,' Leonard replied with a laugh.

As he made his way out of the Teatro Ariston in San Remo that night, Pat Petronelli ran into Leonard. 'Pat,' he whispered, 'I'm going to deny it, but there'll be a fight.'

'I did tell him that,' Leonard recalled with a smile a quarter-century later. 'I guess I said it like a politician: I said there would be a fight. I just didn't say *when*.'

Not even Leonard's closest associates were sure. 'I don't know,' said Ollie Dunlap, 'and, to tell you the truth, I really don't think Ray's made up his mind, either.'

The Hagler camp already had dollar signs dancing in their heads.

Bob Arum, having discovered what he described as a 'mother lode' in the South African 'homeland', supposed that he could sell Hagler–Leonard in Bophuthatswana for 'a trillion dollars'. (Whether either Hagler or Leonard could have been persuaded to perform in a venue that represented a veritable monument to apartheid is a question that never had to be answered. Frankly, I doubt it.)

Hagler's promoter was even contemplating how to get around the nettlesome problem posed by Tony Sibson's impending mandatory challenge, which, according to WBC rules, needed to be formalised within a week or two.

'If José Sulaimán tried to strip Hagler to prevent a Hagler–Leonard match, it would be a joke,' said Arum. 'It would be the end of the WBC. No one would take them seriously.'

It seemed plain enough that Sibson himself was uneager to be an impediment to the proposed megafight. '[Hagler] couldn't turn that down,' said the Englishman. 'As long as they got me a good payday on the undercard, I'd wait in line.'

Seemingly, the only man whose opinion was not solicited in San Remo that night was Obelmejias. At 3 a.m., after we had filed our stories, Jim Fenton of the Brockton *Enterprise* and I walked out of the arena and into the deserted town square to come upon the beaten Venezuelan.

He was a forlorn figure. His face was puffy, and, still clad in his fight robe, trunks and socks, he wore shower clogs on his feet. His driver had apparently abandoned him, leaving the car locked and its formerly distinguished passenger stranded. He quietly found a seat on a stoop before a deserted storefront. His wife eventually approached and tenderly stroked his head. Obelmejias began to sob.

A few miles away, at the Hotel Mediterranee, Hagler's victory party was in full swing. They waited until we got back, and then Arum directed the piano player to strike up the chords to 'God Bless America'.

■ ■ ■

The boxing press, much of it en route to Miami for the Pryor–Arguello fight the following weekend, flocked to Baltimore in anticipation of Leonard's announcement. Howard Cosell was brought in to serve as master of ceremonies. Angelo Dundee was also summoned, as were Muhammad Ali and, of course, Hagler and the Petronellis. Every network in the country sent a film crew, and the event was promoted like a boxing match. Ringside guests ranged from boxing luminaries to Wayne Newton, Orioles star Brooks Robinson, and Donald P. Hutchinson, one of Spiro Agnew's successors as Baltimore County Executive.

Emanuel Steward was also on hand, as were the two reigning light-heavyweight champions, Matthew Saad Muhammad (the former Matthew Franklin) and Eddie Mustafa Muhammad (né Eddie Gregory).

'Whatever you decide, I'm behind you,' Matthew told Leonard.

When Eddie Mustafa followed Saad to the dais, he echoed the sentiments of 'my brother' in counselling Leonard.

The following morning's *Baltimore Sun* reported that 'Matthew Saad Muhammad and his brother Eddie' had supported Leonard's decision.

Dick Young of the *New York Post* boycotted the proceedings, which he described as 'a Barnum & Bailey sideshow'. 'If Sugar Ray Leonard says anything other than that he is through fighting, then the next test he should take is a psychiatric one,' wrote the crusty columnist. 'If he fights again, he is insane, and I just can't bring myself to believe that he is.'

The suspense was prolonged by the reading of congratulatory telegrams from Donna Summer, Richard Pryor and Gerald Ford.

When it came time for his address, Leonard assured the crowd that his eye had fully healed. He thanked Dr Ron Michels, the Johns Hopkins surgeon who had allowed him to see again. He thanked his parents and his wife and his son, his trainer and his lawyer.

He then waxed poetic as he described a fight against Hagler as the match-up each man had wanted for his entire career, one that would not only make each of them rich beyond his wildest dreams, but also establish once and for all the matter of supremacy in the sport of boxing. The smile on Hagler's face seemed to broaden with each sentence, particularly when Leonard pointed his way and said, 'He's the only man who could make it possible.'

Then Sugar Ray dropped the bombshell.

'Unfortunately,' he said, 'It's not going to happen.'

Leonard went on to explain that after consultation with his family, friends and business associates, he had decided to retire.

Hagler was crestfallen, the Petronellis furious.

'I'm surprised,' said Pat.

'I'm shocked,' said Goody.

'I'm disappointed,' said Marvin.

'Leonard had sent us a special invitation, and then he kept calling to make sure we'd be there,' said Goody. 'We were sure it was to announce he was going to fight Marvin. Why *else* would he have wanted us to be there?'

Instead, they had flown to Baltimore to be used as stage props in another Sugar Ray Leonard moment.

On his way out of the arena, Hagler's attorney Steve Wainwright turned to me and made a prescient observation.

'Nothing,' said the Barrister, 'is forever.'

Plans were almost immediately undertaken to revive the Hagler–Sibson mandatory, which took place in Worcester the following February. The outgunned Englishman was stopped in six.

Now, six months after having been snubbed in Baltimore, Hagler found himself relishing the chance to share the ring with Leonard, even if it would only be in a puerile television skit with an eighty-year-old comedian as the referee.

■ ■ ■

A few days before the scheduled appearance, Leonard was rushed to the hospital for an emergency appendectomy, and the boxing skit seemed imperilled. Arum suggested that the producers go ahead with the segment, with Duran replacing Leonard as Hagler's 'opponent'. (The third man in the ring, Hope, had in his youth boxed professionally under the name 'Packy West'.)

Two nights earlier, Angie Carlino and I had been in Atlantic City to cover a fight between Sean Mannion and In-Chul Baek. Mannion was a Boston-based 154-pounder from Ireland, Baek a Korean, and the winner would ostensibly become the WBA's mandatory challenger for the Moore–Duran winner.

Mannion won, and the following morning we drove to Baltimore, where I had been assigned to cover that Saturday's Preakness Stakes. (Deputed Testamony won.) Carlino took a train from Baltimore to Washington, where he hooked up with Hagler.

NBC had dispatched a private plane to fly Hagler and his wife, along with Goody and Pat Petronelli, to Washington. Duran, who had been training in New Jersey, arrived by train.

'Before he left camp somebody else had packed Duran's equipment bag, and when he started to take his stuff out he had two right boxing boots,' Carlino remembered. 'He held them out and stared at them, not saying a word.

'I wore the same size shoe as Duran, and I happened to have a new pair of sneakers I'd never even worn,' said Carlino. 'I offered them to Duran, but he said no. Back then he had an endorsement contract with Viceroy. It said Viceroy on his trunks and on his shoes, and I guess he figured if he didn't wear them he might not get paid. Somehow, he managed to stuff his left foot into the right boot, and he wore it that way throughout the skit. It must have been painful.'

Hagler and Duran shared a dressing-room for the Hope show. As they rehearsed for the skit, Luis Spada noted to Arum, 'I don't believe it. They're almost the same size.'

Indeed, at five foot eight and a half, Duran was just an inch shorter than Hagler and now weighed just a few pounds less. It occurred to both men that a match-up between the middleweight and the long-time lightweight champion might not be such a far-fetched notion after all.

Hagler was a week away from his fight against Scypion, Duran three from his encounter with Moore. By all accounts, the two got on well.

'Duran was always Duran,' said Carlino. 'They joked around together a lot. Once they were getting ready to fight each other things got a little snarly between them, but that weekend they were fine.'

Hagler and Duran were warmly embraced by the rest of the star-studded cast. 'Everybody you could think of was there,' said Carlino. 'George Burns, George C. Scott, Brooke Shields, Sheena Easton, Cheryl Tiegs. Reagan, the president, was there. They all wanted to meet Marvin.'

The Hagler–Duran–Hope skit, more slapstick than boxing, went well. Afterwards, Duran took another train back to New Jersey, while Hagler and his party flew back to the Cape. Or tried to.

'We hit bad weather and couldn't land in Hyannis,' recounted Carlino. 'The plane didn't have instruments, so we couldn't land in Boston or Providence either. Finally they turned around and flew back to Washington.'

Their rooms in a downtown hotel were gone, but the party managed to rent three at a hotel near National Airport. The Petronellis took one, Bertha Hagler another.

'Pat and Goody wouldn't let Marvin sleep in the room with his wife a week before the fight,' said Carlino, 'so Marvin had to bunk with me.'

■ ■ ■

Hagler got back to Provincetown on Sunday, and, six nights later, knocked out Scypion in four in Providence. The most significant aspect of an otherwise unremarkable evening was the fact that it was the first title fight in history to be recognised by three sanctioning bodies.

Following Mancini's fatal beating of Deuk-Koo Kim, the WBC had adopted a 12-round limit for its title matches. Hagler, who held both the WBC and WBA titles, still insisted on fighting 15 rounds, the time-honoured championship limit. As part of a long-standing arrangement, the two organisations alternated the oversight role in Hagler's defences, and although the WBA still had a 15-round limit, it sided with its rival organisation in this instance. Both threatened to strip Hagler if the bout were scheduled for the traditional distance.

Since disposing of Antuofermo in their 1981 rematch, Hagler had defended the middleweight title four more times. That October he had stopped Mustafa Hamsho in an 11-round bloodbath in Chicago. In March 1982 he knocked out Emanuel Steward's middleweight, Cave Man Lee, in the first round, and that autumn in Italy he had stopped Obelmejias, the WBA's top-rated challenger, in five. In February 1983 in Worcester, he demolished Sibson, the WBC's No. 1, in six. Although none of them had lasted that long, all four bouts had been scheduled for fifteen rounds.

In a failed palace coup at a WBA convention the previous winter, New Jersey's Bob Lee had lost out in his bid for the presidency of that organisation, but he remained head of the United States Boxing Association. A few days before Hagler–Scypion, Lee announced the formation of a new world sanctioning body and offered to oversee the 15-round middleweight fight as its first championship bout. (At the time, Lee's hastily formed group was called the USBA-International, but within days it would change its name to the International Boxing Federation.) The WBC and WBA reluctantly came on board and collected their sanctioning fees. Steve Wainwright distributed buttons describing the Hagler–Scypion fight as 'Boxing's First Triple Crown'.

Having successfully defended his championship for the seventh time, Hagler turned up in New York a few weeks later to watch his sparring partner from the Bob Hope special continue his comeback against Davey Moore.

■ ■ ■

Moore had won the WBA version of the 154-pound championship in February 1982 when he knocked out Tadashi Mihara in Tokyo. The other half of the title by now belonged to Tommy Hearns.

Three months after his loss to Leonard in the Showdown, Hearns had initiated his campaign as a junior middleweight by outpointing veteran Ernie Singletary in the Bahamas, a bout that took place in a run-down baseball field outside Nassau on the undercard of what would be Ali's final fight, a ten-round loss to Trevor Berbick.

For The Greatest, it had been a bizarre and bittersweet farewell. Since the amateurish promoters had neglected to provide a supply of extra boxing gloves for the card, cornermen were ordered not to cut off their fighters' gloves, and the same two pairs were passed along from one bout to the next, meaning that Ali probably wore the same sweaty gloves in losing to Berbick that Hearns had used in beating Singletary several hours earlier. And since no one had remembered to bring a bell, the Bahamians borrowed a fair approximation from a neighbouring farm. The conclusion of Ali's storied career was signalled by the tinkling of a cowbell.

In 1982 the Hit Man had knocked out the Mexican veteran Marcos Geraldo in the first round of a February bout in Las Vegas. There were two attempts to make a fight with Hagler, but legal problems and injuries had intervened. Hearns fought next in Detroit that July, where he KO'd an unbeaten middleweight named Jeff McCracken in eight.

Those fights set the stage for a December challenge to Wilfred Benitez in New Orleans. Sharing the bill with another title fight on the Don King-promoted card – Wilfredo Gomez stopped Lupe Pintor in the 14th round of a spectacular WBC junior featherweight bout – Hearns scored a majority decision in becoming just the second man to defeat Benitez.

But he paid dearly for the win: in the eighth round he had rocked Benitez with a right hand. The punch landed with such force that it shattered several small bones in his wrist and popped them through the linear muscles at the back of his hand. Tommy fought the last seven rounds using only his left, but still won easily on two of the three scorecards. Dick Young (146–137) and Tony Castellano (144–139) favoured Hearns by wide margins. The third judge, Lou Filippo, had it unaccountably level at 142–142.

The outcome confirmed yet again what many who had been following his career already knew: that beyond his 'Hit Man' power, Thomas Hearns was a terrific boxer. He had not only beaten the acrobatic Benitez at his own game, but had done it with one hand.

▪ ▪ ▪

After recovering from his appendectomy, Leonard once again found himself in Hagler's neighbourhood when he was invited to address an assemblage of Harvard students. It was Ray's first visit to the Cambridge campus, where in those long-ago post-Olympic dreams he had hoped to go to law school.

'I'd done a lot of public speaking by then and I was comfortable before a microphone,' recalled Ray. 'But I was downright nervous about that one. I kept asking myself, "These kids are about to graduate from *Harvard*. What am I going to tell them?"'

Despite his apprehension, Leonard was a hit.

'You're blessed, and I'm blessed,' Leonard told the students that day. 'We've each been given God-given talents. Mine just happens to be beating people up.'

▪ ▪ ▪

Davey Moore had already made three defences of the WBA title, winning all by knockout. He was a 4–1 favourite against Duran. In a newspaper survey of two dozen boxing writers in town to cover the fight, only four picked Cholo to win. (I was one of them.)

That the champion might be in for a long night was first suggested when he struggled on the scale. Duran made weight with ease; Moore required an extra hour to lose two pounds.

Although Moore was a Bronx-born champion, the loyalties of the Garden crowd were divided, as a massive Hispanic contingent turned out to support Manos de Piedra on his return to the scene of some of his greatest triumphs – on his 32nd birthday. Over 20,000 – the largest Garden crowd since Ali–Frazier II – packed the Mecca of Boxing to watch Duran administer what turned out to be a brutal, one-sided ass-kicking.

Enacting a repertoire of his tricks of the trade, the old master humiliated Moore, bullying him around the ring, spinning him like a top and hitting him with everything from punches to elbows to a thumb (in the opening round) that caught Moore squarely in the right eye, which almost immediately closed.

In the eighth round, after Duran flattened the champion with a straight right, Moore's corner threw in the towel. (It was such a rout that referee Ernesto Magana was widely criticised for not having stopped it earlier.)

Marvelous Marvin Hagler, at ringside, was among the first into the ring to congratulate Duran.

Hagler was also the centre of attention at the post-fight press conference, where he shared the dais with Arum. The middleweight champion was answering a question about his impression of the Duran–Moore fight when a clamour arose in the back of the interview room. A jubilant conga line, headed by Roberto Duran, snaked through the room and headed out the door for what promised to be another all-night party.

Duran paused just long enough to shout, '*Thank you, Teddy!*' at Brenner. He also acknowledged Hagler with a wave of his hand, as if to say, 'And *you*, I'll see later!'

■ ■ ■

As magical as the evening had been, it would be nearly as memorable for a disgraceful episode on the undercard as for Roberto Duran's redemptive triumph.

The supporting acts included a ten-rounder between middleweights Billy Collins Jr and Luis Resto. Collins, from Tennessee, was undefeated at 14–0 but largely untested, while Resto, a Puerto Rican from the Bronx, was 20–8–2. Collins had had several fights on ESPN; I'd seen Resto a few years earlier, when he'd come to Cleveland to spar with Duran before his fight against Nino Gonzalez. Collins was favoured, but I figured he was going to have a tough time beating Resto that night. I couldn't have guessed how tough.

Resto just beat him from pillar to post from start to finish. Collins's face was a mass of lumps and bruises, and he barely finished on his feet. After the fight, as Collins's father/trainer, Billy Sr, shook hands with the winner, he said he 'felt only knuckles'. Collins *père* immediately alerted the New York Commission, and Resto's gloves were impounded.

Once the gloves were examined it became clear that Resto's trainer, Carlos 'Panama' Lewis, had surreptitiously removed the horsehair padding from them. Resto might as well have been hitting Collins with a pair of bricks that night.

Panama Lewis had always been a mysterious figure around the boxing netherworld. I'd first encountered him when he came to Boston with Vito Antuofermo before his second fight against Hagler in 1981. A year later he had famously worked Pryor's corner against Arguello at the Orange Bowl. Between the 13th and 14th rounds, when an aide had handed him the water bottle, HBO's cameras caught him saying 'No, not that one! Give me the other bottle, the one I mixed!' Pryor revived and won the fight. The suspicious bottle was never found.

The boxing commission in Miami was notably lax, and Pryor did not take a drug test after the bout. Artie Curley, Pryor's cut man in the Arguello fight, insisted that the bottle had contained peppermint schnapps 'to settle Aaron's stomach'. (In a home video shot in the dressing-room before the fight, Pryor could be heard repeatedly burping.)

In any case, this time Panama had been caught red-handed. Resto's win was stricken from the books and changed to No Contest. Lewis and

Resto were convicted on charges of assault, possession of a dangerous weapon and conspiracy to influence the outcome of a sporting event. Both were banned from boxing for life. Lewis was sentenced to six years, but served only one. Resto spent two and a half years in prison.

Although prevented from working corners, Panama Lewis continues to pop up in gyms all over the world as an 'adviser'. I still run into him from time to time.

Billy Collins wasn't that lucky. His injuries included a fractured orbital bone and permanent eye damage that prevented him from boxing again. Nine months later, after a night of drinking, he drove his car off a bridge in what his father described as a suicide.

■ ■ ■

After a stopover in Miami, Roberto and Felicidad Duran, accompanied by Bob Arum and his then-wife, Sybil, flew back to Panama. A crowd estimated between 300,000 and 400,000 of his countrymen lined the parade route from the airport to Panama City.

'Colonel Paredes had sent his private plane to pick us up in Miami,' recalled Arum. 'Remember, this was the first time Roberto had appeared in public in Panama since before the No Mas fight, so he wasn't sure what to expect. The Pope had visited Panama just a few months earlier, and there were more people there to greet Duran than had come out for the Pope. After New Orleans these people had been ready to lynch Duran. He'd been an outcast in his own country. Now he was bigger than ever.'

When, a month later, the Hagler–Duran fight was announced for that November, 1,500 spectators, most of them Duran supporters, turned out for the press conference in New York.

'Here's a fight worth $50 million,' marvelled Budd Schulberg, 'that wouldn't have been worth 50 cents six months ago.'

The New York announcement was followed by the obligatory press tour, with Hagler and Duran, each in a private jet, flying around the country to promote the fight. I couldn't tell you what happened on Duran's plane, but when Leigh Montville, Nick Charles, Rich Rose and I flew with Hagler and the Petronellis on the Caesars jet, the poker game commenced at dawn, an hour out of Hyannis, and ended in Los Angeles that night, with somewhat inconvenient interruptions for press conferences in Chicago, St Louis and Denver along the way.

Hagler–Duran was originally slated for the old Dunes hotel, but logistical problems moved it across the street to Caesars Palace. The Dunes remained a player in the promotion, and most of the press corps was assigned rooms there. Caesars needed every available room for the anticipated influx of high-rolling customers.

Hagler and Duran were guaranteed $5 million apiece, with the prospect of doubling that if Arum's predictions of the largest closed-circuit sale in history proved accurate.

At 29, Hagler was at the top of his game and considered the most capable champion in the sport. Duran's recent heroics notwithstanding, the oddsmakers initially established Marvelous Marvin as a 3–1 favourite, but there were those who disagreed.

When *Sports Illustrated* chased down Freddie Brown, Duran's old trainer likened the upcoming fight to Hagler's frustrating draw against Antuofermo in their first fight four years earlier. Freddie had worked the Mosquito's corner that night.

'Vito got right on top of him, pressing him, facing him, making him fight,' Brown told the magazine. 'Hagler doesn't like that. That's why Vito gave him all that trouble – and Duran's a better infighter than Vito. He's as strong as Vito. Duran's a harder puncher and not as easy to hit. I got to pick Duran.'

Hagler embarked upon his traditional spartan existence in Provincetown, where he prepared for the fight with sparring partners Bob Patterson and John Ford. Duran, in keeping with his reclaimed celebrity status, trained in Palm Springs, where his principal sparring partner was a New Jersey southpaw named Charles Boston. Each arrived in Las Vegas a week before fight night and polished off his training at Caesars.

Shortly after the camps had relocated to Vegas, word emerged that Luis Spada had challenged Pat and Goody Petronelli to bet him $100,000 of their own money, even-up, on the outcome of the fight.

As preposterous as it was – had Spada actually been disposed to bet the fight, by now he could have walked over to the sports book and got nearly 4–1 on the same wager – it was reported in several newspapers, and the somewhat bewildered Brothers Petronelli called a press conference of their own to announce their acceptance of the bet.

They never collected. The ploy turned out to have been another misguided publicity stunt cooked up by Arum's press agent Irving Rudd.

The biggest non-fight news of the week came when Caesars Palace announced that it had signed eighty-seven-year-old George Burns to a ten-year contract.

At his workouts, Duran sparred wearing a new helmet-type headgear with slits for the eyes. (A prototype recently developed by Everlast, it looked like one of Darth Vader's discards.) Duran, who had been badly cut in his fight against Nino Gonzales two years earlier, was only too happy to try it out.

One afternoon I watched Duran spar four rounds with Boston from beneath the *Star Wars* headgear and filed this dispatch:

> *Time and again Boston would leap off his feet and lunge as he aimed a right hook at Duran's head, only to watch helplessly as Duran sidestepped and caught him coming in. It was an impressive performance, but a somewhat superficial one. If Marvin Hagler decides to fight off-balance all night on Thursday, then Duran will hit him, too, but one is fairly confident that Hagler's footwork will be considerably nimbler than that of Charley Boston.*

Once Duran finished his workout that day, the headgear was lifted from his face and he noticed Steve Wainwright, seated next to Bo Derek, in the first row of spectators.

Hagler's lawyer wasn't exactly incognito, but when Duran spotted the Barrister he shouted, '*Spy!*'

'*You see that?*' he demanded, in English. '*Now, go to Hagler and tell him!*'

Five days before the fight, the two combatants were doing early morning roadwork on the Dunes Golf Course when they nearly ran into each other somewhere near the 14th green. Hagler not only refused to acknowledge Duran, but also averted his glance, an incident that – with some encouragement from Spada, who quickly spread the tale – was misinterpreted by some as a sign that Duran had intimidated Hagler.

By way of explanation, I wrote in the next morning's *Boston Herald*:

> *Hagler and Duran have shared the stage at innumerable press conferences over the past few months, including one in Los Angeles barely a week ago. They are staying at the same hotel and, less than an hour apart, training at the same facility at the Caesars Sports Pavilion. Recently, Hagler in particular has taken to avoiding Thursday night's adversary like a wary bridegroom on the day of the wedding: you wouldn't necessarily call it superstitious, but then again you might.*
>
> *Since arriving in Las Vegas the middleweight champion has, save for two trips to the mountains to walk in solitude, closeted himself in his room, where he spends most of his time conjuring up malevolent thoughts about Roberto Duran. With the fight just four days away he has, for the most part, withdrawn into his customary pre-fight shell.*

Hagler and Duran weren't the only fighters to avail themselves of the Dunes course that week. One morning our foursome teed off as the first group of the day. When we finished the 17th hole three and a half hours later, we found the 18th tee occupied by Juan Domingo Roldán, the Argentine middleweight who was fighting on the undercard. Roldán was throwing a medicine ball around with members of his entourage.

It was the WBA's turn to administer Hagler's title defence, and the organisation had initially appointed a slate that included South Africa's Stanley Christodoulou as referee and Guy Jutras of Canada, Ove Oveson of Denmark and Yosuku Yoshida of Japan as judges.

A contretemps ensued. The WBC was enforcing a ban against South African participation in its events and, although the organisation theoretically had no say in the administration of Hagler–Duran, José Sulaimán successfully urged the Nevada State Athletic Commission to reject Christodoulou on anti-apartheid grounds.

The WBA's second choice as referee was Isidro Rodriguez of Mexico, but the Petronellis objected on the grounds that Duran was half-Mexican. Rodriguez probably didn't help his cause: shortly after he checked in to Caesars, the first phone call he made was to Duran's room. He, too, was dismissed.

The alternatives were even more unpalatable. Jutras was, at least for a few days, moved from judge to referee, but a quick check of his track record revealed that he had been suspended by the WBA for a year after his abysmal performance as referee in a Eusebio Pedroza–Juan Laporte featherweight title fight, in which he had overlooked 58 separate fouls, including several low blows, on Pedroza's part. Jutras's work that night had been so egregious that the New Jersey commission had overturned the result, although the WBA allowed Pedroza to retain his title.

The other options weren't much better. Arum had seen Oveson work as a referee, and considered him even more inept than Jutras, and Yoshida was not even certified as a referee. A simple solution might have been to use one of Nevada's excellent referees, but the WBA rules at the time precluded assigning a referee of the same nationality as one of the contestants to a world title fight.

'We want a referee who'll be strong and in control of the fight,' said Goody Petronelli. 'Duran has been known to do this job [Goody demonstrated by thumbing himself in the eye] and he's been known to throw a couple down here, too. [This time Petronelli pointed to his family jewels.] If [Jutras] had warned Pedroza and penalised him right away, all that stuff might have stopped.'

'It's difficult enough to prepare for Duran without worrying about the referee, too,' argued Hagler's trainer. 'You can't protect your groin and your head at the same time.'

Hagler seconded the notion that Duran's tactics bore watching.

'Duran is a dirty fighter,' said Marvin, 'and he's gonna get more dirty when he finds himself in trouble. He'll try to do anything he can to win. I just hope we'll get a good referee who'll watch him.'

'*Dirty fighter?*' Duran seemed wounded by the mere suggestion. 'Hagler can no say anything. He use his head like it is a third hand. I am a *cleaner* fighter than Hagler.'

After several days of wrangling the issue was resolved. It turned out that Christodoulou, by dint of his ancestry, could claim dual citizenship, and, after his Greek passport was overnighted to Las Vegas, it was announced that the fight would be refereed by Stanley Christodoulou, of Greece.

The restoration of Stanley the Greek appeared to placate everyone concerned. Four years earlier, Christodoulou had worked Hagler's fight against Norberto Cabrera in Monte Carlo and had done an excellent job, at least in the eyes of everyone save Howard Cosell.

'When I think about that first Antuofermo fight,' said a relieved Petronelli, 'I'd be even more worried if these were Nevada officials.'

'I'm not looking for an edge,' said Hagler. 'I'm just looking for a fair shake.'

■ ■ ■

Hagler liked to say he put himself 'in jail' to prepare for a fight, but his room overlooking the outdoor swimming pool at Caesars hardly resembled a cell. A full-length mirror stared down from the ceiling above the canopied four-poster bed, and you got the impression that an enterprising maid cleaning up after a succession of Caesars' fun-loving patrons could probably retire after a year's work just from the proceeds of whatever high-grade substances earlier occupants had left spilled on the floor.

It was a far cry from the Provincetown Inn. When I visited him at Caesars early that week, I took one look around and laughed.

'If this bed,' I told Hagler, 'could only talk.'

For Hagler, this was all a new experience. He'd fought in Vegas before, but not as the champion. He'd fought for million-dollar purses, but not for one that might approach *ten* million. He'd fought his share of formidable opponents, but this would be the first time he faced a bona fide legend, a sure-fire future Hall of Famer.

'You know,' he told me that day, 'Duran is a very gutsy fighter. He'll fight *anybody*, and I admire that. Guys like Hearns and Benitez and Leonard – if I hadn't been the middleweight champion, they *all* would have been up here. Instead, they've all been sitting on the fence like a bunch of vultures, waiting for me to get old or get beat or retire, and wondering who's gonna be the fool to go against Marvin

Hagler first. Whatever you say about Duran, at least he wasn't afraid to fight me.'

As he prepared to go into battle Hagler traditionally tried to convince himself that he absolutely detested an opponent. Demonising Roberto Duran, who was about to turn him into a multimillionaire, was apparently a stretch.

'Well, he is a bad sport,' said Hagler. 'You never see him give credit or congratulate an opponent after a fight.'

■ ■ ■

Two days before the fight, Caesars hosted a press conference. When Hagler and Duran posed for photographs, they had to be pulled apart after Manos de Piedra waved a menacing fist under Hagler's nose and grunted, '*We fight now?*'

Duran then retreated to a safer distance, where he pantomimed winding up for a bolo punch. This might have been for the benefit of Ray Leonard, conspicuously seated in the audience a few feet in front of the dais.

Hagler seemed amused by Duran's shenanigans.

'And I thought the man couldn't speak English,' he said.

■ ■ ■

That Duran's posse had returned to near-full strength was evident at the weigh-in, where Caesars security guards and Las Vegas police were overwhelmed once the snake-dancing procession reached the Sports Pavilion.

Duran checked in first, and weighed in at 156½. Hagler was just a pound heavier, but it was the lightest he'd been since the Hamsho fight in Chicago.

Spada had allowed Duran to bring his wife Felicidad along to training camp, and she had shared his quarters in Las Vegas. Bertha Hagler, on the other hand, almost didn't make it to the fight.

Along with 180 other fight fans, Hagler's wife and his mother Mae Lang had been booked on a charter flight due to leave Boston's Logan Airport at 8.10 that morning. When the passengers arrived, they were not allowed to board the aircraft. It seemed that the airline broker had failed to make a final payment to the charter company.

Eight hours and $50,000 later, the plane was allowed to depart, and the undercard was in full swing by the time the Brockton contingent arrived at Caesars.

Lest it prove a distraction, Hagler was not informed.

'Marvin is a dedicated fighter,' Mae Lang told the *Boston Herald*'s Lynne Snierson. 'We didn't even let him know about this. We never tell him anything before a big fight, and we certainly didn't want to give him anything to worry about this time.'

■ ■ ■

In the undercard's opening bout, Luis Santana, who a dozen years later would win back-to-back disqualifications in WBC title fights against Terry Norris, knocked out Jesus Gonzalez in two.

Eddie Futch-trained Freddie Roach, who had won the New England featherweight title on another Hagler undercard (Obelmejias I, in Boston), fought undefeated New Mexican Louis Burke in a rematch. The result was the same as their first fight: Freddie was once again outpointed – at least in the eyes of the judges. Roach, who would go on to become a two-time Trainer of the Year once his fighting days were over, saw his record drop to 32–4 with the loss, and told the *Herald*'s Rich Thompson afterwards, 'If I went out and lost that fight, maybe I might get out, but I *didn't* lose the fight. I *live* in Las Vegas, but I'd get a better break if I fought him in Las Cruces.'

In other undercard bouts, Freddie's bantamweight brother, Joey Roach, fought to a draw with Manny Cedeno, and an up-and-coming lightweight named Charlie (White Lightning) Brown won a decision over Oklahoman Frank (Rootin-Tootin) Newton.

The most noteworthy event to take place on the supporting bill came in Roldán's bout against Frank (The Animal) Fletcher in the co-feature.

Roldán was a ruggedly built middleweight, who by 1982 had advanced to the top spot in the WBA rankings. He was little known outside his homeland, and Arum, aware that a Hagler–Roldán fight would be a tough sell, had repeatedly delayed his mandatory challenge by offering step-aside money and featured spots on four consecutive Hagler undercards.

Arum's reasoning was twofold. If he was lucky, Roldán might get beat. And if he didn't, at least the exposure would render him more familiar to American audiences by the time Hagler finally *had* to fight him. Roldán, who a year earlier had never fought outside Argentina, had since performed on Hagler bills in San Remo, Worcester, Providence and, now, Las Vegas.

Roldán dominated the opening rounds of his fight against The Animal, and in the third he caught him with a picture-perfect left hook that sent Fletcher flying, his body parallel to the canvas, out of the ring and into the arms of a startled ringside cameraman. The referee, Carlos Padilla, ruled that Roldán had preceded the punch with a shove and discounted the knockdown.

In the sixth, Roldán landed a left followed by a devastating right to the cheekbone that knocked Fletcher into oblivion. Padilla didn't even bother to count.

When Frank the Animal opened his eyes several minutes later, the ringside physician asked him if he knew where he was.

'The Sands?' guessed Fletcher.

'Juan is the stronger man,' said Roldán's manager/trainer Tito Lectore, who in the 1970s had handled both Carlos Monzon and Hugo Corro. 'He could beat Hagler now.'

'If this hasn't convinced them, then I don't know what else I can do,' said Roldán through an interpreter. 'They can't escape me any more. I finally got my shot.'

Four months later, Roldán would indeed fight Hagler, at the Riviera hotel and casino in Las Vegas, and while he would be stopped in ten, he would be credited with the only knockdown Hagler incurred in a sixty-seven-fight pro career.

■ ■ ■

The 14,600-seat outdoor arena was packed. Ringside tickets had been priced at $600, those in the bleachers furthest from the ring $100, but the scalpers outside were getting two and three times that, and were still doing a brisk business until the opening bell for the main event.

The ringside seats were occupied by the usual mixed bag of big-time gamblers, celebrities (Paul Anka, Susan Anton, David Brenner, John and Bo Derek, Redd Foxx and Red Buttons among them) and boxing luminaries, including heavyweight champion Larry Holmes, former light-heavyweight champs Bob Foster and Joey Maxim, erstwhile welterweight champions Tony DeMarco and Ray Leonard, and a couple of old middleweight champs, Gene Fullmer and Jake LaMotta. The latter was accompanied by his ex-wife, Vicki.

The manner in which the fight would unfold had been unwittingly foreshadowed days earlier, when Hagler told me that he wasn't going to allow Duran to turn it into a brawl. In retrospect, he probably should have done just that himself. Marvelous Marvin was a career-long middleweight, and while Duran had been a fearsome puncher as a lightweight, there was no indication that at 160 he possessed the sort of one-shot firepower that would warrant caution.

Hagler and Duran appeared to sleepwalk through the first several rounds, as the champion, expecting Duran to take the fight to him, awaited his opportunity to counterpunch. Problem was, Duran was doing the same thing. The crowd was growing restive, and Goody Petronelli worried that Marvin might also be boring the judges.

In the early going Hagler was landing the odd jab, a punch he customarily threw with unusual authority, but Duran proved a wily target, sliding from side to side, slipping most of Hagler's attack and smothering the ones that got through.

'This ain't going too well,' Goody Petronelli finally told Hagler, advising him to pressure Duran.

'I was a little tight at first,' Hagler conceded later. 'It took me a few rounds before I could really start putting my combinations together.'

'We never anticipated that he'd fight that kind of fight,' said Petronelli. 'We figured that Duran would be Duran, lean his head against Marvin's chest and try to move him around. Instead, he laid back and tried to counter, and sometimes when you get two counterpunchers, it makes for a stinking fight. Finally, I *had* to send him in.'

In the sixth, the inner beast Hagler described as 'the Monster' made its first appearance.

Switching back and forth between southpaw to orthodox, Hagler rocked Duran on several occasions. A rapid-fire triple-jab snapped Duran's head back, and a left-right combination drove him to the ropes.

Duran would later say that Hagler's switch in gears wasn't the only thing that had changed after five rounds. Late in the fifth, Cholo had landed a right that caught Hagler on the top of the head. 'I felt pain in my hand,' said Duran.

Duran's damaged paw would be one factor as the night wore on. Another would come late in the seventh, when Duran landed a right and – shades of the Davey Moore fight – the thumb of his glove caught Hagler in the left eye. The wound would swell throughout the night.

The crowd, oblivious to either infirmity, came to life in the eighth, and the stadium alternately rocked to chants of '*Doo-ran! Doo-ran!*' from the Hispanics and '*Mah-vin! Mah-vin!*' from the New Englanders.

Once Hagler took the fight inside he seemed to be beating Duran at his own game, and the champion appeared to have seized control in the middle rounds, but in the tenth the bout took yet another turn. Now Duran was in the centre of the ring, Hagler circling warily around him.

'I wanted to show him some boxing and maybe catch him coming in the way he'd sometimes been catching me,' Hagler would later explain. But in almost the same breath he admitted that the rapidly swelling eye had also become a cause for concern.

Had Hagler been willing to stay inside a bit longer, logic suggests that he might well have overpowered Duran, but prudence may have dictated the modification in strategy. The rows of scar tissue Hagler wore like combat ribbons around his eyebrows could provide an inviting target, even for a boxer more observant of the Marquis of Queensberry rules than Roberto Duran.

Duran being Duran, there were several borderline low blows as the fight wore on, none of them lethal, and while Christodoulou cautioned the challenger on several occasions, the referee maintained control without turning himself into a schoolmaster.

By the 12th round, Duran had become cognisant of Hagler's injury and attacked with a fury, zeroing in on the purplish target. Panamanian flags seemed to have sprung up all over the arena, as his supporters urged Manos de Piedra to go for the kill.

'But after the ninth my hands were tired,' Duran recalled afterwards. 'I was a little too tired to finish him in the 12th.'

The sixth, when Hagler looked to be on the verge of taking Duran out, and the 12th, when Duran appeared to have Hagler on the run, had been the only points in which either man was in trouble, but in the 13th Hagler's and Duran's heads collided and the champion came away with blood pouring from two new cuts.

In the Hagler corner the bout had taken on a new sense of urgency. Petronelli realised that the fight might be close. He could hardly have imagined just *how* close.

After 13 rounds, both Yoshida and Oveson had Duran ahead by a point, while Jutras had it even. Had Duran been able to win just one of the final two rounds, he would have become the middleweight champion of the world.

In the 14th, the haematoma below Hagler's eye burst and the blood came spurting out, but, heeding Petronelli's advice, Hagler fought the final six minutes in a controlled fury. Casting off the cloak of caution that had characterised his performance until then, he closed the show by battering Duran around the ring.

'I had to give up my plans for a knockout, but I felt like if I'd had one more round I could have put this man away,' Hagler would say afterwards.

Had Hagler gone on the attack earlier, most ringsiders concluded, he might have made what proved to be his most difficult title defence an easy one.

When the final bell rang, Duran wheeled, glared in Hagler's direction and spat as if to say, 'You didn't hurt me.' But the Panamanian didn't seem surprised by the decision – close, but unanimously in Hagler's favour.

When the final scorecards were tallied, Jutras had Hagler up 144–142, Ovesen 144–143 and Yoshida 146–145. The Japanese official had scored more rounds even (six in all) than he awarded to either man.

Scoring at ringside, I had Hagler up 146–140, a margin more in line with most non-WBA judges who watched the fight that night.

Hagler didn't need to look in a mirror to know he'd been in a fight. It had been the first time he'd had to go the distance in defence of his title, and the cut below his eye reminded him that the old lion named Duran still had some teeth.

'I didn't expect to come out of this one looking pretty anyway,' Hagler said. He held his championship belts above his head and added, 'The only thing that counts is that I'm taking these back home.'

Although the 15-round distance had probably saved him on this night, the WBC would shortly move to vacate its title, citing Hagler's refusal to abide by its 12-round limit and the presence of a referee from an outlaw nation. Only after Wainwright filed a lawsuit on behalf of Hagler was the WBC portion of his undisputed title restored.

'The better man won,' conceded Duran through an interpreter that night. 'But I wasn't disappointed. Hagler didn't do anything special. He's just a strong fighter.'

Still, Duran had landed more punches, and inflicted more damage, than Hagler had absorbed in his seven previous defences put together.

'He caught me a few times with that lead right,' said Hagler. 'But it didn't really bother me. About the 12th, I was concerned when the eye swelled up, but my guys took good care of it. After that, I knew he was going to have to hit me with the ringpost to knock me out.'

At the post-fight press conference Hagler wore sunglasses to mask the damage wrought during the fight, and reiterated his belief (borne out by the films) that the injury had come not from a punch, but from Duran's thumb.

Roberto Duran was learning to speak English.

'He win. I lose. He complaining,' he said with a laugh.

Someone asked Hagler that night whether Duran was the most cunning boxer he'd ever faced. Marvin pondered for a moment before replying: 'I'd call him *experienced*. He's a crafty fighter, all right, but he was a legend, and I beat him. Give me some credit for beating him.'

Although Duran lost the fight, it was Hagler's reputation that took a beating that night. By allowing the fight to turn into a cautious chess match, he had diluted the image of the fearsome destroyer he had so carefully cultivated.

Budd Schulberg suggested that Hagler might want to go back to court to have his name legally changed again, this time to '*Semi-Marvelous*'.

'If I didn't know any better, I'd say Hagler carried him, like in the old days,' Schulberg told Katz that night.

While that view might have been overly suspicious, Arum was clearly a beneficiary of the outcome. Emerging essentially unscathed from the Hagler fight preserved Duran's value for another megafight, against Thomas Hearns, just eight months later.

Sports Illustrated's Bill Nack complained that night that Hagler 'didn't just fight cautiously, he fought *timidly*. A blown-up lightweight was still there at the end.'

By the time his story appeared several days later, Nack had tempered his criticism: 'Hagler proved himself the best middleweight on the block, while Duran showed that he is a fighter for the ages and should again be the object of celebration.'

The criticism would be more than offset by Hagler's career-high payday of nearly $10 million.

'Fighting all those years for peanuts finally paid off,' said Hagler. 'I finally got the big one.'

Duran was also well compensated, earning over $5 million. When a few of us ran into Cholo the next morning, he revealed that he was headed to the hospital to have his right hand X-rayed.

'I put in salts and water all night, and again today,' he said, wincing as he shook his paw. 'Is no good.'

'But,' he added with a grin, 'is good for holding money.'

6

MALICE IN THE PALACE

Hearns–Duran
Caesars Palace, 15 June 1984

THE RIGHT HAND HEARNS had broken on Wilfred Benitez's head remained in a cast until April 1983 and occasioned an eight-month hiatus from boxing, at least part of which was spent at sea.

Hearns owned a 56-foot boat. Each spring he paid a bareboat captain to deliver the *Natasha* (named after his baby daughter) to Detroit from its wintertime slip at the Fort Lauderdale Marina. In the spring of '83, with time to spare, Tommy decided to make the trip himself and spent the better part of a month on a leisurely cruise up the Atlantic coast to the St Lawrence Seaway and onwards to the Great Lakes.

Hearns didn't fight again until that July, when he decisioned Scottish veteran Murray Sutherland in Atlantic City. He didn't make his first defence of the WBC junior middleweight title until February '84, when he outpointed Luigi Minchillo of Italy in Detroit.

Hearns had won six straight since his loss to Leonard, but he had been forced to go the distance three straight times. He had barely used the right against Sutherland, and, said Steward, 'he was even afraid to throw it in sparring'.

The 'Hit Man' appellation seemed suddenly inappropriate, and Hearns began billing himself instead as the 'Motor City Cobra'. Between fights, he became a virtual recluse.

Frederick Lewerenz was Hearns's physician in Detroit, but he might as well have been his psychiatrist.

'You have to understand Thomas,' Dr Lewerenz told *Sports Illustrated*'s Pat Putnam. 'His whole value judgment is based on how hard he can hit. This man actually lives and exists mentally from the power of his right hand. It's his self-image.'

■ ■ ■

Ray Leonard had his own medical issues in early 1984.

Sugar Ray had grown restive in retirement. His ringside work for CBS and HBO kept him close to the sport, but the proximity constantly reminded him how much he missed it.

When Leonard asked Mike Trainer to initiate preparations for his comeback, the direction in which he planned to go was self-evident. The first opponent Trainer contacted was, like Hagler, a left-hander, and was approached about fighting in New England.

Sean Mannion was a rugged southpaw who answered to the *nom de guerre* of 'The Galway Gouger'. Mannion was a former Irish national amateur champion who had boxed for his entire career in the United States, and by 1984 he was rated No. 2 among junior middleweights by the WBA. 'The only stipulation was that the guy had to be free of promotional entanglements and in a position to make a deal,' said Trainer. 'We didn't want to be wrangling with any outside promoters over this thing, and I told [Mannion's manager] Jimmy Connelly that more than once.'

Although it was never announced, Ray's older brother, Kenny, and matchmaker J.D. Brown had undertaken preparations for a new company that would have promoted Leonard's future bouts – including, presumably, a fight against Hagler, had it occurred in 1984. Entering into a contract with an opponent encumbered by promotional baggage might have complicated that plan.

Mannion had been under contract to Top Rank, but that pact had expired with his last fight. Cash-strapped, Connelly apparently tried to use the Leonard offer to squeeze Bob Arum. In a phone call, Arum reminded him that he had worked hard to get Mannion into position for a title challenge and warned him that a loss would imperil his No. 2 WBA rating.

Connelly and Mannion hopped the shuttle to New York that night and, in exchange for a $10,000 signing bonus, agreed to a contract extension with Top Rank.

'It was a pretty stupid move on their part,' said Trainer. 'Mannion would have gotten more money for fighting Ray − $100,000 − than he wound up getting to fight Mike McCallum for the title, and even if he'd lost to Ray but looked good, his career wouldn't have suffered. And when you look at what happened in the two fights, Mannion probably had a better chance of beating Ray, who was coming off the layoff, than he did McCallum, which was zero.'

After Mannion took himself out of the picture, Trainer turned to Kevin Howard, a Philadelphia journeyman with a record of 20–4–1. The bout was scheduled for 25 February at the Centrum in Worcester, Massachusetts, but had to be postponed when Leonard's physical revealed yet another abnormality in his eyes.

Massachusetts Boxing Commissioner Tommy Rawson had asked that Leonard be examined two weeks before the scheduled bout rather than the more standard two days. The detached left retina that had prompted his retirement proved to be fully healed, but in the course of his examination Dr Edward Ryan observed 'some peripheral retina problems' − specifically, a lesion in the retina of Leonard's *right* eye. The imperfection was corrected at the Massachusetts Eye and Ear Infirmary by what Ryan described as 'prophylactic cryosurgery'.

The Howard fight was postponed indefinitely, and Leonard flew back to Baltimore after the operation.

I was at the Winter Olympics in Sarajevo when the postponement was announced, but in Leonard's absence Ryan precipitated something of a firestorm when he told the *Herald*'s Tim Horgan: 'In no way would I recommend that Sugar Ray Leonard ever fight again.'

Once the bout was rescheduled for 11 May, Leonard's handlers trotted out Dr Ryan for the Boston press conference, at which the retinal specialist clarified his remarks to Horgan. What he had meant to say, Ryan explained, was that he didn't think *anyone*, including Leonard, should box at all, whether they'd had an eye injury or not. And although he was predisposed against the sport on general principles, he allowed that Leonard was probably at no greater risk than any other boxer.

After Ryan's address, reporters were informed Leonard would entertain no further questions about his eyes. A British fight scribe in Worcester to cover the bout was moved to observe, 'His bloody eye is the only reason we're *here*!'

'I don't have a licence to practise medicine, but, if I had to guess, I'd say the eye injury went back to the Marcos Geraldo fight,' recalled Leonard years later. 'Something like that can happen in my sport, because there's trauma involved, but it could have happened playing basketball with my kids. An acquaintance of mine recently had surgery for two detached retinas and he never boxed in his *life*.'

After the February bout had been postponed, Kevin Howard was told to sit tight but instead agreed to fight Bill (Fireball) Bradley in Atlantic City on 25 February, and stopped him in six. 'I needed the fight and I needed the work,' explained Howard, who had lost two of his previous three (to Marlon Starling and Mark Medal, sandwiched around a win over the wonderfully named Richard Nixon) and had dropped out of both the WBA and the WBC rankings.

'I knew some people say I took a big risk by taking that fight,' said Howard after arriving in Worcester, 'but to me it wasn't a risk.'

'Some people' included Dan Doyle, the Leonard–Howard promoter, who said that had Howard lost to Bradley 'we would have gotten another opponent', and Howard would have lost out on the $100,000 he had been promised for fighting Leonard.

Leonard, who had reportedly engaged in some hellacious sparring sessions with Simon Brown back in Maryland, toyed with a trio of locals at a Worcester gym the day the press was invited to watch him spar, going a round apiece with Dave Rivello, Keith Stevenson and Jose Ruiz.

Angelo Dundee told Horgan that day that he had been 'flabbergasted' by Leonard's decision to come back. 'I was surprised, because he's financially set, and he was doing very well at what he was doing after he retired,' said Dundee. 'But nothing takes the place of being the best at what you do.'

'He missed the ring,' echoed Kevin Howard. 'He missed the glory, and he missed his fans. I know. I was one of them.'

Although Leonard never mentioned Hagler's name in the run-up

Sugar Ray Leonard
(© Heinz Kluetmeier/*Sports Illustrated*)

Marvelous Marvin Hagler
(© Will Hart)

Thomas 'Hit Man' Hearns
(© Teddy Blackburn)

Robert Duran: Manos de Piedra
(© Stephen Green-Armytage/*Sports Illustrated*)

Not-yet Marvelous Marvin Hagler, circa 1970: 'I had to show him how to hold his hands to pose. He was completely green' – Angie Carlino (© Angelo Carlino)

Leonard–Duran I, Montreal, 1980: 'The man became a legend, and the boy became a man' – Red Smith (© Manny Millan/*Sports Illustrated*)

Leonard–Duran II, No Mas in New Orleans, 1980: 'Leonard could not have shamed
Duran more thoroughly if he had reached over and pulled down his trunks' – Ray Didinger
(© Manny Millan/Sports Illustrated)

Leonard–Hearns, 1981: 'I made a couple of mistakes, and you can't afford to
make mistakes against a fighter of Ray's calibre' – Thomas Hearns
(© International Boxing Hall of Fame)

Hagler–Duran, 1983:
'Fighting all those years
for peanuts finally paid off.
I finally got the big one'
– Marvelous Marvin Hagler
(© Heinz Kluetmeier)

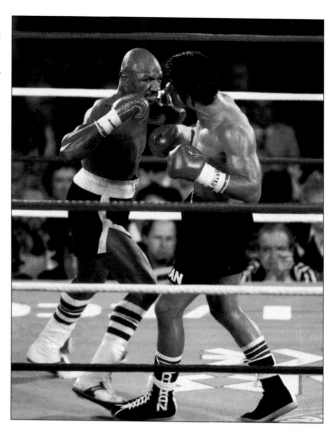

Hearns–Duran, 1984: 'I tried to get under those long arms, and he knocked me crazy with that right hand' – Roberto Duran (© Richard Mackson)

Hagler–Hearns, 1985: 'I've been refereeing for 15 years, and I don't think I've ever seen that much intensity in a fight' – Richard Steele
(© Will Hart/HBO)

Leonard–Hagler, 1987: 'He's a miracle man' – Gil Clancy
(© International Boxing Hall of Fame)

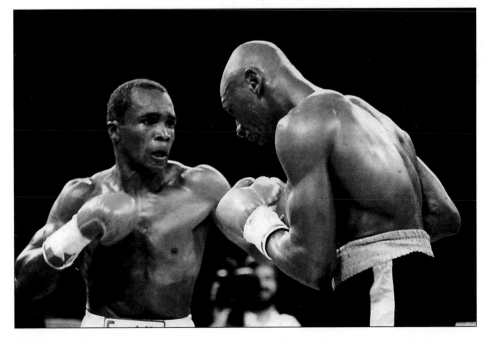

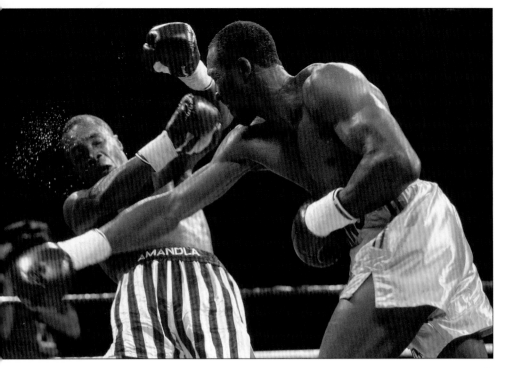

Leonard–Hearns II, 1989: 'I think we both showed what we're made of' – Sugar Ray Leonard
(© John Iacono/Sports Illustrated)

Leonard–Hearns II, 1989:
'That is what makes a great champion!'
– Emanuel Steward
(© John Iacono/Sports Illustrated)

The Hit Man at his place of business – the Kronk Gym:
'Give Tommy Hearns Ray's balance and he probably beats them all'
– Angelo Dundee (© Teddy Blackburn)

Leonard–Duran III, 1989: 'They were better prepared than we were.
It was 38 degrees outside. Leonard had a blanket in the corner and Duran didn't'
– Mike Acri (© Manny Millan)

The Lions in Winter: Hagler, Hearns and Leonard at Ceasars Palace, circa 1995
(© Teddy Blackburn)

Robert Duran in New York, circa 1999 (© Teddy Blackburn)

to the fight, it wasn't far from anyone else's lips. A Hagler–Leonard announcement, Trainer hinted with a wink, 'might come sooner than you think', but Dundee urged caution.

'After this fight we'll evaluate Ray's performance and decide what to do next,' said the trainer. 'It's too early to talk Marvin Hagler. We really won't know a thing until Friday night.'

Hagler seemed decidedly unsympathetic when it came to Leonard's malady.

'If he's foolish enough to step into the ring with me, then I'm foolish enough to rip out his eye,' said the middleweight champion.

Dundee had become something of an expert on boxing comebacks, having overseen at least three of them by Muhammad Ali. 'It's a tougher struggle with a big guy,' said Angelo. 'Plus, Muhammad didn't do *nothing* while he was away. He just got big and husky and put on weight. How much? I was afraid to even look at the scale.

'But Ray *stayed* in shape.'

Although it was a ten-round, non-title fight, HBO paid $2.5 million to showcase Leonard against Howard. It was Ray's first taste of combat in 27 months, and in the fourth round Howard caught him with a hook that knocked him on his backside, leaving him spread-eagled on the ring mat, staring up at the Centrum roof. An embarrassed Leonard made up his mind to re-retire even before he got up.

'I was shocked to see myself on the canvas, and I thought, "It just wasn't there,"' Leonard would explain at the post-fight press conference. 'I knew it wasn't there, and that's when I decided it was time to retire for good. If I didn't feel it tonight, I never will. There's no sense in going on.'

Leonard regained control after the knockdown and was well on his way to winning when referee Dick Flaherty stopped the bout at 2:28 of the ninth.

Although some were critical of Flaherty's stoppage, the referee said that Howard's legs were 'wobbly', and that he would 'rather stop a fight five seconds too soon than one second too late'.

When Howard protested, he only fuelled the referee's argument.

'If they were going to stop the fight, they should have done it when *he* went down,' said Howard. 'I knocked him down and he got up, and he knocked me down and I got up.' Informed that he had, in fact, never been off his feet, Howard shrugged and murmured, 'That's regardless.'

Hagler and the Petronellis had once again been invited to be on hand, and Marvin had fully expected to be called out at the post-fight press conference. Arum had confided that he would have $10 million apiece in the bank for Hagler and Leonard the following week.

'That,' sighed Marvelous Marvin, 'is the story of my life.'

Hagler wasn't the only one who got played that night. Ray also stiffed his sometime employers at Time-Warner, allowing them to get beat on what should have been their own story. When HBO's Larry Merchant interviewed Leonard in the ring immediately after the fight, he asked Ray point-blank whether he might quit.

'I'll have to think it over,' Leonard told him.

Twenty minutes later, Ray walked into the press conference and not only announced his retirement, but also revealed that he had reached the decision midway through the fourth round as he lay on the canvas.

'I wasn't trying to intentionally mislead [Merchant],' Leonard recalled. 'I just wasn't thinking too clearly at that moment. The fight had only been over for a few seconds when he interviewed me.'

'But I'll tell you who was even more disappointed than Marvin – Kenny and J.D.,' added Leonard. 'If I'd kept fighting then, they would have been my promoters. They left a lot of money on the table that night.'

■ ■ ■

Two months before Leonard fought Howard, Hagler had consummated his oft-delayed meeting with Juan Domingo Roldán, stopping 'El Martillo' in the tenth round of their title fight at the Riviera.

Roldán was credited with a first-round knockdown, enraging Hagler, who said he had been tripped. Three months later, at a meeting held on the eve of the Hearns–Duran fight, the Nevada State Athletic Commission levied a $500 fine on the Argentine for having used an ammonia capsule to revive himself on the stool between rounds in the Hagler fight.

'The rules are there to be enforced,' I wrote in reporting Roldán's punishment, *'but it says here they're fining the wrong guy. Did you ever try to snap open an ammonia capsule while wearing boxing gloves?'*

■ ■ ■

Roberto Duran had not fought since his loss to Hagler.

With time off to challenge for the middleweight title, nearly a year had elapsed in which Duran had not defended the 154-pound title he had won from Davey Moore, and he found himself under increasing pressure from the WBA. Reluctant to meet the organisation's mandatory challenger Mike McCallum, he searched for a big-money fight.

In the meantime he was going through his windfall from the Hagler fight in typically profligate fashion. He hired his own orchestra and performed Latino music around Central America. The old entourage swelled, as did his body. Once again Duran ballooned to nearly 200 pounds.

After several months of negotiation, a Duran–Hearns bout was made. Although it loomed as a match-up of two reigning junior middleweight champions, it would not be a unification bout, because the WBA ruled that its title would become vacant the moment Manos de Piedra stepped into the ring against anyone other than McCallum.

Exactly how much the WBA championship was worth without Duran's name attached to it was illustrated when McCallum was left to fight Mannion for the vacant title later that year. The bout went to a purse offer, which was won by Top Rank. Bob Arum's winning bid was $75,000, and in October 1984 he put the fight on the undercard of Hagler's defence against Mustafa Hamsho at Madison Square Garden.

The Hearns–Duran fight was originally scheduled for Nassau in the Bahamas. Both fighters had already gone there to train, but promised local backing failed to materialise. The fight was moved to Caesars in Las Vegas, where it was hastily christened 'Malice at the Palace'.

Caesars had already constructed another huge temporary stadium in anticipation of the heavyweight title unification fight between WBC champion Larry Holmes and WBA titleist Gerrie Coetzee. Since the heavyweight bout fell apart at about the time things began to unravel in the Bahamas, it made for a fairly seamless transition from Nassau to Vegas, but there was no way in the world Hearns–Duran was going to fill a 25,000-seat arena.

Officially the bout was a co-promotion of Shelteron, a consortium put together by Hearns's former publicist Shelly Saltman and Bill Kozerski, a Detroit promoter who had staged many Kronk shows. The chief financial backing came from a Los Angeles automobile dealer named Steve Taub. Taub, a millionaire sportsman who two decades later would enter a colt named Imperialism in the Kentucky Derby, would recall his brief flirtation with boxing as 'the most expensive six minutes of my life'.

A decade earlier, Saltman had been in charge of publicity for Evel Knievel's ill-fated attempt to jump the Snake River Canyon – an event Arum had promoted. Incensed by what Saltman wrote about him in a subsequent book, the motorcyclist vented his displeasure with an aluminum baseball bat, breaking Shelly's left arm and wrist in several places.

Saltman won a $13 million judgment after the attack, but was unable to collect because Knievel declared bankruptcy. The AP's Fast Eddie Schuyler, who didn't have much use for Saltman, suggested that Knievel should have been presented with the Silver Slugger Award.

Hearns was guaranteed $1.8 million, Duran $1.6 million for the bout, which Hearns viewed as a necessary step to force the fight he truly coveted – a match-up with Hagler.

'I don't need to just win, I need to be *devastating*,' said Hearns, who had confidently forecast a second-round knockout and never backed off that prediction.

Steward recalls Hearns's training for the Duran fight as the best of his career. 'We had the best preparation in the world,' said Steward. 'I'd been named an assistant coach with that year's Olympic team, so many of them trained at the Kronk for the Games in Los Angeles. Hearns sparred with Mark Breland every day. He also boxed with Frank Tate and Pernell Whitaker, and Steve McCrory. We had those guys from the Olympics, plus Mike McCallum, John Collins, Milton

McCrory and Hilmer Kenty. They were all sharp, and it must have been one of the best camps in boxing history. Compared to sparring with Mark Breland, Duran was like fighting molasses.'

A few days before the fight, there was a chance meeting between combatants and their entourages at a bank of elevators at Caesars.

'*I kill you! I kill you!*' growled Duran, as he brandished a fist. Manos de Piedra already had his game face on.

'*No mas! No mas!*' replied a laughing Hearns in Motown-accented Spanish.

'For some reason, Duran had always seemed very uncomfortable around Tommy,' said Steward. 'I never fully understood it myself. Once, years earlier, we were out in Vegas when Duran was fighting somebody. We were walking through the casino and came upon Duran, surrounded by a bunch of reporters asking questions.

'Tommy sneaked up behind him and kind of playfully flicked him in the back of his head with his finger. Duran wheeled around with his fists up, as if he was going to attack whoever did it, but when he saw it was Tommy he just put his hands down and walked away, leaving the crowd of people standing there.

'There was something about Tommy that spooked him,' insisted Steward. 'He had his number. Duran tried to intimidate Leonard, he tried to intimidate Marvin, but he never did try it with Tommy. He was always very respectful, even humble, around Hearns. He just didn't seem comfortable in Tommy's presence.'

■ ■ ■

In the days before the bout, Steward predicted, 'No one has ever really tried to hurt Duran, but Tommy *will*.'

If that sounded like a backhand slap at Hagler, it probably was.

'Tommy's hand speed is a lot quicker than Marvin's,' said Steward. 'But the biggest difference is that Tommy's a gambler. Hagler had Duran in trouble a couple of times, but he had so much respect for him that he didn't seize the advantage. Tommy won't worry about getting knocked out. If that happens with him, he'll just throw the dice and take his chances.

'And he might get hit doing it,' added Steward. 'These are both real, macho street-fighters, you know. I can really envision this thing turning into a war, a real toe-to-toe slugfest.'

After his final workout at the Sports Pavilion, Hearns peeled off his gold-and-red Kronk singlet and flung it into the crowd. ('*Grown men happily fell upon one another as they dove for the sweaty garment,*' I described the occasion in the *Herald*. '*It might as well have been Bo Derek's discarded underwear instead of the Detroit boxer's they were fighting over.*')

When Hearns sat down to talk a few minutes later, it was evident that while it was Duran he was fighting, Hagler wasn't far from his thoughts, either.

'I was impressed with Duran in the Hagler fight,' said Tommy. 'I even gave him the decision over Hagler. He dictated the fight. He made Hagler fight the way he wanted him to.'

'As a matter of fact,' sniffed Hearns, 'there wasn't too much Hagler brought out that night that I can use against Duran. Duran dictated the fight against Hagler, but he won't dictate this one. He's going to discover that fighting me is a lot tougher than fighting Marvin Hagler.'

Someone wondered if Hearns might worry that some of what he was saying might find its way back to Hagler.

'I certainly hope so,' Hearns replied with a sly grin.

CBS had the rights to the delayed broadcast, and Ray Leonard was on hand to provide the colour commentary.

'I wouldn't bet this fight,' said the man who had beaten both contestants. 'Duran was the toughest fight I ever had, and Hearns had the best jab of anyone I fought.'

'Duran has to take the fight to Hearns, try to slow him down and mix it up,' supposed Leonard. 'Hearns can make it easy on himself if he stays outside and boxes, but I think they're both capable of knocking each other out. I expect something significant – a knockout, or at least a knockdown – by the fifth or sixth round.'

Hearns said he was glad to have Leonard there, 'because he's a good colour man'.

Leonard, as it turned out, was not at his ringside microphone for Hearns–Duran. Two days before the bout, Juanita went into labour and Ray flew back to Maryland, just in time for the birth of his second son, Jarrell.

■ ■ ■

Hearns opened at 2–1 and a day before the fight was bet down to -$260/+$200, or roughly 13–10, man-to-man. More interesting was the fact that the sports books made it 2–1 that the fight would go the distance.

Hearns had stopped thirty of his first thirty-two opponents, but only two of his last seven. In ten fights going back to Montreal, Duran had dispatched just two opponents – Cuevas and Moore.

On the way to the morning weigh-in, we ran into Eddie López, gorging himself at the breakfast buffet. López would be fighting unbeaten Steward-trained heavyweight Tony Tucker on the undercard, but right now he seemed more interested in his bacon and eggs.

'The only time I'm worried,' confirmed The Animal, 'is when I'm going to court.'

The weigh-in was scheduled for 8 a.m. – the wee hours of the morning, by Vegas standards – on the day of the fight. Despite the unsocial hour, the Sports Pavilion was choked with members of the media, Nevada commission officials, Duran's entourage and, in their gold-and-red regalia, the entire Kronk boxing team.

'I just hope you get this good a turnout tonight,' someone told Shelly Saltman. The neophyte promoter responded with a weak grin. (That night's crowd would number 14,824, and the Hearns–Duran fight would in the final tally lose over $3 million.)

A glowering Duran weighed in at precisely the divisional limit. Hearns was half a pound lighter at 153½.

Padilla was once again appointed as the referee, while the panel of WBC judges was composed of Harry Gibbs, Newton Campos and Hans LeVert. Their services, it turned out, would not be required.

At the rules meeting, Spada requested a waiver of the rule calling for eight-ounce gloves in a 154-pound title fight. Using the ten-ounce gloves Duran wanted might also have benefited Hearns, in that it would have provided an extra bit of protection for his questionable right hand, but when the request was denied, Steward proclaimed it a victory.

'We'd rather have a puncher's glove,' he said.

Steward expressed confidence that Hearns's hand was fully healed and would hold up in battle.

'He hasn't hesitated to cut loose with it in the gym,' said Steward. 'But I'm going to make sure I wrap it good, anyway.'

■ ■ ■

The undercard was a showcase for Steward's Kronk boxers: Jimmy Paul stopped Alvin Hayes in six to win the USBA lightweight title, and Tony Tucker knocked out Eddie the Animal in the ninth round of their fight.

Two other Steward-trained fighters won that night: junior middleweight Đuane Thomas, who two years later would knock out John (The Beast) Mugabi to win Hearns's old WBC title, stopped Tony Harrison in eight, and British middleweight Errol Christie TKO'd Stan White in five. Another prelim saw former WBA lightweight champ Arturo Frias win a ten-round decision over Jose Torres.

In terms of ring accomplishments, Hearns and Duran might have been near-equals, but in this fight, more than any other involving the Four Kings, size mattered.

At six-foot-one, Hearns was the tallest member of the quartet; Duran, at five-foot-seven, was the shortest. More tellingly, the Hit Man enjoyed a 13-inch reach advantage, which figured to make it difficult for Duran to even get close to him with a jab.

Although Duran presented his usual menacing countenance, it rapidly became clear that he was, quite literally, in over his head.

'I will use a ladder if I have to,' Duran had said.

Perhaps he should have brought one along.

'Tommy's style was always going to be good for Duran,' said Steward. 'He mastered in fighting shorter guys, where he could utilise his jab and his reach.'

Physical attributes aside, Steward also wanted Hearns to get inside Duran's head by intimidating him from the outset.

'Whenever I have a fighter going up against a bully, I tell him to bully the bully,' said the trainer. 'Like with Lennox Lewis against Mike Tyson and Andrew Golota: if you whip up on him right away, the bully starts crying.

'In the first round, Tommy pulled Duran's head, stepped on his feet and threw him down. It was all done on purpose, and it got Duran all fucked up, because he was used to being the bully. He never got untracked that night.'

Early in the first, Hearns opened a cut above Duran's left eye with a left uppercut. Cholo, seemingly unhurt, continued to box, as he attempted to analyse the task before him.

Two minutes into the round, Hearns's jab had yet to be a factor. Duran decided to move inside, hoping to neutralise the right. Lowering his head, he lunged towards Hearns, throwing a right hand as he did. The next thing he saw was Hearns's right fist, a split-second before it crashed against his head. Suddenly, the floor was spinning upwards in Duran's direction.

Hearns would say later that he could sense Duran warily eyeing the jab.

'I had him looking for the jab by then,' recalled Hearns. 'And I got him with the sneak right.'

Duran bounced up and even managed an embarrassed grin as he took Padilla's mandatory eight-count, but the instant the referee turned him loose, Hearns pounced again, this time felling Duran with a hard left hook. Duran got up just before the round ended.

'*The bout might have ended there had the bell not intervened,*' I wrote in the *Herald*. '*A wobbly Duran barely made it back to the corner, and when he did it was to the wrong one.*'

In eighty-one fights Duran had been knocked down just twice, both times at the hands of DeJesus, and that had been ten years earlier. Now he had been down twice in three minutes.

As Cholo sat there on the stool, contemplating what had just occurred, he *had* to know what was coming next, even as he pleaded with Spada not to stop the fight.

In my mind it represented an epiphany of sorts. It might not have explained the bewildering turn of events of New Orleans three and a half years earlier – I'd never bought the stomach-ache story – but it surely eliminated the other widely held theory. Duran might have been undisciplined, he might have been arrogant and he might have been, as Steward maintained, a bully, but he was also uncommonly brave.

The man who got up off his stool and charged back at Hearns in the second round in Las Vegas that night was not, and could never have been, a coward.

'You have to keep your hands up!' Spada, stating the obvious, reminded him as he replaced the gumshield.

Duran appeared to have regained his senses, as well as his footing, as the second commenced, but the recovery was illusory. He wrestled Hearns into a clinch and actually landed a couple of punches, but the revival would prove short-lived.

'I had to stop and regroup and get myself together,' recalled Hearns, and for a moment the two seemed to stand still, silhouetted against the sunset, as they studied one another.

Hearns backed Duran up with two quick jabs, and then landed the thunderous roundhouse right to the chin that ended the fight.

Duran, knocked out for the first time in his career, was lifted right off his feet and appeared to lose consciousness before he even hit the deck. When he saw Duran plough face-first into the ring mat, Luis Spada struggled through the ropes and into the ring.

Padilla didn't even see Spada's charge from the corner, but Duran was so obviously indisposed that the referee waved the fight off without a count, instead rolling him over onto his back so he could retrieve the gumshield.

The official end came at 1:07 of the second. The fight had consumed less time than the playing of the Panamanian national anthem. With no one left to hit, a jubilant Hearns trotted happily around the ring, throwing phantom punches at the desert sky.

Once he regained consciousness, Duran was lifted to his feet, and Spada and Plomo literally dragged him back to his stool. Cholo appeared sheepish and embarrassed, but seemed otherwise unhurt. Hearns walked across the ring to embrace him, and then lifted him off the floor.

'I was fighting a legend,' Hearns said that night. 'Roberto Duran is probably the greatest fighter I've ever been in the ring with, but the respect I have for Duran I refused to take into the ring with me.'

Plainly, Hearns was nearly as relieved that he had been able to use his business hand without injury as he was pleased by the victory itself.

'The Hit Man has been away for a while,' said Hearns. 'He's been on vacation, but he's back now. I was able to let the power in my right hand go.'

Hearns used the occasion to call out the middleweight champion.

'In my next fight, I'd like to challenge Marvin Hagler,' he said. 'I could just see him in my mind, shaking like the leafs on a tree.'

Pat Putnam visited Duran in his suite at Caesars later that night.

'My problem was that I brawled with him and lost my head,' said Duran. 'That's when I screwed up. My corner told me something after that first round, but I can't remember what it was because I am still a little dizzy. Damn, I tried to get under those long arms, and he knocked me crazy with that right hand.'

'Now,' added Duran, 'I have to go home to Panama to see what they think.'

Duran's return to his homeland would once again demonstrate the fickleness of his countrymen. The military junta that controlled the Panamanian government had recently honoured him by putting his face on a postage stamp. When he landed in Panama after the Hearns fight, Roberto Duran was promptly arrested and locked up in a Panamanian jail.

Since he was never charged, the cause of his humiliating incarceration was never precisely spelled out. Whether Cholo became obstreperous, as police claimed, or whether the officer in charge was, as has been suggested, a disgruntled bettor who, having lost money on the Hearns fight, determined to break his balls is unclear. Duran was, in any case, released the following morning.

Marvin Hagler's immediate future was already spoken for. An injury had delayed his mandatory rematch against Mustafa Hamsho, but that fight was already on the books for October.

But Hearns's convincing defeat of a man against whom Hagler had struggled just months earlier made it clear what the next big fight for both men would be. As I wrote in the next morning's paper, '*The only questions now are When, Where and How Much?*'

7

THE FIGHT

Hagler–Hearns
Caesars Palace, 15 April 1985

NEARLY A QUARTER-CENTURY LATER, the 1985 fight between Hagler and Hearns remains a high point of boxing in the latter half of the twentieth century. Knowledgeable experts have described it as the greatest short fight in boxing history. Its ferocious first round, which to this day remains the standard against which all others are measured, was undoubtedly the most exciting in middleweight annals, and one of the two or three best opening stanzas of all time.

In an age in which it had already become obligatory to sell every big fight – and many smaller ones – with a catchy slogan, Arum christened the match-up between Marvelous Marvin and the Hit Man as, simply, The Fight.

Events proved Arum prescient. It was, indeed, *The* Fight.

Although its official build-up consumed several months, beginning in late 1984, The Fight had been at least three years in the making. In 1982, with Ray Leonard vacillating towards retirement and Roberto Duran still tainted by the disgrace of his No Mas performance in New Orleans, Hagler and Hearns were the two premier boxers in the game, and a showdown seemed inevitable.

In early 1982 Arum, Hagler's lawyer Steve Wainwright and Emanuel Steward had entered into a unique three-fight contract, pitting Hagler against a trio of middleweights from Steward's Kronk Gym. Under the terms of the arrangement, the middleweight champion would fight, in order, Mickey Goodwin, William (Cave Man) Lee and, in the grand finale of the trilogy, Thomas Hearns. Round One, the Goodwin bout, was to have taken place that March in Italy, with Rodolfo Sabbatini, Arum's silent partner in the middleweight sweepstakes, serving as the co-promoter, but Goodwin broke his hand in training. Lee, considered a less worthy challenger, was rushed into the breach and the fight was moved from San Remo to Atlantic City, where Hagler required barely a minute to send Lee back to his cave.

With Goodwin still indisposed, the decision was taken to go straight to the Hearns fight, which was scheduled for 24 May 1982, in Windsor, Ontario, just across the river from Detroit. The posters were printed, as were the tickets, but the fight didn't happen.

The unravelling of the Windsor fight remains shrouded in mystery. The only way to make the fighters' promised nut was to sell the fight on closed-circuit, but HBO, which had a multi-fight contract with Hagler through Top Rank, believed it had the right of first refusal and filed for an injunction.

In what seemed a transparent attempt to stage an end-run around HBO, the Windsor card was to be promoted not by Top Rank but by 'Bob Arum Enterprises'. (In the past, that corporate name had been used to promote Arum's South African ventures, presumably to shield Top Rank had there been repercussions from anti-apartheid activists.)

The lawyers were poised to have a field day, but the billable hours were somewhat curtailed after it was reported that Hearns had, conveniently, broken the pinky finger on his right hand. 'A day after the injury to Hearns, a federal judge in Los Angeles ruled in HBO's favour,' recalled Arum. 'We would have appealed if Tommy hadn't been hurt, but it would have dragged on for some time and the fight would have been in jeopardy.'

Hagler–Hearns was off, in any case, and would not be revived for nearly three years. Hagler went to Italy later that year and disposed of both Arum's obligation to Sabbatini and the unfortunate Fulgencio Obelmejias in the same evening.

By the time they were scheduled to meet again, the price of poker had gone up. A guaranteed $10.5 million minimum now sat in the pot.

■ ■ ■

The Fight was announced in December 1984 at New York's Waldorf-Astoria. Hagler and Hearns were all smiles, looking more like co-conspirators than adversaries, probably because they shared the knowledge that each would earn more than $5 million from their joint enterprise.

In January and February, Hagler, Hearns and Arum embarked on what its participants would recall as the 'Magical Mystery Tour'. Designed to beat the drums for the closed-circuit sale, the itinerary called for the boxers to visit twenty-two cities in two weeks. The combatants travelled in separate corporate jets.

Caesars owned one of the planes, a state-of-the-art Gulfstream G-II with its own Pac-Man machine. Arum leased a second jet, a Falcon, which was slightly less luxurious and a bit slower. The plan called for Hagler to fly on the Gulfstream when the parties were flying west. Once they reached Las Vegas they would switch aeroplanes. 'But when we got to Vegas, Pat Petronelli called to tell me we had a problem,' recalled Arum. 'Hagler said he was going home if he didn't get to stay on the G-II. He refused to continue the tour if he had to fly on the Falcon.'

'I tried to explain this to Emanuel Steward, but then Tommy had a shit-fit,' said Arum. 'He said *he* was going home if he didn't get to fly in the Caesars plane.'

In the end, Arum had to turn the second plane in and lease another G-II, identical to the first, so that the boxers could have separate-but-equal modes of transportation for the remainder of the tour.

Neither man was exactly a polished public speaker, but Hearns, along with the rest of the Kronk boxing team, had been the beneficiary of locution lessons administered by Steward's resident schoolmarm, Jackie Kallen. He would thoughtfully digest questions and then invariably begin his answer with, 'Well, basically . . .'

'I think,' supposed Leigh Montville, 'Jackie Kallen must have told him, "Tommy, every time you want to say 'motherfucker', stop yourself. Then instead say '*Well, basically* . . .".'

Hearns did his best to sell The Fight on this whistle-stop tour, but seemingly every time he opened his mouth he managed to rankle Hagler with what Marvin perceived to be evidence of disrespect. Hagler habitually tried to psyche himself up for fights by convincing himself that he disliked his opponents, and the Hit Man played right into his hands. Every turn of phrase meant to boost the closed-circuit sale seemed to further antagonise Hagler.

Steward confirms that Hearns did an inordinate amount of trash-talking, 'but it was strictly business'.

'People don't realise how out of character it was for Tommy to do that,' said the Hall of Fame trainer.

All it did was make Marvin Hagler mad.

'That tour did me good,' Hagler said once it was over. 'I might have had some respect for Tommy Hearns before I spent all that time with him, but by the time we got done I came away hating his ass. I respect him as a boxer, but I don't respect him as a person. I'm going to remind him what it's like to be on the bottom and have to work back up again.

'He's on an ego trip, especially after knocking out Duran the way he did after watching me [go the distance] with Duran,' groused Marvelous Marvin. 'Well, he should have fought the winner of that fight, not the loser, 'cause he didn't prove anything. This is the best time for me to get him now, while he's still walking around on that cloud. I'm going to do to him what I did to Alan Minter.'

In retrospect, that was prophetic, at least when it came to the duration of The Fight. When Hagler won the title from Minter in London five years earlier, the slugfest had ended at 1:45 of the third round. The Hearns fight would last but a few seconds longer.

Hagler and Hearns were supposed to have one more face-to-face encounter after the tour ended. On the last day of February, the boxers were summoned to New York, where *Sports Illustrated* would shoot the cover picture for its fight-week issue. Hagler and Hearns had also agreed to participate in the filming of the video for the band Van Zant's upcoming release 'I'm a Fighter'.

Hagler, still battling the effects of a cold he had caught on the tour, telephoned his regrets on the morning of the photo shoot. Hearns was in Los Angeles, where he had attended the Grammy Awards ceremonies and received his Fighter of the Year award at a WBC dinner.

Unaware of Hagler's withdrawal, Hearns boarded a flight for New York, but the United 767 developed mechanical problems and had to return to the gate, where it remained for two hours. When it finally took off, one of the plane's two engines caught fire, forcing an emergency landing in Salt Lake City.

'It could have been,' said Arum, 'the ultimate *Sports Illustrated* jinx.'

The magazine could wait, but in New York, Van Zant had leased Gleason's Gym for the day. The band went ahead with the video, subbing with a pair of New York fighters, Kevin Moley and Alberto Ramos. (Footage shot of Hagler in Provincetown earlier was later spliced in.)

Hearns had intended to fly from New York to Europe to work with his Kronk teammate Milton McCrory, who was defending his WBC welterweight title against Pedro Vilella in Paris, but, said *Sports Illustrated* boxing editor Ted Beitchman, 'Tommy is so shook up right now he may never get on a plane again. They may have to move The Fight to Salt Lake City.'

■ ■ ■

The initial plan had called for Hagler to begin training in Provincetown, as he had for each of his previous 25 fights, before moving to Palm Springs in mid-March, but the champion was nursing such a bad cold that Goody convinced him to proceed straight to the California desert, where the Americana Canyon Hotel had already offered the champion the run of the premises.

In Palm Springs, Hagler sparred with Boogaloo Watts and Jerry Holly, both tall and rangy like Hearns. The Petronellis had also lined up Marcos Geraldo, who had fought both Hearns and Hagler, but when Marcos failed to show up he was replaced by Larry Davis, who didn't last long. Larry fell by the wayside after Marvin busted his eardrum with a left to the head in a sparring session.

Watts, once ranked the No. 2 middleweight in the world, had been the first man to defeat Hagler when he had captured a home-town majority decision in Philadelphia nine years earlier. The controversial loss had been subsequently avenged, and Watts eventually emerged as a loyal and respected member of the Hagler camp. Two years earlier he, along with fellow Philadelphian Buster Drayton, had travelled to Italy to spar with Hagler before Obelmejias II in San Remo. 'Bobby might have been a champion himself if I hadn't been there,' said Hagler of Watts. 'He's smart. He knows who I'm fighting. He'll lay against the ropes, throw overhand rights and hooks to the body, fight in spurts, do all the things Hearns is likely to do.

'And the other kid [Holly], watch him. He's a younger, taller, bigger version of Thomas Hearns, plus he's got something Tommy don't have. He's got guts.'

I didn't think for a moment Marvin actually believed that assessment of Hearns's mettle, but the events of 15 April would surely prove him wrong.

▪ ▪ ▪

The challenge to Hagler had forced a radical departure from Hearns's traditional training *modus operandi*. Steward's Kronk fighters normally sparred against one another, without regard to weight class, and there was such an abundance of talent in the Detroit gym that they usually got all they wanted and more. 'You can't get any better boxing than we give them in our own gym but, except for Milton [McCrory], who can switch up, we just don't *have* any southpaws,' said Kronk assistant trainer Prentiss Byrd.

Hearns trained at the Eden Roc in Miami Beach, where Steward imported a trio of left-handers – middleweights Cecil Pettigrew of Tulsa and Brian Muller (Guyana), along with Kansas City light-heavyweight Charles (Hollywood) Henderson – to prep the Hit Man for The Fight.

Although Hearns had faced a few lefties in his amateur days, only one of his forty-one professional opponents had been a southpaw, the immortal Saensak Muangsurin of Thailand. Muangsurin, said Byrd, 'was a former world champion and all, but he still wasn't no Marvin Hagler'.

Hearns's crash course in left-handedness also had to take into account the fact that Hagler, the best switch-hitter since Mickey Mantle, could, and almost certainly would, switch over to orthodox at moments not even the champion could predict.

'It just kind of takes over, depending on how the fight is going,' Hagler explained. 'I don't even think about it. It just happens.'

■ ■ ■

One afternoon in Palm Springs, the Brothers Petronelli had accompanied Hagler on a brisk walk around the adjacent golf course when they came upon a small grove of citrus trees. A child of the city streets, Marvin couldn't resist.

'I mean, I guess if I'd ever thought about it, I knew oranges grew on trees, but here was all this *fresh* fruit that nobody had ever touched before,' recalled Hagler. 'Pat was saying, "*Naw, come on, Stuff, you're not gonna do it,*" but I said "*Just watch!*"'

The middleweight champion of the world was in short order up the tree and filling a sack with purloined fruit. At that moment a golf cart came puttering along. One of the occupants was Palm Springs's most famous resident.

On Bob Hope's 80th birthday two years earlier, he had briefly shared a ring with Hagler in the boxing skit.

'He couldn't believe this,' said Hagler. 'Bob says, "Marvin, what you *doin'* up there?" and I said, "Hey, I'm picking me some oranges, Bob. That all right?"'

'Next thing you know, he invited me and Pat and Goody over to his house.'

Kirk Douglas also became a frequent visitor to the tent outside the Americana Hotel that served as Hagler's training camp.

Although it was widely assumed that Douglas was, like Hope, a reformed boxer, Old Spartacus revealed that while he had been a college wrestler at St Lawrence, prior to his 1949 role in *Champion*, 'I didn't know the first thing about boxing.'

Douglas told me he had been tutored for that role by the old welterweight Mushy Callahan. Mushy must have done a great job, because Douglas was not only nominated for an Academy Award, but he was convincing enough that for the rest of his life people sought his opinion on pugilistic matters.

He spent a lot of time watching Hagler, but when it came to picking the fight, Douglas was, like a lot of other people, squarely on the fence.

'They're both such marvellous boxers that it's difficult to pick a winner,' said the actor. 'If there's an edge, it's that one guy is moving up in weight class, and you don't know about that. But one thing's for certain: there's going to be an awful lot of talent in the ring on 15 April.'

Despite the seemingly constant presence of celebrities, Hagler was all business in the training ring.

'I'm not here to sign no autographs or make appearances,' he said. 'In fact, I've heard people comment that I'm the hardest worker of any of the champions who've ever trained at this place.'

Still, the surroundings in California were absolutely opulent compared to his familiar digs in Provincetown. Better still, from Hagler's standpoint, it was *free*.

'This didn't just happen overnight, you know,' he told me one day. 'It took me a long time to gain this kind of prestige. I think back to years ago, with me and Pat and Goody sharing one $15 hotel room. This is the way it should be for a champion. It's finally happening to me, but, yeah, I feel like it's something I've earned.

'I'm still me,' he added, 'but I'm not ready to let all of this go.'

Hagler shared the training ring with Donald Curry, who would defend his WBA welterweight title against James (Hard Rock) Green in Dallas two weeks before Hagler–Hearns. Mark Gastineau, the New York Jets' sack specialist, had set up something called 'Mark Gastineau's Intensive Training Camp', at which he pumped iron for the edification of the hotel guests in another part of the tent.

With the fight still nearly a month away, Hagler spent much of his time in seclusion, thinking about Hearns.

'Tommy is a dangerous opponent, and he's going to test me, but I know deep down in my soul that this man cannot whip me,' said Marvin. Hagler attributed Hearns's self-assured demeanour to 'false courage'.

'The thing is, see, I've been shook up, but I've never been hurt. Tony Sibson shook me up with a left hook that I still remember. Even Juan Roldán hit me with a couple of good shots, but that's where the conditioning pays off. I've been able to absorb those kind of shots,' reflected Hagler. 'But Hearns has been stopped and I ain't been stopped. I *know* he can go, but he *don't* know if *I* can go. That's what's going to be worrying him.'

■ ■ ■

Hearns was attempting to become just the second 154-pound champion to win a 160-pound title (Nino Benvenuti had been the first) and, going into The Fight, the Hit Man's credentials as a full-blown middleweight were regarded as questionable.

Hearns had fought five times as a middleweight. Three of the opponents – Mike Colbert, Ernie Singletary and Murray Sutherland – had gone the distance, and Jeff McCracken had still been on his feet when his fight against Hearns was stopped in the eighth. Hearns had dispatched Marcos Geraldo, but it was so obvious the Mexican was in the tank (the 'knockout' punch hit him in the shoulder) that even Emanuel Steward termed the fight 'an embarrassment'.

'We were actually looking to get Tommy some work in that fight, but this guy had obviously decided that he didn't want no part of it coming in. All it did was make the TV people mad at us,' said Steward.

Hearns had packed a killer knockout punch as a welterweight, but the jury was still out at the heavier weight.

'Usually a guy moving up in weight loses some of his punching power,' said Goody Petronelli. 'I don't think I'm giving away any secrets by saying Hearns has had that trouble, too.'

Michael Katz had gone to Miami Beach to watch Hearns train for Hagler. 'One day while Emanuel was off preparing something for Tommy to eat, we discussed the upcoming fight,' said Katz. 'I reminded him that in every fight there's a boxer and there's a puncher, and asked him which he would be in this one.

'Tommy said, "Of course, I'm *always* the boxer, but if I hurt him, then I'm going for the knockout,"' recalled Katz. 'That's when it occurred to me that the conventional wisdom – Hearns early, Hagler late – was probably wrong. Of *course* Tommy was going to hurt him. He was much faster, and he hit like a mule. But I also figured he couldn't *really* hurt Hagler and that by going for an early knockout he might put himself within Marvin's reach – and in harm's way.'

■ ■ ■

Los Bandidos had grown more insistent with each fight. When Hagler's 1984 Madison Square Garden defence against Mustafa Hamsho was slated for 15, the WBC stripped him of his middleweight title, even though Marvelous Marvin made the issue somewhat moot by dispatching the Syrian in three. Hagler took the issue to court, where a federal judge once again ordered José Sulaimán to restore his championship.

Going into this fight, Sulaimán opted for a new tactic: he turned the thumbscrews on Hearns, threatening to strip him of the 154-pound title he had held since 1982, when he captured a majority decision over Benitez in New Orleans.

Officially, the WBC position was that Hearns couldn't fight Hagler without first facing its top-rated challenger, John (The Beast) Mugabi. Unofficially, Los Bandidos let it be known that Hearns would be granted dispensation on the matter, provided Hagler–Hearns was scheduled for 12 rounds and not 15.

While publicly expressing his respect for the traditional 15-round distance, in this instance Steward actually preferred the shorter limit, which he figured would be to his man's advantage. (Remember, had the Leonard–Hearns fight four years earlier ended after twelve, the Hit Man would have won on the scorecards.)

The WBC's decision to lean on Hearns, in any case, produced its desired effect. Rather than face yet another delay, which a Hearns–Mugabi fight would have entailed, the champion's camp reluctantly acceded on the issue, and the Hearns fight became just the second of Marvin Hagler's middleweight championship reign to be scheduled for 12 rounds.

The original panel of judges agreed upon by the WBC and the Nevada State Athletic Commission had consisted of Reno's Herb Santos, Englishman Harry Gibbs and Rudy Ortega of Los Angeles. Pasquale Petronelli vociferously objected to Ortega, who, claimed Hagler's co-handler, might be disposed to favour Hearns. For the record, the objection rested on the grounds that Ortega's big-fight experience had been primarily as a referee, not a judge. Privately, Ortega's cosy relationship with the WBC and its president worried the Hagler camp, as well as his promoter.

'I don't want to see them try to steal it from Marvin,' said Arum.

'It's no secret that José Sulaimán and Emanuel Steward are like cousins,' added Petronelli. 'We've been at odds with Sulaimán for years [mostly on the 15-round issue], so I'm not surprised that they'd try to pull something like this. We're not going to sit by and let them try to railroad The Fight.'

The dispute was aired at a closed-door meeting, and Nevada commission chairman Sig Rogich agreed to replace Ortega. The replacement, according to Arum, was supposed to be Texan Dickie Cole, but by fight time Californian Dick Young was sitting in the third judge's chair.

Not for the last time, the Petronellis apparently outsmarted themselves. On the night of the fight, Young, the replacement judge, scored both completed rounds for Hearns. Santos and Gibbs scored both for Hagler.

Richard Steele, nominated to be the referee, had been at the centre of some controversy for his handling of a Michael Dokes–Randy Cobb fiasco a few weeks earlier. Steele was a casino executive at the Riviera up the Strip (where Arum's arch-rival, Don King, also maintained offices), but neither side objected to his presence as the third man in the ring.

'It's not only *my* biggest fight, it's the biggest fight there's ever *been*,' said Steele. 'Of course I'm excited, but I'm going to try to approach it no differently than if it were another ESPN undercard fight.

'What I have to keep in mind at all times is that these are two human beings I have to protect,' the referee added. 'I want to make sure they can both walk out of the ring when it's over.'

■ ■ ■

When it had been announced in December, The Fight had been posted at 13–10, with Hagler the favourite, but the punters had quickly bet it down to a 6–5 pick, and as the date approached the odds vacillated between one man and the other. Five days before the bout, a big influx of Motown money had temporarily made Hearns the favourite.

Convinced in his own mind that gambling interests had been behind his disputed 1979 draw with Vito Antuofermo, Marvin was almost phobic about betting odds, but one day he overheard me telling someone that Hearns had got a nose in front at the sports book that morning and was now narrowly favoured.

'See,' exclaimed Marvin. 'The pressure is on Thomas Hearns, not me. A lot of people are probably looking at our fights against Duran and figuring he can beat me, and I'm just hoping he's fool enough to believe them, because he's going to find his ass on the deck.

'I'm glad you told me that,' Marvin said with a grin. 'I hope Las Vegas makes him *ten* to one.'

Art Manteris, the sports book director at Caesars, predicted that Hagler–Hearns would be the most heavily bet fight in Las Vegas history and could approach the record set by the Super Bowl a few months earlier.

■ ■ ■

On the Thursday night before the big fight, ESPN celebrated the fifth anniversary of its Top Rank Boxing series with a card at the Showboat. Terrence Alli, who was to have fought Choo-Choo Brown, pulled out on the evening of the fight, citing illness, thus promoting the Brett Summers–Chris Calvin co-feature to main event status.

Summers, a young lightweight trained by Steward, was unbeaten at 22–0, while Calvin, 15–3–2, was a well-travelled Nashville fireman who had battled Hagler stablemate Eddie Curet to a draw at the Boston Garden two years earlier.

Calvin, the self-proclaimed 'Southern Rebel', jumped right on Summers, pummelling him all over the ring in the first. He appeared to have won the fight in the third, when he knocked Summers down three times for what should have been an automatic stoppage, but Joey Curtis bewilderingly ruled one of the knockdowns a slip.

'Joey may be a lousy referee, but he saved the show,' Al Bernstein would say later. (Just a couple of years earlier, Curtis had suspiciously stopped Michael Dokes's fight against Mike Weaver after just 63 seconds.)

Summers was down nine times in all before Curtis stopped the fight in the tenth. The Kronk boxing team, which by then included at least 30 professionals, had been out in force for the Calvin–Summers fight, and they filed out of the arena disappointed with the result.

The rest of us would later shudder at the thought of what might have happened had Joey Curtis, and not Richard Steele, been assigned to work Hagler–Hearns a few nights later.

Once the principals arrived in Vegas, Hearns had halted his sparring on Tuesday – six days before the fight – while Hagler engaged in a few closed-door workouts with Watts and Holly across town at Johnny Tocco's Ringside Gym.

'After Palm Springs,' said Hagler, 'I need to get used to the smell of a gym again.'

Hagler said that the decision to work out privately was not a cloak-and-dagger operation. 'It's not that we've got any secrets,' said the middleweight champion. 'It's just that we're trying to be serious about business. Over at Caesars, every time you fart it winds up on television, and when the corner's trying to tell you something there's always a microphone stuck in your face.'

Emanuel Steward defended his decision to cut Hearns's sparring a week before The Fight.

'We've learned from some of the mistakes we made with the Leonard fight,' said Steward. 'We trained a little too hard for Leonard, but we've learned to adjust.'

In fact, Steward expressed surprise that Hagler was still sparring a few days before The Fight. 'Every trainer knows his own fighter best, and I'd certainly never criticise Goody, but I really think Marvin's working himself too hard,' said Steward. 'I think he's so hyper for this fight that around the sixth round he's going to be exhausted.'

Although Hagler had been a middleweight throughout his career and Hearns was moving up from the lighter weight classes, the Hit Man, at six-foot-one, towered over the champion – whom he tauntingly called 'a midget' – by at least four inches.

Hagler responded by describing Hearns as 'a freak'.

'He ought to be playing basketball instead of trying to fight me,' said Marvelous Marvin.

Apart from obligatory press appearances, Hagler remained sequestered in his room at Caesars. Hearns, on the other hand, strolled around the premises accompanied by his sizeable entourage from Detroit. One evening a few of us were walking through the casino and encountered what I described at the time as 'one of the great mismatches of the week: Thomas Hearns against a craps table'.

Anticipation over The Fight made Hagler–Hearns the casino's hottest affair in years, and 'with an event this big, the whole pecking order changes', explained a Caesars spokesman. A customer with a five-figure credit line might have been accustomed to a two-bedroom suite, but he was going to have to make do with a single room because the million-dollar bettors had first crack at the suites.

The champion's own quarters at Caesars consisted of a two-bedroom suite whose decor was best described as Early American Whorehouse. The walls were purple, with mirrors installed on the ceilings above the beds. A brass plaque, presumably temporary, on the door identified it as the 'Marvelous Marvin Hagler Suite'.

'I guess I'm getting a little seniority around here by now,' Hagler remarked with a laugh when he saw his digs.

By the weekend, the glitterati were flocking to Caesars, and the local press solicited opinions from seemingly all of them. Tom Selleck, Tip O'Neill and Julius Erving were all picking Hagler, while Eddie Murphy, Steve Jobs and Buddy Hackett liked Hearns. Siegfried and Roy were divided in their opinions, while the members of the Fifth Dimension split 3–2 in Hagler's favour.

Even Lee Liberace got into the act.

'Marvelous Marvin Hagler once asked me if I knew how to fight,' Liberace told a Las Vegas magazine. 'I told him that when you dress the way I do, you'd *better* know how to fight.'

Eighty-nine-year-old George Burns joined Kirk Douglas in ducking the issue.

'Hagler and Hearns are both tough,' said the man who once played God. 'I could pick a winner, but I wouldn't want the other one to get mad at me. I may be old, but I want to get older.'

The *Detroit News* even managed to track down Cave Man Lee in the sneezer. Three years earlier, Hearns's one-time stablemate had been knocked out by Hagler in sixty-seven seconds. Now he was doing hard time in the state penitentiary in Jackson, Michigan, after an unsuccessful bank robbery.

'Tell Tommy I love him and I'm pulling for him all the way,' Cave

Man told the *News*'s Mike O'Hara. 'I got twenty bucks riding on him – and in here I only make sixty a month.'

Katz, based on his analysis following the training camp conversation with Hearns, went on the record, picking Hagler in three.

Two days before The Fight, Jake LaMotta was married for the sixth time, around the corner from Caesars at the Maxim's wedding chapel. Sugar Ray Robinson, who had in his heyday engaged the Raging Bull in six brutal fights (and won five of them), was the best man.

Midway through the ceremony a telephone rang. Hearing the bell, LaMotta asked 'What round is it?'

'Sixth,' somebody replied.

ABC's *Good Morning, America* was in town, with plans to originate its programming from a remote location set up in the outdoor ring at Caesars both Monday and Tuesday morning, airing profiles of Hagler and Hearns, with David Hartman interviewing Goody Petronelli and Emanuel Steward on the morning of The Fight. (On Tuesday, Hartman promised to interview the winner, along with special guest Ray Leonard – who was at the time a CBS employee.)

The weigh-in took place the morning of the fight and, given the verbal sparring that had preceded the bout, the final pre-fight encounter proceeded with dignity. Hagler weighed 159¼, Hearns half a pound more.

The two exchanged glances, but no words, and quickly repaired to their respective rooms.

■ ■ ■

The celebrity-studded audience at the outdoor arena numbered 15,200 on Monday night, but the closed-circuit numbers would, in Arum's estimation, fall short of his expectations. Although an estimated 1.2 million viewers bought Hagler–Hearns, it fell shy of the 1971 record set by the Joe Frazier–Muhammad Ali 'Fight of the Century'.

While an undistinguished undercard played out in the stadium a hundred yards away, Hagler sat sequestered in his dressing-room. He could hear the whoops and hollers from Hearns's quarters down the hall, where seemingly the entire Kronk team had gathered.

'That's all right,' Marvin told Tony Petronelli. 'He can't take them all into the ring with him. It's just going to be me and him.'

'I never got a chance to finish wrapping Hearns's hands the way I wanted to that night,' revealed Emanuel Steward. 'While I was in the middle of wrapping his hands, an argument broke out between Tommy's brother, Billy, and one of the security people, and I had to leave in the middle of my wrapping to go take care of that.'

With over $10 million committed to the main event, there evidently wasn't much left for the preliminary fighters. For an event of its magnitude, The Fight was accompanied by a disappointing undercard.

The Kronk Gym split its two fights among the supporting acts. Light-heavyweight Ricky Womack outpointed David Vedder, while the up-and-coming Luis Santana scored an upset when he stopped Steward-welterweight Darrell Chambers in three. Angelo Dundee-trained heavyweight Alex Williamson fought to a draw with Canadian Willie deWit. In what was supposed to be the co-feature, Eddie Futch-trained Cuban junior welter Irleis (Cubanito) Perez was awarded a decision over Pat Jefferson. The crowd lustily booed the decision.

Hearns and his substantial entourage marched in to the strains of 'Hail to the Victors', the University of Michigan fight song. Hagler chose John Philip Sousa's 'Stars and Stripes Forever' for his entrance music.

Before the fighters were introduced, Doc Severinsen did a solo rendition of the national anthem. Even as Severinsen's trumpet notes were echoing through the outdoor stadium, Billy Hearns was taunting Hagler from across the ring. Seemingly oblivious, Marvin continued to shadow-box.

'I saw him,' recalled Hagler later. 'I was thinking right then, "*All you're gonna do is get your brother's ass kicked!*"'

The opening bell finally rang, unleashing eight minutes of mesmerising action. Hagler and Hearns tore out of their respective corners and were immediately consumed in a war in which no quarter was given, and none expected.

Less than ten seconds into The Fight it had already become apparent that whichever way this one ended, the judges' opinions weren't going to matter. Hagler and Hearns engaged with an unsurpassed ferocity, Tommy firing rights at Hagler, who, head down, resolutely marched straight at his taller foe, winging right-hand jabs and hooks from his southpaw stance.

The conventional wisdom had been that at some point it would come down to a test of Hearns's right hand and Hagler's head, and with Marvin charging right at Tommy, that anticipated encounter wasn't long in coming. Early in the wild first round, Hearns rocked Hagler with a right uppercut that momentarily appeared to have stunned the champion, but Marvin continued to surge forwards.

'I wanted him to know who was the boss from the opening bell,' Hagler said later. 'I knew I could take everything he had.'

With a minute left in the first, Hagler was pursuing Hearns towards the challenger's corner when Hearns landed a right that opened a deep cut to Marvin's forehead. Blood spewed forth, but by the end of the round Hagler had trapped Hearns in his own corner and was landing almost at will. Just inside the ten-second mark, Hagler landed a right-left combination that appeared to shake Hearns to his boots.

'At first I was wondering when this guy was gonna stop punching, but I was sorry to see that round end,' Hagler reflected later. 'I hated to give Tommy a chance to go back to his corner and recover.'

The furious first round had delighted the crowd, and drew comparisons to some of the great opening stanzas in the annals of pugilism – Graziano–Zale, Torres–Tiger, Frazier–Quarry and Dempsey–Firpo – but in the corner between rounds Goody Petronelli had other matters on his mind.

'Don't worry about the cut,' he told Hagler as he swabbed away at the wound.

'Close your eyes,' he warned the champion as he poured Adrenalin solution into the cut.

Hagler's cut was nearly in the centre of his forehead, and while his bald pate accentuated the appearance of the gore as it spread across his glistening head and ran down into his face, it could have been much worse had the wound been to one side or the other. As it was, the blood flowed almost straight down between his eyes and not into one or the other.

Because he was the one who was bleeding, Hagler's corner was the focus of attention, but across the ring there was also cause for concern.

'When Tommy came back to the corner after the first round, he told me, "My hand's broke,"' recalled Steward. 'I said, "What do you mean? Is it sore?"'

'No,' said Hearns. 'It's *broke*.'

It was, said Steward, but 'the idea of quitting never entered my mind. That just wasn't who Thomas Hearns was.'

Hagler charged out of his corner to land a long right, but Hearns avoided further damage by retreating. Then, with Hearns on the run, Hagler briefly, but inexplicably, switched to an orthodox attack. That interlude consumed no more than half a minute; there were other times in the fight when he waded in with such a two-fisted attack that it would have been difficult to tell *which* hand he was leading with.

Hearns, who had fought the first as if he expected it to be a one-round fight, was much more cautious in the second. Attempting to maintain his range, he did his best to jab away at Hagler from a safer distance.

Late in the second Hearns appeared to be in full retreat, doing his best to counterpunch against Hagler's charge, but his own rights were increasingly wild. Hagler's jab seemed to be finding its mark, as the champion repeatedly cut off the ring to take away Hearns's avenues of escape. A Hagler left caught Hearns off-balance and momentarily appeared to stagger him. The challenger's spindly legs were beginning to look suspect.

'*Box, Tommy! Box!*' shouted Steward.

'It's pretty tough to box,' said Ralph Citro, the boxing record-keeper working as the cutman in Hearns's corner, 'when you're being attacked by a swarm of bees.'

Towards the end of the round Hagler trapped Hearns on the ropes, as he had in the first. Just before the bell Marvin landed a right-left combination followed by another right hook. All three punches appeared to find their mark.

Hearns wobbled back to his corner, and Petronelli went back to work on the cut between rounds.

'I was a little worried that they might stop it because of the cut,' Hagler confessed later.

As the third began, Hagler again switched to an orthodox stance, and then further confounded Hearns by landing three straight right-hand leads.

Steele had allowed the third to begin, but half a minute into the round the blood was pouring so copiously from Hagler's cut that he halted the action and brought the ringside physician, Donald Romeo, into the champion's corner.

'[The doctor] asked me if I could see all right and I said, "Sure, I can see fine,"' recalled Hagler. (The champion would later claim that he told Romeo, '*I ain't missing him, am I?*', but the rejoinder was almost certainly supplied after the fact by Pat Putnam. Tapes of the doctor's visit to the corner suggest that if Hagler actually did utter that now classic line, he must have been an even better ventriloquist than he was a boxer.)

Allowed to resume, Hagler and Hearns went right back at it.

'I've been refereeing for 15 years, and I don't think I've ever seen that much intensity in a fight,' Steele would say afterwards.

Just beyond the midpoint of the third, Hagler, in pursuit of Hearns, caught the Hit Man off-balance with a lunging straight right to the head. Hearns, dazed, went reeling across the ring in stutter-steps, finally coming to a halt when he believed himself to be out of harm's way. As Hearns began to turn his head, the traces of one of those brief '*Hey-I'm-not-hurt!*' smirks had just begun to form on his lips when he realised that Hagler had chased him across the ring and was right on top of him.

Hagler landed two crushing rights, punctuated by a left that missed mainly because Hearns had already begun to fall. The first of the right hands started Hearns on his trip to the canvas. The second ensured that he would have great difficulty getting back up.

Hearns hit the deck flat on his back, staring up at the desert sky. It initially appeared that he might not get up at all, but he struggled to his feet and barely made the count. One glance at the blank expression on Hearns's face was all Steele needed to stop the bout. As he cradled Hearns in his arms, the beaten fighter sagged, and the referee, realising he was all that was holding the Hit Man erect, gently lowered him back to the canvas, where he remained for another minute or two.

'It was really the only way to fight a guy like Tommy Hearns,' Hagler would later recall. 'I had to go inside and work him. I told you I'd cut him down like a tree, and I did just that.'

As Hagler celebrated across the ring, QB Hines, the gentle Kronk giant, bent over to pick up Hearns and carried him, like a baby, across the ring. QB was incongruously clad in a white dinner jacket, a red boutonnière in his lapel, and the picture of the big man holding Tommy appeared in papers all around the world.

Rudimentary computerised statistics of the day revealed that Hagler and Hearns had unleashed a combined 339 punches in just eight minutes of boxing, and that each had landed well over half the punches he threw. Hagler connected on 96 of 173, Hearns 94 of 166.

'I want to give Tommy all the credit in the world,' said Hagler afterwards. 'He put up an excellent fight. He came out the only way he could if he wanted to take something away from a champion.'

Emanuel Steward would say years later that Hearns fought the last five minutes of the eight-minute dance on raw courage alone.

'After the first round,' said Steward, 'his hand was broke and his legs were gone. But that night Tommy told me not to mention anything about the hand. He said he didn't want to take anything away from Hagler's victory. That's the kind of guy Tommy was.

'So we wrapped it real good and put ice on it. Tommy didn't even go to the hospital that night because word would have leaked out. We gave him some pain pills, but he didn't see a doctor about it until we got back to Detroit.'

'He came in, took my best shot and fought his ass off,' said Hearns of Hagler.

'It was a roll of the dice,' said Citro. 'They both had to gamble. Hagler gambled and won, Hearns gambled and lost. I think he just punched himself out.'

In Citro's medical opinion, Hagler's wound would have forced a stoppage had Hearns been able to last another round or two. 'A cut like that just spurts blood all night long,' he said. By the time Steele stopped it, Hagler was also sporting a cut across the bridge of his nose.

Once he revived, a weary Hearns, accompanied by Steward, made his way along the corridor in the Sports Pavilion and presented himself in Hagler's dressing-room to offer his congratulations.

The trash-talking of the past few months was quickly forgotten as the two adversaries embraced.

'You've got a lot of class coming in here like this,' Hagler told him before promising, 'If I had lost, I'd have done the same thing.'

The two gladiators hugged again.

'I want you to keep on winning, Marvin,' Hearns told the champion. 'You were the better man tonight – but we both deserved that $5 million.'

Actually, Hagler's end came closer to $10 million, despite the disappointing take in some areas of the country.

'We did very well in most places,' said Arum. 'It fell off a little in the South and didn't do as well as we expected in Texas. The Northeast, especially New England, did very, very well. But Chicago sucked.' In contrast to the approximately 200,000 buys The Fight engendered in the New York area, Chicago had only 20,000.

When she laid eyes on her father for the first time in weeks the next morning, three-year-old Charelle Monique Hagler ran her finger over the bandage on his head.

'Daddy got a boo-boo,' she said.

As it turned out, Tommy had one, too. When he got back to Detroit, X-rays confirmed what Hearns had known after the first round. He had broken a bone in his right hand.

Even though by most estimates it had been one of the most exciting fights of all time, not even its promoter seemed interested in a rematch. The devastating manner in which Hagler had finished Hearns effectively squelched talk of a return bout.

'I couldn't sell it,' said Arum. 'Even though The Fight was a big success, in order to sell a rematch we would have to convince people that if they fought again the result would be any different. Who would pay to see it?'

■ ■ ■

Two years later Gene Mayday, the proprietor of Little Caesars sports book on the Strip, told the *Boston Herald*'s Mike Globetti that the Hagler–Hearns fight had resulted in a half-million-dollar bloodbath for his establishment.

'All the money towards the end went to Hearns and actually made him the favourite,' Mayday told Globetti, but several well-heeled Hagler supporters ('close friends' of the middleweight champion, the bookmaker described them) had swooped in to bet Hagler by knockout in the early rounds.

Little Caesars' original line for a Hagler third-round KO had been 25–1.

'His people started betting it at $1,000 or more a pop, so it went down,' said Mayday. 'But, hell, they kept betting it. 22–1. 20–1. They still kept betting it. We got *killed*.'

■ ■ ■

In the aftermath of Hagler's devastating performance, speculation reigned over the question 'Who's next?'

The most likely suspect immediately took himself out of the running.

'If I ever needed a reason to stay retired, that was it,' said Ray Charles Leonard.

At Hagler's victory party at Caesars a few hours after the fight, I was approached by Butch Lewis, who promoted light-heavyweight champion Michael Spinks. Lewis wanted to put together a fight between the two champions.

'Gee, I don't know, Butch,' I told him. 'Do you really think Michael can make 160?'

The idea of a Hagler–Spinks fight did appeal to Tommy Hearns, who urged Marvin to consider it.

'Sure,' snorted Hagler. 'So you can move up and have the middleweights?'

The most obvious challenger was James Shuler, 21–0 and ranked No. 1 by both the WBC and WBA, but the public barely recognised his name. The hope was that his anonymity might be overcome with more high-profile exposure before Hagler had to engage him in a mandatory defence.

As it turned out, Shuler would only have two more fights. (In the first of them, later that summer, he won a decision over Hagler's sparring partner Jerry Holly.)

A day after The Fight, Arum had set his sights on the next foe: the undefeated Ugandan John (The Beast) Mugabi.

'Mugabi is the hot fighter right now, and he's the one the TV people want,' agreed Pat Petronelli. 'We can always make a deal with Shuler, put him on the undercard and promise him the winner.'

'Mugabi is a dangerous knockout specialist,' said the promoter. 'People would *want* to see that fight.'

8

THE SUPER FIGHT

Leonard–Hagler
Caesars Palace, 6 April 1987

The devastating nature of his win against Hearns finally brought Hagler the acclaim he had sought. When the Boxing Writers Association of America voted for the recipients of its awards for 1985, Marvelous Marvin was the overwhelming choice as Fighter of the Year. At the same dinner at which Hagler was honoured, I received the Nat Fleischer Award for Excellence in Boxing Journalism. There was little doubt in my mind but that my election had come on Marvin's coat-tails.

The following spring Hagler would engage in a fight that unwittingly provided the springboard for the match-up he'd dreamed of since 1973 – a chance to confirm his greatness against Sugar Ray Leonard. Nobody could have guessed it at the time, but his 1986 fight against John (The Beast) Mugabi would be the last he would ever win.

* * *

BORN IN UGANDA, JOHN Mugabi had come of age amid the repressive regime of Idi Amin Dada and won a silver medal at the 1980 Moscow Olympics. When he turned professional and relocated to London under the aegis of Mickey Duff, Mugabi was rechristened 'The Beast' and fought primarily in Europe before Duff shifted his operations to the United States in late 1982.

Over the next three years, the Beast ate his way through a collection of respectable, though decidedly second-tier, American middleweight and junior middleweight contenders. In one of those early fights, Duff matched Mugabi against a solid opponent, Curtis Ramsey, on a card promoted by Don King.

'I'd been telling Don that I had a boy who was going to be a champion,' recalled Duff. 'I kept pestering him to use Mugabi on the undercard of a show he was running in Atlantic City.'

'Put him in tough,' Duff told King. 'I don't mind.'

'I had to fly back to England on business, so I left Mugabi in the hands of [trainer] George Francis, and told George to ring me collect the minute the fight was over,' said Duff. 'So here I was, sitting at home in London when George called to tell me John had knocked out Ramsey in the first round. He said he hit him with a punch that was so hard it knocked Ramsey *and* the referee, Larry Hazzard, right out of the ring and onto the press table.

'Oh, by the way,' Francis added, 'Mr King would like a word with you.'

'Hey, Mickey,' said King over the transatlantic line, 'I'm *in! Heh-heh-heh!* That is the *meanest* motherfucker I've ever seen in my *life*.

'You know,' King continued, 'I had a little talk with Mugabi after the fight and he says he wants to go with me, but of course I told him you and me were in this together.'

'I let him get it all out,' said Duff. 'And then I said, "Don, if that conversation took place, then you must be fluent in Swahili, because the lad doesn't speak a word of English."'

By August 1985, Mugabi's record stood at 25–0 and he had risen to No. 1 in the WBA's world rankings. Not one of his opponents had lasted the distance.

Bob Arum had initially slated the Hagler–Mugabi fight for November 1985, but after the champion injured his back in training, the bout was rescheduled for Monday, 10 March, at Caesars Palace.

Despite the Beast's fearsome credentials, Hagler was a better than 3–1 favourite and at a pre-fight news conference at Caesars promised that he would 'feast on the Beast'.

'Look, I realise this man Mugabi's got a dream,' said Hagler. 'I had my own dream once, but these things are not easy to come by. I can see him eyeing my clothes and checking out my jewellery, but I spent a long time in this game before I could even put food on the table.'

Mugabi, with former lightweight champion Cornelius Boza-Edwards serving as his interpreter, suggested that the 32-year-old champion's time had come and gone, and that he was ripe for the taking.

'Mugabi,' Hagler turned to face his adversary, 'you better be nice to me. You keep calling me an old man, you're only going to make me meaner.'

Despite his credentials, few boxing types gave Mugabi much chance against Hagler.

'I think Hagler will stop him inside six rounds,' supposed Ray Leonard. 'Marvin's just got too much artillery for him, and I'll tell you something else: Hagler's used to all of this, but I think the atmosphere is going to get to Mugabi. He'll be in awe.'

■ ■ ■

Hagler–Mugabi was televised not by HBO but by rival Showtime, which inaugurated its 'Showtime Championship Boxing' series with the bout. That night's undercard included another middleweight fight of significance: Thomas Hearns had been matched against undefeated James Shuler for the NABF title.

Shuler was 22–0, although the roster of his victims was comparable to Mugabi's. He had reached the No. 1 spot in the WBA rankings the previous year, only to be overtaken by Mugabi.

Like Hagler, Hearns had not fought since their eight-minute war eleven months earlier. Arum, hoping that the victor's stock would be boosted by a high-profile win, had 'guaranteed' the Hearns–Shuler winner the next shot at Hagler.

Shuler was trained by the venerable Eddie Futch, who reckoned that the beating Hagler had inflicted on the Hit Man a year earlier might have increased his man's chances. 'There's no question that a man can't get destroyed the way he got destroyed and not have some residual damage,' said Futch.

'The only damage was to my ego,' maintained Hearns. 'It was bruised, all right, but that's just like my car. It hurts, but you can take it to the body shop and get it fixed.'

■ ■ ■

In preparation for the Beast, Hagler sparred with brother Robbie Sims, along with Alex Ramos and Bobby Patterson. In his final session at Johnny Tocco's Gym the Thursday night before the fight, Patterson caught Hagler off balance and floored him with a left hook. Hagler dismissed the incident, claiming that it had been a slip, but, when pressed, Goody Petronelli concurred with the assessment of the handful of reporters who had been present: had the knockdown occurred in a real fight, Marvelous Marvin would have taken a count from the referee.

Lest anyone attach too much significance to the workout knockdown, Johnny Tocco noted that two years earlier a sparring partner named Larry Davis, wearing 16-ounce gloves, had flattened Mugabi in the same ring. Freddie Roach recalled that he had been present when a journeyman named Dennis Fikes knocked Mugabi *out* in a training session.

A day before the championship fight, Sims was matched against John Collins in what was supposed to be the *pièce de résistance* of that afternoon's NBC *Sportsworld* presentation. Collins, a highly regarded middleweight prospect from Chicago once trained by Emanuel Steward, had lost just once – to Tony Sibson – in 36 pro fights.

The network wound up with a lot of time to fill, as Sims scored a first-round TKO. Afterwards, Arum announced plans to match Hagler's brother against Roberto Duran that summer.

'Robbie was always a hell of a prospect,' said the promoter, 'but he always screwed around too much. This time we put his fight on at the same time as Marvin's and sent them to training camp together in Palm Springs. With Marvin around, he *had* to behave himself.'

■ ■ ■

On Monday morning at the Sports Pavilion, Hagler weighed 159½, Mugabi 157. Mills Lane, the Reno district attorney who had refereed Hagler's 1979 draw with Antuofermo, was appointed to work Hagler–Mugabi, while Richard Steele drew the Hearns–Shuler fight. Carlos Padilla was named to work Richie Sandoval's bantamweight title defence against Gaby Canizales.

Although few expected the verdict would go to the scorecards, an all-Nevada slate of Dave Moretti, Dalby Shirley and Jerry Roth was assigned to judge the main event.

In his first taste of combat since being knocked out by Hagler a year earlier, Hearns required just over a minute to dispose of Shuler. The Hit Man got Shuler's attention with a series of early jabs before catching him with a left hook that forced the Philadelphian to drop his hands. Tommy drove his opponent into a neutral corner with a right hand, and then delivered another big right that sent Shuler to the floor. Shuler showed little interest in getting up as Steele counted him out.

The other featured bout on the undercard produced a frightening outcome. Canizales knocked Sandoval down five times in seven rounds, the last of which left the champion twitching in convulsions as Padilla and ringside physicians tried to remove his gumshield.

Following the seizure, Sandoval was rushed to Valley Hospital, and although he recovered, it was his last fight. Arum offered him a job as a publicist-cum-translator with Top Rank in exchange for a promise he would never fight again, and Sandoval, sensibly, accepted.

Canizales, who visited Sandoval in the hospital the next morning, joined most ringsiders in criticising Padilla's handling of the fight.

'I think he should have stopped it after the second knockdown,' said the new champion. 'I knew I'd really hurt him then, and he was ready to go.'

Padilla – the man, remember, who had stopped Leonard–Benitez with six seconds on the clock – lamely explained: 'If I stop the fight too early, then the crowd is not allowed to see it to its conclusion.' (When Katz spoke to him later that night, the referee claimed that it wasn't *his* job, but that of Sandoval's corner, to stop the fight.)

There had been two ambulances stationed outside the dressing-rooms. One of them had been used to rush Sandoval to the hospital and the other was revving up its engines to take James Shuler there as well. Shuler revived and walked out of the arena under his own steam that night, but a week after his first loss he was dead at 26, killed in a motorcycle accident. Thomas Hearns not only flew to Philadelphia for the funeral but returned the NABF belt he had won from Shuler so that his fallen foe could be buried with it.

■ ■ ■

It had rained for much of the day and throughout the undercard, and the nearly 15,000 in attendance had been issued plastic garbage bags to protect their expensive clothing. The downpour subsided just before Hagler (to the strains of James Brown's 'Living in America') and Mugabi entered the arena.

Marvin Hagler successfully defended his middleweight title for the 12th time that night, but it was scarcely the cakewalk many had anticipated.

In an attempt to confuse Mugabi, Hagler opened up from an orthodox stance, but the Beast hardly appeared to notice. 'I came out right-handed early just to try and confuse him, but then I had to retreat a little bit and try to wear him down,' Hagler recalled later.

Hagler appeared to have the Ugandan in a world of trouble in the sixth, when he battered him around the ring, but by the end of that round the champion was also bleeding from the nose. 'I got caught with a lot of shots,' admitted Hagler, 'but that was mainly because I had to take the fight to him.'

Lane took a point from Hagler for a low blow in the seventh, and as the evening wore on with Mugabi still on his feet, chants of '*Beast! Beast!*' began to emanate from the crowd.

Although Hagler was landing right jabs virtually at will, he was repeatedly frustrated when he tried to set up the left behind it. Time and again, Hagler's sweeping left flew over Mugabi's head.

Hagler appeared to have the Beast on the run again in the ninth, but Lane halted the action and took Mugabi back to his corner for repairs on some loose tape on one of his gloves.

Recognising the respite as a fortunate break, Duff, even as he re-wrapped Mugabi's glove, told his fighter, 'Congratulations. You just got back in the fight.'

By the 11th, Hagler's right eye was nearly closed, but the war of attrition had taken its toll on the challenger. Midway through the round, Hagler landed four straight punches – a right, a left and two more right hooks – that ended the fight.

The Beast reached out and tried to grab the ring rope as he fell to the canvas, but once he hit the floor there was no getting up. The best he could do was roll over into a sitting position as Lane counted him out.

'If he had gotten back up and [Lane] had let him go on, the man could have been badly hurt,' said Hagler.

■ ■ ■

When he was interviewed by Al Bernstein in the ring immediately afterwards, Hagler suggested that the Mugabi fight 'might have been my last'.

'Aren't you going to miss me?' he asked the broadcaster.

That night the Petronellis met with Hagler in his suite to discuss his future.

'Right now, he's tired, he's sore and he hurts, but I think he'll be ready to fight Tommy Hearns again in November,' said Pat Petronelli. 'I just told him, "Hey, *you're* the one that's hurting right now. Goody and me, we ain't got a pimple on us, so you take your time and make up your mind."'

'This guy's been fighting for a long, long time, and he was in one of his toughest fights last night,' said Goody the next morning.

I had covered every one of Hagler's dozen defences, and I'd seen ominous signs in the Mugabi fight that I'd never seen before. Two days later, my column on the back page of Wednesday's *Boston Herald* summarised my position:

> ### IT'S TIME TO QUIT, MARVIN
> *Against Mugabi, for the first time in memory, Marvin Hagler found himself unable to accomplish things he wanted to do in the ring. Time and again – on perhaps 15 occasions in all – Hagler threw the jab ahead of a sweeping left, only to watch the punch, one that would have connected two or three or five years earlier, either sail wide of the mark or whistle over the Beast's head.*
>
> *And when he took the fight to Mugabi to throw his once-lethal and well-practised combinations, the routine was repeatedly interrupted by hard counterpunches that Hagler once would have been able to avoid.*
>
> *Marvin Hagler's place in history is already secure, and the thinking here is that the time to get out is now.*

233

The Petronellis did not disagree with my assessment, but, said Pat, 'You know you can't push Marvin into anything.'

'I still think he's going to keep fighting,' added the manager, 'but if he decides he wants to retire, we'll certainly respect that, too. We've all had a great ride and if that's what he wants, it'll be fine with us.'

■ ■ ■

With Hagler–Mugabi on Showtime, Ray Leonard was not part of the broadcast team. He watched the fight as a civilian, from a seat near ringside, where he sat drinking beer with Ollie Dunlap and the actor Michael J. Fox. As the bout wore on, he found himself noticing the same things I had noticed.

'When the fight was over, we ran into Whoopi Goldberg and we all wound up going to a party in somebody's suite,' recalled Dunlap. 'There was a party going on all around him, but Ray was sitting there by himself. You could see he was thinking, and then all of a sudden he turned around and said to Michael Fox: "*Know what? I can beat this guy!*"'

'Ray,' Ollie asked gently, 'how many drinks you had, anyway?'

'Plenty, and I'm going to have another one,' said Leonard. 'But I'm telling you, I can beat Hagler.'

Later that evening, Leonard telephoned Mike Trainer, who told him he was nuts. 'We'll talk about it when you get home,' said Trainer, who went back to bed. When Ray phoned again the next day, the lawyer realised it hadn't just been the booze talking. By the following week, Ray had quietly returned to the gym.

■ ■ ■

'A couple of months after the Mugabi fight, Mike Trainer and I opened our restaurant, Jameson's, in Bethesda, and Marvin came down for the grand opening,' said Leonard. 'I picked him up at the airport, and we sat around together having a few drinks.'

'So what's next?' Leonard recalled asking Hagler.

'I don't know, Ray, I'm finding it hard to get motivated,' replied Hagler.

'No shit,' agreed Leonard, as he poured another glass of champagne for Hagler.

'The two of us sat up all night, drinking and talking,' said Leonard. 'We never discussed the fight, but I knew I'd already baited the hook by planting it in his head.'

A few weeks later, Trainer relayed a proposed challenge to Bob Arum, who passed it on to the Petronellis. There was no immediate response from Hagler.

■ ■ ■

While he awaited Hagler's answer, Arum had other things on his mind. Three months after Hagler–Mugabi, the promoter was staging a summertime show at Caesars Palace, one he had christened the 'Triple Hitter'.

Designed to appeal to a wide cross-section of boxing fans, the bill included two world championship bouts – Ireland's Barry McGuigan defending his featherweight title against Argentine Fernando Sosa, and a WBC 154-pound title bout between Hearns and Mark Medal – along with what figured to be a grudge match, with Hagler's younger brother Robbie Sims fighting the ageing Roberto Duran.

Enormously popular in his homeland, McGuigan had managed to unite all of Ireland with a deliberately apolitical agenda that appealed to Catholics and Protestants alike. 'The Clones Cyclone' had a huge following in Britain as well: over 25,000 had packed Queens Park Rangers' stadium in London the night he defeated Eusebio Pedroza to win his championship. Now he was testing American waters for the first time as champion, and Arum made the wee Irishman the centrepiece of a cross-country promotional tour.

At one stop in Boston, the Triple Hitter line-up, *sans* Duran, appeared before a group of inner-city schoolchildren in Roxbury. After Hearns and Sims addressed the children, Sosa's remarks were relayed by an interpreter.

When it came McGuigan's turn to speak, it became apparent that the youngsters were having difficulty grasping his Hibernian brogue. Hearns playfully leapt to the microphone and began to 'interpret', explaining to the children: '*What Barry say . . .*'

The tour was barely over when Sosa was diagnosed with two detached retinas and scratched from the card. His place as McGuigan's challenger was assumed by Steve Cruz, an unknown and largely untested boxer from Texas, who worked as a full-time apprentice plumber by day. Cruz wore the logo 'Fort Worth Plumbing and Heating' on his trunks.

At least 3,000 of McGuigan's countrymen came to Las Vegas to witness his introduction to America. McGuigan's father Pat, a professional entertainer who traditionally sang 'Danny Boy' (in lieu of national anthems) before his fights, was booked for a weekend-long engagement at Caesars' Olympia Lounge.

June 23 1986 proved to be one of the hottest days in Las Vegas history, and one of the blackest nights in the annals of Irish boxing. Overcome by the 110-degree heat and badly dehydrated, a legless McGuigan was knocked down three times, two of them in the final round. He barely finished on his feet before collapsing and, after losing his title, was taken by ambulance to a Las Vegas hospital.

In the main event, Hearns stopped Medal in the eighth round of their title fight. In the other bout, Sims won a split decision over Duran in what was widely assumed to have been the final fight of Cholo's career.

■ ■ ■

Leonard had proposed that he would emerge from retirement for one fight and one fight only – against Marvelous Marvin Hagler, for the middleweight championship of the world. There would be no tune-up fight, and the notion of discussing options was utterly moot. Even if he beat Hagler, Leonard insisted, he would never defend the title.

Hagler was torn. Leonard was the one fight he'd always coveted, but four years later he still resented the way Ray had played him at that Baltimore retirement ceremony, and he felt he had been an ill-used pawn in the Kevin Howard comeback fight as well. How could he be sure this wasn't just another ruse?

Hagler also saw it as a no-win situation. Beating a one-eyed welterweight who'd fought just once in five years would hardly put an exclamation mark on his career. In fact, if he went on to break Carlos Monzon's record and the Leonard fight was one of them, future boxing historians might mark his achievement with an asterisk.

And although he insists to this day that he never considered the possibility that he might *not* win, somewhere in Hagler's mind he must have realised what effect losing to Leonard under these circumstances might have had upon his legacy.

While a Leonard fight figured to make him millions, there was another, unspoken, reason for Hagler's misgivings over the prospect of Ray's return to the limelight.

Between Leonard's absence and the sensational nature of his win over Hearns, Hagler had by the mid-1980s become the sport's most visible active practitioner. Playing off his menacing demeanour and fearsome reputation, an advertising agency had imaginatively cast him in a series of deodorant commercials (for Right Guard) in which Marvin, playing the genteel country squire, eloquently delivered lines like 'One wouldn't want to offend, would one?' and 'Anything less would be uncivilised.'

These commercials had been well received, but Leonard was unquestionably the King of the Q-Factor, and his return to the ring threatened to displace Hagler's new-found position.

Duran and Hearns, by contrast, never made a significant impact on Madison Avenue. Duran's opportunities had been limited by the language barrier (his only significant exposure had come in playing the foil to Leonard in those 1980 soft drink commercials), while Hearns sometimes had nearly as much trouble with English as Duran did. Early in his career, Kronk publicist Jackie Kallen had arranged auditions for Hearns to endorse several Detroit-based products, Stroh's beer and Vernor's soft drinks among them, but Tommy had so hopelessly bungled his lines in the studio that the commercials never made it to the screen.

▪ ▪ ▪

Leonard would later suggest that the 109 days it took Hagler to accept his challenge was an indication that the champion wasn't sure he wanted to fight him at all.

'Oh, yeah?' Hagler bristled. 'Well, how come it took Ray *four years* to make up his mind? He didn't want me *then*.'

Hagler's agreeing to fight was only the first step. Months of negotiations culminated in a record purse of $23 million, of which Hagler was guaranteed $12 million.

It was just the third time in Leonard's career (Benitez and Duran

II were the others) that he would be paid less than his opponent, but Hagler's representatives made several concessions in other important areas that more than offset the cosmetic difference in the purses.

The date was set for 6 April 1987. Although other venues were briefly discussed, there was no realistic possibility that a fight of this magnitude could take place anywhere other than Caesars Palace.

The bout agreement called for a 20-foot ring, which favoured the participant who was quicker afoot. And when Hagler insisted on a 15-round fight, Trainer replied that if it weren't scheduled for 12 rounds there would *be* no fight.

Leonard even reserved the right to choose the gloves, normally the prerogative of the champion.

'I'm surprised Leonard didn't get to choose the colour of Hagler's trunks, too,' cracked one observer. 'He got everything else he wanted.'

Once the terms had been arranged, the two embarked on a 12-city press tour, including an appearance with Bob Hope at Caesars, where the comedian plugged the bout as 'a fight for the common man – two millionaires trying to beat each other's brains out'.

Hagler abandoned the tour halfway across the country, accusing Leonard of creating a 'circus atmosphere' by joking about the fight.

'Just because he's America's sweetheart,' Hagler had complained, 'doesn't mean that I'm a bum.'

Hagler was not alone in being put off by Leonard's style.

'Leonard's arrogance is overwhelming,' wrote the estimable British fight scribe Harry Mullan. 'He must always be Prince Hamlet, and his fellow professionals attendant lords. He retires and un-retires at will, and shoves other contenders who have paid their dues out of the queue to allow him to make another grand entrance, at the top, in a title fight.'

Leonard appeared alone at several Midwestern stops and jokingly addressed 'Hagler' questions to an empty chair.

'Hagler misinterpreted what I said in November,' protested Ray. 'That was fun and games, to help the promotion. I had an obligation to fulfil. I knew that as time went by it would turn serious.'

Marvin didn't rejoin the press tour until it hit the west coast.

Hagler spent ten weeks training for the Leonard fight, by far the most extensive preparation for any bout of his career. 'I'm a perfectionist, you know,' he said. 'I put a little more effort into each and every one of my fights. In that respect, I'm still learning. Hey, I feel young. I feel as though I'm 21 again.'

Marvin once again trained in Palm Springs, where he had an unexpected visitor. J.D. Brown, a knowledgeable scholar of the sweet science who had served as matchmaker for several Sugar Ray Leonard promotions during Leonard's retirement, was dispatched on an espionage mission to the champion's camp.

Brown dyed his hair grey, donned horn-rim glasses and went unrecognised by Hagler or any of his people. For three days, he watched Marvelous Marvin spar and filed away mental notes of everything he heard Goody Petronelli tell him. On the day he left, just to prove that he'd been there, he had his picture taken with Hagler as the middleweight champion signed autographs for a waiting queue.

The Hagler camp was furious when word of Brown's spy mission became public, but, Ollie Dunlap pointed out, 'Remember, Ray had worked on the telecasts of a whole bunch of Marvin's fights, so a lot of it was a psyche job, too.'

'Ray had been away for so long he wanted any edge he could get,' said Brown. 'I was supposed to go and critique Hagler, bring back a report of what he did in training. The first thing I noticed that impressed me was that he had no entourage: when Marvin walked into the gym, he was carrying his own bag.

'But,' said Brown, 'I did notice a couple of things. One was when I watched him spar with the Weaver Triplets [Floyd, Lloyd and Troy Weaver, the younger brothers of former heavyweight champion Mike Weaver]. They were young junior middleweights, too quick for him, and when they'd flit around the ring it pissed Hagler off. "*Stop running and fight, you little bitch,*" he'd snarl at them. So I knew Ray could frustrate him by doing the same thing.

'Another thing I noticed was that as soon as the bell rang Hagler moved straight to the centre of the ring. That was his domain. That's where he wanted to be. So I knew that if Ray got there first, Marvin wouldn't like it.'

Leonard, in the meantime, was training on Hilton Head, a resort island just off the coast of South Carolina. Dundee, who usually came in to polish off the final few weeks of sparring, arrived at the resort on 28 February – over five weeks before the fight.

After each day's workouts, the two met to discuss strategy. Dundee reminded Leonard that although Hagler was a left-handed boxer, he was a natural right-hander, and that his significant power lay on that side.

The conventional approach when fighting a southpaw is to move to the right, but, Dundee told Leonard, 'You don't fight this guy the way you fight a regular southpaw. Keep moving to the left.'

Although Dundee and Mike Trainer would have their differences in the bitter divorce that followed the Hagler fight, in its immediate aftermath the lawyer, recalling those long sessions at Hilton Head, would tell Bill Nack, 'I can't give Angie enough credit. Ray's talent was there, but Angie helped choreograph it. He stepped in and filled a void.'

Throughout the long weeks of work, as he tried to whip his body back into fighting trim, Leonard kept reminding himself, 'Ray Leonard couldn't do this, but Sugar Ray Leonard *can*.'

The question was: could he ever be Sugar Ray Leonard again?

■ ■ ■

A former Irish national middleweight champion, Dr Terry Christle completed his studies at the College of Surgeons in Dublin, but before embarking on a medical career he wanted to give professional boxing a try. In 1983, with eight pro fights in England and Ireland under his belt, he had flown to the United States and made his way to the Petronelli Gym, and sought out the men who had taken Hagler to the middleweight title to supervise his postgraduate programme.

Christle had a boxing pedigree. His brother Mel, a Dublin lawyer, had been an All-Ireland heavyweight champion and to this day chairs the Boxing Union of Ireland. Another brother, Joe, had also been a professional heavyweight.

Billed as 'The Fighting Physician', Christle had made his US debut in December '83 and had won all five of his fights on American soil.

'We weren't taking many chances with Terry,' admitted Pat Petronelli. 'He was always going to be a better doctor than he was a fighter, and we weren't going to jeopardise his medical career by getting him hurt. We tried not to put him in too tough – and for years we wouldn't even let him *spar* with Marvin.'

In Palm Springs, Christle finally got his chance when Goody ordered him to put on the headgear and get into the ring with the champion.

Hagler had been under the weather for several days. He and Christle went a lacklustre two rounds, and it became apparent that Marvin was not himself. He repaired to his room after the workout, where, at Goody's request, he was examined by Dr Christle. It may have been the first time in boxing history that one of his sparring partners administered a physical to a reigning champion.

When Terry emerged from his consultation with his patient, the Petronellis were eagerly awaiting his diagnosis. Was Marvin all right?

'Not unless you know of a cure for the common cold,' reported Christle, who proposed a few days of bed rest for the middleweight champion.

Bob Arum had arranged for a media delegation a hundred strong to travel to Palm Springs for what was supposed to be Hagler's final sparring session. He was not pleased to hear that there would be no further workouts. He was even more irate when he learned that activity had been suspended on the instructions of the Fighting Physician.

'Get us a *real* doctor,' demanded Arum. 'I want a second opinion!'

The Petronellis listened to Dr Christle and not Arum. Marvin didn't emerge from his room again until it was time to leave for Vegas.

■ ■ ■

With the bout scheduled exactly a week after the 1987 NCAA basketball championship game, many sportswriters flew directly to Las Vegas from New Orleans on Monday (a full week before the fight), a trip we likened to taking the shuttle from Sodom to Gomorrah.

A media throng of over 500 was waiting outside Caesars Palace when Hagler and his travelling party arrived from Palm Springs on Tuesday, six days before the fight. When the champion, wearing a blue tracksuit, sunglasses and a white baseball cap bearing the legend '*No Mercy*', stepped out of his white Lincoln limousine, he was greeted by a costumed Caesar and Cleopatra, along with several faux centurions.

'Caesar' read a proclamation in which he described Hagler as 'the undisputed middleweight champion of the world', but just a few hours earlier that designation had ceased to be accurate.

Although the WBC had approved Leonard as an opponent, the WBA had not and ordered its title vacated. Once again Hagler had gone to court, but that morning in Boston federal judge Robert Keaton had declined Hagler's request for an injunction forestalling the move, effectively formalising the WBA's decision to vacate the title.

'So what else is new?' said Hagler. 'They tried to take away my title before the Hamsho fight, and they tried to strip me when I fought Scypion.'

'We're disappointed, but we're not totally surprised,' said Pat Petronelli. 'Right now I'm sorry we ever got involved with the WBA. We've done them nothing but good, and they turn around and do this.'

Morris Goldings, who had replaced Steve Wainwright as Hagler's lawyer, said he would appeal the judge's ruling, but the champion's camp did not seem optimistic.

'This isn't the first time,' said Petronelli. 'We'll just keep whacking away in court and see what happens, but neither Marvin nor Goody and me are going to lose any sleep over it. You know how important those belts are to Marvin, but we've always said they can only be won or lost in the ring. That's why he's not getting too excited about it.'

Leonard's camp seemed even less distressed by the news.

'It doesn't concern us at all,' said Mike Trainer. 'That particular title wasn't ever part of this deal anyway.'

On Thursday, another federal judge, Bruce Selya of the first US Circuit Court of Appeals, rejected Hagler's appeal, saying that the fighter 'failed to land any forceful blows' in his attempt to forestall the WBA action. '*Marvelous Marvin Hagler has been less successful in the court than in the ring,*' wrote Selya in his opinion. '*We need spar with this matter no further.*'

By vacating its one-third of the title, the WBA effectively turned Hagler–Leonard into a WBC title fight. While the IBF took no action, neither did it sanction the bout, meaning that it would continue to recognise Hagler as champion if he won. If he lost, it, too, would vacate the title.

■ ■ ■

By eschewing a tune-up bout, Leonard would enter the ring not having been fought for nearly three years, but he had not been entirely inactive. In the months leading up to the Hagler fight, he had engaged in several 'simulated' 12-round bouts back in Maryland.

'I trained for nearly a year before the Hagler fight,' recalled Leonard. 'I didn't even know who some of these guys were, mostly guys J.D. Brown brought down from gyms in New York. They'd wear headgear and use ten-ounce gloves; I used fourteen-ounce gloves and no headgear. They might go three or four rounds apiece, but I went all twelve. I was trying to reproduce the competitive nature of a real fight. I wanted to get that feel back.'

Did it *feel* like a real fight?

'Yes,' said Leonard. 'Except I didn't get paid.'

So who won in those simulated fights?

'Hey, it was my gym,' said Leonard with a grin. 'They were home-town decisions.'

■ ■ ■

Correctly anticipating that he would be grilled about the inherent risk to his eyesight, Leonard had prepared a statement, replete with medical testimony, copies of which were distributed before his first meeting with the media at Caesars. That session was preceded by an announcement that Leonard would not entertain any questions about his eyesight.

No sooner had the floor been thrown open to questions than Pat Putnam raised his hand from the back row of what had to be the largest ballroom in press conference history.

'Hey, Ray,' he shouted. 'How many fingers am I holding up?'

In addition to the concessions he had made on the length of the bout and the size of the ring, Hagler had agreed to the Leonard camp's request for 'thumbless' gloves.

The Reyes gloves the boxers would wear could more properly be described as 'thumb-attached'. The extra bit of stitchery had been incorporated as a precautionary device to prevent one boxer from accidentally gouging the other with a stray thumb. Dundee was quick to proclaim the adoption of the weapons an edge for Leonard.

'It's going to take away Hagler's best weapon,' claimed the 65-year-old trainer. 'If Juan Roldán hadn't got thumbed, he would have beaten Marvin. Take away the thumb and Roldán wins the title.'

Goody Petronelli smiled when he heard that.

'We were using the same Reyes gloves in the Roldán fight we'll be using for this one,' revealed Hagler's trainer.

That Leonard was reluctant to answer questions about his eyesight didn't mean Hagler couldn't talk about it.

'I'm not really thinking about his eye,' insisted the champion. 'That's his business. He's the one who made the decision to fight. Look, this is a dog-eat-dog business. It's a *man's* sport. If it was me, do you think he'd come up to me and say, "Oh, Marvin, there's something wrong with your *eye*?"'

Somebody asked Leonard whether he would consider saying '*No mas*' if he experienced problems with his eye.

'I don't speak Spanish,' he replied.

That was demonstrated the next afternoon when Juan Roldán, who would be fighting James Kinchen on the undercard, showed up at the gym to watch Leonard spar. Afterwards he was introduced to Leonard and the two engaged in a brief conversation, with Dundee serving as the interpreter.

■ ■ ■

When Dundee discussed the impending match-up, he sounded as if he were training David to fight Goliath.

'Hagler is a monster,' he said. 'It boggles the mind that he hasn't lost in 11 years. And here's this little kid trying to beat him.'

Dundee recalled that this was hardly the first time a fighter of his had been given little chance, citing the then-Cassius Clay's challenge to the awesome Sonny Liston, Carmen Basilio's to Sugar Ray Robinson and Willie Pastrano's to Harold Johnson.

'Basilio beat Robinson and *nobody* thought he was going to do it,' recalled Dundee. 'He opened him up with the jab. [The original] Sugar Ray said, "How's this little midget going to hit me?" And he hit him with the jab. Got inside him and beat him.'

Someone noted that a more apt historical analogy might be the ageing Joe Louis's quixotic attempt to recapture the heavyweight title from Rocky Marciano, then at the top of his game.

'Joe Louis didn't have the athletic ability that Ray has,' said Dundee. 'Ray is always in condition. He's never been *out* of condition.'

'Remember, everyone thought Hearns was going to knock Leonard's block off,' noted Dundee. 'It turned out Ray was the puncher in that fight, and he'll be the puncher in this fight, too. Ray is the puncher because he hits you with shots that you can't see. Those are the ones that hurt. Those are the ones that get you out of there.'

In talking up his man's chances, Dundee had alluded to the fact that Hagler had been extended beyond ten rounds in his fights against Duran, Roldán and Mugabi.

'Yeah?' growled Hagler, when apprised of Dundee's observation. 'Well, I'm still here, ain't I?

'The object of this game is to get out of trouble,' he added. 'I expected to get hit by Mugabi, and I certainly expected to get hit by Tommy Hearns. I'd say that Hearns has better speed than Leonard.

'Besides,' said Hagler, 'I've got more knockouts than Leonard has had *fights*.'

∎ ∎ ∎

In 1982, Leonard had been part of an HBO crew that had visited the Petronelli Brothers' Gym to tape a preview for Hagler's second fight against Obelmejias. For reasons that are not entirely clear, Leonard had allowed himself to be photographed, a self-satisfied smirk on his face and clutching a fistful of money. With the thumb of his other hand, he could be seen gesturing over his shoulder to a sweaty Hagler, standing in the ring behind him.

Five years later, the photo had become a motivational prop. Taped to a mirror in the Marvelous Marvin Hagler Suite at Caesars, it was the first thing Hagler saw each morning, the last thing he saw before he went to bed at night.

'Do I resent Ray Leonard? Sure I do,' Hagler nodded one day as he sat in his suite. 'I don't think he has any business being in the ring with me right now, but I've just got to prove that to the world.

'Just thinking about it,' he gestured toward the photo, 'makes me mean.'

■ ■ ■

With every newspaper and every television network in the English-speaking world on hand in Vegas, there was no question that wasn't going to be asked. At a session with the press at the Sports Pavilion one afternoon, an enterprising scribe outdid himself when he asked Hagler, '*If you were a dog, what kind of dog would you be?*'

The middleweight champion actually gave it some thought before replying: 'Some combination of German shepherd, Dobermann pinscher and pit bull.'

'*There does not seem to be much doubt,*' we wrote in recapturing the moment, '*that he had decided that Leonard is a poodle.*'

A few weeks earlier, Thomas Hearns had stopped Dennis Andries to win the WBC light-heavyweight title. On Wednesday, the Hit Man showed up in Vegas and, pressed for a prediction on the fight between his old adversaries, forecast a Leonard upset.

'Don't make no difference to me,' said Hagler with a shrug. 'He's jealous, I guess. It's a free country; he can say what he wants. I just hope the result is the same as when I fought Tommy.

'Am I at the same peak I was for that fight? Well, I've got to be even meaner,' replied Hagler. 'For the Hearns fight, we had a good strategy, and we've got a good game plan for this one. I just hope the strategy we've got for Leonard works the same way.

'He can do whatever he wants to. We'll accommodate him,' said Hagler, whose subsequent vow would come back to haunt him: 'I *am* going to take control of this fight. I'm not going to let Leonard dictate it.'

'I will not let him dictate the fight,' vowed Leonard. 'If he comes out full steam, he can only do it for one or two rounds. He can't keep it up.'

■ ■ ■

Hagler–Leonard would be the tenth middleweight title fight held in Las Vegas. Beginning with his fight against Sugar Ray Robinson back in 1961, Gene Fullmer had been a participant in the first three, while Hagler had fought in five of the other six. The Super Fight was Hagler's third headline appearance in a row at Caesars and the fourth time in four years he had topped the bill there.

'It's getting better,' he said. 'You know, before the Duran fight here I was a little bit tight. For the Hearns fight, I was a little less so. For this one, I'm confident. I know what's ahead for me.'

Leonard was conducting public workouts at the Golden Gloves Gym, while Hagler sparred behind closed doors at Tocco's.

On Tuesday afternoon, the *Boston Herald*'s Mike Globetti was among a host of witnesses at the gym when sparring partner Quincy Taylor surprised Leonard, rocking him with an overhand left that, wrote Globetti, 'seemed to shake the former champion'.

'*Oh, Jesus!*' cried John Madden, the football coach-turned-TV broadcaster and fight fan extraordinaire, who had been sprawled on a folding chair, as he sat bolt upright.

Although Leonard and his handlers would, for public consumption, make light of the episode, Leonard would recall that 'when Quincy hit me with that punch, it knocked the shit out of me. I was hurt, and he was so surprised that he just backed away.'

If Hagler had an Achilles heel at all, it was probably the build-up of scar tissue that described his eyebrows and rendered him vulnerable to cuts. Leonard's initial battle plan had been to go after the champion early, hoping to inflict damage that might lead to an early stoppage. The punch from his sparring partner revised that strategy.

'I thought, if this guy can hurt me, Hagler will *kill* me,' Leonard told Tim Dahlberg. 'Thank God Quincy hit me, because I changed the plan.'

'I think what I brought back from Palm Springs helped Ray formulate his strategy,' said J.D. Brown. 'But Quincy Taylor changed it even more.'

Over at Tocco's, Hagler was sparring with old standby Bob Patterson, along with the Weaver Triplets, who had been brought in from Pomona, Califonia, to emulate Leonard's speed. (Pat Petronelli described them as 'the three Weaver twins'.)

'They've done everything,' said Goody Petronelli of Floyd, Loyd and Troy. 'They even stuck out their tongues and taunted Marvin. They did everything we expect Leonard to do.'

'It's been tough,' Floyd Weaver acknowledged. 'We knew it would be hard working against Hagler, but it's *real* hard. He didn't hold nothing back, and we didn't either. We took a lot of bruises to the body, and Troy got a broken nose.'

■ ■ ■

Hagler and Leonard weren't the only ones besieged by the press each day. Demands upon their respective cornermen were so incessant that Arum's publicists found themselves arranging press conferences for Dundee and the Petronellis.

'Hagler's been a great fighter, God bless him, and I've got a guy who's not even supposed to be fighting,' said Dundee. 'He's been away; he was lousy in his last fight. It's never been done before, but you can't compare this to any other fight or any other fighter. Only Ray Leonard could do it.'

'I respect the Petronelli brothers,' Dundee told a flock of reporters that day. 'They go with their fighter like Charlie Goldman and Rocky Marciano, like Whitey Bimstein and Rocky Graziano.'

Being showcased for the media gave the Petronellis an opportunity to trot out their Abbott and Costello act, with Pat playing Lou to Goody's taciturn Bud.

When Goody was asked about the worst cut he'd ever had to repair, he didn't even get to answer.

'I'll tell you exactly when it was,' Pat interrupted. 'You know that scar above Marvin's left eye? Well, six years ago he was hanging a shower curtain in his bathroom. He slipped and hit the sink when he fell. Took 14 stitches.'

To demonstrate that there were no hard feelings, Pasquale Petronelli and Dundee agreed to meet for dinner after the fight, with the loser picking up the tab and the winner choosing the menu. Dundee's choice was linguine with clam sauce, Petronelli's *pasta e fagioli*, spaghetti and meatballs.

■ ■ ■

The weekend of the fight saw Al Bernstein make his debut as a crooner. The ESPN commentator, who would also work the closed-circuit telecast of the Super Fight, opened to rave reviews as a headline act in Caesars' 'Festival of Jazz' when he played the Olympia Lounge – the same venue in which Pat McGuigan had performed ten months earlier on the weekend of his son's ill-fated Las Vegas debut.

Caesars was the epicentre of the boxing world that weekend, and the casino scheduled Friday and Saturday cards leading up to Hagler–Leonard on Monday night.

Iran Barkley headlined an ESPN card on Friday night, facing Jorge Amparo of the Dominican Republic. Amparo held the WBC youth title and the previous year had improbably emerged from a fight in Jakarta as the Orient–Pacific champion as well. Unimpressed, Barkley promised to relieve him of 'this old tuna-fish belt he have'.

'I came here to beat him up just for signing the contract,' said the Blade.

Barkley won an unpopular decision despite receiving a nasty gash above his left eye that bled over the last half of the fight.

Terry Christle, who had treated Hagler in Palm Springs, might as well have used a scalpel on Albuquerque's Sam Houston on the ESPN undercard, opening up four gashes on his opponent's face before Davey Pearl stopped it in the fourth round.

(It would be Dr Christle's last pro win. Later that summer he lost for the first time, dropping a decision to Dave Tiberi in Atlantic City. He promptly retired from the ring with a record of 13–1–1 and devoted himself thereafter to the practice of medicine.)

A heavyweight bout on the Friday night show saw Orlin Norris knock out Texan Eddie Richardson in two.

On Saturday afternoon, CBS televised a live card headlined by a junior middleweight clash between a pair of former champions, Donald Curry and Carlos Santos, won by Curry when Carlos Padilla disqualified Santos for 'repeated head-butts' in the fifth round. The network also carried a one-hour *Sports Saturday* special dedicated to Hagler–Leonard, with John Madden and Gil Clancy analysing Monday night's match-up.

Although CBS had no direct involvement with the Hagler–Leonard telecast, its usual boxing broadcast team of Tim Ryan and Gil Clancy would man the microphones for the live closed-circuit telecast. HBO had paid $3 million for 'up to three' replays, while ABC, which had purchased the rights to the *delayed*-delayed broadcast, would also have a crew at ringside.

■ ■ ■

The heightened security measures surrounding Hagler's preparation directly precipitated the goofy episode that would be recalled in Boston newspaper lore as 'Cameragate'.

My newspaper, the *Boston Herald*, had dispatched three sportswriters and two photographers to the Super Fight. The first shutterbug, Rick Sennott, arrived just in time to learn that Hagler's gym workouts would be off-limits. Since I was nominally the team leader and perceived as being the closest to the champion's camp, I was asked to intercede with the Petronellis to get Sennott into the gym, but Pat and Goody, fearing that it would open the doors for a host of similar demands, refused the request.

Back in Boston, the desk wouldn't take no for an answer.

'I don't care how you do it,' I was told. 'Just *do* it.'

Thus was born Plan B. Although outsiders had been barred from the workouts, I knew Angie Carlino, who had been with Hagler since his amateur days, would be in the gym. Angie and I approached Goody Petronelli with a proposal: what if Carlino borrowed Sennott's camera and took a few shots of Hagler in training?

'Well,' said Goody, 'I guess if Angie did it, it would be OK.'

That night Carlino shot a roll of film with the *Herald* lensman's Nikon, which he then slipped through the door to Sennott, who was waiting outside.

Not content with this modest victory, the desk back home trumpeted the pictures in the next morning's edition with a banner headline proclaiming them '*Exclusive Herald Photos*'.

The arch-rival *Boston Globe* and Hagler's home-town Brockton *Enterprise*, outraged at having been scooped, protested to the Hagler camp.

Then, at Hagler's final shakeout on Saturday night, someone at Tocco's detected a clicking sound and, upon investigating, discovered two cameras secretly mounted above the ring.

The Petronellis' immediate assumption was that the cameras were part of an espionage mission orchestrated by Leonard's camp. The cameras were confiscated and the film immediately destroyed.

Leonard's people insisted that they had had nothing to do with the cloak-and-dagger operation. 'You sure Allen Funt didn't put those cameras in there?' laughed J.D. Brown.

As it turned out, the Leonard camp's hands were indeed clean. The cameras had been installed by a *Boston Globe* photographer, Jimmy Wilson, in an apparent attempt to even the score for the *Herald* 'exclusive'.

Even as a tearful Wilson pleaded for the return of his cameras, *Globe* sports editor Vince Doria (whom I somewhat gleefully described as 'the Oliver North of the episode') acknowledged his role as the choreographer of the bungled subterfuge.

'It was just an effort to get our cameras into the gym,' confessed Doria. 'Closing the workouts in the first place was ridiculous. If they'd opened it up for ten minutes on Wednesday, we could have gotten all the photos we needed.'

As embarrassing as it was for the *Globe* – Jimmy Wilson eventually got his cameras back – the real victim turned out to be Angie Carlino.

Blaming Hagler's personal photographer for the subsequent developments, Pat Petronelli angrily ordered Caesars official Rich Rose to revoke Carlino's ringside credential. Banished from the champion's entourage, Angie, who had been with Hagler throughout his career, watched his final fight from the stands.

■ ■ ■

A poll in one Las Vegas newspaper found that 60 of 67 journalists covering the fight favoured Hagler. One of them was Leonard's long-time HBO broadcast colleague Larry Merchant, who picked Hagler in nine.

'I wouldn't go onto an operating table if I knew the surgeon hadn't been practising regularly for five years,' said Merchant. 'In any highly skilled profession, it's impossible to maintain the same level of effectiveness when you've been away that long.'

Pat Putnam, who at one point had agreed to collaborate on Leonard's autobiography, agreed with Merchant.

'A man can't train in a tuxedo for five years and expect to beat the middleweight champion of the world,' said Putnam. 'Hagler in three – unless he hurries.'

'Hagler in four or five,' said Budd Schulberg. 'I think he'll be able to force Leonard to fight, and if that happens, he's just too big for him.'

'Every time I look at Leonard,' said the *New York Times*'s Dave Anderson, 'I keep thinking about Kevin Howard.'

Among the dissenters was Tom Cryan, who had flown from Dublin to cover the fight for the *Irish Independent*.

'I can't see Leonard even taking this fight unless he thought he had a good chance of winning it,' said Cryan. 'I can't see either fighter knocking the other out, so I'm saying Leonard by decision.'

Michael Katz, who had moved from the *Times* to the New York *Daily News*, had also picked Leonard. 'In the Hearns fight, I saw that Marvin's legs were no longer there after the first round, and in the Mugabi fight it was clear that his reflexes were fast fading,' said Katz. 'He was taking shots he never would have been subjected to before.'

Katz had already written a piece for one of the London papers, in which he picked Leonard, but, as the fight drew near, the Wolf Man's resolve seemed to be wavering.

'When Larry Merchant heard I was waffling on my original pick, he suggested I write a column for the *Daily News* revealing that I'd changed my mind,' recalled the Wolf Man. 'He said it would be the only thing fight fans talked about in New York – and he was right about that. I looked like a genius in England and a schmuck in my own home town.'

Hagler and Leonard shared three common opponents, and reporters chased down each of them in the days before the Super Fight.

'Sugar Ray,' said Marcos Geraldo, the Mexican middleweight who had gone the distance with both men. 'He's got more class, more boxing ability. He's more refined.

'There won't be a KO because both are very experienced. Sugar Ray doesn't have enough punch to knock out Hagler, but he can win on points. Sugar is smarter and he is going to make Hagler look bad.'

Duran and Hearns were divided in their opinion.

'I fought both and I should know,' said Duran. 'Leonard has no chance.'

Hearns was already on record, picking Leonard. 'The layoff will affect Ray, but I think he'll be able to overcome it,' said the Hit Man. 'I've seen how well he thinks in the ring. He's the better boxer. If he boxes, goes side-to-side and gets that head movement going, he wins; but if Ray's plan is to go toe-to-toe, I think it's a mistake.'

Undoubtedly at the urging of some editor back in Boston, the *Herald* even solicited the opinion of former heavyweight champion Ivan Drago. Dolph Lundgren, citing the conventional wisdom, liked Hagler. 'I don't think Ray will move as much as people think he will,' supposed Lundgren. 'I think Leonard will stand there and try to go toe-to-toe with him, and eventually Hagler will just be too strong.'

■ ■ ■

Both corners had undergone some revision since each man last fought. Dave Jacobs had buried the hatchet and returned to the Leonard camp, and would work the corner with Dundee and Janks Morton.

And while Goldings had displaced Wainwright as Hagler's attorney, Tony Petronelli would take the Barrister's place manning the spit bucket in the champion's corner.

'Back when I was fighting main events, he'd come into the arena with me,' reminisced Petronelli. 'Instead of him working for me, I work for Marv now.'

The younger Petronelli recalled for reporters that week that back in 1978 he had nearly been matched against Leonard in the Boston fight Dickie Ecklund wound up getting. 'He was a hotshot out of the Olympics, and they were fighting him up the east coast,' said Tony. 'He would've beaten me. He was a great fighter, and I was just a good one.'

Both Morton and Jacobs disputed this version of events.

'No way did we ever look at [Petronelli],' said Morton. 'His name was never mentioned.'

'Maybe we *should* have,' added Jacobs. 'Ecklund turned out to be a tough one.'

■ ■ ■

The final press conference at Caesars' Colosseum Room ('a "room" double the size of the *real* Coliseum,' noted Frank Dell'Apa) brought Hagler and Leonard together for the first time since the previous

8 December in San Francisco, just before Hagler jumped ship on the tour for good.

Leonard seemed strangely subdued, responding to most questions with one-word answers. Hagler arrived wearing a legionnaire's *chapeau*, replete with side-flaps, and kept his sunglasses on as he joked his way through the session.

'Is my hair OK?' he asked at one point. And when someone asked what advice his trainers had imparted, Marvin replied, 'They tell me that once I climb through the ropes, I'm on my own.'

When Leonard was asked about his 'toughest fight', he replied, 'Bruce Finch'. (Although he had stopped Finch in three, that was the fight, it turned out, in which he had detached his retina.)

On Sunday, publicist Irving Rudd handed out to the assembled media the menu for the meal Leonard had ordered up for his post-weigh-in repast: chicken smothered in gravy and onions, creamed-style corn, fresh greens on rice, corn bread, iced tea and fruit cocktail.

And what did Hagler plan to eat?

'Leonard,' said Unswerving Irving.

■ ■ ■

A crowd of 3,000 turned out on the morning of the Super Fight to watch Hagler and Leonard weigh in at the Sports Pavilion. Ring announcer Chuck Hull introduced the principals, who never got within ten feet of one another.

To a mixture of cheers and boos, Leonard went first, doffing his sweatsuit top before he weighed in at 158.

Hagler, who had worn a white T-shirt lettered 'CHAMPION' to the ceremony, removed the garment, as well as the hefty gold chain he wore around his neck, before he stepped on the scale.

'Marvin loses five pounds without his Mr T starter kit,' cracked Akbar Muhammad.

Hagler's weight was announced at 158½.

Neither man appeared to acknowledge the other's presence.

For Hagler, whose weight hadn't varied since his amateur days, it was business as usual, but Leonard's heft represented a career high. He was not only 40 pounds bigger than he had been for his first amateur fight, but weighed nearly 20 more pounds than he had when he made his pro debut against Luis Vega a decade earlier.

'All of that weight is natural,' publicist Charlie Brotman pointed out to Frank Dell'Apa. 'No weights. He worked out for a year, hitting the speed bag, really banging the heavy bag, jumping rope, sparring, sit-ups. Look at his legs: I don't know about the other guy, but Ray's legs are really solid.'

'All I know about legs,' Pat Petronelli responded, 'is that you can run faster forward than backward. And our guy is ready to go forward.'

Shielding itself in advance from criticism, the Nevada State Athletic Commission trotted out a retinal specialist, Louis Angioletti, who attested to the soundness of Leonard's eyesight.

'I found him perfectly fit,' said Dr Angioletti. 'Boxers have a greater risk by virtue of their profession, but Ray Leonard has no greater risk than any other boxer on the card, before or after his fight. That's the bottom line.'

Associated Press scribe Fast Eddie Schuyler was moved to note that 'the commission probably told Leonard that if something happened to his eye, he could be a judge'.

At the pre-fight rules meeting, Dundee complained to the commission about the location of Hagler's protective cup.

'He wears his trunks so high because he wears the damn cup up around his ribs,' said Dundee. 'I saw a photo in the *New York Times Magazine* recently where Hagler was posing in a pair of shorts, and it was the first time in my life I'd ever seen Hagler's navel. I was beginning to wonder if he *had* one.'

Richard Steele, who had performed creditably in Hagler–Hearns two years earlier, was named the referee, with no objection from either side.

The original panel of judges was to have comprised Lou Filippo, Dave Moretti and Harry Gibbs, but the Petronellis, still seething over Hagler's treatment in London after the Minter fight seven years earlier, objected to the Englishman's inclusion on the panel.

'*We want a Mexican judge!*' demanded Pat Petronelli.

He got one. Gibbs (who two years earlier had worked Hagler–Hearns without incident) was replaced by Jose Juan (Jo Jo) Guerra.

Gibbs didn't even stay for the fight. He packed his bags and flew home to England, arriving just in time to watch Leonard–Hagler on television.

Although it was voiced by his co-manager, the challenge to Gibbs appears to have had the full support of Hagler himself.

'I have nothing against the English people,' the champion explained, 'but, you know, if you get bad food in a restaurant, you don't want to go back there no more.'

■ ■ ■

The capacity of the outdoor stadium at Caesars was supposed to be 15,236, but the officially announced attendance would be 15,366. Tickets, with a $700 top for ringside, had long been sold out, though 2,000 of the best seats were never offered to the public. The host casino held that many back for its preferred gambling customers.

Hagler–Leonard was such a hot ticket that some of the A-list celebrities had been consigned to the bleachers, but Caesars released a list of guests that included the usual suspects – Jack Nicholson, Gene Hackman, Tom Selleck, Billy Crystal, Bo Derek and David Brenner from the world of entertainment, Muhammad Ali, John McEnroe and Wilt Chamberlain from the world of sport – but a host of others, ranging from Timothy Hutton, Willie Nelson and Joan Collins to Chevy Chase, Tony Danza and the Pointer Sisters.

Action on the bout was so heavy that Lou D'Amico, the sports book manager at Caesars, said, 'No question, Leonard–Hagler couldn't be outdone unless we built a stadium out back and got them to play the Super Bowl here.'

The Aladdin, a hostelry down the street formerly owned by Wayne Newton, reopened just three days before Hagler–Leonard, after having had its gaming licence revoked two years earlier.

'We didn't plan our reopening around the fight,' said Aladdin spokesperson Barbara Shimko. 'But we sure don't mind the windfall.'

By fight time, Hagler remained the favourite, but the odds had been bet down to 5–2.

What was unquestionably the highlight of the undercard came during the first televised bout, between Lupe Aquino and Davey Moore.

At the beginning of the second round, a round-card girl who identified herself to Michael Globetti as Alechia Patch was negotiating her way into the ring between the ropes when she leaned too far forwards and one of her breasts flopped out of her top.

The unintended nudity was greeted by considerably more applause than either Lupino or Moore had received. (When she climbed through the ropes a round later and her boobs *didn't* fall out, she was booed by the crowd.)

'Tell me I'm not embarrassed,' Ms Patch told Globetti. 'It's not the kind of exposure I was looking for. I was climbing through the wires and I looked down and, oops, I was in trouble!'

Arum said he was paying the round-card girls $75 apiece for the night's work, 'but they get to sit in $700 seats'.

There was no indication that Moore was distracted by Alechia Patch's wardrobe malfunction, but the former champion was stopped by Aquino in the fifth. In the principal undercard bout that followed, Roldán bounced back from his loss to Hagler with an impressive ninth-round TKO of James Kinchen.

Two young New England boxers had performed earlier in supporting roles: Brian Powers, a welterweight fighting out of the Petronelli Gym, outpointed Celio Olivar in a four-rounder, while twenty-one-year-old Micky Ward, a junior welterweight from Lowell whom Teddy Brenner was touting as 'the best New England prospect since Hagler', ripped open a gash above Kelly Koble's right eye with a left hook on the way to a fourth-round TKO that raised Ward's record to 13–0.

■ ■ ■

Marvelous Marvin Hagler was probably more confident of victory in the Leonard fight than he had been for any of his previous twelve defences, and nothing that happened over the twelve rounds the two men shared in the ring that night disabused him of that notion. He was, in fact, so dismissive of Leonard's threat that he allowed the fight to slip away from him.

Twenty years later, an incautious man could walk into the wrong Boston saloon and with just two words – '*Leonard won*' – almost guarantee himself an invitation to step outside.

What unfolded that night was not unlike a baseball game between teams operating under diametrically opposite philosophies: one relying on the long ball, the other employing bunts, stolen bases, sacrifice flies and perhaps even the hidden-ball trick. If, at the end of nine innings, the latter has more runs on the scoreboard than the former, it wins.

Leonard understood the rules of the game they were playing that night better than did Hagler.

And Marvin never did hit a home run.

For reasons that have never been entirely clear, Hagler attempted to confuse Leonard by abandoning his southpaw attack to box out of an orthodox stance, and stubbornly clung to that strategy even after its futility had been demonstrated.

Hagler never adequately explained his decision to come out right-handed, but Michael Katz offered an explanation as plausible as anything else we've heard.

'Marvin told me once that he not only wanted to be the best worker on the assembly line at the shoe factory and the best bricklayer at Petronelli Brothers Construction, but that in addition to being the best middleweight in the world as a southpaw, he wanted to be the best from an orthodox stance as well,' recalled the Wolf Man. 'I think he may have been trying to prove that against Ray.'

The result was that the champion lost each of the first four rounds on the scorecards of two judges, as well as on my unofficial tally for the *Boston Herald*.

Calling the fight on the pay-per-view telecast, Gil Clancy prophetically told colleague Tim Ryan 'If [Hagler] loses this fight because he gave away the first two rounds, he won't be able to live with himself.'

In the corner between rounds, Goody Petronelli could be heard directing Hagler to 'rough him up', although at this point Leonard didn't have a mark on him.

In the fourth, Leonard even embarrassed Hagler by winding up and throwing a right-handed bolo punch, although the blow landed waist-high and inflicted no damage.

The fight took a turn in the fifth when Hagler erupted with a display of aggression. Dictating to his desk back in New York over a ringside telephone, the Associated Press scribe Ed Schuyler described the final minute of the round:

'*Hagler got in a left to the head, then a hook to the body. Hagler landed a short left to the face. Hagler got in a good left to the head in Leonard's corner. Hagler got a good right and left to the head with 30 seconds left. They were finding the range. Hagler had Leonard against the ropes. Hagler landed a right at the bell.*'

The intervention of the bell appeared to annoy Hagler. A look of disgust on his face, he gave Leonard a disdainful shove.

In my own hastily composed report of the fight for the following morning's paper, I noted that 'as the bell sounded, ending the round, Leonard woozily eyed Hagler and then stumbled – no, *staggered* – back to his stool'.

In a conversation a few months later, Leonard recapitulated that moment.

'I was definitely in trouble,' he told me. 'I thought I was gone. But then when I passed him on my way back to the corner I looked Marvin in the eye, and I realised at that moment, "He doesn't even *know* I'm hurt! He doesn't know it!" I knew I had him right there.'

The odd aspect of this epiphany was that it came at the conclusion of the first round Leonard had decisively lost. All three judges scored the fifth for Hagler.

'*Any delusions that the corner had been turned were quickly laid to rest in the next round,*' I wrote in the *Herald*. '*As Hagler pressed the attack, Leonard was a veritable will-o'-the-wisp, dancing about as Hagler's mighty blows flew harmlessly all around him, pausing just long enough to land an effective flurry of his own just before the bell.*'

'If I was Leonard,' Clancy suggested in the eighth round, 'I'd load up and try to nail Hagler now. Hagler is getting over-confident – and he's gasping now, too.'

But at this point Leonard wasn't listening to the television analyst. He didn't even seem to be listening to Angelo Dundee.

'Ray is a smart fighter, maybe the smartest,' Dundee would later recall this interlude. 'He's such an intelligent guy that you had to assume in the corner he knew just what he was doing.'

'After Marvin gave away the first six or seven rounds, I knew he was figuring he had to finish strong to win a decision,' explained Leonard.

In the ninth, Hagler once again appeared to have Leonard in a world of trouble, but Ray rallied with a flurry at the end of the round.

The timing of Leonard's flashy eruptions was hardly an accident. In anticipation of the possibility that many rounds might be there for the taking, Ollie Dunlap, manning a stopwatch in the corner, had been directed to alert Leonard when 30 seconds remained in the stanza.

Hagler had won the middle rounds, or won them everywhere save on the scorecard of Jo Jo Guerra, anyway, but he was clearly in for a fight.

Although Hagler seemed to be landing the more telling blows, Leonard was landing more punches, and over the final third of the fight Ray would play the master toreador to Marvin's increasingly enraged bull. It was as if Leonard had an invisible jet-pack on his back, and when he sensed immediate malevolent intentions on Hagler's part, it triggered some psychic button that whooshed him backwards out of harm's way.

'That was the plan,' Sugar Ray would say later, 'to cross his wires, to frustrate him and make him mad. You look back at that fight and you'll see that Marvin rarely threw combinations, except when he had me on the ropes. He hardly ever put two punches together. He was totally out of synch.'

Indeed, as Hagler tried to manoeuvre Leonard to the ropes in an attempt to force the fight inside, Dundee shouted from the corner to Steele, '*Watch that bald-headed sucker's head!*'

In the corner after the tenth, Dundee told Leonard, 'Six minutes to the title! Man, you can do six minutes in your *sleep*, can't you?'

'He's a miracle man, doing what he's doing right now, and he's winning in my opinion,' said Clancy on the telecast, adding that Hagler needed to win each of the last two rounds to win the fight.

In the 11th, Hagler nailed Leonard with a right jab, and followed with a combination. Leonard responded with a flurry of his own, took a step backwards and then lashed out to catch Hagler with a right-hand lead. For the first time all night, he seemed to be getting the better of the infighting, even when he was backed against the ropes.

As the 12th and final round commenced, Dundee dispatched Leonard from his corner with a shout of, 'Three minutes, champ!' As he rose from his stool, Leonard held his gloves above his head in an unmistakable gesture of confidence. Hagler sneered and mocked him by raising his own gloves.

Once again Hagler dutifully stalked his quarry, and once again Leonard avoided any serious engagement. In those final minutes, an expression of scorn etched on his face, Hagler seemed to be talking to Leonard.

'He was,' referee Steele would later confirm.

'But,' added the ordained minister, 'they were words I wouldn't repeat.'

Well into that final stanza, Sugar Ray actually looked to his corner and shouted, '*How much time?*'

'One minute!' Ollie shouted back, and with that Leonard raised his right glove in triumph as he danced away. Hagler, snarling and huffing in pursuit, disdainfully raised his own glove.

At the final bell, Leonard attempted the same celebratory backflip he had enacted in the Superdome ring once he realised Duran had quit. This time he miscalculated and landed flat on his back. He had to be carried back to his corner.

Even as he was being towelled off and awaiting the verdict, Leonard swears that he looked out into the audience and already saw money changing hands.

'What that meant was that in the eyes of some people I'd "won", just because I was still there at the end,' recalled Leonard. 'From the third round on, I'd been looking out in the audience and I could tell from the expression on some guys' faces they were saying, "Shit, he's *still* there!" An amazing number of people didn't think I would be.'

Clancy, on the closed-circuit telecast, described Leonard's as 'the greatest performance I've ever seen by any boxer', and Steele pronounced it 'the greatest fight I've ever been involved in'.

In the moments between the conclusion of the fight and the announcement of the decision, there had been a near-fistfight between two other old rivals. Although Don King had not been involved in the promotion, his allegiance was clear-cut: Hagler was Bob Arum's fighter and Leonard was not, and, sensing the possibility of an upset, King had begun to climb the steps into Leonard's corner to join in the celebration.

Arum, behind him, tried to pull King back down the steps but succeeded only in ripping the pocket of King's expensive sports coat.

The rival promoters squared off but were quickly separated by a Caesars security guard, who restrained King and began to pull him away.

King turned on the peacemaker, calling him 'a lousy black motherfucker', but he never did make it into the ring.

'That man had nothing to do with the fight,' fumed Arum, who got high marks from ringsiders for his display of bravery in the brief set-to, but refused to gloat.

'I'm not going to drop in any way, shape or fashion to that guy's level,' said Arum.

The writers at ringside that night were as divided as the judges turned out to be. Scoring for the Associated Press, Schuyler had Hagler winning 117–112, while I had Leonard narrowly ahead. Since my newspaper used the AP's round-by-round for the press run that hit the streets immediately after the fight, readers who picked up the *Herald* bulldog edition must have been bewildered to read side-by-side accounts of a fight with two different winners.

As they awaited the decision, Hagler appeared concerned that it had come to this. He hadn't wanted to leave it in the hands of the judges. Leonard, on the other hand, seemed positively serene.

'I thought I'd won the fight, but I didn't really care that much one way or the other,' he said. 'I'd proved something to myself. It was exciting. The event itself was exciting, and the anticipation on people's faces right then told me that whatever the judges said, it had lived up to their expectations.'

Filippo scored the fight 115–113, or 7–5 in rounds, for Hagler. Moretti had the same score, but in Leonard's favour. The third judge, Guerra, had it 118–110 for Leonard – a whopping 10–2 margin so utterly at variance with reality that Pat Petronelli would proclaim 'that JoJo Guerra is a disgrace. He ought to be put in jail. Ask Leonard if *he* thought Marvin Hagler only won two rounds.'

Angelo Dundee did not seem to disagree with this assessment. 'Unfortunately,' Leonard's trainer would say the next morning, 'one of the judges wasn't with us last night.'

Ironically, of course, Guerra had been empanelled only because Petronelli had demanded 'a Mexican judge'. Harry Gibbs, who had flown back to England after being dismissed from the tribunal, watched the fight on television and scored it for Hagler.

In mid-ring, Leonard approached a crestfallen Hagler. And as he attempted to embrace the ex-champion, he whispered 'You're the champ' into his ear.

Hagler would claim that Leonard was admitting, 'You won the fight.'

'We're still friends, right?' asked Leonard.

When Marvin didn't respond, Ray repeated the question. 'We're still friends?'

Hagler was still staring off into space.

'It's not fair,' he finally murmured.

Interviewed in the ring, Leonard pronounced it 'a special conflict', adding, 'To me, Marvelous Marvin Hagler is still the middleweight champion of the world. It wasn't his belt I wanted. I just wanted to beat *him*.'

In his dressing-room, Hagler was almost inconsolable.

'I beat him,' murmured Marvin. 'I beat him, and he knows it. I told you about Vegas. They stole it. I stayed aggressive, and I won the fight. He told me himself, "*You beat me.*" I feel in my heart that I'm still the champ.'

Well over an hour elapsed before Hagler and his small entourage vacated the dressing-room and began the long march back to the hotel. The crowd had long since dispersed to the gaming tables, and elsewhere on the grounds a Leonard victory party was already underway.

The arena was deserted but for the clean-up crew. In the parking lot outside, a beer truck was loading up the remaining inventory from the concession stands. As Hagler passed by, he called to one of the workers, 'Hey, man, how about a six-pack?'

The fellow loading the truck didn't even hesitate.

'You're the champ, Marvin,' he said, and handed over two cases of Budweiser for Hagler to take back to his suite.

Six years, six months and ten days after it had begun on a rainy night in London, Marvin Hagler's championship reign had come to an end.

■ ■ ■

The decision was immediately controversial. Two decades later, the debate has scarcely abated.

After filing our post-fight stories, a dozen scribes reconvened in the bar at the Flame Steakhouse late that night, and a lively discourse ensued.

The argument continued in the pages of several national magazines, and a few years later the editors of a British boxing anthology entitled *Come Out Writing* twinned divergent views (mine from *Boxing Illustrated*, Hugh McIlvanney's from *Sports Illustrated*) in sort of a point/counterpoint debate entitled 'The Rumble of Dissent':

'Clearly, there is room for philosophical argument on both sides: Leonard's punches never did any real damage, other than to pile up points, while Hagler's were clearly more lethal – when they managed to connect,' I wrote. 'In terms of "clean punches", the fight was no better than a wash. "Aggression?" Hagler was obviously the aggressor for most of the night, but the operative word in this category is supposed to be effective aggression. And it seemed to me that Leonard's mastery of another category of supposedly equal importance, "defence", was at least sufficient to offset any supposed edge Hagler might have built up here.

'With the first three categories more or less a push, then it seemed, and still seems, to me that in the fourth – "ring generalship" – there was a clear-cut dominance on the part of Leonard. It was Leonard who dictated the terms under which this battle was waged. It was Ray who was able to lead Marvin around by the nose, forcing him to fight Leonard's fight rather than his own. Leonard did what he wanted to do and denied Hagler what he wanted to do for the better part of the evening.'

The Boxing Bard of Scotland was passionate in his response to the judges' verdict. 'Ray Leonard's real accomplishment lay in pulling off an epic countertrick, one that was a testament to the mischievous richness of his intelligence and the flawlessness of his nerve. The natural priority of most fighters is to seek to dominate their opponents, but, throughout the thirty-six minutes of this match, Leonard was far less concerned with impressing Hagler than with manipulating the minds of the judges,' wrote McIlvanney.

'His plan was to catch their attention with isolated but carefully timed flurries of flashy punches, relying on these superficially dramatic though rarely telling flourishes to blur the officials' appreciation of how much time he was spending in retreat (and, occasionally, headlong flight) from the relentlessly chasing Hagler.'

Even Hagler's corner seemed to have retrospective misgivings.

'Marvin should have come out stronger,' conceded Pat Petronelli. 'That was a mistake. But the fight should have been 15 rounds. Leonard was out on his feet at the end, exhausted. A championship fight should be 15 rounds, but Leonard's people wouldn't do it.'

'I beat him and you know it,' moaned Hagler. 'How can they take the title from the champion on a split decision when the other guy won't fight?

'*A split decision*,' he insisted, '*should go to the champion.*'

■ ■ ■

The morning after the fight Leonard was having breakfast in the Café Roma at Caesars when he was joined by John Madden.

'Madden was a big fight fan,' said Leonard. 'He'd been at the gym the day Quincy Taylor put me on Queer Street, and he didn't think there was any way I could win. That morning he sat down across the table from me and just stared, as if he couldn't believe what he was looking at. He looked at me for about five minutes and never said a word. Then he got up and walked away.'

'My heart really went out to Marvin,' said Leonard. 'I honestly wish there was some way I could have beaten him and then said, "Here's your belt." That title meant the world to Marvin. It was his identification, and he'd finally been getting the recognition he thought he should have. Marvin's stock rose while I was retired. He'd started doing commercials. Where was he going to go now?'

'I'm going to discourage him from fighting again,' said Pat Petronelli. 'He doesn't need it.'

In Hagler's mind, a rematch would have been a logical conclusion to the conspiracy theory. 'I believe the boxing world wants me back,' he said, 'and the only way they could keep me here was with a rematch.'

Under the circumstances, Arum was reluctant to push Hagler towards a hasty decision. 'I don't know how things will work out, but it's a fight I'd like to see again,' allowed the promoter.

In the days following the fight, Leonard was not among those pressing for a rematch. On Monday night, he had hinted at one direction in which he might go when he said, with a nod to Hearns's newly acquired light-heavyweight title, 'I'll see you six months and fifteen pounds heavier from now.'

■ ■ ■

Ten days after the Super Fight, sportscaster John Dennis of Boston's WNAC-TV reported that the Nevada State Athletic Commission was investigating a report that an unidentified gambler who had bet a large sum of money on Leonard had improperly influenced one of the judges to swing the fight to the challenger.

I subsequently recapitulated the episode in the pages of *Boxing Illustrated*:

> As it turned out, an investigation was not under way, but following the widespread circulation of John Dennis's story, Nevada officials were forced to initiate one. In order to avoid potential conflict-of-interest charges, Nevada commissioner Duane Ford turned the matter over to a special investigator representing the state attorney general's department.
>
> It did not require the services of Sherlock Holmes to discern that the gambler in question was sometime fight manager Billy Baxter and that the judge whose ethics had been called into question was not Guerra but Moretti. After an investigation lasting several months, both men were completely exonerated.

The appearance of impropriety stemmed from the fact that Baxter and Moretti had discussed going into business together in a planned gymnasium in Las Vegas. Although it was never conclusively determined who had leaked the 'fix' story to Dennis, Leonard's people suspected that it had been someone in the Hagler camp, or perhaps even Arum himself.

The episode did not exactly smooth the way for a rematch.

'What gets me,' Mike Trainer told me at the time, 'is that Ray never uttered a peep after he lost the first fight to Duran – one that in our minds was equally disputable. All this bellyaching, all this complaining, all these excuses; it's made Ray very disappointed in Marvin. He hasn't been a very good sport about the whole thing.'

The combatants would continue to exchange recriminations in the weeks following the fight.

'He called me a sissy,' complained Leonard, irate that Hagler did not respect him.

'He fought like a girl,' muttered Hagler.

Months later Hagler was back in Vegas, doing the colour commentary for a middleweight fight between Sumbu Kalambay and Iran Barkley. Afterwards he partied at a nightclub called Botany's, where he had a chance encounter with Leonard in the men's room.

'Some fight, huh?' said Leonard, attempting to make small talk.

He got only an icy stare in return. As Hagler walked away, it was clear that there would be no rematch.

Ollie Dunlap suggested that had Hagler simply emerged from the Super Fight saying, '*Well, I thought I won, but I guess the judges saw it differently. Let's do it again,*' Ray might have said 'sure'.

'As it was,' said Dunlap, 'everything Hagler and his people did over the next several months only soured Ray on the idea of fighting again – or at least fighting Marvin again. But this whole sour-grapes attitude they've had since the moment they stepped out of the ring is not going to have its desired effect, I can tell you that. If they really wanted to fight Ray again, the last thing they should have been doing was running around telling people they got robbed and that the fight was fixed and all that bullshit.'

Leonard convened another press conference, this time in Washington, to announce that he was relinquishing the WBC middleweight championship and that – for the fourth time, if you include his post-Olympic announcement – he was retiring from the ring.

'Why should we believe you *this* time?' he was asked. 'You're retired now, but will you *ever* fight again?'

'No,' Ray replied, but then broke into a grin. 'But you guys know me . . .'

Even in retirement, though, Leonard left the door open for a possible Hagler fight. That autumn, he told a Washington television interviewer, 'If Marvin wants to fight me, he has to come to me and talk about it first.'

A few weeks later Leonard appeared on the *Oprah Winfrey Show* in Chicago, where he told the hostess, 'Hagler never gave me credit. I beat him fair and square. He made allegations that some of the officials in Nevada were corrupt and what have you. I think it's unprofessional, and I want to beat him up.'

Hagler refused to rise to the bait.

'Let Leonard go get another belt first,' he said. 'If he really wanted to fight again, why did he give up the title?'

'All Marvin has to do is call me up,' said Ray.

'If I ever do call him,' grumbled Hagler, 'it'll be collect.'

'A myth has grown up that Hagler wanted a rematch and I wouldn't give it to him,' Leonard reflected years later. 'That's bullshit. I knew the value of a rematch and, having beaten him once, I felt I'd beat him even easier the second time.

'But as you know, Marvin is stubborn. When he says no, he means no, and he won't change his mind no matter what.'

■ ■ ■

In the aftermath of the Leonard fight, Hagler decided to take a long family vacation. He bought a van that would accommodate the entire brood and asked Angie Carlino to come along as his driver.

'Marvin and Bertha had been having trouble even before the Leonard fight,' said Carlino. 'Part of the reason for the trip was that he was hoping to patch things up with her. We spent nearly two months driving across the country and back – me, him, Bertha and the kids – from New England out to the west coast and then back again.

'He was trying to be as incognito as a guy as recognisable as him could be, just trying to get away from everything. Bob Arum kept trying to contact him. It was no secret that Arum wanted him to fight again,' recalled Carlino. 'On the last part of the trip we were driving through Canada, and in Montreal a reporter asked him about fighting Davey Hilton up there. Marvin said, "I don't know if I'm ever going to fight again," and he sounded like he meant it.

'From Montreal, we drove down to New Hampshire. I dropped Marvin at his place there and drove Bertha and the kids back to Hanover. A few weeks after we got back from the trip, Bertha filed for divorce.'

Bertha Hagler's divorce petition was filed in Hingham District Court on 30 June 1987. Shortly thereafter she retained the services of a noted Los Angeles celebrity attorney, thereby cementing yet another bond among three of the Four Kings. Between divorce and custody proceedings, Hagler, Leonard and Hearns shared another common opponent besides Roberto Duran: across a negotiating table, the three of them all went eyeball to eyeball with Marvin Mitchelson.

Hagler eventually packed up his bags, moved to Europe, and never fought again.

9

THE WAR

Leonard–Hearns II
Caesars Palace, 12 June 1989

IN A PREDICTABLE AFTERMATH of the Leonard–Hagler fight, the middleweight title was shortly fragmented almost beyond recognition. For nearly seven years Hagler had reigned as the undisputed champion, but in a few short weeks that October, three new champions were created.

On 10 October at Caesars Palace, American Frank Tate outpointed Canadian Michael Olajide for the IBF title. On 23 October in Livorno, Sumbu Kalambay, an Italian-based middleweight from Zaire, won a decision over New Yorker Iran Barkley to claim the WBA version. And, less than a week later, at the Las Vegas Hilton, Thomas Hearns became the third member of the triumvirate when he knocked out Juan Domingo Roldán to win the WBC championship vacated by Leonard.

It was Hearns's fourth world title, but his reign would be short-lived. In his first defence he was matched against Barkley the following June. By the end of two rounds, the Blade was bleeding badly and Hearns looked to be on his way to an easy night.

Then in the third he walked right into a stunning right hand. It may have been the best punch Barkley ever threw.

Once again Hearns's chin proved his undoing. Only by force of will did he rise from the knockdown, but he was floundering around the ring, and when Barkley decked him again, Richard Steele wisely stopped it at 2:39 of the round. The fight would be voted *The Ring* magazine's Upset of the Year.

The reigns of the new crop of 160-pound champions were uniformly brief: Kalambay lost the WBA title the night he fought Mike McCallum in his first defence, and Tate lost his IBF belt to Michael Nunn in his second.

Barkley, having scored one monumental upset over Hearns, himself became the victim of one in his first defence. On 24 February 1989, in what would be acclaimed as *The Ring*'s Fight of the Year, Barkley was floored in the 11th round and lost his title on a split decision – to a 37-year-old Roberto Duran.

Another title became available with the establishment of the World Boxing Organisation, a spin-off sanctioning body established by a breakaway WBA faction headed up by Puerto Rican attorney Francisco Valcarcel. In the new body's first-ever middleweight title fight, Doug DeWitt won a split decision over Robbie Sims to become the WBO champion. (DeWitt would lose it a year later to Nigel Benn.)

'Hagler came back to the states and went to Atlantic City for his brother's fight,' said J.D. Brown. 'It was the first time I'd seen him since *Sports Illustrated* ran that story about me spying on him in Palm Springs. Marvin looked like he wanted to choke me.'

▪ ▪ ▪

The original agreement between Sugar Ray Leonard, Inc. and Angelo Dundee had long expired. The maestro had returned to work the Howard and Hagler fights on the assumption that it would be under terms similar to his original arrangement. Angelo appears to have been satisfied with the pay cheque he received from the Howard fight, but was plainly insulted by the $150,000 he was paid after the Hagler blockbuster.

Cable television and the emerging pay-per-view industry had dramatically altered the boxing landscape in the decade since Dundee had first worked with Leonard. On one hand, Angelo was realistic enough to recognise that it would be ridiculous for a trainer to expect 15 per cent – or even 10 per cent – of the profligate purses now being tossed around. On the other hand, 1 per cent seemed humiliating.

When an entreaty from his lawyer to Mike Trainer elicited no response, Dundee decided to move on.

Contrary to widespread assumption, Dundee never resigned. When Leonard decided to end retirement number four by coming back to fight Donny Lalonde in 1988, Dundee was one of the first members of the old team to whom he reached out.

'I had my lawyer send Mike Trainer a letter saying that I wanted a contract,' said Dundee. 'This time I wanted to know exactly how much I was being paid.

'We never got a response.'

When Leonard went into training for the Lalonde fight, Janks Morton had been promoted to chief second. Angelo would never work with Ray again.

Although Leonard himself must have signed off on the decision, to this day Angelo Dundee blames Trainer for the rift.

■ ■ ■

Donny Lalonde was an unlikely boxer. Uncommonly handsome, he had worked as a model and actor, and in his spare time composed thoughtful poetry. Canadian by birth, he had come under the aegis of Dave Wolf, the former sportswriter who had turned Boom-Boom Mancini into a household name. Wolf had repackaged Lalonde as the 'Golden Boy' (years before the world had heard of Oscar De La Hoya) and turned him into a marquee prizefighter.

In 1987, Lalonde had won the vacant WBC light-heavyweight title with a second-round TKO of Eddie Davis in Trinidad and Tobago. The following spring he successfully defended it, stopping former WBA champion Leslie Stewart, a Trinidad native, in Port of Spain.

As a result of negotiations for the Lalonde fight, Leonard once again emerged with a decided advantage. The WBC had recently joined the other sanctioning bodies in establishing a 168-pound super-middleweight division. Leonard and Trainer managed to persuade Wolf and Lalonde that history was there to be made were the fight the first ever to be simultaneously contested for world titles in two divisions.

The WBC happily sanctioned Lalonde–Leonard as its inaugural

super-middleweight title fight. Although the Golden Boy's light-heavyweight title would also be on the line at Caesars Palace, Lalonde's agreement to fight at 168 pounds was a significant concession by the naturally bigger man.

The Lalonde–Leonard fight on 7 November 1988 was preceded by a junior welterweight title bout between Roger Mayweather and Vinny Pazienza. Mayweather, the champion, won rather easily, but the final bell precipitated a wild melee. An enraged Pazienza pushed past referee Mills Lane and continued to swing away, and both corners spilled into the ring to join the fracas.

By the time security could restore order, Pazienza's 66-year-old trainer, Lou Duva, was bleeding profusely from a cut on his forehead. He was lifted off the floor, and a stretcher was summoned. I was no more than 20 feet away, but the confusion of bodies had rendered it impossible to see what had happened. Someone suggested that it had been a punch from Mayweather that decked Duva.

When Lane descended the ring steps, I raced over to enquire: 'Mills, did Mayweather actually hit Lou?'

'Yeah,' drawled the referee. 'But it was the 12th round. He didn't have much left.'

■ ■ ■

In the early going of Leonard's fight against Lalonde it appeared that Sugar Ray had bitten off more than he could chew. Donny Lalonde might not have ranked among the pantheon of great or even good light-heavyweights, but he was a light-heavyweight nonetheless, while Leonard had strayed 21 pounds above what had been his optimal fighting weight.

When Lalonde floored Leonard with a short right in the fourth, it was looking like *déjà vu* – in this case, Kevin Howard – all over again. Although Leonard bounced up and took Richard Steele's eight-count, by the time the round was over, Ray was bleeding from a cut to his nose.

But Leonard recovered and got back into the fight, and after eight rounds he led on two scorecards, while the third still had Lalonde in front. In the ninth, Lalonde appeared to have badly staggered Leonard, but Ray responded with a left hook that finished off the Canadian.

Sugar Ray had won his fourth and fifth world titles on the same night. As when he won the junior middleweight championship from Ayub Kalule and the middleweight title from Hagler, Leonard would abdicate the light-heavyweight title without ever defending it.

The super-middleweight title, on the other hand, he hung onto. It would become an important bargaining chip in the next phase of his plan.

■ ■ ■

Hoping to beat Leonard to the punch as the first man to win world titles in five different divisions, Hearns had scheduled a fight against Fulgencio Obelmejias, Hagler's old Venezuelan foe, who now owned the WBA super-middleweight title. They were to face off at the Las Vegas Hilton on 4 November – three nights before Leonard–Lalonde.

A few weeks before the bout, Obelmejias suffered a rib injury in training and withdrew from the bout. James Kinchen, a respectable pug from San Diego with a 45–4–2 record, replaced Obelmejias as Hearns's opponent, and the newly created World Boxing Organisation agreed to recognise the Hearns–Kinchen winner as *its* first 168-pound champion.

The WBO had yet to establish much credibility in the boxing world, but Bob Arum noted, not unreasonably, that to dismiss the WBO as 'a joke' suggested that the other organisations were not.

Although Hearns built up an early lead, in the fourth round Kinchen followed a big right hand with a left hook that put Tommy on the floor. He got up woozily, barely able to stand.

Hearns's inability, or unwillingness, to clinch had cost him the first Leonard fight, but in the intervening years he had apparently learned his lesson well. He got through the round only by seizing Kinchen in what I described as a 'Motown Death Grip'.

'I was holding him like he was my woman,' Tommy confessed afterwards.

Mills Lane, who had to keep prying Hearns loose from Kinchen, was not as amused – particularly when he was nearly throttled by the same stranglehold Hearns was applying to Kinchen. After numerous warnings, the referee took a point from Hearns ('The best point he ever spent,' noted Tommy's hometown scribe, Mike O'Hara) and appeared to be within an eyelash of disqualifying him altogether.

Hearns, in any case, survived the round and, ultimately, the fight. Although the verdict came in the form of a narrow majority decision (Bill Graham and Cindy Bartin scored it for Hearns 115–112 and 114–112, while Larry Rozadilla had it even at 114–114), the Hit Man prevailed.

The victory set the stage for a long-awaited rematch with Leonard the following June. The first time they had met, each owned a share of the welterweight championship. This time it would also be a unification bout, with both the WBC and WBO super-middleweight titles on the line.

■ ■ ■

Leonard prepared for Hearns II in Palm Beach – less than an hour's drive north of Dundee's home in Pembroke Pines.

Ray was working with his third trainer in as many fights. Following Dundee's acrimonious departure after the Hagler fight, Janks Morton had walked away after the Lalonde bout.

Morton had moved to Phoenix, where he occupied himself with other boxers – among them former heavyweight champion Greg Page and Canadian heavyweight contender Donovan (Razor) Ruddock – during Leonard's several retirements.

For public consumption, he had departed for reasons similar to those voiced by Jacobs seven years earlier. Off what he'd seen in the Lalonde fight, he, too, had urged Ray to retire, and declined to countenance his further participation in the ring.

There was a lingering suspicion that, like the Dundee situation before, this was a rift that probably could have been resolved by money. Those closest to Ray suggested that Morton had erred in attempting to haggle with Trainer over his proposed fee, rather than taking his case directly to the boxer himself.

'But Janks had another problem,' a Leonard associate confided. 'He'd known Ray since he was a little boy, and he still tended to talk down to him. Ray doesn't like that.'

Now, to supplant Jacobs in the corner, Ray turned to a man he'd known as long as any of them – Pepe Correa, the man who'd helped

Jacobs start the boxing programme back in Palmer Park 18 years earlier.

When Correa left Palmer Park ('for personal reasons', he says), he established an inner-city boxing club called The Latin Connection at 14th and Columbia in Washington. Among his pupils there had been Simon Brown and Maurice Blocker, both of whom would become world champions. Outside the District of Columbia, few boxing people even knew Correa's name before he joined the Leonard camp, and he didn't make many new converts once he had the spotlight. Not only was he replacing Angelo Dundee, a revered figure in boxing circles, but he was telling anyone who would listen that it was no great loss, because 'I'm a better trainer than he is, anyway.'

Leonard was still in Palm Beach when he publicly confirmed for the first time that he and his wife had separated.

The couple had actually split nearly a year earlier, but, with Leonard in camp, Trainer learned that the media was looking into the story of the marital break-up. 'I sat down with Ray and told him, "You probably ought to announce it yourself. It's the only way you're going to keep the *Washington Post* out of your bushes,"' said Trainer.

Charlie Brotman was instructed to issue a statement. When the item broke into print several days later, it was buried in a two-part *Post* series on Leonard, and merely mentioned in passing that the couple had separated 'some time earlier'.

Juanita and their two sons had actually visited Leonard in Palm Beach and planned to fly to Vegas to attend the Hearns fight together.

'It was a mutual decision, and it's been a very amicable arrangement,' said Trainer, who had handled his share of divorce cases over the years. 'If all separations were like this, I'd be broke.'

■ ■ ■

For nearly two months Leonard and Hearns periodically interrupted their training to appear at Arum-arranged press conferences around the country. Although their rematch had been christened 'The War', one of Arum's public relations geniuses had suggested that the two gladiators cast themselves as spokesmen addressing world issues.

In Chicago, Leonard and Hearns announced that they were

declaring 'War on Crime on Public Transportation'. In Los Angeles (where Arum presumably wasn't counting on many pay-per-view buys from either the Crips or the Bloods), the theme became 'War on Gangs'. In Hearns's home town, the subject was one nearer and dearer to many Detroiters' hearts – 'War on Imports'.

'I understand Tommy's been working a lot on a bicycle,' teased Leonard at one of the press stops. 'But the thing about it is, people don't punch you while you're riding a bicycle going backwards. Sooner or later his legs are going to say, "I don't know about you, but I'm *tired*" – and when those legs give out, the fight is *over*.'

When Leonard described Hearns as 'a shot fighter', Tommy responded: '*You* more shot than *I* am.'

According to Trainer, 'the biggest mistake Hearns made was agreeing to play cards with Ray on the press tour. Ray suckered him in, and before Tommy knew what had hit him, he'd lost $2,000 playing "in-between" on the Caesars plane.'

Leonard had been guaranteed $14 million, Hearns $11 million, but Arum was predicting that closed-circuit and pay-per-view revenues might gross between $60 and $80 million, 'which', noted Pat Putnam, 'would send the boxers' purses soaring to national-debt levels'.

Moreover, although the fight was for a 168-pound title, the bout agreement called for both contestants to weigh 164, with financial penalties should either exceed that.

In what was probably a calculated approach, both boxers tended to downplay comparisons between The War and their earlier meeting.

'I don't punch that hard any more,' admitted the 33-year-old Leonard.

'I don't remember shit about the first fight,' said Hearns. 'I've had a lot of fights since then [sixteen in all; Leonard, remarkably, had engaged in just four]. You shouldn't even *think* about that fight in '81. It was a long time ago.'

Asked why the return bout had been so long in the making, Hearns replied, 'I think he was waiting around for me to slide. And after viewing my last couple of fights, he thinks it's time.'

But in a more pensive moment, Hearns admitted that he was still haunted by the first fight.

'Eight years of pain, with a little monster following me around,' he described it. 'This whole thing is about payback. [Leonard] knows how bad I want him.'

■ ■ ■

Four days before The War, at the final pre-fight press conference at Caesars, the Hearns camp dropped a bombshell by invoking the 'S' word. Leonard's upper body appeared conspicuously more bulked-up than it had been for the Lalonde fight the previous autumn, and Tommy, for one, suggested that he might have had some help.

'I've been working on my legs, but you been working on your body,' Hearns told Sugar Ray. 'I think you want to be a bodybuilder. The way you pumped up, you look like you been taking *steroids* or something!'

Nervous titters of laughter greeted the Hit Man's taunting, but when Emanuel Steward repeated the charge it was no longer a joking matter.

'I'm seriously considering asking them to test both boxers for steroids,' said Steward. 'I've been hearing rumours for some time. A source told me Leonard had been using steroids.'

The steroid question became the burning issue for the day. Reporters flocked to Dr Elias Ghanem, the chairman of the Nevada State Athletic Commission, and to NSAC executive director Chuck Minker. 'It's not part of our testing procedure, and I see no reason to test for it at this time,' said Ghanem, but Minker appeared to take it more seriously, allowing that testing 'might be considered' if either camp requested it at the following day's rules meeting.

'I haven't especially been working on my body,' said Leonard. 'I'm 33 years old, and that's what happens when you're 33.'

Although Leonard laughed off the accusation, Mike Trainer was outraged.

'What Hearns said and what he did was, well, good theatre. It's actually flattering that Ray looks that good, and I'm just glad Tommy noticed,' said the lawyer.

'But that's a cheap shot coming from Emanuel. I'll tell you what we'll do: we'll each put up $100,000, and they can test Ray before the fight, after the fight and they can take a break after the sixth round and test him then, too. We'll see how good his "sources" are.'

Trainer added that he wouldn't even ask Hearns to take a test. 'Tommy,' he said, 'doesn't look like *he*'s been taking steroids.'

When Leonard was asked if he had any objection to the inclusion of steroid testing in the pre-fight exam, he replied, 'Not at all.'

'How do you do it, anyway?' he asked.

A urinalysis, somebody guessed.

'In that case,' said Ray, 'can I do it right now?'

■ ■ ■

Hearns had engaged James Kinchen, his most recent opponent, to spar with him in Las Vegas.

This time nobody even bothered with trying to put a disguise on J.D. Brown; the espionage was conducted right out in the open. One afternoon, Roger Leonard had walked right into the Sports Pavilion and taken a seat in the audience assembled there for Hearns's public workout. Ray's brother subsequently delivered a blow-by-blow assessment of the engagement.

'Incidentally, that was no low blow,' Leonard twitted Hearns about an incident Roger had seen in the sparring session. 'In fact, I'm gonna throw the same damn punch.'

Kinchen was due in Atlantic City, where he was fighting Stacy McSwain two nights later, but Steward offered manager Wes Wambold an extra $2,500 if he would stick around for one more sparring session. Kinchen went three rounds with Hearns on Wednesday and flew to Atlantic City on the morning of 8 June. He stopped McSwain in five that night.

■ ■ ■

After losing to Leonard, Donny Lalonde – a poet, vegetarian, actor, and sometime Bob Dylan consort – had announced his retirement from the ring on the grounds that he could no longer reconcile causing deliberate pain with the rest of his philosophical outlook.

Lalonde had arrived at this epiphany in mid-ring during a New York sparring session with Hector Rosario.

'There was just this tremendous sense of guilt about hurting another human being,' he recalled in Vegas that week. 'And this was a *sparring partner*. The thought stayed with me from that day on, and the more I thought about it, the more I realised it was not a good thing to be in a boxing ring in that frame of mind.'

Lalonde voiced his opinion that instead of fighting each other, Leonard and Hearns should join him in retirement.

'Personally, I think it's quite unfortunate,' said the Canadian, who had earned $5 million for being knocked out by Leonard the previous November. 'I suppose the biggest question I have deals with motivation: *Why* are they fighting again? I mean, between them, they must have made well over $100 million, so if it's about money, you're talking about extreme greed.

'And if it's *ego*, my God, with all these two have accomplished, if they don't feel good about themselves by *now* . . .'

Steward seemed to admit that Lalonde had a point.

'If Tommy was fighting anybody but the senior-circuit guys, I'd hate to see him fight again at all,' said Steward, who promised, 'He will not fight any of the younger fighters, period.

'There aren't that many of the old fellows left, anyway,' added Steward. 'Duran, Hagler – I still say he's going to come back – and maybe another rematch with Ray if this is a really great fight. But Tommy can't get himself motivated to fight these younger guys, and the rewards for fighting a guy like Barkley or Nunn just don't measure up to the risks involved.

'What's Tommy got to gain compared to what he's got to lose? He can't get up for these guys, and if he beats a Michael Nunn, people will just say, "So what?"'

Hearns was asked whether he might walk away from the sport if he avenged his loss to Leonard.

'Naw,' he replied. 'I would like to have a rematch with Marvin Hagler. But Barkley doesn't really mean as much to me.'

■ ■ ■

Bob Arum had brazenly predicted an unprecedented viewing audience of one billion, but by Thursday he was beginning to waver. His fanciful projection had apparently included an unspecified number of viewers in China, but five days after the tanks rolled into Tiananmen Square, the state-controlled television stations in that nation did not seem to be running many Leonard–Hearns promos.

'You can't trust those Orientals,' said Arum. 'They'll do anything to upstage you.'

Most of his audience groaned. Arum's Japanese-American wife, Sybil, rolled her eyes in embarrassment.

'I'm a promoter, and it's my business to hype fights,' Arum said that day. 'But this is worth considering: when they met in Manila, Muhammad Ali was nine months older than Ray Leonard will be Monday night. Joe Frazier was a year older than Tommy Hearns, and had lost two of his last three fights. But on 1 October in 1975, I saw the greatest fight I've ever seen in my life!'

By 1989, Arum was virtually at war with NBC in general, and with Dr Ferdie Pacheco in particular. The network was backing away from its commitment to boxing, and the Fight Doctor, who had approval on the matches NBC did buy, had been shunning Top Rank's fights.

After Arum charged that Pacheco knew 'next to nothing about boxing', the Fight Doctor responded by describing the Leonard–Hearns match-up as 'a battle of two sinking battleships'.

■ ■ ■

Although the 15,000-capacity stadium guaranteed that the audience would only be 60 per cent of that for the 1981 Leonard–Hearns fight, tickets were the hottest commodity in the country.

Six days before the fight, authorities in Detroit arrested a man they described as 'a very high-level drug dealer' and found him to be in possession of a pair of $800 ringside tickets.

Noting that 'our office is obligated by law to preserve the value of the property seized during the pendency of the action', and recognising that the ducats would be worthless after Monday night, Wayne County Prosecuting Attorney Marshall Goldberg contacted Arum for advice on how to proceed.

'Send them back,' Arum told him. 'I'll sell them again.'

■ ■ ■

Hearns shook out at the Sports Pavilion on Saturday, and despite shadow-boxing six rounds in 100-degree heat appeared to be bone dry.

'When you're not sweating like that, it means you haven't been taking liquids,' noted Evander Holyfield. 'That usually means you've got a weight problem.'

It seemed unlikely that Hearns would have difficulty making 168, but every ounce over 164 would reduce his purse.

A month earlier, Eddie Futch had broken his leg in an automobile accident. His top assistant, Freddie Roach, had taken charge of Futch's stable of boxers while he recuperated. The 77-year-old trainer was at Caesars for Hearns's final shakeout and reflected on Monday night's fight.

'I like Leonard, of course,' said Futch. 'Hearns has had just too many tough fights later, with Roldán, Barkley and Kinchen, and his legs are showing the wear and tear from them. His chin, which never was great, figures to get him in trouble.

'But Hearns can still punch,' added Futch. 'He'll be dangerous for three or four rounds. Leonard can't afford to get hit like he did against Lalonde, but he should win around the eighth or ninth.'

Although no one accused him of being a spy, another of Leonard's Washington neighbours, Georgetown basketball coach John Thompson, dropped by to watch Hearns's final workout. UNLV coach Jerry Tarkanian was also conspicuous by his presence during the week leading up to the fight. Tark the Shark had a minority interest in a couple of Las Vegas-based boxers, Kenyan welterweight Robert Wangila and American bantamweight Kennedy McKinney.

■ ■ ■

There would be four men in each corner on the night of The War. Steward, Prentiss Byrd and Walter Smith had all been there for the first Leonard–Hearns fight. The only new face was that of Ralph Citro, the cut man who had replaced Don Thibodeaux.

In Leonard's revamped corner only Ollie Dunlap remained from the first fight, and Ollie was the first to admit, 'I don't even *understand* boxing. I just yell a lot, and in between rounds I hand up the bucket.'

Correa, who was the chief second, said of being reunited with Leonard, 'I've been in and I've been out. I'm kind of like the Billy Martin of this camp.' (A peripatetic baseball manager, Billy Martin had been hired and fired five times by the New York Yankees. Martin was killed in a car crash later that year.)

Dave Jacobs, of course, had been wearing a Kronk jacket when Leonard and Hearns fought in 1981. Those three would be joined by cut man Eddie Aliano.

Aliano and Citro had each worked over 100 world title fights, but, said Citro, 'Way back when Eddie fought, I was *his* cut man. He was such a lousy fighter I had to teach him to be a cut man too.'

Aliano didn't argue with that, but he pointed out that this was not the first time he and Citro had eyed each other from opposing corners.

'I stopped Hearns with Barkley,' said Eddie.

That having been duly noted, the Hearns brain trust appeared to have a considerable edge in big-fight experience. Pepe Correa had worked a few title fights with IBF welterweight champion Simon Brown, but this would be his first exposure to the international limelight.

■ ■ ■

Arum, visions of a full-fledged Seniors Tour dancing in his head, ensured the presence of Hagler and Duran at the Leonard–Hearns fight by hiring them to work on the English and Spanish closed-circuit telecasts.

Duran was unabashedly rooting for Leonard in the hope of a rubber match of their series. (A rematch with Hearns, on the other hand, did not seem to appeal to Cholo.)

'Leonard has to win so he can fight me. It's 1–1 with me and Sugar,' Duran said through his interpreter, 'so I think Leonard owes me a fight. I want to fight Leonard and nobody else.'

Asked why he was still boxing at his advanced age, Duran cheerfully replied, 'For the money.'

Hagler, who would man a microphone alongside Tim Ryan and Gil Clancy, didn't arrive until Sunday, the day before the fight. Although he was on the promoter's payroll, Hagler didn't sound much like a man trying to sell Leonard–Hearns to the public.

'*War?*' Hagler snarled. 'The war was between me and Tommy. This is not war. This is a chess-and-chequers game.'

'You know,' added Hagler, 'these guys have been watching me

fight for a long time. When I fought Duran, Hearns was watching. Then once I exposed Hearns, he started getting banged around by everybody else. That's the only reason Leonard is taking this fight now.'

Although he said he found it difficult to pick a winner, Hagler, who never lost a rematch, pointed out that 'once you've defeated a fighter before, it not only gives you confidence, but the knowledge of how to do it. The other guy isn't going to be able to do much different.'

Hagler added that 'if Tommy tries to bang Leonard out right away, he's making a big mistake. He was winning their first fight until he got stopped – and this one is only twelve rounds.'

Marvelous Marvin seemed to be enjoying retirement. He had already completed shooting on his first movie.

'My hardest job is staying out of the boxing game,' he said. 'I've got nothing left to prove.'

But 'you never say never', allowed Hagler.

'Who knows?' he managed a laugh. 'If these guys beat each other up bad enough, it might make it easier for me to think about returning.'

■ ■ ■

Arum and the imaginative Caesars Palace publicity crew had distributed souvenir plastic army helmet liners advertising The War. To the best of my knowledge, nobody ever got Leonard or Hearns to wear one, but when I ran into Duran at poolside one afternoon he happily donned a helmet. When Cholo strolled through the casino wearing it later that day, I was moved to note in the *Herald* that he looked 'for all the world like one of General Noriega's enforcers'.

The arrival of the Fight Mob at Caesars for Leonard–Hearns II coincided with a convention of 18,000 Southern Baptists in Las Vegas that week. On the Strip just outside Caesars, flag-waving Baptists were trying to pass out '*Jesus Loves You*' literature to drug dealers from Detroit, while, a few feet away, a rather jaundiced-looking Vegas wino offered pamphlets advertising a local escort service. A taxi driver taking a boxing writer to Tocco's Gym over the weekend reported that his cab company had just ferried two carloads of Baptists out to The Ranch – a legal brothel on the outskirts of town.

The weekend before the Leonard–Hearns rematch, my *Herald* colleague Michael Gee surveyed several local sports books for a story on the gambling aspects of the fight and discovered that Leonard was a 7–5 favourite in some betting parlours, while others gave the slight edge to Hearns. Ray was 2–1 to win by either knockout or decision, Tommy 3–1 by knockout, 5–1 by decision.

Gee discovered more than 32 betting propositions on offer, including a 15–1 price on a Hearns first-round knockout, 10–1 on a Leonard first-round KO. Interestingly, the story, which ran across three columns, did not address the possibility of a draw.

Gee was, however, standing in the sports book at Caesars the next day when he came upon what he described as 'two young men just off the plane from Copenhagen', staring intently at a large television set as a replay of the Leonard–Hagler fight played on the screen.

'Is there still time to get a bet on this fight?' asked one of the Danes.

Gee briefly considered offering a man-to-man wager before informing the visitors that the fight they were watching had been over for a couple of years.

■ ■ ■

Over the course of the week most of the questions surrounding The War revolved around Leonard – his inactivity, the relative inexperience of his corner and the red-herring steroid issue – but on Sunday morning the shocking news from Detroit struck Vegas like a lightning bolt and suddenly made Thomas Hearns the focus of attention.

Less than 48 hours before Hearns was supposed to enter the ring against Leonard, a 19-year-old girl had been shot dead at Tommy's suburban Southfield home. And the boxer's youngest brother had been charged with the murder.

Police described it as 'a boyfriend-girlfriend thing'.

When Tommy departed for Las Vegas, he had left his 22-year-old brother, Henry, in charge of the house. Shortly after midnight on Saturday, at what appeared to have been a party gone awry, an argument broke out between Henry Hearns and his girlfriend, Nancy Barile.

'Mr Hearns ordered the victim into a room she didn't want to go to,' Oakland County Prosecutor Lawrence Kozma would describe the shooting at Henry Hearns's arraignment.

According to Kozma, a witness had heard Henry Hearns threaten, 'I'm going to blow your brains out.'

'The victim's brains were, in fact, blown out,' added the prosecutor.

Although Thomas Hearns was by all accounts a solid citizen – even after becoming a professional boxer he had served as an auxiliary policeman in Detroit – his entourage had always included some unsavoury types.

Shortly before the Iran Barkley fight, Tommy's former girlfriend Kimberly Craig (the mother of his daughter Natasha) had been killed by a shotgun blast while sitting in her car in Detroit.

A year or two earlier, a Kronk hanger-on and sometime Hearns bodyguard named Rick Carter had been wounded in a bungled assassination attempt. When the assailants learned that they hadn't finished the job, they broke into the ward and gunned down 'Maserati Rick' in his hospital bed.

And, of course, there had been the gun-cleaning incident at the Caesars swimming pool before the first Leonard fight.

Back in 1980, just before Hearns was to fight Eddie Gazo in his final tune-up before the title fight with Pipino Cuevas, Tommy's father had died. On that occasion Steward kept the news from Tommy until after the fight, but there would be no shielding him from this tragedy.

'I doubt if something like this could affect Tommy this close to the fight,' said one long-time Detroit friend of the Hit Man. 'But the way it affects his mom *might*. There's nobody in the world he cares more about, and she's taking this pretty hard.'

Hearns resolved that it would be business as usual. Steward and publicist Jackie Kallen arranged for round-the-clock security – not for the boxer's protection, but to shield him from the swarming media. Otherwise Tommy meticulously followed the schedule Steward had already plotted out for him.

Tommy's mother, Lois Hearns, at the boxer's urging, remained with him in Las Vegas. (Another brother, John Hearns, a UNLV student, was dispatched home to represent the family at Henry's arraignment on Monday, the morning of the fight.)

Tommy stayed in his suite watching the Pistons play the Lakers in the NBA Finals that afternoon, and then slipped off to Tocco's for some light shadow-boxing. He didn't return to Caesars that night. He and Steward quietly spent the night in a private residence, just as they had planned to do.

Shortly after word of the shooting reached Vegas, Arum had raced to the press room to assure the media that the show would go on.

The promoter said he had spoken to Hearns during the day and reported that the fighter 'had never even considered' pulling out of the fight.

'He said, "I've waited eight years to knock out Sugar Ray Leonard, and nothing will deter me,"' reported the promoter. 'He was blocking out everything. The only thing that concerned him was how and when he'd put Leonard on his ass Monday night.'

On Monday morning, Henry Hearns was charged with first-degree murder. At the arraignment, Nancy Barile's parents expressed their displeasure that people seemed to be less concerned with their daughter's fate than with how it might affect Tommy Hearns's chances against Leonard.

At Monday morning's weigh-in at Caesars, Leonard dropped his guard long enough to console Hearns.

'I totally lost it when I went to Tommy to express my condolences,' said Leonard, as he recalled the exchange. 'It was completely out of character for me. I should have waited till after the fight and then done it. Fighters need to remain in that zone. That's your job. But I'd stepped outside it.

'When I went back to the house where we were staying after the weigh-in, I already knew I was in for a long night,' added Leonard.

'I felt flat, bland. I could barely eat. "What's going on?" I found myself wondering. I guess my biorhythms must have been low or something, because there's a way you're supposed to feel before a fight, and I didn't feel that way.'

Henry Hearns would be convicted of second-degree murder. Thomas Hearns would pay $685,000 to settle a wrongful-death suit brought by the victim's family.

Oddly, the betting line barely budged when news of Hearns's troubles began to circulate around Vegas. In fact, as had been the case with nearly all of the Hit Man's big fights, a late rush of Hearns money poured through the sports book windows in the 24 hours immediately preceding the fight.

■ ■ ■

On the morning of the fight, it was apparent that any concern over the weight had been misplaced. Hearns removed his outer garments, but he stepped on the scale still wearing a pair of blue terrycloth shorts and a formidable gold chain, and weighed 162½ – five and a half pounds under the divisional limit.

Had Hearns weighed in excess of 164 he would have incurred financial penalties; now people were wondering whether he should be entitled to a refund.

Leonard removed his Franklin Sports warm-up suit but retained a pair of black bathing trunks and a green, black and red tank top, with the legend 'FREE SOUTH AFRICA' in gold letters across the top. Leonard weighed 160 – five pounds less than he had for Lalonde.

As Nevada's senior and most prominent referee, Mills Lane had been expected to draw the Leonard–Hearns II assignment, but Lane had encountered such difficulty trying to pry Hearns loose from Kinchen that the NSAC guarded against a repetition by appointing the larger and stronger Richard Steele.

None of the 'Three Blind Mice' who had worked the 1981 fight were on the panel of judges for the rematch. (Minker and Ford had been promoted to supervisory positions.) Nevadans Dalby Shirley and Jerry Roth were named to the tribunal, with New Jersey's Tom Kaczmarek occupying the third seat.

The question of a post-fight steroid test never came up at the rules meeting, even though the commission seemed prepared to order one had either side requested it.

'The subject was never brought up,' shrugged Minker. 'Emanuel knows how to ask.'

■ ■ ■

With the fight scheduled for the off-day between Games Three and Four of what would be a Detroit sweep in the 1989 NBA Finals, Michael Gee was shuttling between Vegas and Los Angeles. On his

Monday-morning return from LAX, Pat Morita, Olivia Newton-John and Cathy Lee Crosby were all on the same flight.

Pistons coach Chuck Daly also dashed over from LA on Monday, presumably to root for the Hit Man.

'I'm just looking for a knockout punch,' Daly, whose team would score one of its own the following evening, told Gee.

▪ ▪ ▪

'This was my first time covering a big fight in Vegas, and nothing had prepared me for the heat,' recalled Gee. 'A few days before the fight, one of the sidepiece screws in my glasses broke while I was in the press room. It was late in the morning, and I asked someone if there was a LensCrafters in the area so I could get them fixed and was told that there was in fact one located about half a mile away.

'I got up to leave Caesars and walk over when [Caesars publicist] Andy Olson stopped me. He personally escorted me to the entrance and put me in a cab, saying, "No writers are dying of sunstroke on my watch." It was 109 outside at the time.

'So, on Monday evening I was supposed to write a sidebar on light flyweight Michael Carbajal, who was facing Eduardo Nuñez in the fourth bout of the evening. In my naivety, I was in my seat for the first fight. The only people there to watch the fights were the 300 or so gambling addicts who'd bet on them.

'Anyway, the action in the first three fights consisted entirely of each man attempting to manoeuvre his opponent into the east side of the ring, where he'd be blinded by the sun. It made for some pretty weird-looking fights.'

The first two bouts of the evening showcased a couple of Leonard protégés: Canadian middleweight Dan Sherry and light-heavyweight Andrew Maynard, the 1988 Olympic gold medallist, who registered TKOs over John Tunstall and Stephen Schwann.

The third fight saw Ray Mercer, the former army sergeant who had won the heavyweight gold medal in Seoul, win his sixth pro fight by knocking out Ken Crosby.

Carbajal, a future Boxing Hall of Famer, stopped Nuñez in four, while another future world champion, 17-year-old Mexican lightweight Manny Medina, scored a fifth-round TKO over Jorge Cazares.

The other two prelims saw a pair of Arum-promoted, Tarkanian-backed boxers win six-round decisions – Robert Wangila barely edged veteran Buck Smith, and Kennedy McKinney outpointed David Moreno.

Celebrities were periodically introduced from the ring.

Chuck Daly got the biggest round of applause, presumably from the Motown fans, and then only, wrote Michael Gee, 'after a photo finish with Kirk Douglas'.

Gee noted that 'because this was a carefully crafted promotion, there was a celebrity for every taste. Nobody made a sound when George Peppard was introduced. Saddest of all was *Hollywood Squares* host John Davidson, who was roundly booed.'

Also in the audience that night were Don Rickles and Jerry Lewis, Tom Selleck and Mr. T, Dionne Warwick and Ed Marinaro, Lou Gossett and Barry Switzer.

And while no Pistons or Lakers players joined Daly at ringside, a number of NBA stars from non-competing teams were in attendance, including Michael Jordan, Charles Barkley, David Robinson and Chris Mullin.

The Pointer Sisters were also seated at ringside, and just before the main event performed the national anthem.

In keeping with the socially conscious 'Free South Africa' theme Leonard had initiated at the weigh-in, Ray made his ring entrance wearing a red-and-white robe with a single word – *AMANDLA* – written across the back. A Zulu term meaning 'power', it had been adopted as a slogan in anti-apartheid demonstrations. Once he shed the robe, the waistband of his red-and-white candy-striped trunks bore the same legend.

Hearns was attired in the gold Kronk livery he had worn against Duran and Hagler. (Both he and Leonard had worn white trunks in 1981.)

Once the bell rang, noted Pat Putnam, 'neither seemed in a hurry to earn his astronomical payday'. Hearns, whose dominant weapon figured to be his jab, repeatedly came up short with it, noted Putnam, 'as though fearful of exposing a chin that had failed one recent test and barely survived two others'.

'From the time the fight was announced, most writers were saying that Hearns was shot, that he shouldn't fight, that he might get hurt,' remembered Leonard. 'Throughout training camp people kept telling me the same thing. I kept telling them that Tommy would rise to the occasion because he was fighting me, but I don't know whether I convinced myself. I'd gotten in shape, but I didn't feel threatened, and I think in my mind I was thinking, "Hey, Tommy's just one punch away from getting knocked out."'

Midway through the third round, Leonard, who had been rather indifferently chipping away at Hearns without significant effect, lowered his head and moved inside to throw a two-punch combination to the midsection. Hearns responded with a short right that stopped Leonard in his tracks, and followed it by slamming another right to the side of the head.

As the crowd gasped, Leonard tumbled to the canvas. More embarrassed than hurt, he bounced to his feet, assured Steele he was all right and endured a mandatory eight-count.

Hearns chased Leonard around the ring for the remaining half of the round, but Ray survived without further damage and recovered sufficiently to win the next round.

In the fifth, Leonard rocked Hearns with a right to the head and a hook to the chin. Hearns staggered backwards until he came to rest against the ropes, which he used to steady himself as he endured Leonard's onslaught.

'*For a solid minute Leonard flailed away at his wounded quarry,*' read my account of round five in the next morning's *Boston Herald*. '*During this episode, he hit Hearns with everything but the ring post, but failed to put him down, and toward the end of the round Leonard appeared as vitiated as Hearns, having punched himself out in the spirited but vain attack.*'

When Hearns staggered back to his corner after the rounds, Steward told him, '*That* is what makes a great champion!'

Leonard seemed to have edged his way into control, but in the seventh Hearns jolted him again, this time with a right hand.

In the ninth, Hearns was cautioned by Steele for a low blow, after which Leonard delivered his own warning, a shot that was patently aimed below the belt, but not at a critical spot.

Although a right from Leonard opened a cut below Hearns's right eye in the tenth, Citro's quick work in the corner between rounds minimised the damage, and in the 11th Hearns stunned Leonard with a huge overhand right. Ray went scurrying towards a neutral corner with Tommy in hot pursuit. When he caught up with him, two hammering rights and a left put Leonard on the floor again.

This time the bell saved Leonard.

'He was *dead*,' said Hearns. 'But you know what? He came back. I didn't think he had such a great heart.'

'After two knockdowns, I didn't know what the judges were thinking,' Leonard would later reveal. 'I figured I'd better give them something else to think about.'

Leonard proceeded to stage a 12th round that was a fair approximation of the 13th in their fight eight years earlier, battering Hearns all around the ring. Hearns's legs appeared even more spent than they had in the Kinchen fight, and he could offer but token resistance. Steele was eyeing Hearns warily, and appeared to be on the verge of stopping it when the final bell intervened. A plainly relieved Hearns managed to smile, revealing a blood-drenched gumshield.

With Leonard having made two trips to the canvas, much of the audience assumed that the underdog Hearns had won. Most of the scribes scoring at ringside also had Hearns slightly ahead (in our case, the margin was 113–112), but a significant minority scored it for Leonard. (Ed Schuyler's Associated Press card had it 113–112, Leonard.) An air of suspense still gripped the arena when Michael Buffer announced the scorecards that counted – those of the judges.

Roth also scored it for Hearns, 113–112, while Kaczmarek had Leonard winning by the same narrow margin. The third official, Shirley, scored it 112–112: the result was a draw, one that by any standard seemed just.

'*For the better part of 12 rounds Ray Charles Leonard and Thomas Hearns bombarded one another in a test of wills,*' read my account in the *Herald*. '*It was a spirited and savage, if technically imperfect, match in which the advantage repeatedly changed hands, and at its conclusion three judges determined that it had been a fight neither deserved to lose.'*

Seven years, seven months and twenty-seven days had elapsed since their first fight, and if both Leonard and Hearns had slipped a bit with the passage of time, they had fallen to nearly the same place. The War revealed that, if anything, they were more evenly matched than ever.

There were the predictable cries of 'robbery!' and worse from the crowd, but not from either of the competitors.

Leonard allowed that he was 'very pleased by the outcome'. Hearns believed he had won, but when he added with a shrug, 'I guess the judges saw it differently,' he was hardly the picture of outrage.

The razor-thin margin by which Leonard had pulled out the draw – Dalby Shirley scored the fifth 10–8, despite the absence of a knockdown – led to almost immediate talk of a rematch, though none of it came from Leonard.

'I want to go back, relax and think,' said Leonard, who sounded like a football coach when he added, 'I haven't looked at the film yet.'

Another school of thought held that since The War seemed a perfectly appropriate note for both men to go out on, Leonard and Hearns should *both* retire.

'We're talking about some serious stuff here,' said Bob Arum. 'It's a fundamental question. This is an extremely tough sport. If you have the money, do you have to take chances?'

'Look,' Arum tried to explain, 'this was a great night for boxing. It definitely had redeeming social value. But nobody *makes* them fight. If a guy needs money, sometimes he has to keep fighting, but for a fighter like Ray Leonard, who's meant so much to boxing, to risk permanent injury at this stage would be unconscionable.'

Leonard and Hearns were mutually gracious when they jointly met with the press the following morning.

'Tommy came into this fight seeking redemption,' said Leonard, 'and he got that.'

'When I woke up this morning my mind was clear,' said Hearns. 'I was laying there in bed thinking, "Hmm, I wonder who *Ray* is thinking about this morning?"'

'I still *love* this man,' added Tommy.

Asked if he believed he had won the fight, Leonard diplomatically replied, 'I think we both showed what we're made of.'

The sports books, which had been under siege from Hearns bettors in the hours before the fight, were even more relieved than Leonard by the outcome. Although the result was a push, refunding winning bets on both fighters was a small price to pay compared to the bath they would have taken had the verdict gone to Hearns.

And as it turned out, many of those refunds were never collected anyway. Thousands of boxing fans, believing their bets on Leonard and Hearns had been lost, discarded their betting slips that night. That proved to be a windfall for the Caesars clean-up crew the next morning. The stoopers made a fortune.

10

UNO MAS

Leonard–Duran III
The Mirage, Las Vegas, 7 December 1989

SIX MONTHS LATER, LEONARD was back in the ring again. It was his shortest hiatus between fights since 1981.

A third fight with Hearns or another against Hagler might have been even more lucrative, but this time Ray set his sights on Duran.

Ray appeared to want no part of Hearns, and a Hagler rematch seemed even less likely. Although Marvelous Marvin had yet to officially retire, and in fact had taken to periodically lobbing verbal hand grenades from Italy, the enmity between the rivals was so pronounced that each seemed inclined, out of spite, to deny the other the huge payday a second fight would have produced.

Duran had been chasing Leonard for years, pointing out that their rivalry stood 1–1 and needed to be settled with a rubber match. Of course, if Duran were motivated by the prospect of evening scores, he had lost to Hearns as well, but Cholo was no more anxious to fight the Hit Man again than was Leonard.

Although much of the shine had gone off the 38-year-old Panamanian, he remained the only man alive to have beaten Leonard, and there was just enough lustre left in their fading reputations to make a Leonard–Duran match-up – the tie-breaker no one had wanted to see nine years earlier – a viable proposition.

Although Leonard had 15 million reasons for fighting Duran, he claimed an even more important motivation for returning to the ring. 'When my two sons look at the tapes of my last fight,' he said, 'I don't want them looking at that damn draw with Hearns.'

Leonard prepared with an almost monastic camp in Safety Harbor, Florida. The old entourage had been pared from twenty-one to six. Dave Jacobs was gone again, this time for good. For the Duran fight, Pepe Correa would be the lone voice in the corner.

While both men tried to play down the residue of the events in New Orleans nine years earlier, the fight's promoters seemed happy enough to use the No Mas fight as a selling point. Lest anyone miss the point, Leonard–Duran III would officially be entitled Uno Mas.

It would be the first time since 1980 that a bout involving two of the Four Kings was staged anywhere other than Caesars Palace. Steve Wynn, the owner of the Golden Nugget in downtown Las Vegas, had just completed construction of the Mirage, a sparkling new hotel on the Strip, replete with a periodically erupting volcano outside and a shark-filled aquarium in the lobby. Wynn was so anxious to christen his new hostelry by luring the Leonard–Duran fight from Caesars that he outbid his deep-pocketed rivals with a pre-emptive multimillion-dollar site-fee offer.

Arum was the lead promoter, but he and Trainer had buried the hatchet, and each man seemed to welcome the innovative concepts of the other. Wynn's involvement was another matter.

This time there was no press tour, and the television advertising blitz commenced only a few weeks before the fight. Although it made not a few closed-circuit exhibitors and cable system operators nervous, the promoters were convinced that they were on the right track.

'Running ads months before a big fight doesn't really sell tickets,' Arum explained. 'The purpose of the early commercials and the promotional tours was mainly to attract exhibitors – and to keep them in line. They want some reassurance that you're helping them out, but for this fight, you didn't need it.'

'Before the [second] Hearns fight, for instance, you had to sell Tommy,' noted Trainer. 'The public perception was that Hearns was somehow an unworthy opponent, but once you put the two of them out in front of people where they could see Hearns express his confidence, it helped change that image.'

'The reverse was true when Ray fought Hagler,' Trainer added. 'Everybody thought Ray was nuts for coming back. Since nobody gave him a chance, you had to build *him* up. But for this fight, you didn't have to sell either guy to the public.'

The advertising campaign was supposed to kick off a month before the fight, with the first scheduled spot slated for NBC just before the final race on the Breeders' Cup telecast, but Wynn was dissatisfied with the footage of the Mirage and ordered the spot pulled from the air.

Once the commercials did begin to air, they didn't cost the promoters a dime. Trainer had come up with a scheme by which Budweiser and the Mutual Broadcasting System were brought in as sponsors. (They were the 'official beer' and the 'official pre-fight radio station'.) What might have looked like pre-fight TV promos were, in fact, Anheuser-Busch commercials. (In return, the Bud logo would be conspicuously displayed on the ring mat.)

Still, Leonard had been guaranteed $13 million and Duran $7.6 million. With a $20 million nut on the line, one would have thought the promoters were a bit worried about their money.

'No,' chuckled Mike Trainer. 'We're just going to count it.'

■ ■ ■

Although Wynn had operated successful casinos in Atlantic City and in Las Vegas, the Mirage was his first venture on the Strip. (It would shortly be joined by its next-door neighbour, Treasure Island.) The hotelier was a relative neophyte when it came to the boxing game, and Arum shortly became annoyed by what he considered the casino magnate's constant interference.

'Steve Wynn thinks he invented the wheel,' fumed Arum. 'This fight should have been held at Caesars Palace.'

'I blame Bob Halloran for part of that,' Arum reflected years later. (Wynn had persuaded Halloran, the long-time president of sports for Caesars World, to move down the street and head up *his* boxing operation.) 'For years when he was at Caesars, he'd been trying to tell them, "Why do we need promoters? Why don't we put on the fights ourselves?" Henry Gluck, who was the chairman of the board, was smart enough to realise that was the last thing in the world they needed. Whether it was Top Rank or Don King or somebody else, Caesars allowed the promoters to do what they do best, which was to promote.'

At the urging of Halloran, who had decided that Michael Nunn was the heir apparent to Hagler as the next great middleweight, Wynn had already attempted to sign the IBF champion to a long-term promotional contract that would have tied him exclusively to the Mirage. And the week before the Leonard fight, Wynn went behind his putative partners' backs in an attempt to steal Duran away as well.

'I had a guy from Chile named Alfonso Riat assigned to the Duran camp,' Arum recalled two decades later. 'He served as an interpreter, and as a liaison with Duran's people, much the way Ricardo Jimenez does for me now.'

'A lot of people, including Wynn, thought Duran was going to win that fight. A week before the fight he approached Riat and told him that after Roberto won the title he should dump his promoters and throw in with him,' said Arum. 'Wynn didn't realise Riat worked for me. He thought he worked for Duran. So of course Riat patiently listened to his proposal and then came straight back and told me about it.

'Wynn had no experience in boxing whatsoever,' sighed Arum. 'A year after we did the Leonard–Duran fight, he put on the Holyfield–Buster Douglas fight himself. He lost a fortune.'

■ ■ ■

The Mirage's outdoor stadium, designed for a capacity crowd of 16,300, was still under construction as the fight approached. Leonard had opened as a 3–1 favourite, but a few days before the fight the odds had dropped to slightly under 2–1.

Of course, the way Leonard sarcastically poor-mouthed his chances probably contributed to the rush of Duran money.

'I'll try to move,' Leonard, feigning concern, said at the press conference. 'They say it's not there any more, and I really won't know until the seventh round or so. I've slowed down a great deal. I'm susceptible to being hit by the right hand. It's got me puzzled right now. I've just got to get back to the gym and figure out something.'

The fight would be Leonard's second defence of the WBC super-middleweight title, and while he said, 'I'm seriously considering the possibility that this will be my last one,' this time he knew better than to write it in stone.

'I've made a promise to myself never to announce retirements again, because they don't seem to last that long,' Ray said. 'The best way to do this is to just fade into the sunset. I guess if you don't see me in another ten years, I won't be fighting any more.'

Leonard closed his workouts to both the press and the public, but Duran had been publicly sparring for weeks at a ring set up at the Tropicana casino.

Cholo had engaged the services of a new trainer, Carlos Hibbard. Panamanian by birth, Hibbard described himself as an 'Israelite' and had a gold filling in a front tooth shaped like the Star of David. He had been a gypsy cab driver in New York and a sometime salsa singer in Florida, and while he had worked with some kick-boxers in the gym, Duran was the first boxer he had ever trained.

'Roberto almost got out of boxing on a real sour note,' Hibbard described their initial encounter. 'I was singing in Miami, some months after the Robbie Sims fight, and when I met Roberto I told him that in watching that one, he'd run out of gas, but that it looked to me like the reflexes were still there.

'I told him what I thought I could do, which was first of all putting him on a concentrated weight-loss programme,' said Hibbard. 'Roberto likes Miller Lite. And Budweiser, too.

'He went back to Panama for the holidays, and when he got back to the states, we started. No gym, just exercise, some extra therapy and lots of roadwork. Then I said, "Now, let's get back to the gym and see what we've got."'

That was Carlos Hibbard's version of Duran's reincarnation, anyway. In *Hands of Stone*, Duran described the pivotal moment to Christian Giudice as an evening drinking in the company of a pair of prostitutes.

'I love whores,' Duran explained. 'The hookers told me, "You need to screw with us and then go out and beat the living shit out of that black man." They start kissing me and I told them, "You're right." I

299

come home and tell my woman that it's the last time I drink. Then I start to sharpen myself, and by now I'm praying for the rematch.'

In Las Vegas, however, Duran said, 'I give Carlos not 99 per cent, but 100 per cent of the credit for where I am today.'

'Roberto had always blown up after every fight, some worse than others,' noted Hibbard. 'He's a human being, remember, and he almost lost it all. After New Orleans he had few friends, and he was real down.'

'I have won two world titles since then,' interjected Duran. 'But still all people ask me about is No Mas. I always knew I would fight him again some day.'

A week or so before the Leonard fight, Angie Carlino dropped by the Tropicana to watch Duran spar.

'I was just a fly on the wall. He didn't even know I was there,' reported Carlino. 'I don't speak much Spanish, but all I know is whenever he started talking about Leonard, every other word was *maricón*.'

■ ■ ■

Three days before the bout, Duran went three rounds with sparring partner (and future opponent) Carlos Montero at the Mirage, and then agreed to a brief meeting with the press. When one enterprising scribe asked Manos de Piedra if he was 'still hungry', Duran all but elbowed Riat off the stage to answer the question himself.

'I am hungry now,' said Cholo. 'I must eat some eggs and some hams.'

How Leonard, who was training behind closed doors, fared against his sparring partners remained a matter of speculation, but word did leak out that he had accidentally decked Pepe Correa. The trainer, wielding the mitts while Leonard practised combinations, got caught and flattened by an unexpected punch.

Leonard seemed uncharacteristically distant and moody in the days preceding the bout. Seemingly every day, as a fresh wave of reporters arrived from around the world, he found himself enduring some variant of the same question: *Why are you still doing this?*

'My motivation,' he explained at one media gathering, 'is instinctive. I just get upset with people continually trying to psychoanalyse me.

They're trying to look inside my head and find out what makes Ray Leonard tick, and it bothers me. It would bother anybody.'

'They say wealthy men shouldn't be fighting,' said Trainer. 'But Ray Leonard fights because he enjoys the sport, not for the money.'

Leonard seemed almost as annoyed by the frequent No Mas references as Duran was.

'In New Orleans, Duran became the story,' Leonard complained. 'All everyone talked about was him quitting. He got more attention for quitting than I did for winning the fight.'

Although the bout was for Leonard's 168-pound title, the contractual weight limit was 162 pounds. Should either contestant have exceeded that, he would have paid a heavy financial penalty.

Not only were Leonard and Duran nine years older and fifteen pounds heavier, but the Tale of the Tape revealed that between their first fight in Montreal and their final encounter in Las Vegas, Duran's waist size had gone from 30 inches to 34.

▪ ▪ ▪

The fighters and much of the media had already arrived in Las Vegas a week before the fight, when came the shocking news from London that promoter Frank Warren had been shot. Warren was standing on the pavement outside the Broadway Theatre in Barking, where he was running a boxing card, when an assailant wearing a ski mask opened fire and then, leaving the promoter for dead, made good his escape.

Warren had no dearth of known enemies. Mickey Duff was promoting a show of his own that night across town at the Elephant & Castle. When he was informed of the shooting, Mickey said, 'Thank God I'm *here*, else I'd be the chief suspect!' (Terry Marsh, the former IBF light-welterweight champion, was later arrested and charged with the shooting, but when the case came to trial he was acquitted by a London jury.)

While Leonard and Duran prepared for the third bout of their trilogy, the undefeated young heavyweight champion was also in town. Mike Tyson, slated to meet cruiserweight champion Evander Holyfield the following spring, was sparring at Tocco's Gym for a tune-up bout in Japan against a journeyman heavyweight named Buster Douglas.

Although most fight writers were picking Leonard, Ray's dubious performance against Hearns, coupled with Duran's against Barkley, had convinced some experts that Cholo had a better-than-middling chance. Among them were Duran's 90-year-old ex-trainer Ray Arcel, 83-year-old promoter Chris Dundee and Harold Conrad, the 77-year-old press agent widely assumed to have been the model for Budd Schulberg's Eddie Lewis character in *The Harder They Fall*.

'The guys from his own generation,' noted Katz, 'are picking Duran.'

Although he was estranged from the Leonard camp, Chris Dundee's younger brother liked his former pupil's chances. 'Ray can lick him, but he's got to keep punching straight up the middle,' said Angelo Dundee. 'He can't come in there winging punches the way he did with Lalonde and Hearns, else he's gonna lose.'

Having had six months to digest the films, Leonard had determined that his performance against Hearns could be written off as 'an off night'. Still, he had been down three times in his last two fights. The suggestion was that if Leonard had slipped as much since the Hearns fight as he had between Lalonde and Hearns, he could be in for a long night.

And Roberto Duran seemed to have something else in his favour: he had been campaigning as an old fighter for a lot longer than Leonard had. If everything else was equal on Thursday night, guile and treachery might prove to be the difference.

■ ■ ■

A few days before Uno Mas, Bob Arum was threatened with arrest by representatives of the US Treasury Department. Although Arum was a former Justice Department attorney who had been introduced to the sport via an investigation into boxing, the feds were now threatening to clap him in irons should even one minute of the Leonard–Duran fight appear on a Panamanian television station controlled by that nation's strongman, General Manuel Noriega.

Two months earlier, Arum had peddled the television rights to a state-controlled Panamanian station. Relations between the George H.W. Bush administration and Noriega had subsequently deteriorated to the point that the US had ordered a full-fledged embargo.

Arum dodged the bullet by repackaging the Panamanian rights to the privately owned Telemundo Canal 13, which in turn reimbursed the government-owned station, getting the promoter off the hook and ensuring that Duran's countrymen could watch the bout.

The feds had a busy week in Vegas. Two years earlier the IRS had mistakenly issued Duran a $1.6 million refund, and Cholo had cashed the cheque and long since spent the money. Now the government was prepared to gain restitution by attaching Duran's purse from the Leonard fight. That the feds meant business was confirmed over the weekend preceding the fight. IRS agents looking to settle a back-tax beef raided Redd Foxx's Vegas home and carted off everything from jewellery to television sets. By the time the agents left, Redd's house looked like the set of *Sanford and Son*.

■ ■ ■

The Nevada State Athletic Commission named Richard Steele to referee the bout, while the NSAC and WBC agreed on a slate of officials that included local Jerry Roth, Joe Cortez of New Jersey and Belgian Bob Logist.

The Duran camp voiced some displeasure at the fact that there were two US judges but no Latin American representative.

'Duran might as well *be* an American,' said Trainer. 'He's lived more of his adult life here than he has in Panama. He's made 98 per cent of his money here, and when he couldn't go back to Panama after the second fight with Ray, he chose to live in Miami.

'Besides,' noted the lawyer, 'Roth is the judge who scored the last fight for Hearns.'

In the days before the weigh-in it had become clear not only that neither man would have a problem making the 162-pound contractual limit, but that each might actually enter the ring as a middleweight.

On the morning of the fight, Leonard weighed 160, Duran 158. Since Duran still held the WBC 160-pound championship, under the time-honoured rules of boxing that title would be on the line as well.

When I approached WBC president José Sulaimán on the matter, he replied that Duran's middleweight title would 'absolutely' be at stake in the fight.

This proved to be unsettling news for Mike Trainer. The contract he had drawn up for the fight was for the super-middleweight title only, and specifically *excluded* Duran's belt.

'As far as Ray is concerned, the contract is for his title only,' Trainer told reporters. 'That's what the contract specifies. Ray has no interest in winning Duran's middleweight title. He's already won one of those.'

Trainer then blamed me for having ignited the controversy by bringing the rule to Sulaimán's attention.

'I guess this all got started a few days ago when some writer [this one] with a knowledge of boxing history brought up the situation to José,' said Trainer, labelling the weight issue a 'misunderstanding'.

A Las Vegas newspaper described the canon as 'a little-known rule'. Actually, that the champion could lose his title in a fight in which both boxers were within the prescribed weight was a principle encoded in the sport since the days of the Marquis of Queensberry, which is why champions historically had been careful to ensure that one belligerent or the other was over the weight even in scheduled 'non-title' fights.

'I just wish somebody in our camp had known about it before the weigh-in,' said Duran's adviser/promoter Mike Acri.

Had one boxer or the other been even half a pound over 160, Duran's claim on the middleweight title would not have been threatened. This could have been easily accomplished by mounting the scale with a roll of silver dollars in his pocket – a ruse Leonard himself had used in the Lalonde fight.

After reviewing the language of the WBC rules, Sulaimán clarified his position. Duran would 'definitely' lose his WBC title if he lost to Leonard in a 160-pound fight, but Leonard would not necessarily win it. 'That,' said Sulaimán, 'would be up to our executive committee.'

WBC executive Steve Crosson somewhat grandiosely announced that the organisation would 'neither expect nor accept an additional sanctioning fee'.

■ ■ ■

At a meeting with Arum and Trainer a few days earlier, Steve Wynn had revealed his intention to accompany the Grand Opening with a marching band and a fireworks display. Arum shrugged and said, 'Fine. Have what you want.'

It was so cold on the appointed night that the musicians' horns nearly froze to their lips. The fireworks, on the other hand, commenced without warning just after the conclusion of the undercard, producing post-combat flashbacks in a pair of ex-Marines among the ringside scribes. Unsure whether the explosions signalled incoming artillery fire or a mutiny by Duran's bodyguards, Pat Putnam and the *Boston Globe*'s Ron Borges both dived for cover.

Leonard had wanted to wear tights underneath his trunks to protect against the December desert chill, but the Nevada commission denied the request. Correa brought along a large blanket, in which Leonard was swaddled between rounds, and when Sugar Ray entered the ring wearing a balaclava, he looked like a Ninja warrior, or perhaps a second-storey man.

'I had that ski mask, and towels underneath my robe,' recalled Leonard. 'I was wrapped up like an Eskimo.'

'They were better prepared than we were,' said Mike Acri. 'It was 38 degrees outside. Leonard had a blanket in the corner and Duran didn't. Not only that, our guys kept putting an ice pack on Roberto's neck between rounds.'

'Every time I'd look over in the other corner between rounds they were throwing water on Duran,' recalled Leonard. 'It's a wonder he didn't start growing icicles.'

It didn't take Duran long to realise that if he hoped to avenge the events of New Orleans nine years earlier he probably should have brought along a gun. He wasn't going to get close enough to Leonard to hurt him any other way.

While his tactics may have lacked aesthetic appeal, Leonard's game plan virtually guaranteed a lopsided victory. He danced, he moved, he lashed out from his preferred range. For the better part of the evening Duran looked like a snarling dog, tethered to a post in the middle of the ring while a cruel boy poked at him with a stick.

In this fight, Manos de Piedra might as well have changed his nickname to *Piernas de Piedra* – Legs of Stone. Unable to cut the ring off on Leonard, Duran was reduced to imprudent charges, which were invariably smothered as Leonard clinched. Ray danced, mugged and teased his old rival.

Duran drew first blood in the fourth round, when he butted Leonard in the face, splitting his lower lip, but his efforts seemed otherwise futile.

For five rounds Leonard outran and outmanoeuvred Duran, and when Leonard finally elected to engage in the sixth, he outbrawled him as well. Possibly in response to the restive taunts of the crowd, he caught Duran coming in with two left hooks, slammed a right and a left off his head and, shades of New Orleans, enacted a mocking shuffle. Then he predictably wound up as if to throw a bolo punch, but this time, instead of throwing the jab as he had nine years earlier, he banged the windmill punch off Duran's head.

Duran responded with a sheepish grin.

Leonard had apparently determined to use this fight as an excuse to hand Duran a dose of his own medicine. Sugar Ray repeatedly hit Duran on the break, threw what were seemingly deliberate low blows and even paused – out of the sight of referee Richard Steele – during one clinch to give Duran an apparent noogie.

Only occasionally did Leonard deign to take the fight to the trenches, and when he did it was usually on his own terms. Near the end of the ninth he caught Duran with a combination followed by a pair of jolting left hooks, and he closed the tenth by pummelling his foe with a flurry of punches.

As a restive crowd chanted, '*Bullshit! Bullshit!*' Leonard was eventually forced into action, and in the 11th he ventured near enough to incur more damage than Duran had inflicted in their first two meetings combined. Duran picked off a right-hand lead, lowered his head and charged into Leonard. Blood immediately spurted from Leonard's forehead, and Correa shouted at Steele that his man had been butted again.

It certainly *looked* as if he had been, but replays later revealed that the cut had been inflicted by a Duran uppercut.

Aliano was unable to do much with the cut between rounds, so Leonard fought most of the final stanza on his bicycle. Had Duran been able to open the cut with four rounds, rather than four minutes, left in the fight, it might have proven troublesome, but, as it was, Leonard successfully avoided contact until less than a minute before the final bell, when a Duran right ripped open yet another cut – this one above the right eye.

This time it was the crowd who said 'No mas'. Long before it was over, 16,305 voices were voicing their displeasure, and at the final bell they booed victor and vanquished alike.

'Ray was reluctant to fight Duran, and he turned off a lot of fans,' said Tommy Hearns's cornerman Prentiss Byrd. 'Ray didn't give the people what they paid to see.'

There was little suspense to the reading of the verdict: Logist didn't give Duran a single round, scoring it 120–110, while Roth (119–109) gave him one and Cortez (116–111) four. My scorecard had Leonard winning 118–111.

CompuBox's punchstats appeared to bear out the judges' opinion: Leonard had landed 227 of the 438 punches he threw that night. Duran had thrown even more – 588 – but had missed with 504 of them.

Said Acri: 'One wouldn't, and the other couldn't.'

'I fought my kind of fight,' said an unapologetic Leonard. 'I heard the boos, but I'm not going to change the things that got me here. I'm not Marvin Hagler. I'm not Tommy Hearns. I'm Sugar Ray Leonard, and I fought the way I wanted. I'm proud of my performance tonight, and I fought the only way I knew how.'

So, for that matter, had Duran. 'I knew he was going to come in here and clown around,' groused Legs of Stone. 'I came to fight and he didn't. He was just running around out there. When he did hit me, I hit him back.'

'I think a lot had to do with the fact that Duran is 38 years old,' supposed Leonard. 'Duran is a veteran and he came to fight, but I figured if I stayed outside I was out of harm's way. The outside was *my* territory.'

Carlos Hibbard blamed Steele for having abetted the snooze-fest. 'That Siamese twin of a referee worked against Roberto all night,' complained Duran's trainer. 'He never let him get inside and punch his way out of a clinch. He *made* him stay on the outside.'

But Acri conceded that the fight had for the most part been just what most newspapers called it the next morning – a bore.

The two old foes managed an embrace before they went their separate ways that night.

'Leonard won the fight,' said Duran. 'The judges saw it that way. I am going to say goodnight and have some champagne and go back to Miami.'

Sugar Ray Leonard didn't drink any champagne that night. He went to Valley Hospital, where it took 60 stitches to repair the damage Duran had done to his face, a reminder that the old dog had some teeth in him yet.

The audience appeared to share Duran's view of the proceedings, but Bill Nack's *Sports Illustrated* piece the following week lauded Leonard for his disciplined approach.

'The 12-round fight had all the beauty of a bullfight, but without the expected horror of the kill,' wrote Nack. 'Still, the fans didn't like it. Leonard gave them artistic perfection when they wanted heated battle, and they booed lustily. Most fight fans would not spend a dime to watch Van Gogh paint *Sunflowers*, but they would fill Yankee Stadium to see him cut off his ear.'

■ ■ ■

When he met with reporters the following morning, he looked more like Ray Charles than Ray Charles Leonard. The dark glasses could not mask the patchwork of stitches on his face.

'I could have fought and won and been untouched,' reflected Leonard. 'I could hear the crowd. They wanted to see us toe-to-toe, you know, bang-bang, like Hearns and Lalonde. But that's just not my fight. I wanted to box and not get hit, and if I'd been smart I'd have just stayed out there instead of trying to accommodate the demands of the public.

'The best way to beat Duran was to score points,' he said. 'If I'd fought him inside all night long, I think I still could have won, but it would have been a much uglier – and much closer – fight.'

■ ■ ■

Bob Arum was still fuming at Wynn the morning after the fight.

'He thinks this is Alice in Wonderland,' the promoter grumbled. 'He thinks he can buy anything he wants.

'I think Mr Wynn is going to discover that loyalties in boxing run deeper than they do in the casino business,' said Arum. 'It may be easier and simpler than building a big hotel. Maybe it's easier and simpler than raising $600 million by selling 18 per cent junk bonds, but it's still a very complicated business.'

In a not-so-oblique reference to Wynn's overture to Riat, Arum said, 'I'm going to watch my ass. I don't think it's right when I'm promoting a fight here that one of his staff propositions someone who's working for me that he thinks is working for one of the fighters. In my view, that's disruptive.'

Although the live gate for Uno Mas had topped $9 million – at the time the largest in boxing history – Wynn still lost a few million on the fight.

Leonard was non-committal on the subject of retirement. ('Right now I'm not even going to think about it. I'm going to go home and enjoy the holidays.') But few, including Arum, expected him to fight again. Ray had enriched himself by another $17.6 million, but a man who had been cut just once in thirty-six previous fights had sustained three cuts in one night, and had not appeared to enjoy it.

Duran's guarantee had been $7.6 million (four times what he had earned in the first fight in Montreal), but Cholo got out of town with considerably less. Between its normal tax bite and the other $1.6 he owed the IRS from the erroneous refund, the government took almost $3.5 million off the top.

And by this stage of his career Duran had become a boxing version of the Max Bialystock character in Mel Brooks's *The Producers*: he'd raised capital by selling off pieces of his only asset, which in this case wasn't *Springtime for Hitler*, but himself. The usual manager's and trainer's shares came to 30 per cent, and the courts had upheld Luis Spada in his claim for a share of Duran's earnings. Between them, Duran's promoters Mike Acri and Luis De Cubas, and his previous promoters Jeff Levine and Gerry Cooney, were entitled to over a million dollars.

However much Duran got out of Las Vegas with, it seemed a fairly safe bet that it wasn't going to last long.

'Duran will keep fighting,' predicted Arum. 'Duran wants more money, because Duran likes to spend money. We'll look for guys who want to stand toe-to-toe and fight Duran.'

Marvin Hagler, who had been at ringside as a commentator for the closed-circuit telecast, was asked by Gil Clancy about coming out of retirement for a rematch with Leonard.

'I'd like to be smart and say no,' said Hagler, 'but if they want to wave $20 or $25 million in my face, who knows?'

But it seemed clear enough that the era of the mega-paydays had vanished that night.

The most immediate casualty of the evening was a guy who hadn't even fought. Hearns had hoped to face the winner, but the anticlimactic manner in which Leonard–Duran III had played out left him without a natural rival.

'I guess,' sighed Prentiss Byrd, 'the only thing left for Tommy is to be a cruiserweight.'

In fact, the whole fanciful notion of a protracted Seniors Tour involving Leonard, Hagler, Hearns and Duran seemed to have evaporated amid the chorus of boos that serenaded Leonard's exit at the Mirage after what would be the last win of his career. The era of the Four Kings had ended, not with a bang but a whimper.

There would be other fights for Hearns and Duran, and even a few for Leonard, but the members of the fabled quartet would never face one another again.

11

APRÈS LE DÉLUGE

'It was a great time to be a fighter, and a magical
time to be a fight fan.'
– Tim Dahlberg, *Fight Town*

ON 20 DECEMBER 1989, 12 days after Leonard–Duran III brought
down the curtain on the rivalry among the Four Kings, American
forces bent on overthrowing the regime of Manuel Noriega invaded
Panama in what the US government called 'Operation Just Cause'.
Charged with drug trafficking, the Panamanian strongman took refuge
in the Vatican Embassy. American troops attempted to drive him out
by blasting Van Halen's 'Panama' and George Benson's 'Nothing's
Gonna Change My Love For You' around the clock from loudspeakers
set up across the street. On 3 January, Noriega surrendered and was
transported to the United States, where he was eventually tried,
convicted and imprisoned at a federal penitentiary in Miami.

El Chorillo, the Panama City slum in which Roberto Duran had
been raised, was utterly destroyed during the invasion. 'We turned
Chorillo into an ash tray,' said journalist Kevin Buckley, whose book
Panama: The Whole Story recounted the American intervention.

A few weeks later, Duran's old manager Carlos Eleta Almaran was
released from a federal prison in Atlanta, and the drug and money-
laundering charges that had led to his arrest were dismissed. Eleta's
lawyer, Gregory B. Craig, told the *New York Times* that the dismissal of
charges 'confirms the truth of the situation, that Mr Eleta was and is
innocent of all the charges that were brought against him'.

311

Duran continued to box until beyond his 50th birthday. After losing to Leonard at the Mirage, he had 26 more fights, in which he went 18–8. The last of them, ironically, was a 2001 loss in Denver to Hector Camacho, the same man who had ended Leonard's career. Cholo might have been tempted to fight on beyond the Camacho loss, but in October of that year he was injured in a car accident in Argentina, where he had gone to promote his latest salsa CD. Several broken ribs and a collapsed lung accomplished what no man had been able to do. Manos de Piedra went out with a career mark of 103–16, with half the losses occurring after he had turned 40. When Duran was inducted into the Hall of Fame in 2007, Hagler flew in from Italy to join the festivities at Canastota.

One of Duran's sons had a brief flirtation with the fight game. Roberto Jr won his first five bouts, but in 2004 he lost a decision to another novice, Nicasio Sanchez, in Panama City and never boxed again.

■ ■ ■

Shortly after the Leonard fight, a disappointed Marvin Hagler moved to Italy. He would never lace on a pair of gloves again. In 1989, he co-starred (with Francesco Quinn and Brian Dennehy) in *Indio*, a spaghetti-adventure film directed by Antonio Margheriti. Marvelous Marvin's character was a Rambo-like half-Indian former Marine named Sergeant Jake Iron. (Sgt Iron was resurrected two years later for *Indio 2: La Rivolta*.) In 1997, Hagler starred with John Savage and Jennifer Youngs in another Italian-made film, *Notti di paura*. He works occasionally as a ringside analyst for both Italian and British television.

Married to Kaye Guarrera, Hagler continues to live an expatriate existence in Milan. 'He's become more Italian than I am – and I was *born* there,' said Hagler's old foe Vito Antuofermo. ('That,' supposed Michael Katz upon hearing Antuofermo's observation, 'could be because so much of Vito's blood rubbed off on Marvin.')

Marvelous Marvin's transmutation to continental *bon vivant* seems all the more remarkable because of the distance he travelled to get there from Newark and Brockton. On his first journey to Monte Carlo nearly 30 years ago, Marvin seemed genuinely surprised to discover that the denizens of San Remo and Nice, less than 50 miles apart, spoke entirely different languages, and reflected his astonishment by telling me, 'I've even heard that the Chinese and the Japanese can't even understand each other!'

That Hagler was going to be a world champion seemed to me a foregone conclusion. That in his dotage he would occupy a box at La Scala was somewhat less predictable.

Somewhat reclusive, Hagler also maintains a summer cottage in the White Mountains of New Hampshire, where he returns each summer to vacation with his children. Having finished his career with a 62–3–2 record, he was elected to the Boxing Hall of Fame in 1993, his first year of eligibility. He frequently returns to Canastota in June for the annual induction ceremonies.

'I run into Marvin from time to time when I'm in Europe,' said Emanuel Steward. 'He seems very content to me, happy in his role in life. He drinks a bottle of red wine a day, but he gets up at five in the morning to run and still looks in shape. I bet he doesn't weigh more than 175 today.

'The only dissatisfaction in his life, I'd say, is that he's still bitter about the Leonard decision. He still believes he won that fight and that they stole something from him. I doubt if he'll ever get over *that*.'

In *Boxing Illustrated*'s 1990 poll of boxing writers to select the Fighter of the Decade, Hagler, with 297 points, outstripped Leonard, who was second with 248. (Hearns, with 88 points, was ranked seventh, Duran (76) eighth, with Mike Tyson, Larry Holmes, Julio César Chávez and Salvador Sánchez in between.)

■ ■ ■

After his rubber match with Duran, Ray Leonard had two more fights. He lost them both and was badly embarrassed on both occasions.

And his HBO broadcasting career came to an end even before his ring career did.

In July of 1990, seven months after Duran III, the newly divorced Leonard, accompanied by bodyguard James Anderson, travelled to London for the All-England Championships. HBO had the broadcast rights to the early rounds of the Wimbledon fortnight, and Ray spent several days watching the tournament unfold, hobnobbing with the players by day and partying his way through London by night.

On the day of the Wimbledon final that year, a number of high-ranking network executives, including Chairman Michael Fuchs with his date and HBO Sports president Seth Abraham and his wife Lynn, had taken their places in their Centre Court box, expectantly awaiting the arrival of their celebrity guest.

Leonard and Anderson never showed up, but a pair of scantily clad ladies bearing their tickets did, precipitating a mini-scandal that would have repercussions back in the Time-Warner offices in New York.

'Their attire was totally inappropriate,' said Abraham. 'I mean, you don't have to wear a *gown* to Wimbledon, but they were dressed like, well, a couple of hookers.'

There was a good reason for that. They *were* a couple of hookers.

'It just wasn't cool on my part,' said Leonard. 'I think I was just hung-over and wasn't thinking. I think James got in more trouble than I did over it. He was supposed to keep me from doing shit like that.'

'Did that end my HBO career? I don't know,' Leonard reflected. 'It could have.'

'I spoke to Ray about it when we got back to the States,' said Abraham. 'Yes, some people were upset about it, but as far as it being a cause and effect for our ending our relationship with Ray, it wasn't.

'A few months later Mike Trainer began negotiating for the Terry Norris fight, and as the process went on it became clear that he was pretty aggressively shopping the fight to Showtime. That, frankly, miffed me. Ray's contract was up for renewal at the time and I finally told Trainer, "This just won't do. We can't have an HBO announcer fighting on Showtime," so that's how it ended.'

In his penultimate comeback fight, Leonard challenged for Norris's WBC junior middleweight title at Madison Square Garden in February 1991. He was knocked down twice – in the second and seventh – and lost a runaway decision. One judge didn't score a round for Leonard, and another awarded him just one.

Ineligible for the Hall of Fame until five years after the Norris fight, Leonard was elected in a landslide in 1997. Between his election and that June's induction, a 40-year-old Leonard came out of mothballs one more time to engage Camacho in a fight that was billed for the IBC middleweight title. Leonard was stopped for the only time in his career when the bout was halted in the fifth. Apart from the decision to Duran in Montreal, those last two fights were the only losses of his 36–3–1 career.

'I don't regret either of those fights, just the way they turned out,' said Leonard. 'I should have won them both.'

'The Norris fight was right after my divorce, and my head wasn't in the right place,' said Sugar Ray. 'And not to discount Terry Norris's talents, but if I'd been even 75 per cent physically I could have beaten him. When I was training for that fight, I got a hairline fracture in one of my ribs sparring with Michael Ward. The doctors told me it would only heal with rest, but I kept sparring, wearing a flak jacket, hoping it would be all right. Just before the fight a doctor gave me four shots of Novocain in my ribs, but it didn't help enough. Norris just beat the shit out of me.

'Camacho should have been a great fight, and I would have knocked him out if I'd been healthy,' continued Leonard. 'Before that fight I started working with Billy Blanks as a strength and conditioning coach. I had the bright idea that I'd start lifting weights at the tender age of 40. I tore a calf muscle doing squats, and in the fight my leg wouldn't support me. It's probably just as well, because if I'd beaten Camacho they were already talking about me fighting Oscar De La Hoya. I'm just as glad that didn't happen.'

Leonard has since dabbled in promotion (heading up Sugar Ray Leonard Boxing, which for a time regularly staged ESPN2 shows) and in 2004 joined forces with Sylvester Stallone, Jeffrey Katzenberg, Mark Burnett and Jeff Wald to produce a made-for-TV reality series called *The Contender*. (Former Kronk Gym staffers Prentiss Byrd and Jackie Kallen were affiliated with the programme in its first season on NBC; for its third, by which time it had migrated to ESPN, Pepe Correa had come on board as a trainer.) Leonard is also a partner in the Planet Hollywood restaurant chain.

Leonard remains in demand as a motivational speaker (he recently shared a dais with former Secretary of State Colin Powell, addressing a throng of 15,000) and devotes his leisure time to improving his golf game. He is a member at Riviera Country Club in LA, where he maintains a 14 handicap.

Divorced from Juanita in 1990, Leonard walked down the aisle for the second time when he married Bernadette Robi, the daughter of Platters singer Paul Robi (and the ex-wife of one-time Super Bowl MVP Lynn Swann) in 1993. The couple had been introduced by the saxophonist Kenny G at a Luther Vandross concert five years earlier, and when Ray proposed, he presented his wife-to-be with a $340,000 engagement ring. 'Marvin Hagler,' he joked, 'paid for this.'

The wedding guests included Thomas Hearns. Ray and Bernadette Leonard have two young children and live in Pacific Palisades, California.

▪ ▪ ▪

Hearns, who won the WBC middleweight title Leonard had vacated and lost it to Iran Barkley in his first defence, found it even more difficult to leave the ring. Although Hearns never again approached the level to which he had risen against his great rivals, he did win one more legitimate world championship (the WBA light-heavyweight title, which he lost – once again to Barkley – in his first defence) and two lesser ones, the WBU and IBO cruiserweight belts. He won 15 of the 17 bouts in which he engaged after the 1989 draw with Leonard, the last of them a stoppage of Shannon Landberg in Auburn Hills in 2006.

Hearns won't be eligible for election to the Hall of Fame until the Class of 2012 – and that's if he doesn't fight again – but his place in Canastota is secure. Although his destruction of Duran was the only recorded win in his four encounters within the Leonard–Hagler–Duran nexus, he was the loser in two of the greatest fights in the annals of the sport. It wasn't just that Hearns gave both Leonard and Hagler hell; their fights against Hearns virtually defined the greatness of both men.

The two Barkley losses are generally regarded to have been an aberration, and his only other loss came at the age of 42, when he broke a leg in the second round against Uriah Grant. The Hit Man otherwise beat everyone who was put in front of him – the best of his own generation, and a couple of other generations, too.

'One night a few years ago, Tommy and I were in London to open up a new Kronk Gym there, and Marvin Hagler showed up,' recalled

Steward. 'Marvin asked Tommy what he was up to and Tommy told him, "I still want to fight."

'"Man, are you *crazy*?" Hagler told him. "You ought to think about doing something else. You need to get *on* with your life."

'Then Tommy asked Marvin what he was doing, and Marvin told him he was making these movies in Italy where he was some kind of Rambo-type character, and Tommy asked, "How much do you make for doing that?"' related Steward.

'When Marvin told him, "I got about $175,000 for doing the first one," Tommy said, "Man, that ain't enough money," and Marvin said, "Tommy, it's not always about the money. It gives you something to do, and it keeps your name out there."'

After a standout basketball career at American University, the Hit Man's son, Ronald Hearns, somewhat to the displeasure of his father, opted to follow in Tommy's footsteps. By June of 2008, billing himself as the 'Motor City Cobra' (one of his father's discarded nicknames), Ronald had accumulated an 19–0 record as a middleweight.

■ ■ ■

Angelo Dundee, who had been in Muhammad Ali's corner throughout his career from start to finish, did not complete the journey with Leonard. The rupture following the 1987 Hagler fight was never repaired. Dundee remained involved in the sport, however, and in 1994 the man who had been in Ali's corner for his 1974 Rumble in the Jungle against George Foreman was in Foreman's when he upset Michael Moorer to become, at 45, the oldest heavyweight champion in history. Inducted into the International Boxing Hall of Fame in 1994, Dundee, now 84, lives in Florida with his wife, Helen.

Marvelous Marvin Hagler was Goody Petronelli's first world champion, but also his last. Although Petronelli developed the skills of middleweight Steve Collins (and worked his corner in his unsuccessful 1990 WBA title challenge to Mike McCallum), the Irishman had returned to his homeland and European management by the time he won the WBO middleweight and super-middleweight championships. Twenty years after Hagler's last fight, Goody continues to train boxers in Brockton, with his most prominent moment on the world stage coming in 2005, when his Irish heavyweight, Kevin McBride, scored a stunning upset that sent Mike Tyson into retirement.

Although he eventually parted ways with Tommy Hearns, Emanuel Steward's career has flourished both in and out of the ring. A man who had made his reputation developing local boxers from their amateur days became one of the most sought-after hired guns in the game, and has trained 32 world champions, including Lennox Lewis, Oscar De La Hoya, Evander Holyfield, Julio César Chávez and Jermain Taylor.

In late 2007, Steward's stable included a pair of world champions – heavyweight Wladimir Klitschko and welterweight Kermit Cintron – along with Irish middleweight prospect Andy Lee, whom he signed out of the 2004 Olympics. He also serves as a ringside commentator for HBO, and in July of 2007 he combined the roles, working the corner during Cintron's Atlantic City knockout of Walter Matthysse before hastily changing into his tuxedo to join the cable network's broadcast team for that evening's main event, Alfonso Gomez's career-ending knockout of Arturo Gatti. Steward was elected to the Hall of Fame in 1996.

'I've done it every way there is,' said Steward. 'I took two kids, eight and ten years old, from the same *block* – Thomas Hearns and Milton McCrory – and turned them into world champions. And I've had the experience of being brought in when it looks like a guy's career is all messed up.

'I had Holyfield after he'd been beaten by Riddick Bowe, and Lennox after I knocked him out with another fighter [Oliver McCall]. I got involved with Julio César Chávez after he'd lost his first fight; Oscar after he'd looked bad in a controversial win over Pernell Whitaker,' said Steward. 'I was never fortunate enough to get the superstars where somebody would pay them millions of dollars and then give them to me. The only time I ever got those guys is when their careers were in trouble, but in almost every case I succeeded with them.'

A disappointed Ray Arcel never worked with Roberto Duran again after the 1982 Benitez fight, but he remained in the game for a few more years, and teamed up with fellow Hall of Famer Eddie Futch to train Larry Holmes for his 1982 fight against Gerry Cooney. Holmes was the last of Arcel's heavyweight champions; James J. Braddock had been the first. Arcel, who trained 20 world champions in all, was inducted into the Hall of Fame in 1991. He died, at age 95, in 1994.

Freddie Brown lapsed into such depression after the No Mas fight that he never worked another corner. Nestor (Plomo) Quinones remains active on the boxing scene, most recently working with Cuban lightweight champion Joel Casamayor.

■ ■ ■

The oft-told tale of the once-famous boxer who winds up punch-drunk, dead broke or both tends, alas, to be more the rule than the exception. Joe Louis spent time in a mental institution and, with the IRS on his tail, found himself hustling a buck in the wrestling ring, just like the fictional Mountain McClintock in Rod Serling's *Requiem for a Heavyweight*, before playing out his days as window dressing at Caesars Palace. Mike Tyson made over $400 million in the ring but was virtually penniless by the time he last went off to prison. Late in his life, Sugar Ray Robinson was so afflicted by Alzheimer's – quite possibly boxing-related – that he scarcely knew where, or even who, he was.

Happily, none of the Four Kings wound up punch-drunk, and none of them wound up dead broke. Two decades later, Leonard, Hagler and Hearns are all millionaires. Duran, despite having squandered several fortunes, lives comfortably.

From the outset of Leonard's career – just about the time the $21,000 with which the original investors in Sugar Ray Leonard, Inc. had been repaid – Mike Trainer began to lay the foundation for the fighter's financial future. Trainer (who did not take a percentage from his earnings, but rather billed his young client on an hourly basis) began to salt away a portion of the income from Leonard's purses, endorsements and television advances in long-term investments: T-bills, blue-chip stocks, tax-free bonds and real estate tax shelters.

In chronicling his early career, Sam Toperoff noted that Sugar Ray Leonard had amassed a net worth of over $3 million before he even fought 'a truly first-class opponent'.

And as Trainer pointed out at the time, Leonard could have

retired after the first Duran fight in 1980 and lived comfortably off his investments – and he made almost $100 million *after* that. Despite a more than comfortable lifestyle (and a divorce that didn't come cheaply), Leonard left boxing with more money than he would ever need. Neither his multiple comebacks nor his subsequent dabblings in the promotional field and his involvement with *The Contender* was undertaken because he was strapped for cash.

'I live in an incredible neighbourhood and my kids go to great schools,' said Leonard. 'Mike Trainer set me up to be secure for the rest of my life. Anything I do now, I do it because I enjoy it. I enjoy *The Contender* because it gives me a chance to be around the sport, even though those kids look at me as an old granddad of yesteryear.'

Leonard's investment strategy looked like that of a riverboat gambler alongside Marvin Hagler's. Peter Mareb, the Brockton adviser who handled Hagler's money during his championship reign, avoided the tax-shelter dodge altogether, preferring instead to pay the IRS off the top, leaving any subsequent investments free and clear of subsequent tax liability. Hagler has been able to live like a movie star despite having only made three films in twenty years.

'When he was still fighting, even though he was making millions, Marvin didn't change his lifestyle much,' said Arum. 'He provided for his future very well – and Goody Petronelli was even more conservative than Marvin was. Whatever he made from his share of Marvin's purses, Goody put in the bank. He lived on his Navy pension cheque.'

Pat Petronelli's fortunes, on the other hand, came to a sadder end. Gamblers by nature (he and his son Tony owned and trained a string of low-rent claimers they raced on the New England fairgrounds circuit), Pat and Tony lodged a significant portion of their earnings from the Duran, Hearns and Leonard fights with attorney Morris Goldings, who had promised them a substantial return on the investment.

They had retained the mild-mannered lawyer because he represented a contrast to Steve Wainwright's flamboyance, and the scholarly Goldings was regarded as a pillar of the community. It was shocking, then, when in early 2001 Goldings was accused of having embezzled as much as $17 million from client accounts maintained by his Beacon Hill law firm, Mahoney, Hawkes and Goldings.

Goldings initially checked himself into a mental hospital but eventually stood trial, where he pleaded guilty to 25 counts of mail fraud, wire fraud and money laundering. Sentenced to three years in prison and three years of supervised probation, he was ordered to make restitution of $12.3 million. Goldings was disbarred, and Mahoney, Hawkes and Goldings dissolved into bankruptcy.

Pasquale and Anthony Petronelli filed a lawsuit seeking $1.6 million they claimed Goldings had misappropriated, but received only a small fraction as the result of the bankruptcy settlement.

Newspaper accounts of the episode carefully noted that Hagler's money was not involved.

In 2000, Thomas Hearns returned to big-time boxing as the promoter of Tyson's fight against Andrew Golota at the Palace in Auburn Hills, Michigan. His old acquaintances were pleased to discover that, rumours to the contrary, the always quick-witted Hearns was not only *not* punchy but perhaps funnier than ever in his entrepreneurial role.

Although Tyson–Golota tickets moved so slowly that Hearns had to slash prices on the eve of the fight, he maintained his sense of humour. He even had *Tyson* laughing – and this was in a week during which the hot topic of debate was whether Tyson should be allowed to fight on liquid Zoloft.

'I never got involved in Tommy Hearns's money; he had other people helping him invest it,' said Emanuel Steward. 'But you can see that he's very comfortably fixed. He has a big, beautiful house on about ten acres, and he buys a new Bentley every year.'

In addition to his palatial estate in Southfield, Hearns maintains residences in Phoenix and in Henderson, Nevada, just outside Las Vegas, along with a 46-foot boat he keeps in the Detroit River.

Roberto Duran's capacity for extravagance was legendary, but when it came to money, he wasn't even the most profligate member of his own family.

'Duran's wife was a crazy gambler,' said Bob Arum. 'She'd bet on *anything.*'

After taxes, Duran's take from the No Mas fight in New Orleans had been nearly $6 million. Carlos Eleta told Christian Giudice that he had placed $2 million in a 'ring-fenced' escrow account in a Panamanian bank that was supposed to provide for Duran's future. Both Roberto and his wife, Felicidad, had signed a consent form that supposedly put the money beyond reach for ten years, but by 1982 Felicidad Duran persuaded Colonel Ruben Paredes – the pro-tem strongman who ruled the country between Torrijos's death and Noriega's consolidation of power – to accompany her to the bank and get someone there to hand over the money.

'His wife bet thousands and thousands of dollars daily,' Eleta told Giudice. 'His friends took money from him. I just lost control of him.'

Less than two years after the New Orleans fight, the nest egg was gone. But for Duran it had always been a matter of easy come, easy go.

'In 1989, after the Barkley fight, the IRS mistakenly issued Roberto a $1.6 million refund,' Mike Acri told me. 'He went through some of it right away, and then decided to take what was left – $800,000 – back to Panama. He split it up in $100,000 bundles, which he, his family, and a few of his friends put in their carry-on luggage. When they got to the airport, there were more carry-on bags than there were passengers, so they wouldn't let them carry one bag on. They checked it as luggage. The airline "lost" the bag with the hundred grand in it. He never saw it again.'

■ ■ ■

The conclusion of the rivalry among the Four Kings precipitated an almost immediate decline in the sport. There have been 'big' fights since, but none has recaptured the magical aura created by their internecine battles.

Mike Tyson, who had won the WBC heavyweight title in 1986 and unified it over the next two years, appeared to be positioned to assume the standard-bearer's role for the sport, but in February 1990, just two months after Leonard–Duran III, Tyson was knocked out by a journeyman named James 'Buster' Douglas in Tokyo. Before he got another crack at his title, Tyson was arrested on rape charges and spent over three years in an Indiana prison. After his release, his career continued on a downward spiral that often verged on self-parody.

It has now been more than ten years since Tyson held any part of the heavyweight title, yet he probably remains the most recognisable boxing name to the man on the street, evidence of the way the sport distanced itself from the mainstream sports fan after the era of the Four Kings.

There were flashes of brilliance from individual boxers, men like Oscar De La Hoya, Julio César Chávez and Pernell Whitaker, Roy Jones, Riddick Bowe and Lennox Lewis, but in the absence of great natural rivalries, none captured the imagination of the public the way the Four Kings had.

The middleweight division was particularly hard-hit. Beyond the fragmentation of the title, the division lost two of its more promising practitioners when Briton Michael Watson and Emanuel Steward-trained WBC champion Gerald McClellan suffered career-ending brain injuries at the hands of Chris Eubank and Nigel Benn in fights in London in the 1990s. Both were rendered paraplegics.

What had been a glamour division was also affected by the establishment of yet another bastard weight class, the 168-pound super-middleweight division. Men who earlier might have had to train religiously to maintain a 160-pound fighting trim could now compete for world championships without having to be as committed.

Although the American public never enthusiastically embraced the super-middleweights, the 168-pounders, at least in their WBO guise, became stars in Great Britain, where Benn, Eubank, the Irishman Steve Collins and current super-middleweight champ Joe Calzaghe would rule for 15 years without the title ever leaving the British Isles. American middleweights Roy Jones and James Toney made only a brief stopover at 160 pounds, shortly graduating to super-middle and then to light-heavyweight.

The system in place today almost discourages the development of great natural rivalries like those that engaged Leonard, Hagler, Hearns and Duran. Promoters, sanctioning bodies and even cable networks protect their interests with options and exclusivity agreements, ensuring that many of the top fighters never face one another. In any other business, or in a more respectable sport, this might be considered restraint of trade.

'The climate was different back in the '70s, because unless you were Don King, promoters didn't sign fighters to exclusive contracts,' said Russell Peltz, then the matchmaker at the Spectrum in Philly, who now serves in an advisory capacity for ESPN. 'Because we had no vested interest in protecting a fighter's record, we could make the best fights, which was all we wanted to do.

'In those days at the Spectrum we had to persuade 10,000 people we had a good product. Today all you have to do is convince Kery Davis [of HBO] or Ken Hershman [Showtime].'

■ ■ ■

The writer Pete Hamill once asked the great trainer Gil Clancy about the vacuum created after Leonard, Hagler, Hearns and Duran departed centre stage. Clancy, a New York schoolteacher before he immersed himself in boxing, had a one-word explanation:

'Crack.'

It may be oversimplifying the case, but a good argument could be made that the crack epidemic of the early 1990s consumed an entire generation of inner-city kids who might have become boxers.

The ones who weren't using crack were selling it, and they quickly figured out that there was a lot more money to be made peddling quick-fix drugs than in training in gyms for hoped-for preliminary bouts. This in turn led to violent turf wars, in which the alpha males who a generation earlier might have settled their differences in the ring were now shooting each other over the right to sell crack on a particular street corner.

Which is not to say that the world of drugs was unknown to the Four Kings. Testimony at the divorce trials of both Leonard and Hagler included allegations of cocaine use, though there was never any suggestion then that drugs had interfered with their training or preparation for a fight.

After Leonard's 1991 loss to Terry Norris, he pleaded with Randy Gordon, then the chairman of the New York State Athletic Commission, to be excused from taking a post-fight drug test. Since the NYAC was aware of the local anaesthetic that had been administered to mask the rib injury, there was plainly a concern that a urinalysis might reveal something more incriminating.

'When I threatened to have a commission doctor draw blood with a horse-needle, Ray finally agreed to pee for me,' said Gordon. 'He passed.'

But remember, in those pre-crack days, cocaine was almost regarded as glamorous, the signature recreational substance of the rich and famous, and in the late 1980s its use was endemic among athletes of many sports.

'People don't realise that when I first retired I was still in my 20s,' said Leonard. 'I had the fame and the money and a lot of time on my hands, and cocaine was enticing. It wasn't just movie stars and baseball players who were doing it, it was lawyers and politicians, too. But I admit it. I experimented. More than I should have.'

Leonard, in any case, hasn't gone near drugs for over 15 years now, and a few years ago the man who once prided himself on his wine cellar also gave up drinking. 'The triumph,' he said, 'comes in where you are now, not what you've done.'

Although drugs were prevalent among the entourages of both Hearns and Duran, there have been no allegations that either man dabbled. Duran's capacity for alcohol was legendary, but he was almost phobic about drugs, which he had watched kill many friends and acquaintances on his journey from Chorillo to the limelight.

'My repeating a story he once told me led to a falling-out between me and Roberto,' recalled Acri. 'I'd told Christian Giudice about an incident where Duran picked up this girl and took her back to his room, where she smoked a bunch of marijuana before he screwed her. Apparently it was rapturous sex, and she got so excited that she was hyperventilating and gasping for air. He was naturally pleased with himself, but he had to ask her, you know, "Was it me or was it the drug?"

'"Neither one," she told him. "I have asthma."

'Well, when that got into the book, he was really pissed off at me,' said Acri. 'Not about the girl or the sex – in fact, Duran told me that story in front of his wife – but because the way it came out in the book suggested that he had also smoked the marijuana.'

■ ■ ■

'While it was taking place, I didn't have the sense of what an historical era it was,' said Emanuel Steward, as he wistfully recalled the time of the Four Kings. 'I had no idea at the time it would be the greatest rivalry in history. I guess back then I just assumed that other boxers would come along to replace the Leonards, the Haglers, the Hearns and the Durans, but that didn't happen.

'Today's boxers just fight for money,' said Steward. 'Wherever they can make the most money, they go up and down in weight divisions. They're businessmen. Every fighter is his own manager. They're interested in maximising their earnings, but they're not interested in becoming good prize-fighters.

'Leonard, Hagler, Hearns and Duran was a great, great era, but remember, Ray, Marvin and Tommy all had substantial amateur backgrounds, and Duran had been fighting since he was 16. They had a foundation today's boxers don't seem to have, and I blame the trainers for that,' said Steward.

'When I came along,' continued Steward, 'the guys up there were Eddie [Futch], Jackie McCoy, Angelo, Arcel, Freddie Brown, but there haven't been that many true trainers come along since then. You've got guys everybody runs to. People put money up for a fighter and they say, "Hey, Buddy, will you train this guy?"'

'Nowadays, you've got promoters and managers and publicists. You've got nutritionists, and strength and conditioning coaches, and the guy who's the expert in how to jump over the sticks and then jump back over the sticks, but nobody who really teaches boxing.'

Steward sees his share of fights in his role as an HBO commentator but finds himself turned off by much of what is served up these days.

'Not long ago Andy Lee came in when I had a fight on television between two former light-heavyweight champions,' recalled Steward. 'He asked me what I thought, and I had to admit I wasn't even paying attention. I was reading a book and I was paying more attention to the book than to what was on TV. It was just awful. I told Andy, "See, this is why people aren't watching boxing any more." There are no exciting fights. Nobody punches, nobody wants to take chances. As a boxing person, I don't even care about a lot of these fights any more.'

It could be argued whether the television networks abandoned boxing or boxing abandoned the networks, but where Leonard, Hagler, Hearns and Duran had established their early reputations with weekend appearances on ABC, CBS and NBC, by the mid-1990s all three networks had forsaken the sport. Boxing aficionados could still find weekly shows on ESPN and USA, and big fights on HBO and Showtime, but the absence of weekend afternoon programming rendered boxing a virtual stranger to armchair America, a condition that obtains to this day. A contemporary man-on-the-street survey would be hard-pressed to turn up one person in fifty who could even *name* the middleweight champion.

Similarly, *Sports Illustrated* not only covered all nine of the fights between Leonard, Hagler, Hearns and Duran but featured seven of them on its cover. America's premier sports magazine rarely covers fights at all nowadays. The *New York Times*, which had at least two staffers on hand for each of the Four Kings' internecine fights, hasn't had a regular boxing writer for the past half-dozen years, and rarely covers fights even in New York.

■ ■ ■

A fundamental precept of baseball, the dynamic between the pitcher and the hitter, is based on deception and the knowledge that being hit by a ball thrown at 90 mph is going to hurt. At its most elementary level, the curve ball is effective when it leads the batter to flinch from a pitch he thinks is coming straight at him, only to have it break over the plate. A fearsome slugger is discouraged from becoming comfortable at the plate by a pitch judiciously directed at his belly button. An untimely home run is likely to be followed by a pitch at the ensuing batter's chin, just to remind him of the possibility of pain.

In the boxing ring, pain is not merely a possibility, but a certainty. The most accomplished of boxers is still going to absorb his share of punches, and they are going to hurt. (Remember that one punch in the nose sufficed to keep eight-year-old Ray Leonard away from the gym for five years.) The courage to persevere in the face of that pain distinguishes the boxer from the ordinary man, but the ability to avoid debilitating punishment can be the difference between a good boxer and a great one.

The evidence suggests that Leonard, Hagler, Hearns and Duran were superior defensive fighters – at least when they weren't fighting one another – and they were all to a degree gifted with that intangible boxing quality known as 'chin' – the capacity for tolerating punches that might render another man senseless.

Although no authority in either the boxing or medical fields was ever able to conclusively demonstrate a connection, an MRI administered to Hagler following a training-camp injury in the early 1980s revealed that he was possessed of an abnormally thick skull. (Tommy Hearns, who broke his right hand hitting that skull, would probably argue that it was a factor in Marvelous Marvin's resiliency.) The fact remains that in 67 professional bouts, Hagler tasted the canvas just once – in the Roldán fight, from what Marvin to this day maintains should have been ruled a slip.

After being knocked down just twice in his career before he met Hagler, Leonard was dropped on several occasions (including twice by Hearns) over his last few fights, but was never knocked out. (The only fight he failed to finish, his final one against Camacho, was halted by the clemency of the referee.)

Duran had engaged in eighty-two fights before he was knocked out in one – by Hearns, in 1984.

And while Hearns was stopped by both Leonard and Hagler, it could be reasonably argued that on both occasions it was not his chin, but his legs, that betrayed him.

'Ray was always going to beat Tommy,' Angelo Dundee once told me. 'For one reason – balance. Some guys are blessed with it, some guys aren't. You give Tommy Hearns Ray's balance and he probably beats them all.'

■ ■ ■

Those only casually acquainted with the sport seem amazed when they watch two boxers beat each other to within an inch of their lives, only to warmly embrace when the final bell rings. The bond of mutual respect, and even genuine affection, between men who have experienced this unique form of combat can be bewildering to those outside the fraternity. So it is with Leonard, Hagler, Hearns and Duran, who not only shared a glorious decade on the world stage together but made each other rich. It's hard to carry a grudge under such circumstances.

'We still all run into each other now and then,' said Sugar Ray

Leonard. 'When I see Hagler, it's civil, like, "How you doing?", but that's all. Marvin now is like Marvin then. He was always old-school. He never had an entourage, he carried his own bags. He's like that today. He does things his own way. He marches to his own drummer. Marvin and I talk, but it's short talk.

'Tommy Hearns was at my wedding, and I see him at birthday parties and boxing events and we have a good time together. Tommy's always smiling and joking and happy-go-lucky, but somewhere in the back of his mind I know he's still hoping I'll come back and fight him for a third time, even after all these years.

'And when Duran and I are together we can even joke around a bit,' said Leonard.

The subject of No Mas has never come up between them, and, says Leonard, it never will. But a few years ago the two did find themselves together in Mexico City for a WBC convention. Leonard was having breakfast in the coffee shop when Cholo walked in.

'Hey, Roberto,' Leonard beckoned with a smile, 'come over here. Come over here and sit down, goddamn it!'

As the two old rivals sat across the table from one another, Leonard said, 'I need to know something. We're older, we've got kids and grandchildren, so you can tell me now. Did you really hate me as much as you seemed to hate me back then?'

'*Ray, Ray, no no no no!*' said Duran, looking offended. 'I was only acting.'

'*Acting?*' Leonard laughed. 'Well, you must have been a damned good actor, then, because you sure convinced me!'

329

APPENDIX

RING RECORD OF SUGAR RAY LEONARD

1977

2 February	Luis Vega, Baltimore	W6
14 May	Willie Rodriguez, Baltimore	W6
10 June	Vinnie DeBarros, Hartford	TKO3
24 September	Frank Santore, Baltimore	KO5
5 November	Augustin Estrada, Las Vegas	KO5
12 December	Hector Diaz, Washington DC	KO2

1978

2 February	Rocky Ramon, Baltimore	W8
1 March	Art McKnight, Dayton	TKO7
19 March	Javier Muniz, New Haven	KO1
13 April	Bobby Heyman, Landover	RTD3
13 May	Randy Milton, Utica	TKO8
3 June	Rafael Rodriguez, Baltimore	W10
18 July	Dick Ecklund, Boston	W10
9 September	Floyd Mayweather, Providence	TKO10
6 October	Randy Shields, Baltimore	W10
11 November	Bernardo Prata, Portland	W10
9 December	Armando Muniz, Springfield	RTD6

1979

11 January	Johnny Gant, Landover	TKO8
11 February	Fernand Marcotte, Miami Beach	TKO8
24 March	Daniel Aldo Gonzalez, Tucson	KO1
21 April	Adolfo Viruet, Las Vegas	W10
20 May	Marcos Geraldo, Baton Rouge	W10
24 June	Tony Chiaverini, Las Vegas	RTD4
12 August	Pete Ranzany, Las Vegas	TKO4
28 September	Andy Price, Las Vegas	KO1
30 November	Wilfredo Benitez, Las Vegas	TKO15
	(won WBC welterweight title)	

1980

31 March	Dave Green, Landover	KO4
	(retained WBC welterweight title)	
20 June	Roberto Duran, Montreal	L15
	(lost WBC welterweight title)	
25 November	Roberto Duran, New Orleans	TKO8
	(regained WBC welterweight title)	

1981

28 March	Larry Bonds, Syracuse	TKO10
	(retained WBC welterweight title)	
25 June	Ayub Kalule, Houston	TKO9
	(won WBA junior middleweight title)	
16 September	Thomas Hearns, Las Vegas	TKO14
	(retained WBC and won WBA welterweight titles)	

1982

15 February	Bruce Finch, Reno	TKO3
	(retained WBA and WBC welterweight titles)	

1983

Inactive

1984

| 11 May | Kevin Howard, Worcester | TKO9 |

1985–6

Inactive

1987

| 6 April | Marvin Hagler, Las Vegas | W12 |
| | *(won WBC middleweight title)* | |

1988

| 7 November | Donny Lalonde, Las Vegas | TKO9 |
| | *(won WBC super-middleweight and light-heavyweight titles)* | |

1989

12 June	Thomas Hearns, Las Vegas	D12
	(retained WBC and won WBO super-middleweight titles)	
7 December	Roberto Duran, Las Vegas	W12
	(retained WBC super-middleweight title)	

1990

Inactive

1991

| 9 February | Terry Norris, New York | L12 |
| | *(for WBC junior middleweight title)* | |

1992–6

Inactive

1997

| 1 March | Hector Camacho, Atlantic City | TKOby5 |

Career record 36–3–1; 25 KOs

RING RECORD OF MARVELOUS MARVIN HAGLER

1973

18 May	Terry Ryan, Brockton	KO2
25 July	Sonny Williams, Boston	W6
8 August	Muhammad Smith, Boston	KO2
6 October	Dornell Wigfall, Brockton	W8
26 October	Cove Green, Brockton	TKO4
17 November	Cocoa Kid, Brockton	KO2
6 December	Manny Freitas, Portland	TKO1
18 December	James Redford, Boston	KO4

1974

5 February	Bob Harrington, Boston	KO5
5 April	Tracy Morrison, Boston	TKO8
4 May	James Redford, Brockton	TKO2
30 May	Curtis Phillips, Portland	KO5
16 July	Bobby Williams, Boston	TKO3
13 August	Peachy Davis, New Bedford	KO1
30 August	Ray Seales, Boston	W10
29 October	Morris Jordan, Brockton	TKO4
16 November	George Green, Brockton	KO1
26 November	Ray Seales, Seattle	D10
20 December	D.C. Walker, Boston	KO2

1975

15 February	Dornell Wigfall, Brockton	KO6
31 March	Joey Blair, Boston	KO2
14 April	Jimmy Owens, Boston	W10
24 May	Jimmy Owens, Brockton	WDQ6
7 August	Jesse Bender, Portland	KO1
30 September	Lamont Lovelady, Boston	TKO7
20 December	Johnny Baldwin, Boston	W10

1976

13 January	Bobby Watts, Philadelphia	L10
7 February	Matt Donovan, Boston	TKO2
9 March	Willie Monroe, Philadelphia	L10
2 June	Bob Smith, Taunton	TKO5
3 August	D.C. Walker, Providence	KO6
14 September	Eugene Hart, Philadelphia	RTD8
21 December	George Davis, Boston	TKO6

1977

15 February	Willie Monroe, Boston	TKO12
16 March	Reggie Ford, Boston	KO3
10 June	Roy Jones Sr, Hartford	TKO3
23 August	Willie Monroe, Philadelphia	KO2
24 September	Ray Phillips, Boston	TKO7
15 October	Jim Henry, Providence	W10
26 November	Mike Colbert, Boston	KO12

1978

4 March	Kevin Finnegan, Boston	TKO9
7 April	Doug Demmings, Los Angeles	TKO8
13 May	Kevin Finnegan, Boston	TKO7
24 August	Bennie Briscoe, Philadelphia	W10
11 November	Willie Warren, Boston	TKO7

1979

3 February	Ray Seales, Boston	TKO1
12 March	Bob Patterson, Providence	TKO3
26 May	Jamie Thomas, Portland	KO3
30 June	Norberto Cabrera, Monte Carlo	TKO8
30 November	Vito Antuofermo, Las Vegas	D15
	(for WBA and WBC middleweight titles)	

1980

| 16 February | Loucif Hamani, Portland | KO2 |
| 19 April | Bobby Watts, Portland | TKO2 |

17 May	Marcos Geraldo, Las Vegas	W10
27 September	Alan Minter, London	TKO3
	(won WBA and WBC middleweight titles)	

1981

17 January	Fulgencio Obelmejias, Boston	TKO8
	(retained WBA and WBC middleweight titles)	
13 June	Vito Antuofermo, Boston	TKO5
	(retained WBA and WBC middleweight titles)	
3 October	Mustafa Hamsho, Rosemont	TKO11
	(retained WBA and WBC middleweight titles)	

1982

7 March	William (Cave Man) Lee, Atlantic City	KO1
	(retained WBA and WBC middleweight titles)	
30 October	Fulgencio Obelmejias, San Remo	TKO5
	(retained WBA and WBC middleweight titles)	

1983

11 February	Tony Sibson, Worcester	TKO6
	(retained WBA and WBC middleweight titles)	
27 May	Wilford Scypion, Providence	KO4
	(retained WBA and WBC and won IBF middleweight titles)	
10 November	Roberto Duran, Las Vegas	W15
	(retained WBA, WBC and IBF middleweight titles)	

1984

30 March	Juan Roldán, Las Vegas	TKO10
	(retained WBA, WBC and IBF middleweight titles)	
19 October	Mustafa Hamsho, New York	TKO3
	(retained WBA, WBC and IBF middleweight titles)	

1985

| 15 April | Thomas Hearns, Las Vegas | TKO3 |
| | *(retained WBA, WBC and IBF middleweight titles)* | |

1986

10 March	John Mugabi, Las Vegas	KO11
	(retained WBA, WBC and IBF middleweight titles)	

1987

6 April	Ray Leonard, Las Vegas	L12
	(lost WBC middleweight title)	

Career record 62–3–2; 52 KOs

RING RECORD OF THOMAS HEARNS

1977

25 November	Jerome Hill, Detroit	KO2
7 December	Jerry Strickland, Mt Clemens	KO3
16 December	Willie Wren, Detroit	KO3

1978

29 January	Anthony House, Knoxville	KO2
10 February	Robert Adams, Detroit	KO3
17 February	Billy Goodwin, Saginaw	TKO2
17 March	Ray Fields, Detroit	TKO2
31 March	Tyrone Phelps, Saginaw	KO3
8 June	Jimmy Rothwell, Detroit	KO1
20 July	Raul Aguirre, Detroit	KO3
3 August	Eddie Marcelle, Detroit	KO2
7 September	Bruce Finch, Detroit	KO3
26 October	Pedro Rojas, Detroit	TKO1
9 December	Rudy Barro, Detroit	KO4

1979

11 January	Clyde Gray, Detroit	TKO10
31 January	Sammy Ruckard, Saginaw	TKO8
3 March	Segundo Murillo, Detroit	TKO8
3 April	Alfonso Hayman, Philadelphia	W10

20 May	Harold Weston, Las Vegas	TKO6
28 June	Bruce Curry, Detroit	KO3
23 August	Inocencio De La Rosa, Detroit	RTD2
22 September	Jose Figueroa, Los Angeles	KO3
18 October	Saensak Muangsurin, Detroit	TKO3
11 November	Mike Colbert, New Orleans	W10

1980

3 February	Fighting Jim Richards, Las Vegas	KO3
2 March	Angel Espada, Detroit	TKO4
31 March	Santiago Valdez, Las Vegas	TKO1
3 May	Eddie Gazo, Detroit	KO1
2 August	Pipino Cuevas, Detroit *(won WBA welterweight title)*	TKO2
6 December	Luis Primera, Detroit *(retained WBA welterweight title)*	KO6

1981

25 April	Randy Shields, Phoenix *(retained WBA welterweight title)*	TKO12
25 June	Pablo Baez, Houston *(retained WBA welterweight title)*	TKO4
16 September	Ray Leonard, Las Vegas *(lost WBA welterweight title)*	TKOby14
11 December	Ernie Singletary, Nassau	W10

1982

27 February	Marcos Geraldo, Las Vegas	KO1
25 July	Jeff McCracken, Detroit	TKO8
3 December	Wilfred Benitez, New Orleans *(won WBC junior middleweight title)*	W15

1983

| 10 July | Murray Sutherland, Atlantic City | W10 |

1984

11 February	Luigi Minchillo, Detroit	W12
	(retained WBC junior middleweight title)	
15 June	Roberto Duran, Las Vegas	TKO2
	(retained WBC junior middleweight title)	
15 September	Fred Hutchings, Saginaw	TKO3
	(retained WBC junior middleweight title)	

1985

15 April	Marvin Hagler, Las Vegas	TKOby3
	(for WBA, WBC and IBF middleweight titles)	

1986

10 March	James Shuler, Las Vegas	KO1
23 June	Mark Medal, Las Vegas	TKO8
	(retained WBC junior middleweight title)	
17 October	Doug DeWitt, Detroit	W12

1987

7 March	Dennis Andries, Detroit	TKO10
	(won WBC light-heavyweight title)	
29 October	Juan Domingo Roldán, Las Vegas	KO4
	(won vacant WBC middleweight title)	

1988

6 June	Iran Barkley, Las Vegas	TKOby3
	(lost WBC middleweight title)	
4 November	James Kinchen, Las Vegas	W12
	(won vacant WBO super-middleweight title)	

1989

12 June	Ray Leonard, Las Vegas	D12
	(for WBC and WBO super-middleweight titles)	

1990

| 28 April | Michael Olajide, Atlantic City | W12 |
| | *(retained WBO super-middleweight title)* | |

1991

11 February	Kemper Morton, Inglewood	KO2
6 April	Ken Atkins, Honolulu	TKO3
3 June	Virgil Hill, Las Vegas	W12
	(won WBA light-heavyweight title)	

1992

| 20 March | Iran Barkley, Las Vegas | L12 |
| | *(lost WBA light-heavyweight title)* | |

1993

| 6 November | Andrew Maynard, Las Vegas | TKO1 |

1994

| 29 January | Dan Ward, Las Vegas | KO1 |
| 19 February | Freddie Delgado, Charlotte | W12 |

1995

| 31 March | Lenny LaPaglia, Detroit | TKO1 |
| 26 September | Earl Butler, Auburn Hills | W10 |

1996

| 29 November | Karl Willis, Roanoke | KO5 |

1997

| 31 January | Ed Dalton, Inglewood | KO5 |

1998

| 6 November | Jay Snyder, Detroit | KO1 |

1999

| 10 April | Nate Miller, Manchester | W12 |

2000

8 April	Uriah Grant, Detroit	TKOby2

2001–4

Inactive

2005

30 July	John Long, Detroit	TKO9

2006

4 February	Shannon Landberg, Auburn Hills	TKO10

Career Record 61–5–1; 48 KOs

RING RECORD OF ROBERTO DURAN

1968

23 February	Carlos Mendoza, Colón	W4
14 May	Juan Gondola, Colón	KO1
15 June	Manuel Jimenez, Colón	KO1
30 June	Eduardo Morales, Panama City	KO1
10 August	Enrique Jacob, Panama City	KO1
25 August	Leroy Carghill, Panama City	KO1
22 September	Ulises De Leon, Panama City	KO1
16 November	Juan Gondola, Colón	KO2
7 December	Carlos Howard, Panama City	TKO1

1969

19 January	Alberto Brand, Panama City	TKO4
1 February	Eduardo Frutos, Panama City	W6
18 May	Jacinto Garcia, Panama City	TKO4
22 June	Adolfo Osses, Panama City	TKO7
21 September	Serafin Garcia, Panama City	TKO5
23 November	Luis Patino, Panama City	TKO8

1970

28 March	Felipe Torres, Mexico City	W10
16 May	Ernesto Marcel, Panama City	TKO10
18 July	Clemente Mucino, Colón	KO6
5 September	Marvin Castaneda, Puerto Armuelles	KO1
18 October	Ignacio Castaneda, Panama City	TKO3

1971

10 January	Jose Angel Herrara, Monterrey	KO6
21 March	Jose Acosta, Panama City	KO1
29 May	Lloyd Marshall, Panama City	TKO6
18 July	Fermin Soto, Monterrey	TKO3
13 September	Benny Huertas, New York	TKO1
16 October	Hiroshi Kobayashi, Panama City	KO7

1972

15 January	Angel Robinson Garcia, Panama City	W10
10 March	Francisco Munoz, Panama City	TKO1
26 June	Ken Buchanan, New York *(won WBA lightweight title)*	TKO13
2 September	Greg Potter, Panama City	KO1
28 October	Lupe Ramirez, Panama City	KO1
17 November	Esteban DeJesus, New York	L10

1973

20 January	Jimmy Robertson, Panama City *(retained WBA lightweight title)*	KO5
22 February	Juan Medina, Los Angeles	TKO7
17 March	Javier Ayala, Los Angeles	W10
14 April	Gerardo Ferrat, Panama City	TKO2
2 June	Hector Thompson, Panama City *(retained WBA lightweight title)*	TKO8
4 August	Doc McClendon, Hato Rey	W10
8 November	Ishimatsu (Guts) Suzuki, Panama City *(retained WBA lightweight title)*	TKO10

| 1 December | Tony Garcia, Santiago de Veraguas | KO3 |

1974

21 January	Leonard Tavarez, Paris	TKO4
16 February	Armando Mendoza, Panama City	TKO3
16 March	Esteban DeJesus, Panama City *(retained WBA lightweight title)*	KO11
6 July	Flash Gallego, Panama City	TKO7
2 September	Hector Matta, Hato Rey	W10
31 October	Jose Vasquez, San Jose	KO2
16 November	Aldalberto Vanegas, Panama City	KO1
21 December	Masataka Takayama, San Jose *(retained WBA lightweight title)*	KO1

1975

15 February	Andres Salgado, Panama City	KO1
2 March	Ray Lampkin, Panama City *(retained WBA lightweight title)*	KO14
3 June	Jose Peterson, Miami Beach	TKO1
2 August	Pedro Mendoza, Managua	KO1
13 September	Alirio Acuna, Chitre	KO3
30 September	Edwin Viruet, Uniondale	W10
20 December	Leoncio Ortiz, Hato Rey *(retained WBA lightweight title)*	KO15

1976

4 May	Saoul Mamby, Miami Beach	W10
23 May	Lou Bizzarro, Erie *(retained WBA lightweight title)*	KO14
31 July	Emiliano Villa, Panama City	TKO7
15 October	Alvaro Rojas, Hollywood *(retained WBA lightweight title)*	KO1

1977

29 January	Vilomar Fernandez, Miami Beach	KO13
	(retained WBA lightweight title)	
16 May	Javier Muniz, Landover	W10
6 August	Bernardo Diaz, Panama City	KO1
17 September	Edwin Viruet, Philadelphia	W15
	(retained WBA lightweight title)	

1978

21 January	Esteban DeJesus, Las Vegas	TKO12
	(retained WBA lightweight title; won WBC lightweight title)	
27 April	Adolfo Viruet, New York	W10
1 September	Ezequiel Obando, Panama City	KO2
8 December	Monroe Brooks, New York	KO8

1979

	(relinquished lightweight titles in January)	
8 April	Jimmy Heair, Las Vegas	W10
22 June	Carlos Palomino, New York	W10
28 September	Zeferino Gonzalez, Las Vegas	W10

1980

13 January	Joseph Nsubuga, Las Vegas	TKO4
24 February	Wellington Wheatley, Las Vegas	TKO6
20 June	Ray Leonard, Montreal	W15
	(won WBC welterweight title)	
25 November	Ray Leonard, New Orleans	TKOby8
	(lost WBC welterweight title)	

1981

9 August	Nino Gonzalez, Cleveland	W10
26 September	Luigi Minchillo, Las Vegas	W10

1982

30 January	Wilfred Benitez, Las Vegas	L15
	(for WBC junior middleweight title)	
4 September	Kirkland Laing, Detroit	L10
12 November	Jimmy Batten, Miami	W10

1983

29 January	Pipino Cuevas, Los Angeles	TKO4
16 June	Davey Moore, New York	TKO8
	(won WBA junior middleweight title)	
10 November	Marvin Hagler, Las Vegas	L15
	(for WBA, WBC and IBF middleweight titles)	

1984

15 June	Thomas Hearns	KOby2
	(for WBC junior middleweight title)	

1985

Inactive

1986

31 January	Manuel Zambrano, Panama City	KO2
18 April	Jorge Suero, Panama City	KO2
23 June	Robbie Sims, Las Vegas	L10

1987

16 May	Victor Claudio, Miami Beach	W10
12 September	J.C. Gimenez Ferreyra, Miami Beach	W10

1988

5 February	Ricky Stackhouse, Atlantic City	W10
14 April	Paul Thorne, Atlantic City	TKO6
1 October	Jeff Lanas, Chicago	W10

1989

24 February	Iran Barkley, Atlantic City	W12
	(won WBC middleweight title)	
7 December	Ray Leonard, Las Vegas	L12
	(for WBC super-middleweight title)	

1990

Inactive

1991

18 March	Pat Lawlor, Las Vegas	TKOby6

1992

30 September	Tony Biglen, Buffalo	W10
17 December	Ken Hulsey, Cleveland	KO2

1993

29 June	Jacques LeBlanc, Bay St Louis	W10
17 August	Sean Fitzgerald, Bay St Louis	KO6
14 December	Tony Menefee, Bay St Louis	TKO8

1994

22 February	Carlos Montero, Marseilles	W10
29 March	Terry Thomas, Bay St Louis	TKO4
25 June	Vinny Pazienza, Las Vegas	L12
18 October	Heath Todd, Bay St Louis	TKO7

1995

14 January	Vinny Pazienza, Atlantic City	L12
10 June	Roni Martinez, Kansas City	TKO7
21 December	Wilbur Garst, Fort Lauderdale	TKO4

1996

20 February	Ray Domenge, Miami	W10
22 June	Hector Camacho, Atlantic City	L12

31 August	Ariel Cruz, Panama City	KO1
27 September	Mike Culbert, Chester	TKO6

1997

15 February	Jorge Fernando Castro, Buenos Aires	L10
14 June	Jorge Fernando Castro, Panama City	W10
15 November	David Radford, Temba	W8

1998

31 January	Felix Jose Hernandez, Panama City	W10
28 August	William Joppy, Las Vegas	TKOby3
	(for WBA middleweight title)	

1999

6 March	Omar Eduardo Gonzalez, Buenos Aires	L10

2000

16 June	Pat Lawlor, Panama City	W12
12 August	Patrick Goossen, Yakima	W10

2001

14 July	Hector Camacho, Denver	L12

Career Record: 103–16–0; 70 KOs

AFTERWORD AND ACKNOWLEDGEMENTS

ALTHOUGH I WAS AN eyewitness to all nine fights between Leonard, Hagler, Hearns and Duran and have relied on (and quoted from) my notes, recollections and clippings from well over a hundred stories I wrote at the time – for the *Boston Herald* and *Herald American*, as well as for several boxing magazines – I am indebted to a number of secondary sources.

Remarkably, only one of the subjects treated herein has been the subject of a comprehensive biography encompassing his entire ring career, and Christian Giudice's *Hands of Stone* was a valuable resource in filling out the enigma that is Roberto Duran. I have attempted to credit him where I have quoted directly from that book, but I would be remiss if I did not acknowledge the critical nature of Giudice's work in recounting the background, and dispelling some of the tales, surrounding an almost mythic figure.

Sugar Ray Leonard was the subject of several biographies, three of which were written for the children's market. Bert Rosenthal's *Sugar Ray Leonard: The Baby-Faced Boxer* and James Haskins's *Sugar Ray Leonard*, both written for a juvenile audience, were published in 1982. A children's book also called *Sugar Ray Leonard*, authored by S.H. Burchard, was published in 1983 and concluded with the 1982 Baltimore retirement ceremony. Alan Goldstein's excellent *A Fistful of Sugar* was published even earlier, and while it takes the reader as far as the first two Duran fights, it was rushed into print to emerge before

Leonard's 1981 fight against Hearns, too early, alas, to capture the critical second phase of Leonard's career. Sam Toperoff's *Sugar Ray Leonard and Other Noble Warriors* is not, as the title suggests, exclusively about Leonard, and gets its subject only as far as the 1984 Kevin Howard fight. (It would have been interesting to see how Toperoff dealt with Leonard's subsequent encounters – with Hagler, Hearns II and Duran III.)

Marvin Hagler was also the subject of a short (48 pages) biography written for younger readers. Published in 1985, Carolyn Gloeckner's *Marvelous Marvin Hagler* emerged before the Hearns and Leonard fights had taken place.

Happily, though, the era is well represented in the work of a number of outstanding contemporaneous boxing scribes, Michael Katz, Hugh McIlvanney, John Schulian, Budd Schulberg, Dave Anderson, Vic Ziegel and the late Harry Mullan among them, and revisiting their coverage (along with Pat Putnam's and Bill Nack's *Sports Illustrated* accounts) of the fights between the Four Kings was invaluable in the preparation of this book.

When I began to cover the sport, record-keeping was decidedly imprecise. *The Ring*'s record book was often unreliable, and in many cases newspapers abetted exaggerations by accepting promoters' often fanciful estimates of a given fighter's record. That situation was improved considerably by the emergence of FightFax in the 1980s, and has been rendered virtually obsolete by today's online resources – particularly Boxrec.com, which I found myself consulting almost daily as I worked on this book.

I would also like to express my gratitude to each of the following for sharing their time, expertise and memories: Ray Charles Leonard, Thomas Hearns and Roberto Duran; Seth Abraham, Mike Acri, Dave Anderson, James Anderson, Bob Arum, Amiri Baraka, Al Bernstein, Teddy Blackburn, J.D. Brown, Kevin Buckley, Michael Buffer, Prentiss Byrd, Angie Carlino, Nick Charles, Jose (Pepe) Correa, Lou DiBella, Ray Didinger, Dan Doyle, Angelo Dundee, Ollie Dunlap, Steve Farhood, Leonard Gardner, Julius (Juice) Gatling, Christian Giudice, Bobby Goodman, Randy Gordon, Ross Greenburg, Bob Halloran, Pete Hamill, Thomas Hauser, Stan Hochman, Jerry

Izenberg, Michael Katz, Jay Larkin, Jim Lawton, Hugh McIlvanney, Wally Matthews, Larry Merchant, Leigh Montville, Mike O'Hara, Reinaldo Oliveira, Andy Olson, Goody Petronelli, Freddie Roach, Lee Samuels, Budd Schulberg, Ed Schuyler, John Scully, Rick Sennott, Emanuel Steward, Steve Taub, Jose Torres, Mike Trainer, Steve Wainwright, Jeff Wald, Alex Wallau and Jim Watt.

Thanks as well to Joe Fitzgerald, Mike Carey, Tom Gibbons, Jack Thompson, Peter Drumsta and Bob Sales, my old bosses at the *Boston Herald*, who at various times were responsible for paying my way to cover all nine fights between the Four Kings, as well as to Michael Gee, Tim Horgan, Richie Thompson, Eddie Gray, Frank Dell'Appa, Kevin Cullen and Mike Globetti, *Herald* colleagues who rode shotgun on some of those journeys, and to Marvelous Marvin Hagler, who made it all possible.

Colin Wilkins of the library staff at the *Boston Herald* was particularly helpful in retrieving and assembling my own newspaper coverage of the fights described here, as was Richard O'Brien of *Sports Illustrated*, who rooted out back issues containing that magazine's coverage of the era. Thanks as well to Jim Mahoney of the *Boston Herald*, Karen Carpenter of *Sports Illustrated*, Janet Indelli and Pam Waring of HBO, and Scott Mosher of Ambient Studios for helping me to pull the illustrations together, and, of course, to ace boxing shutterbugs Teddy Blackburn, Angie Carlino, Stephen Green-Armytage, John Iacono, Will Hart, Heinz Kluetmeier, Richard Mackson and Manny Millan, whose photos grace these pages.

Thanks are also due to Bill Campbell at Mainstream, who embraced the *Four Kings* project even in its embryonic stages, and in particular to Deborah Warner, my editor at Mainstream. Thirty-five years spent in the newspaper dodge had produced a deep-rooted mistrust that held editors to be the natural enemy of writers, but Debs quickly disabused me of that apprehension with her enthusiasm and her expertise. Her work on this book was so caring, thoughtful and thorough that I now find myself wincing when I contemplate what *Four Kings* might have been like without her.

Two Dr Kimballs – my wife Marge and my mother Sue – proofread the manuscript and galleys, and Emily Snider coordinated some difficult logistics to arrange sit-downs with Ray Leonard in some far-flung and unlikely locales.

My everlasting gratitude to the Wolf Man, who as ever had my back at each step of the way, and to Tom Frail of *Smithsonian*, my old editor from the Boston *Phoenix*, whose editing of the manuscript made this a much better book. Thanks as well to Farley Chase of the Waxman Agency, who encouraged me at every turn and shepherded *Four Kings* from concept to finished product.

And thanks, in memoriam, to Patrick Francis Anthony Nolan Putnam.

George Kimball
New York City

BIBLIOGRAPHY

BOOKS

Anderson, Dave *In The Corner* (William Morrow & Co., New York, 1991)

Brenner, Teddy (with Barney Nagler) *Only the Ring Was Square* (Prentice Hall, Englewood Cliffs, N.J., 1981)

Buckley, Kevin *Panama: The Whole Story* (Touchstone Books, New York, 1991)

Burchard, Sue *Sugar Ray Leonard* (Harcourt Brace Jovanovich, New York, 1983)

Dahlberg, Tim *Fight Town: Las Vegas – The Boxing Capital of the World* (Stephens Press, Las Vegas, 2004)

Dundee, Angelo (with Mike Winters) *I Only Talk Winning* (Contemporary Books, Chicago, 1985)

Fried, Ronald K. *Cornermen: Great Boxing Trainers* (Four Walls Eight Windows, New York, 1991)

Giudice, Christian *Hands of Stone: The Life and Legend of Roberto Duran* (Milo Books, Wrea Green, Lancs., UK, 2006)

Gloeckner, Carolyn *Marvelous Marvin Hagler* (Crestwood House, Mankato, Minn., 1985)

Goldstein, Alan *A Fistful of Sugar* (Coward, McCann and Geoghegan, New York, 1981)

Haskins, James *Sugar Ray Leonard* (Lothrop, Lee and Shepard Books, New York, 1982)

Heinz, W.C. and Nathan Ward (eds) *The Book of Boxing* (Total/Sports Illustrated, Kingston, N.Y., 1999)

Hughes, Bill and Patrick King *Come Out Writing: A Boxing Anthology* (Queen Anne Press, London, 1991)

Liebling, A.J. *The Sweet Science* (Penguin USA, New York, 1991)

McIlvanney, Hugh *McIlvanney on Boxing* (Beaufort Books, New York, 1982)

Mullan, Harry *Fighting Words* (Colebridge Associates, Kent, 1993)

Myler, Patrick *A Century of Boxing Greats* (Robson Books, London, 1997)

Newfield, Jack *Only in America: The Life and Times of Don King* (William Morrow & Co., New York, 1995)

Rosenthal, Bert *Sugar Ray Leonard: The Baby-Faced Boxer* (Children's Press, Chicago, 1982)

Schulberg, Budd *Ringside: A Treasury of Boxing Reportage* (Ivan R. Dee, Chicago, 2006)

Schulian, John *Writers, Fighters and Other Sweet Scientists* (Andrews & McMeel, Kansas City, 1983)

Toperoff, Sam *Sugar Ray Leonard and Other Noble Warriors* (McGraw Hill, New York, 1987)

MAGAZINES

Inside Sports
'Roberto Duran in New York', Vic Ziegel, 30 June 1980
'Park Avenue Desperado', Robert Friedman, 30 June 1980

Sports Illustrated
'Right on for Roberto', William Nack, 30 June 1980
'The Big Bellyache', William Nack, 8 December 1980
'On Top of the World', Pat Putnam, 28 September 1981
'I Am Still a Pistol', William Nack, 7 November 1983
'Marvelous Was Something Less than Marvelous', William Nack, 21 November 1983
'There Was No Doubting Thomas', Pat Putnam, 25 June 1984
'Better than a Barroom Brawl', Pat Putnam, 8 April 1985
'Eight Minutes of Fury', Pat Putnam, 22 April 1985
'Everything I Did Worked', William Nack, 20 April 1987
'Let the World Know I'm OK', William Nack, 28 September 1987
'Another Classic', Pat Putnam, 19 June 1989
'One for the Ages', Pat Putnam, 18 December 1989

Time
'A King-Size Scandal in the Ring', 2 May 1977

NEWSPAPER ARCHIVES

Boston Herald
New York Post
New York Times
Philadelphia *Bulletin*
Philadelphia *Daily News*

INDEX

ABOUT THE AUTHOR

GEORGE KIMBALL WAS AN eyewitness to all nine of the fights between Leonard, Hagler, Hearns and Duran. A familiar face at ringsides all over the world, Kimball has covered nearly 400 world title fights in a four-decade sportswriting career. He was the 1985 recipient of the Nat Fleischer Award for Excellence in Boxing Journalism from the Boxing Writers Association of America, and spent a quarter-century as a sports columnist for the *Boston Herald*, from which he retired in 2005. Kimball has covered boxing since the eras of Muhammad Ali and Joe Frazier, and was the only journalist to cover every fight of Marvelous Marvin Hagler's middleweight reign from start to finish. For the past 11 years, he has written the weekly 'America at Large' column for Dublin's *Irish Times*, and is a regular contributor to *Boxing Digest* and ESPN.com. Kimball has received numerous awards for his boxing, golf, baseball and Olympic Games coverage, and also covered the New England Patriots and the NFL from 1970 to 2005. He has two children, Darcy and Teddy Kimball, stepsons Kim, Chris and Jeremy Seeger, and four grandchildren. A member of the European Club in Brittas Bay, Ireland, and the St Andrews Golf Club in Scotland, he lives in New York City with his wife, Marge Marash, M.D.